ARMIES OF PESTILENCE

Armies of Pestilence
The effects of pandemics on history

Yet know my master, God omnipotent
Is mustering in his clouds on my behalf
Armies of Pestilence.

Richard II, Act III , Scene III – Shakespeare

Dr. R.S. Bray

The Lutterworth Press
Cambridge

The Lutterworth Press
P.O. Box 60
Cambridge
CB1 2NT

British Library Cataloguing in Publication Data:
A catalogue record is available from the British Library.

ISBN 0 7188 2949 2

Printed and bound in Great Britain by
Biddles Ltd, Guildford and King's Lynn

Contents

List of Maps

Acknowledgements

A work such as this requires the devoted services of excellently staffed libraries. I should like to thank the long-suffering and highly efficient staffs of the Lyon Playfair library of the Imperial College, both at South Kensington and Silwood Park, of the library of the London School of Hygiene and Tropical Medicine and of the library of the Department of the History of Medicine of the Wellcome Trust. All have rendered me uncomplaining service of the highest order in the face of much unreasonableness. My son Dr. Michael Bray, in conjunction with the Library of CIBA AG. in Basel were able to fill some late-discovered gaps.

Though this has been a somewhat solitary work I have benefited greatly from discussions and correspondence with the late Emeritus Professor Leonard Bruce-Chwatt, Sir Ian MacGregor, Dr. Andrew Wilkins, Dr. Peter Kessler, Dr. Brigitte Franke, Dr. Ann La Berge, Dr. Paul Slack and Dr. Michael Bray. My brother Dr. John Bray was kind enough to read critically the manuscript and make valuable comments and criticisms. To keep the family note my brother-in-law Mr. Michael Page ran a cold editorial eye over the manuscript, greatly to its benefit. The other quality required of a family is patience and my wife has displayed this quality to the highest degree. She has shown faith, she has been hopeful and above all she has been charitable with a pre-occupied husband.

PREFACE

Health care in the affluent West has now shifted from the infectious diseases of the nineteenth and preceding centuries and the children's diseases of the early twentieth century to the problems of old age, cancer, heart disease, congenital abnormalities and physical accidents.

During earlier centuries infectious disease in the form of calamitous pandemics were a great regulator of populations and thus an arbiter of the forms of society. While it is true that these great plagues, such as bubonic plague, smallpox and cholera have now receded, even in the case of smallpox, disappeared, they may return. After all they came from somewhere in the first place and may do so again. Four possibilities face us:-

The first is that a brand new infectious agent may engulf us, transmitted quickly and efficiently and by a protected means. That such a possibility exists we know from painful present experience, as we are in the midst of just such a pandemic, partly hidden from the West, as Africa is bearing the main brunt of AIDS. AIDS is an awful warning to any complacency about our ability to handle any infectious disease pandemic. Africa may yet suffer a demographic slump due to AIDS of an order to compare with Europe under the scourge of the Black Death.

The second possibility is an atomic catastrophe leading to destruction of all of our present means of infectious disease control, such as sewers, vaccines and insecticides. If the present disaster camps are anything to go by, such a holocaust could lead to the re-introduction of such diseases as typhus and cholera, possibly in a new form which a dimly remembered prevention technique could not control.

The third possibility arises out of the known phenomenon of mutation. A well-known pandemic disease such as plague could revisit us in a mutant form, more swiftly transmitted, more deadly and unresponsive to our armoury of drugs and vaccines.

Finally pandemic disease could be re-awakened by the modern techniques of immunosuppression and by diseases, such as AIDS, which render the patient immuno-incompetent. It has been suggested that AIDS might bring about the re-appearance of *Yersinia* infections (plague) or rickettsial infections (typhus), so far without proof of actual occurrence.

It would be as well therefore, if the great pandemics of the past and their effects upon man and his organisations were not forgotten and allowed to slip into the limbo of ill-remembered folk-lore and ill-understood behaviour which even today lurk in our collective mythology and behaviour patterns, breaking out in odd ways and in response to inappropriate situations.

Early man, the nomad, the hunter-gatherer, was sparsely distributed. Even after the Agrarian Revolution no great population concentrations were immediately apparent. Man was not, therefore, subject to the great epidemics which require a certain level of crowding to get up and running. It was city life which provided the conditions for cholera and influenza.

Sir MacFarlane Burnet took as his text:-

"Why do not all the city-dwellers die early of infectious disease?"

The answer lies in man's ability to acquire immunity to infectious diseases. It is the main concern of man's remarkably successful immune system to rid him of foreign bodies such as the agents of disease. It should also be added that it is also a major concern of many agents of disease to circumvent man's immune system. This immune system operates with more or less success in all known infectious diseases, only in rabies and AIDS is this response so inadequate that death intervenes (1). It is the little hiccups in the system which are so important.

Ashurn wrote in 1947 :-

'Someday, perhaps, a giant of learning will weave the massive tapestry of the influence of disease on all human history'.

This is not that book. I do not possess, for instance, the necessary skills to enquire of the many primary sources and much of this enquiry uses secondary, even tertiary sources. Perhaps, however, this book might be taken as the first stumbling steps towards that book and may give encouragement to the giant of learning. It might provide some indication of the extent of the bibliography and its errors may provide some guidance among the pitfalls. The main intention of this book is to try to convince historians that omission of disease from their calculations is a major sin; that the statement that X's army was decimated by disease and so retreated is insufficient without some attempt to identify the disease and some informed calculation about its probable source and effects.

As always in a book involving geography the question of place names arises. Where the location is well-known in history I have used the name current at the time of the incident. Where it is less well-known I have used the present-day name for the locality.

INTRODUCTION

Of all the human diseases which will be considered in this book only one is thought to be as old as man – malaria. Parasites occur in the blood of chimpanzees and gorillas which are virtually indistinguishable from those causing malaria in people. It must be assumed therefore that we acquired malaria parasites from our ape ancestors at the time when our stock separated away from the higher ape stock.

All the other epidemic diseases considered here, plague, cholera, smallpox, typhus, yellow fever and influenza, are thought to be late-comers to the bodies of people and are the result of certain critical numbers of people coming together. Informed opinion has it that these great pandemic diseases (malaria is usually endemic) require a certain amount of crowding of people before they can achieve an epidemic state.

So it is usually claimed, with justice, that while man was a widely scattered hunter-gatherer he was free of the major communicable diseases other than malaria. When man became an agriculturalist and pastoralist and collected together in groups he became prey to infectious diseases.

The other general remark, which can be made at this point, is that all of these diseases were to begin with, zoonotic; that is to say they commenced as diseases of animals and were transmitted from those animals to man. Subsequently most were transmitted from man to man, losing the original animal reservoir from their life-cycle. It is generally assumed that continuing zoonoses are by nature endemic, that is only sporadically distributed and of medium to low incidence in the human population as they are transmitted to man only occasionally even if constantly. Thus yellow fever transmitted from monkeys to people will give rise to only sporadic disease in man. Yellow fever only becomes epidemic when it is transmitted man to man by local mosquitoes. Medical biology has not yet reached the state of exact laws perceived and proclaimed by man so any general statement made here is subject to exceptions and in science the exception does not prove the rule in the sense of confirming it; on the contrary it disproves the rule.

Arising out of what has just been said about zoonoses the great surprise is that pandemic plague should have been a zoonosis involving the rat as it was found to be in late nineteenth and early twentieth century pandemic. The surprise is so great that doubt should be cast on the supposition that all plague pandemics must have been bubonic plague exclusively and this question will be discussed in greater detail later.

CHAPTER 1
Early Civilisations

I will also do this unto you, I will even appoint over you terror, consumption and the burning ague, that shall consume the eyes and cause sorrow of the heart: and ye shall sow your seed in vain, for your enemies shall eat it.

The Bible, Leviticus 26: 16

It was Apollo, son of Zeus and Leto, who started the feud when he punished the King for his discourtesy to Chryses, his priest, by inflicting a deadly plague on his army and destroying his men.

Homer, *The Ilaid*

At his dawn man can be assumed to have been free of the great epidemic diseases in their epidemic form. Indeed, as written evidence is always our best guide to the past diseases of the soft tissue of man, we can do little other than make this comfortable assumption. Skeletal remains give us some idea of whether the corpse was knocked on the head or had some major bone disease, but apart from that all other evidence is arguable.

Early written evidence is only a little more reliable as we have to interpret from a wholly alien concept of disease. There is, for instance, the story that the Hittite Empire disappeared coincidentally with a wave of disease, possibly smallpox. The evidence for this is tenuous in the extreme and other explanations involving the 'sea people', the fall of the Mycaenean civilisation and the invasion from the north of the Gasga people have proved more attractive to historians as an explanation for the fall of the Asia Minor empire. It might be noted that Diodorus Siculus (Book V, para 82) wrote that prior to the establishment of Troy an ancestor of Priam called Macares was trying to annex the Dodecanese Islands while a plague was devastating the mainland opposite. This, however, seems a little early for the fall of the Hittites. It is Hare (1954) who claims that the evidence for a major epidemic, possibly smallpox, at the fall of the Hittite Empire is to be found in a cuneiform tablet.

There are numerous references to major plagues in Greek mythology including (1) Homer's 'deadly plague' sent by Apollo to punish Agamemnon's discourtesy to his priest Chryses in the opening chapter of the *Iliad*. Homer also sings of the disease of the 'dog-star' time which is taken by many to be aestivo-autumnal fever, a form of malaria, but, as de Zulueta (1987) says, it is doubtful if this form of malaria was present in any great amount in Asia Minor in the years before Christ.

Equally early Chinese records afford us no examples of history-making epidemics at this time though they knew malaria. Nor does King Ashurbanipal's famous library furnish us with any evidence of such plagues having any disastrous consequences in the early days of the civilisations of the Tigris/Euphrates basin. The greatest source of medical information of those early days are the medical papyri of the Egyptians. Once again, while much valuable information has been gathered from them concerning the presence of individual diseases, there is no evidence of any major epidemics. Malaria was undoubtedly present, the story that Horus suffered from it and was cured by the waters of the Nile should be discounted, but it does not seem to have reached epidemic proportions, despite a certain seasonality which can always be dangerous with malaria. One would have expected epidemic malaria to dampen the very obvious enthusiasm to be seen in the waterfowl hunting expeditions pictured on the walls of the tombs at Thebes.

The next great source-book to be considered is the Bible with its vengeful leading character, Jehovah. There is no shortage of blains, fevers, eruptions, plagues, emerods, burning agues, consumption, pestilence and inflammation which were to be visited by an angry tribal god upon his disobedient subjects or, in better times, their enemies. The Egyptians, a favourite target, were visited by a plague held by some to be smallpox on no very firm grounds. What might be called Jehovah's home on earth had a very profound effect upon the Philistines (I, Samuel, 5.). It will be remembered that Israel had been worsted in battle with the old enemy at Ebenezer. The victorious Philistines carried off the Ark of God and deposited it as a trophy of war in the temple to their god Dagon. Next day the statue of Dagon was found to have fallen on its face and its head and shoulders broken off. Then the Philistines who had captured the ark 'were smitten with emerods' by the hand of the Lord. The Philistines were much exercised as to what to do with such a dangerous item of booty and sent it off to Gath. No sooner had it arrived than the hand of the Lord was turned against Gath and its citizens were likewise smitten with emerods.

The Philistines were determined to send the Ark on to Ekron, whose citizens, not unnaturally, would have none of it. The Philistines took council of their wise men and decided to send the venomous object back to its rightful owners who had signalled a willingness to receive it with a handsome 'trespass offering', consisting of five golden emerods, and five golden mice 'that mar the land'. So they loaded the Ark with the trespass offering onto an ox-cart and sent it to the field of Joshua at Bethshemesh, leaving it and scampering off as fast as possible, no doubt hoping that the Ark's properties would continue to plague the Israelites. The Israelite peasants were in the fields harvesting when they saw the Ark, which they then unloaded and frugally used the wood of the cart to make a fire and the oxen were roasted as a burnt offering to Jehovah. The Levites arrived and took charge of the Ark. Jehovah, far from being grateful for this homecoming, smote the Bethshemeshites and went on in a petulant fury to smite a further fifty thousand and seventy.

This tale has given the medically minded of Bible commentators a field-day. Many have seized upon the mice and emerods and equated them with rats and buboes to come up with bubonic plague. As all this is to be found in a sacred text a great amount of passionate ink has been employed on its explanation. Much learned thought and a fair modicum of nonsense has been lavished on the interpretation of mice as rats and emerods as buboes. The great German commentator Preuss has translated emerods rather noncommittally as swellings, easily transposed as buboes or haemorrhoids. One quite extraordinarily silly commentator claims a universal practice of buggery among the Philistines to support his contention that this plague was dysentery which acted on Philistine anuses critically weakened by inveterate buggery to produce haemorrhoids (2). More serious commentators have noted that Josephus says it was only seventy Bethshemeshites and others who died and they were killed by lightning (which would hardly have reduced the credulity). Conrad, on careful examination, finds the whole question of enormous complexity but weighs in against a diagnosis of bubonic plague. Pollitzer (1954B), the great plague expert, doubts the claim of bubonic plague for the Plague of the Philistines.

Castiglione, the Italian medical historian, believes that both the Philistine plague and the defeat of Sennacherib (II Kings, 19, 32-6) were due to plague. He does himself little service by this last attribution. According to the Bible Sennacherib, King of Assyria, was advancing on Jerusalem, but the Lord said that 'he shall not come unto the city' and sent an angel to smite the camp of the Assyrians, killing 185,000 Assyrians and bringing into being Byron's stirring poem. Sennacherib went back to Ninevah. Some have taken this account from the Bible and coupled it with Herodotus (II, 141) whose account is of an Assyrian army defeated by the Egyptians near Sinai because mice gnawed through their bowstrings on the night before the battle (3). Pestilence plus mice equals bubonic plague which is pretty far-fetched even if one ignores the accuracy of the Bible and Herodotus in medical matters. The actual battle took place, not outside Jerusalem, but as Herodotus writes in the area nearer the Egyptian border though not as Herodotus claimed on the Egyptian border to the east of Alexandria and involved not the Israelites but the Egyptians.

Ignoring the Assyrian campaigns of 720, 716 and 713 BC it would seem that Sennacherib moved down the coast of Phoenecia to Philistia reducing rebellious cities in these his domains as he went. He met an Egyptian army moving north in support of the Judean rebellion and defeated them at Eltekeh. He then set about forty six cities of Philistia and Judah winning a victory at Lakish. From there he sent a small flying column against Jerusalem, investing it and exacting tribute from it, but without taking it. Sennacherib then returned to Assyria and, as grandiloquent as his victims, claimed the capture of 200,150 people.

It does not seem possible at this distance in time to determine with any accuracy the nature of the 'Plague of the Philistines' though informed opinion does seem to favour dysentery, nor does it seem worth doing so for our purposes, whatever the sacerdotal importance a sacred text may lend it, as it involved only a minor tribal war. It can be left to the Talmudic scholars. The Bible holds two more accounts which might be of interest to the purpose of this book. There are those who attribute the coma of the son of the Shunammite (II Kings, 4, 34), who was revived by Elisha, to cerebral malaria. This seems unlikely, given our present understanding of the geographical distribution of cerebral malaria at that time. There remains the pestilence wished upon the people of Israel by David as his punishment for numbering the people (II Samuel, 24, 10-25). No one has any serious suggestion as to what this disease might have been though Mignard was in no doubt when he depicted it as bubonic plague.

It has been claimed that the Orphic poems of approximately the sixth-century BC mention malaria and this seems to be true. Russell reports that very early Chinese writings give an excellent picture of the symptoms of malaria. It is described by them as being caused by three devils, one with a bucket of cold water, one with a stove and one with a hammer, as good a representation as any of the rigour, the fever and the headache of malaria.

It is in the fifth and fourth centuries BC that we begin to encounter more or less accurate descriptions of disease from the Greeks. There is little doubt that the final nail in the coffin of Persian pretensions in Greece and the Mediterranean world was driven home by dysentery when Zinnser reports that it reduced the army of Xerxes from a reputed 800,000 to 500,000. Another source has Darius also checked by dysentery. In both cases it might be claimed with justification that Greek and European culture owe their continued existence to Greek arms and dysentery. From this time in Ancient Greek history two great descriptions of disease have come down to us, the first is Thucydides' description of the 'Plague of Athens' in his *The Peloponnesian War* of the fifth-century BC and the second is the collection known as the Hippocratic writings of the fifth and fourth centuries BC and their classic description of several well-known diseases of today as well as some of arguable provenance.

Thucydides provides us with one of the most remarkable descriptions of an epidemic in medical literature; remarkable for its accuracy of description, for its detailed inventory of the epidemiology and for the vividness of the language, all at a time of fanciful, muddled and animistic descriptions of natural disorders and disasters. The most remarkable fact today about the Plague of Athens is that, despite the clarity of this notable description, modern medical science is quite unable to put a label on it. The disease is one that has either now altered or disappeared, or it is one, the identity of which, continues to baffle the best of modern epidemiologists and diagnosticians.

Just listen, for a moment, to the accurate fluidity and astonishing detail of Thucydides' account of the Athenian Plague:

> At the beginning of the following summer the Peloponnesians and their allies, with two-thirds of their total forces as before, invaded Attica, again under the command of the Spartan King Archidamus, the son of Zeuxidamus. Taking up their positions, they set about the devastation of the country.
>
> They had not been many days in Attica before the plague broke out among the Athenians. Previously the plague had been reported from many other places in the neighbourhood of Lemnos and elsewhere, but there was no record of the disease being so virulent anywhere else or causing so many deaths as it did in Athens. At the beginning the doctors were quite incapable

of treating the disease because of their ignorance of the right methods. In fact mortality among the doctors was highest of all, since they came more frequently in contact with the sick. Nor was any other human art or science of any help at all. Equally useless were prayers made in the temples, consultations with oracles, and so forth, indeed, in the end, people were so overcome by their sufferings that they paid no attention to such things.

The plague originated, so they said, in Ethiopia, in upper Egypt, and spread from there into Egypt itself and Lybia and much of the territory of the King of Persia. In the city of Athens it appeared suddenly, and the first cases were among the population of Piraeus, so that it was supposed by them that the Peloponnese had poisoned the reservoirs. Later, however it appeared in the upper city, and by this time the deaths were greatly increasing in number. As to the question of how it could first have come about or what causes could be found adequate to explain its powerful effect on nature, I must leave that to be considered by other writers, with or without medical experience. I myself shall merely describe what it was like, and set down the symptoms, knowledge of which will enable it to be recognised, if it should ever break out again, I had the disease myself and saw others suffering from it.

That year, as is generally admitted, was particularly free from other forms of illness, though those who did have any illness previously all caught the plague in the end. In other cases, however, there seemed to be no reason for the attacks. People in perfect health began to have burning feelings in the head; their eyes became red and inflamed; inside their mouths there was bleeding from the throat and tongue, and the breath became unnatural and unpleasant. The next symptoms were sneezing and hoarseness of voice, and before long the pain settled in the chest and was accompanied by coughing. Next the stomach was affected with stomachaches and vomitings of every kind of bile that has been given a name by the medical profession, all this being accompanied by great pain and difficulty. In most cases there were attacks of ineffectual retching, producing violent spasms; this sometimes ended with this stage of the disease, but sometimes continued long afterwards. Externally the body was not very hot to the touch, nor was there any pallor: the skin was rather reddish and livid, breaking out into small pustules and ulcers. But inside there was a feeling of burning, so that people could not bear the touch of even the lightest linen clothing, but wanted to be completely naked, and indeed most of all would have liked to plunge into cold water. Many of the sick who were uncared for actually did so, plunging into the water-tanks in an effort to relieve a thirst which was unquenchable; for it was just the same with them whether they drank much or little. Then all the time they were afflicted with insomnia and the desperate feeling of not being able to keep still.

In the period when the disease was at its height, the body, so far from wasting away, showed surprising powers of resistance to all the agony, so that there was still some strength left on the seventh of eighth day, which was the time when, in most cases, death came from internal fever. But if people survived this critical period, then the disease descended to the bowels, producing violent ulceration and uncontrollable diarrhoea, so that many of them died later as a result of the weakness caused by this. For the disease, first settling in the head, went on to affect every part of the body in turn, and even when people escaped its worst effects, it still left its traces on them by fastening on the extremities of the body. It affected the genitals, the fingers, and the toes, and many of those who recovered lost the use of these members; some, too, went blind. There were some also who, when they first began to get better, suffered from a total loss of memory, not knowing who they were themselves and being unable to recognise friends.

Words indeed fail one when one tries to give a general picture of this disease; and as for the sufferings of individuals, they seemed almost beyond the capacity of human nature to endure. Here, in particular, is a point where this plague showed itself to be something quite different from ordinary disease: though there were many dead bodies lying about unburied, the birds and animals that eat human flesh either did not come near them or, if they did taste the flesh, died of it afterwards. Evidence for this may be found in the fact that there was a complete disappearance of all birds of prey: they were not to be seen either around the bodies or anywhere else. But dogs, being domestic animals, provided the best opportunity of observing this effect of the plague.

These, then, were the general features of the disease, though I have omitted all kinds of peculiarities which occurred in individual cases. Meanwhile during all this time there was no serious outbreak of any of the usual kinds of illness; if any such cases did occur, they ended in the plague. Some died of neglect, some in spite of every possible care being taken of them. As for a recognised method of treatment, it would be true to say that no such thing existed: what did good in some cases did harm in others. Those with naturally strong constitutions were no better able than the weak to resist the disease, which carried all away alike, even those who were treated and dieted with the greatest care. The most terrible thing of all was the despair into which people fell when they realised they had caught the plague; for they would immediately adopt an attitude of utter hopelessness, and, by giving in in this way, would lose their powers of resistance. Terrible, too, was the sight of people dying like sheep through having caught the disease as a result of nursing others. This indeed caused more deaths than anything else. For when people were afraid to visit the sick, then they died with no one to look after them; indeed there were many houses in which all the inhabitants perished through lack of any attention. When, on the other hand, they did visit the sick, they lost their own lives, and this was particularly true of those who made it a point of honour to act properly. Such people felt ashamed to think of their own safety and went into their friends' houses at times when even the members of the households were so overwhelmed by the weight of their calamities that they had actually given up the usual practice of making laments for the dead. Yet still the ones who felt most pity for the sick and dying were those who had had the plague themselves and had recovered from it. They knew what it was like and at the same time felt themselves to be safe, for no one caught the disease twice, or if they did, the second attack was never fatal. Such people were congratulated on all sides, and they themselves were so elated at the time of their recovery that they fondly imagines that they could never die of any other disease in the future.

A factor which made things much worse than they were already was the removal of people from the country to the city, and this particularly affected the incomers. There were no houses for them, and, living as they did during the hot season in badly ventilated huts, they died like flies. The bodies of the dying were heaped one on top of another, and half-dead creatures could be seen staggering about in the streets or flocking together around the fountains in their desire for water. The temples in which they took up their quarters were full of the dead bodies of the people who had died inside them. For the catastrophe was so overwhelming that men, not knowing what would happen next to them, became indifferent to every rule of religion or law. All the funeral ceremonies which used to be observed were now disorganised, and they buried the dead as best they could. Many people, lacking the necessary means of burial because so many deaths had already occurred in their households, adopted the most shameless methods. They would arrive first at a funeral pyre that had been made by others, put their own dead on it and set it alight; or, finding another pyre burning, they would throw the corpse that they were carrying on top of the other one and walk away.

Thucydides goes on to describe the general state of disorder and degeneration which the plague brought down on the head of Athens and the failure of Hagnon's army besieging Potidaea due to the plague. Hagnon's Athenian reinforcements infected the troops already present at the siege who had been plague-free. Thucydides says that Athens bore the major brunt of the plague but other populous cities also suffered. The plague carried off its major prize when it claimed Pericles himself.

How one's heart goes out to Thucydides. Here is no vengeful Jehovah visiting nameless epidemics upon the people he made in his own image, for the least offence. Here is no transmission of leprosy by bricks and mortar. Here is no vague description of a tribal god supposed to be the bearer of pestilence and figured as a fly. Here is no credulous Herodotus with his plague of bow-string-eating mice. Here is only dispassionate description of known events in common language and high honour. Just look at what he tells us:

1. The plague had been reported elsewhere but only in Athens after the inhabitants of Piraeus and the local countryside had crowded into the city did it reach high incidence and virulence.
2. It was incurable.
3. It attacked particularly those who tended the afflicted.
4. It originated in Ethiopia then Upper Egypt ('so they say'). Such was the influence of Thucydides that a disproportionate number of subsequent epidemics were claimed to have come from the same source.
5. It was not water-borne.
6. It affected all classes, both sexes, the healthy and the weak alike.
7. It was not a relapse or a sequel of another disease.
8. It started with headache and inflamed eyes, the buccal cavity was affected

and bleeding and the breath became unpleasant.

9. The patient started to sneeze and suffered from laryngitis.
10. The lungs became affected, then the digestive tract accompanied by vomiting.
11. There was no great fever despite the patient's impression of internal heat. There was some indefinite neurological involvement.
12. The skin was reddened and small spots appeared.
13. There was a great feeling of thirst, and combined with the impression of heat caused a desire to plunge into cold water and to drink a great deal, neither brought relief.
14. Death usually occurred on the seventh or eighth day despite the apparent haleness of the body.
15. Survivors of this crisis went on to dysentery.
16. Those who recovered were immune to further attacks but frequently had lost their extremities, their capacity to breed, their sight or their memories. There was no cross immunity gained from other common diseases though the plague may have caused some increased resistance to other diseases.
17. Scavenging animals spurned the dead bodies, or if they did eat the dead bodies they died themselves. (Did Thucydides influence Boccaccio? see Chapter 6)
18. The people showed all the signs of collective despair with a breakdown of public and private morals.
19. The pandemic was associated with crowding.
20. It was a highly infectious communicable disease.
21. The disease afflicted Athens for 16 years.

Such information about a disease was not communicated in Europe with such richness for nearly another two thousand years. Yet it is totally beyond the wit of modern medical science and medical scientists to put a name to this disease. That is perhaps not entirely true as a legion of names have been advanced for it, what is lacking is any form of agreement. Most odd of all is the fact that the Hippocratic corpus does not mention it. MacArthur says that more ink has been spilt over the nature of the Plague of Athens than blood was spilt in the Peloponnesian War, and then, goes on to spill some more; though to some purpose (4).

MacArthur (1959) is certain that the Athenian Plague was typhus and his arguments are persuasive, and only become the more so when one reads the misdirected criticisms attacking this view. Shrewsbury (1950), maintaining his form and with his usual vituperative wrongheadedness, claims that the diagnosis of typhus is hopelessly wrong as there were no lice in Athens. As both Aristophenes and Aristotle mention lice and fleas, this does no more than reveal Shrewsbury's ignorance of fifth-century BC Athens. Shrewsbury said it was measles, not a view which has gained any support. Some have pointed out Thucydides' belief that the disease was communicable (5). A great number of possibilities have been canvassed (6).

Cartwright (1972) listed all the diagnoses made up to 1972 which included a malignant form of scarlet fever, bubonic plague, typhus, smallpox, measles, anthrax and a now unknown disease without committing himself. More recently ergotism, bubonic plague, measles and even typhus were ruled out of court according to Longrigg while smallpox was given a fair wind. The most recent diagnosis, by Langmuir et. al., has been influenza complicated by a fulminating *Staphylococcus* infection, claiming that the enterotoxic form of *Staphylococcus* would explain the intestinal symptoms.

I have no intention of entering these lists, claiming insufficient training, but leave the last word with the thoughtful terms of Poole and Halliday who list all of the objections to all of the diagnoses made and postulate that at the end of the day there are four possibilities:

1. It was and is a presently known disease or a mixture of two or more known diseases.
2. It exists today only in some remote and unknown corner of the world.
3. It is now extinct. A theory which they favour.
4. The disease has changed, which they find quite possible as would any bacterial geneticist.

No one, in the world today, with the epidemic of AIDS spreading as it is, can doubt the ability of an epidemic of a disease to spring up *de novo*, whether the underlying organism existed previously or not. What remains certain is that we have a clear case of a disease affecting history. Pericles himself warned the Athenian people that they could not win a war on land and the Plague of Athens ensured that; the Peloponnesians, who were not affected by the plague it seems, were able to have their way on land with only a few exceptions. It was Pericles' tactic to win at sea and keep the sea lanes open to the Athenian colonies and trade, much as Great Britain was to do in modern times. Such sea power could deliver troops where they were most needed or most likely to gain an advantage. Even then the Athenian Plague played a part as the fleet was attacked and hampered by it.

The war moved to Sicily and the Athenian colonies there but not before the Athenian Plague had killed 300 knights, 45,000 citizens, 10,000 freedmen and slaves and Pericles; and Athens had been forced into an unfavourable peace settlement. So passed the golden age of Periclean Athens, though the final blow was not to fall until a little later in Sicily where again disease was to play its part. Once again Thucydides is our authority with a little help from Diodorus Siculus (XII, 82). In 413 BC the Athenian general Nicias, after some disastrous dithering, found his troops too weakened by disease to resist or attack the Syracusan troops under Gylippus. The Athenians were said to have lingered too long in a swamp. This general site outside Syracuse was to become famous for the defeat of armies afflicted with disease be it smallpox, influenza or malaria. In very nearly the same place a Carthaginian army, almost wiped out by disease, was defeated by the Syracusans only 17 years later in 396 BC, thus ending the Magonid dynasty in Carthage as well as ending Carthaginian aspirations in Sicily for a time.

Two centuries later in 213 BC Carthage tried to secure Sicily, the great grain producer of the western Mediterranean, for the Carthaginian cause in the first Punic War against Rome. The combined Carthaginian and Sicilian force approached Syracuse garrisoned by Romans. The combined army, learning nothing from history, camped on the marshy Anapus River and a terrible epidemic broke out among them. The Sicilians deserted and the Carthaginians were almost entirely destroyed by the epidemic alone. The Romans who had also been infected were less affected as they were on higher ground and had better discipline and sanitation. They retreated into Syracuse, according to Livy (XXV, 4-11), where the shade revived them from the autumnal heat. Diodorus adds that the Romans had been in the area longer, as if they had gained some immunity to the disease in question. It is tempting to ascribe these outbreaks to malaria because of the marsh and the effects of local geography and because of local immunity or at least knowledge, however no one else has done so which leaves the suggestion rather exposed to the objection that malaria would be unlikely to destroy so completely an army in such a short space of time. What remains clear is that epidemic disease or diseases prevalent in the lands to the north and west of Syracuse defeated Athenian colonial pretensions, rang the Athenian Empire's death knell and kept Sicily from the hands of Carthage with enormous consequences in the feeding of Rome, the outcome of the Punic wars and Rome's subsequent domination of the Mediterranean.

Before one comes to the fall of the Roman Empire and the part played in those events by epidemic disease, it is necessary to examine the last great enterprise of Ancient Greece. This was the attempted harmonisation of Hellenic art and culture with that of Persia and near Asia by Alexander the Great. What turned him and his army back at the banks of the Beas?, what killed him? There can be no doubt that, at the Beas (7), the Greeks turned back at the urgings of the Greek soldiers themselves and because they had reached the very edge of the Achaemenid Empire, but was there a medical reason for such urgings? We hear remarkably little about the health of Alexander's army from the recorders who were pupils of Aristotle. It would seem reasonable to suppose that on the banks of the Beas the Greeks would be suffering from malaria. More importantly perhaps they would be likely to be suffering the miseries of dysentery (which had carried off the Buddha at the age of 80 in India in the previous century) even if their love of cleanliness may have prevented typhus. Their allies may have been relatively immune to these local diseases which would add to the feeling of isolation and plain homesickness which afflicted this remarkable army. There is no reason to believe that Asiatic cholera would have played any part.

One might safely hazard a guess that one of the points made by the Macedonian soldiers to Alexander in favour of a return home would have been the poor health of the army as a whole. Alexander's death has been attributed to malaria, but the reasons for supposing the attribution are flimsy.

CHAPTER 2
Rome

Pestilence and famine contributed to fill up the measure of the calamities of Rome.
   Gibbon, *The History of the Decline and Fall of the Roman Empire*

When the Roman Empire and its fate are mentioned the name of Gibbon inevitably arises and Gibbon was no friend to any overemphasis on disease as a contributory factor in the fall of the Roman Empire. He had his own candidates for that role. Consideration of the rise of Rome allows an escape from under the shadow of the great man. Such a consideration can only lead to wonder that it ever got off the ground. How did the infant state, long before it was a republic let alone an Empire, ever survive the terrible plagues and pestilences that attended its birth and early years. Livy has hardly any room left for history after he has enumerated the pestilences. No sooner had Romulus been left sole ruler after the death of Tatius than a plague fell upon the land, causing sudden death, barren cattle and a rain of blood. Rome was very nearly finished off in its infancy by disease and the Camerians. From then on as Pope Gelasius was to observe epidemics arose in Rome with the frequency of the seasons and those epidemics slew thousands which infant Rome could have ill-afforded.

Livy records a pestilence which laid Rome so low that it was unable to defend itself against the Volsci and the Aequi, who, finding so little to conquer and plunder, retired (from the epidemic too if they had any sense). That was in 463 BC; there was another pestilence in 433 BC, another in 430 BC and so on and so on. How, then, in the face of such attacks of disease and in a known malarious area (and what was Aeneas thinking of? he had been warned of the unhealthiness of the area) did the Roman Empire arise? One of the obvious conclusions which arises from the considerations of this book will be that: while epidemics may have profound effects upon systems, governments and state in decline, they have little or no effect upon the same institutions when on the rise. In the concluding chapter of this work this point will be addressed again and an explanation sought.

The fall of the Roman Empire! The very title gives pause as one must now examine a phenomenon already examined by one of the great minds of our culture. Gibbon, while giving passing mention to major epidemics and pandemics in the Roman Empire, ascribes no import to them (except perhaps Justinian's plague which is the subject of the next chapter). He does not even give the Antonine plague any relevance to the decline of his beloved Antonine rule. He makes note of the Antonine plague, the Aurelian plague and the role of disease in the barbarian incursions but gives them no special importance. The major stumbling block to any consideration of the two major plagues of the west Roman Empire is the inability to give a certain name to the disease causing them. This precludes any assumptions based on a known epidemiology, though assumptions must be made, if only on suppositions.

Five major pestilences have been identified by Castiglione in the period from Augustus Caesar to the ascent of Justinian to the eastern purple:

1. AD 79, after that eruption of Vesuvius which engulfed Pompeii and Herculaneum, an epidemic spread all over the Campagna, killing tens of thousands daily (?). Some have described this outbreak as malaria consequent on the destruction of the drainage systems. This is dubious and will be discussed in a later chapter on malaria.

2. AD 125, the so-called plague of Orosius. Orosius was a fifth-century historian who reported that this epidemic killed 800,000 in Nubia and a further 200,000 in Utica. Virtually nothing is known about this pestilence some, believe it was bubonic plague. Orosius, who was repeating some earlier work, certainly overestimates the total population of the North African littoral of the time.

3. AD 164-180, the Antonine plague or Galen's plague began with the soldiers serving on the eastern frontiers of the Empire with Verus, the co-Emperor with Marcus Aurelius (although this plague occurred during the reign of Marcus Aurelius, the Aurelian plague is later and belongs in the reign of Aurelian among others). It spread rapidly on the return of the infected soldiers and reached Rome itself in 166. Thousands died daily in Rome and Marcus Aurelius himself died of it. Galen is said to have fled from it but he was recalled by the joint Emperors Marcus Aurelius and Verus to advise on the control of the pandemic. Galen's behaviour during this epidemic has been discussed with heat by various protagonists and bids fair to becoming a minor literature on its own. Galen left us no recognisable diagnosis, though what he does say, has led most to believe it was smallpox, others believe it may have been typhus or true plague. Gibbon says that the populace favoured the just indignation of the gods directed at the Christians.

4. AD 251-266, the Aurelian plague or the plague of Cyprian, which raged during the reigns of Claudius Gothicus and Gallienus, began to abate during the reign of Aurelian. No sooner had the Empire begun to recover from the effects of the second-century plague when this plague struck. Many think it too was smallpox, and, indeed, a recrudescence or a prolongation of the previous pandemic. Among the population of Alexandria those of 14 to 80 years old after the plague were equal in numbers to those of 40 to 80 years old prior to the plague, which given the life expectancy of those days is a very considerable death toll. Gibbon computed that half the population of Alexandria had perished. This plague also struck the invading Goths who had by then gathered together in such concentration of numbers as to fall victim to epidemic crowd diseases. This plague struck down Claudius Gothicus, who was succeeded by Gallienus.

5. AD 312, another pestilence, thought once again to be smallpox and, therefore, essentially the same pandemic as before. Little is known about this outbreak, except that it ushered in Constantine the Great.

By rights we should know most about the 166 pandemic since it involved one of the sacred cows of medicine – Galen himself, whose views on disease were to survive and prevail into the nineteenth-century. Littman and Littman (1973) provide us with a confident opinion as they have done with the Athenian plague. They put the outbreak as starting in late 165 or early 166 among the troops of Verus in Mesopotamia and lasting until at least 180, with a recrudescence in 189. They quote Niebuhr's famous opinion that:

the ancient world never recovered from the blow inflicted upon it by the plague which visited it in the reign of M. Aurelius,

and they quote the opinion of Seeck that over half of the population of the Empire perished in the pandemic. They feel that the case for believing the disease to have been smallpox is strong despite the equivocal and sketchy description of Galen. The question then arises whether this plague and its continuations had any decisive effect on the decline of the Roman Empire of the West.

The main opinion to be considered is that of Boak though many others (1) also deserve study. Boak with Parker in some sort of support, believes that the outbreak of disease in 166 and its continuation was critical to the decline of the Western Roman Empire.

In his *Manpower Shortage and the Fall of the Roman Empire* Boak advances the view that the decline commenced in the mid-second-century and certainly by 193. In this he has Grant's (1968) concurrence. It is central to Boak's argument that he puts the halt in the growth of the population of the Western Roman Empire at the death of Marcus Aurelius, when the pandemic had had a grip on the Empire for some 20 years. Boak sees this population check as lasting from 193 to 235, that is through the Severan dynasty and until the ascent of Maximin. At this point Boak postulates a distinct downward dip in critical portions of the population, when the agricultural classes and the *curiales* were drafted in large numbers into the ever hungry and disproportionately large army. This situation was to hold until the ascent of the Diocletian, who, with Constantine I, was able to stem, if not cure, the population decline with a series of economic and social reforms. Here Grant (1968) disagrees, but only in timing, as he puts the beginning of the stemming of the population decline in the prior date of the reigns of Claudius Gothicus and Aurelian. It is equally central to Boak's hypothesis that the lack of peasants to till, plant and harvest and the lack of *curiales*, the municipal officers, to administer the day to day duties of the towns led to an inability to hold off the invasion of the barbarians.

The critical periods were, in his opinion, a population check by 193 and a progressive decline in population in the period 235-285. This decline put Rome on the slippery slope of population loss where each shortage of numbers feeds interdependent shortages elsewhere and Peter is robbed to pay Paul. Critical to this, in his opinion, was the extensive recruitment into the army of barbarians. These views received some contemporary support from Dio Cassius, who says that after Marcus Aurelius the Empire descended from a kingdom of gold to a kingdom of iron and rust.

It is immediately obvious from the foregoing account of the Roman pandemics that these dates of population crises fit roughly with the culmination of the pandemics, that is immediately after the first Antonine plague and during the subsequent Aurelian plague. If the latter was only a flare-up of the former then the disease would have been rumbling along at an endemic but deadly level. It has to be said that despite this Boak does not ascribe to disease the prime place in the population decline. He is meticulous in stating his belief that there was no one single major cause for the check and decline. To my mind, however, the timing gives disease a position of great importance. If disease directly is not to be held responsible then the only other cause can be a lowering of the birth rate and it is held here that the primary cause of that would be the low expectancy of any quality or duration of life due to the pandemic.

Needless to say Boak has his detractors. Finley is not enamoured of Boak's figures and his consequent comparative demography. He disagrees with Boak's central thesis that population decline leads to manpower shortage and hence to breakdown, citing the belief that many governments have resorted to the Roman methods of recruitment since that time without demonstrating proof of manpower shortages. Nor does Finley accept the recruitment of barbarians either into the army or preliminarily as *coloni* as a proof that there was either a population or a manpower shortage in the Roman Empire. Finley writes:

No one will deny that the plagues and disorders of the third-century cut the population of the western Empire. That is not the issue.

He sees the issue as whether the Empire recovered from these demographic disasters, and obviously he believes that it did. Finley concludes that manpower shortage, while important, is not a solution of the problem of the fall of Rome. While Finley is excellent in criticism, he is less convincing when advancing his own contentions. Will is sympathetic to Boak's thesis but warns against dogma or simple single explanations.

Gilliam provides us with a most thoughtful and scholarly treatment of the question. He notes the views of the German historians – Niebuhr in the last century and Seeck in this – that the Antonine plague was the turning point of the Roman Empire of the West. He notes, too, that the standard text of our time by Parker writes of the plague as leaving many districts depopulated and contributing, perhaps more than any other factor, to the decline of the Empire. Gilliam makes first the point that there is not enough evidence to diagnose the disease accurately or to determine the death toll due to it. He proceeds to make a complete review of the sources available, noting that the Antonine plague was followed by another plague in 189 which may have been a flare-up of the original plague. It was during this second episode that Dio Cassius wrote of as many as 2,000 Romans dying in a day. A careful consideration of all the sources leads Gilliam to conclusions different from those of Boak, largely due to uncertainties concerning populations and their relation to recruitment to the army. He also points out that the legalised entry of barbarians into the Empire (central to Boak's argument that this spelt a manpower shortage) was nothing particularly new at the time of the post-Antonine era.

Gilliam, like Boak, refers to the Black Death with its death toll of at least 20% in its first three years in England and claims that nothing like this occurred in the latter half of the second-century in the Roman Empire. He computes that a 1% death toll would spell 500,000 deaths and 2%, a death toll of one million and assumes that there is no evidence for more. Here it is necessary to part company with Gilliam. Not only does this argument ignore any drop in birth rates due to uncertainty over the future but the Black Death figures used are for the first three years of a long decline due, arguably, to continuing disease and while they represent a check on population growth the actual downward slope is later. The Antonine plague lasted from 166 to the death of M. Aurelius in 186 and returned in the reign of the next Emperor, Commodus, in 189. It lasted in all 30 years, long enough for a check and the commencement of a decline. Gilliam's 2% death rate is an underestimate even on his own evidence.

Gilliam accepts that the decline of the Roman Empire was under way by the death of Marcus Aurelius, but notes that:

> even if one agrees that depopulation became an important aspect of the process of the third-century and later, he may doubt that this plague contributed significantly and was a decisive factor on a long continuing development'.

He requires more proof of its devastation before accepting Boak's thesis.

The Littmans (1973) produce a critical examination of Galen's writings on the Antonine plague and conclude that the case for believing it to have been haemorrhagic smallpox is overwhelming. They go on to say that Gilliam has laid to rest the idea of an overwhelming pandemic but find his figure of a 2% death-rate too low (as well they might, having just pointed to the outbreak of smallpox in Minneapolis in 1924–5 which included haemorrhagic and purpuric cases. This pandemic produced an 84% death rate among those who caught these forms of smallpox). They argue for a 7-10% death-rate. This seems to me to be picking figures out of a hat. How does one argue from an 84% case death-rate to an overall one of 7-10%? It is known that immunity would have modified the outbreak eventually but there is no way of computing the eventual death toll, let alone the effect on the birth rate. It should be remembered that confluent smallpox caused the disappearance of whole Red Indian confederations.

The figures of the Littmans spell a total death-rate of about 4,000,000 and there is no internal medical reason why this should not have been 10,000,000. The Littmans compare the Antonine plague with the plague of Athens which they claim was also smallpox (1969).. As this last is unproven, to say the least, it is difficult to find the comparison convincing. They are on firmer ground when they compare the Antonine plague with better-known smallpox outbreaks. They quote 25% as the average death-rate for smallpox cases though it can reach 60–80% (this is going to depend on the number of immunes in the population). It must be remembered that the Romans would have been a non-immune population like the Amerindians, and Amerindians went on suffering from smallpox without, it seemed, any diminution of attack for centuries. I can see, therefore, no medical reason why the death rate figure should not be anything up to 80% depending on the proportion of the population infected, the number of effective immunes (which should rise as the pandemic continued), the proportion of severe disease and the speed of spread among a still relatively sparse population.

The Littmans conclude that even at a 7–10% death-rate the Antonine plague was not a decisive event in Roman history without giving any reasons for such a dogmatic conclusion. All this omits consideration of three important factors, first that the death toll may have been much higher than is assumed, second that the plagues seem to have continued on into the reign of Aurelian and it may be that it was this very continuation which is critical to the demographic decline's slipping beyond easy recall, and third the difficult question of confidence and its effect on birth-rates.

It is accepted that high birth rates result temporarily from a confidence in a society producing sufficient for the family, usually by the lowering of the age of marriage; the reverse side of the medal must be that loss of confidence in the future, both in terms of child death-rates and the ability of society to ensure living standards and a reasonable life expectancy, will temporarily lower birth-rates by way of marriage at greater ages. If a plague so decreases the confidence of a people that population will commence to limit their increase by less breeding and it seems that the fecundity of the Romans did drop in the latter half of the second-century and the third-century in Rome at least.

Salmon addresses to some degree this last point. Basing himself on new researches into the longevity of populations in classical times, he also disagrees with Boak. He feels that insufficient notice has been taken of Christianity as a stabilising factor in a declining birth-rate. He comes, however, to no definite conclusions of his own concerning the importance of the population decline of the period 193 to the end of the third-century in the Western Empire.

A number of other authors have had their say in passing without giving the subject any exhaustive thought. Henschen believes that the decline of the Roman Empire was due to smallpox, malaria and epidemic typhus. Cartwright (1972) believes the Antonine plague to have been smallpox but admits that view is not universal. Hare (1967) takes the same view. Crawfurd in his delightful book on the effects of disease on art and literature notes that one Roman author thought the Aurelian plague so virulent that even a single glance could cause it. Castiglione and Colnat thought that a greater role for disease should be allowed in the discussion of the decadence and decline of the Roman Empire.

Maenchen-Halfen reminds us that the effect of the disease was not wholly unidirectional. By the end of the fourth-century the barbarians were beginning to come together in such numbers as to become susceptible to infectious epidemics. Even before then the Aurelian plague had so devastated regions of the Empire that the Alamanni and the Burgundians, on crossing the Rhine to plunder, found the land too poor to support their army and they fled back over the Rhine, back, that is, to the state described by Tacitus of never living in cities and with houses far apart dotted here and there.

In 383 the Visigoths were weakened by a raging epidemic. Ruga, King of the Huns, was killed in about 435 and his army scattered by a plague. Attila, after his defeat at the *Locus Mariacus* in 451 turned back to Bohemia and then down into Italy across the Julian Alps and though he took Aquileia, Milan and Pavia and even reached Rome, he had to retire hastily from the city, not so much because of the entreaties of Pope St Leo but to save his diseased and ill-nourished troops from further travail. He crossed back over the Po to his eventual death from angiorrhexis. This part of Italy became known as the *Regio Funestus* as 50 years earlier Alaric's Visigoths had been struck down by an epidemic there near

Verona, as they had been a few years earlier in Arcadia.

A hundred years later the Franks were to suffer similarly on the Po. In 447 the Huns again had to retreat in the face of an epidemic when they were besieging Constantinople itself, a capital which often seemed to rely on disease among its would-be conquerors as an epidemic caused the withdrawal of the hitherto victorious Arabs in 717 with incalculable consequences for the Byzantine Empire and Europe.

Marks and Beatty in their excellent *Epidemics* state their belief that the Aurelian plague coming on an Empire not yet recovered from the ravages of the Antonine plague depopulated the land of peasants, the army of men and the economy of workers. The 310–312 outbreak added its contribution and deepened the depopulation and the economic inflation. The Christians saw it as a just reward for Maxentius, who had persecuted them. Marks and Beatty, obviously influenced by Boak, believe that the epidemics were a prime cause of the decline of the Western Empire. Conrad thought that the 189 plague was the same as the Antonine plague. He traces the Cyprian (=Aurelian) plague to Nice in 250, spreading to North Africa, thence to Italy, Greece and the Balkans by 269, but he does not hazard any guess as to what it might have been.

The belief expressed here is that the Antonine, Aurelian and the 312 plagues were a *primus inter pares* cause of the decline of the Roman Empire of the West. The belief has been propounded that when a state is on an upward curve in power and population, in dominance and expansion, then pandemics have little or no effect on their progress. Rome provides a supreme example. Plutarch and Livy inform us that the young Rome was subject to epidemic after epidemic, sometimes so bad that they could not defend themselves, as against the Hernici in 265 BC and against the Volsci and the Aequi as mentioned before. Yet Rome was to prosper while the Etruscans disappeared. This same Rome fell having gone into a population decline at a time when epidemics were ravaging it. It is held here that these epidemics were critical to the population loss and that demographic decline was critical to the decline of the Empire, but it is inherent in this argument that an epidemic, of itself, does not, of necessity precipitate a decline, though it does or may do so when associated with other unknown factors which can affect confidence and cause a drop in the birth-rate.

One major misconception concerning epidemic or pandemic disease should be mentioned here as it is common to many of the classical writers as well as those of a later date. There is a phrase, much beloved by historians, the translators of the Bible and the chroniclers. It is 'famine and pestilence'. This gives the convenient even comfortable impression that the one follows the other as night the day. Little could be further from the truth as far as it is known today. The Greeks did better with *loimos meta limon* (pestilence then famine). There is no established evidence for the common belief that protein-calorie malnutrition can predispose a person to infectious disease with the possible exception of some work done on measles in malnourished subjects, though this may owe more to an avitaminosis due to lack of Vitamin A, which can, however, be interpreted as a form of malnutrition.

It has to be said that the belief is not confined to the non-medical world, it is an article of faith with the nutritionists, stated at frequent intervals without benefit of proof. There is some evidence that severe malnutrition may impair certain immune functions of the body but absolutely no evidence that that impairment is critical to the body's ability to respond adequately to any particular infection, or that malnutrition has indeed precipitated an infectious disease in a patient except perhaps measles. Indeed some of the few facts we do have point in exactly the opposite direction. Malaria is known to be inhibited by a form of avitaminosis caused by a shortage of para-amino-benzoic acid in the body of the host; more importantly, malaria in mice has been shown to be inhibited by protein malnutrition and malaria in humans by a shortage of iron. Malnutrition kills few people of itself but does damage the killer malaria parasite.

There is a correlation between malnutrition and an over-growth of unwanted bacteria in the gut but which is cause and which is effect is anyone's guess. The general misapprehension arises because the season of disease often coincides with the season of little or no food and because hunger drives people together into masses ideal for the spread of infectious disease. The nutritionists proclaim that it is axiomatic that malnutrition of itself at least increased the number suffering from an infectious disease in any given population. I wish they would prove it as I am inclined to believe it is sometimes true; but until they do so the case is 'not proven'.

To return to the Roman Empire, by the sixth-century the Western Empire had disappeared under waves of Huns, Visigoths, Ostrogoths, Vandals, Alans, Burgundians, Lombards and Franks. In the east in Constantinople, however, a renaissance was occurring under the energetic leadership of the Emperor Justinian and his exceptional general Belisarius. Their war aim was to oust the barbarians from the confines of the former Roman Empire and re-establish it in all its former glory. Belisarius had reconquered North Africa from the Vandals and had swept up the Italian peninsula and was taking Italy from the Ostrogoths. Justinian had secured his rear by buying off his chief enemy, the Great King of Persia, with an affordable tribute and achieving an uneasy 'permanent' peace. In 542 the Persians broke the peace, but a far worse enemy was to break the peace, push back the Persians and bring all Justinian's hopes to utter ruin. Its name was *Yersinia pestis*. Bubonic plague stepped onto the world stage.

CHAPTER 3
Plague
Justinian's Plague (part 1)

During these times (AD 452) there was a pestilence, by which the whole human race came near to being annihilated. . . . And this disease always took its start from the coast and from there went up into the interior.
Procopius *History of Wars* II, XXII, 1-7

Justinian's Plague has been called possibly the most disastrous event in the history of man. If it was not, then its brother, 'The Black Death', certainly was. Listen to Gibbon, who usually gives disease scant notice:

during three months, five and at length ten thousand persons died each day
at Constantinople; that many cities of the East were left vacant: and in several
districts of Italy the harvest and the vintage withered on the ground.

One must set the scene for the greatest and most powerful of the actors in our drama – *Yersinia pestis*. Now that we are examining a specific disease it is necessary to give some information on the aetiological organism, the vector if any, and the natural history and symptomatology of the disease. True plague *(sensu strictu)*, our subject now, as opposed to the generic term, is a bacterial disease caused by *Yersinia* (= *Bacillus* = *Pasteurella*) *pestis*, usually transmitted by a flea. The disease in man in the nineteenth and twentieth centuries took one of three forms:

1. Bubonic Plague
2. Pneumonic Plague
3. Septicaemic Plague

(in descending order of frequency in the nineteenth and twentieth centuries and ignoring the rare meningeal plague).

The first, bubonic plague, is acquired from an infected rat via a rat flea, and is characterised chiefly by the appearance of greatly enlarged lymph nodes, known as buboes, occurring mostly in the armpits and the groin, more rarely on the upper thigh and the neck. Bubonic plague kills about 70% of its victims. The buboes appear where the lymph nodes drain the site of the infective flea bite: thus if an infected flea bit the leg the bubo appears in the groin or more rarely the upper thigh; if the flea bit the hand or the arm then the bubo swells up in the armpit; and so on. The vector (transmitting agent) of *Y. pestis* in bubonic plague is the tropical rat flea *Xenopsilla cheopis*, and more rarely other genera and species of rodent fleas.

Present theory has it that the flea's alimentary canal becomes blocked by the exuberant growth of *Yersinia* so that, if the flea wishes to feed successfully it must clear this blockage. It does this by regurgitating the mass of organisms during the feeding process and these are thereby inoculated into the skin of the animal upon which the flea is attempting to feed, thus transmitting the infection. This is a somewhat naive and simplistic description for these days of highly complicated physiological and molecular explanations of biological phenomena. The regurgitation process is hardly the same as a human consciously clearing his throat and has more to do with the relaxation of pumping muscles which suck up the blood when the flea senses a lack of success followed by a clearing of the obstruction due to the back flow consequent on the sudden cessation of pumping.

A very great deal of hard work has gone into the identification of the offending flea in the differing areas of the world and the differing rodents involved in bubonic plague outbreaks. An infected flea, which has acquired the infection by feeding on an infected rodent, may live for several months though the life-span of a blocked flea is much shorter. The major reservoir animal of bubonic plague is the black rat *Rattus rattus,* though other rodents, even rabbits or predators of rodents such as coyotes, may be involved in differing ecosystems. Plague usually kills all of its hosts, humans, rats and fleas, when the disease is epidemic or epizootic (epidemic among animals).

The symptoms of bubonic plague appear in two days to one week after the infective bite, exceptionally two weeks. There may be preliminary feelings of dizziness, depression, aches, chills, giddiness, palpitations and dull pain at the eventual site of the bubo. The bubo develops quickly usually a day after the first symptoms of illness. The bubo may be of the size of an almond or as large as a goose's egg and may be very painful or relatively painless. The fever then commences with temperatures as high as 40.5°C. The pulse rate increases, there is an intense thirst and prostration sets in. The patient may become delirious. Coma, convulsions, violent twitchings, urine retention and other symptoms of an involvement of the nervous system may follow. Vomiting may be frequent and both diarrhoea or constipation may occur.

All these symptoms may abate, the bubo burst, discharge pus, slough off and the patient recover. Sometimes papules are present which may develop into pustules ('blains'). The disease may develop into pneumonic plague. Death may intervene in anything from 20% to 95% of infected persons. After death haemorrhagic spots or patches may appear on the skin, usually black in colour. *Y. pestis* is susceptible to attack by chloramphenicol, streptomycin, tetracyclines and sulphonamides though resistant strains have appeared. An anti-plague serum exists. Vaccination is available and has been shown to be effective with the American Army in Viet-Nam but not with the indigenous Viet-Namese.

The next form – pneumonic plague – is a very deadly form of the disease, killing up to and over 90% of cases. It occurs when the major site of infection is the lungs and the transmission is by droplets of sputum from another victim of pneumonic plague. The prime sign of pneumonic plague is blood-stained sputum. The highest incidence of pneumonic plague tends to be in winter, possibly because at that time other respiratory diseases are present and assist the transmission of pneumonic plague by adding their share of coughing and sneezing. I am anything but happy with this explanation as respiratory diseases are not confined to the winter months, though it does seem that pneumonic plague was greatly more prevalent in winter months. The significance of winter may have more to do with crowding together for warmth than with other respiratory diseases.

Pneumonic plague overcomes man so quickly in modern experience that buboes are not given time to appear. Pollitzer and Li (1943) have shown that in the modern pandemic, droplet transmission could not sustain an epidemic of pneumonic plague for longer than one season or so and that modern pneumonic plague outbreaks die out of their own accord, presumably as the lung infection grew less severe with each succeeding patient and coughing ceased to be a major feature. Even the most disastrous epidemic of pneumonic plague in this century only lasted from autumn to the following spring. The disease commences with rigour, malaise, headache, vomiting, fever and extreme prostration. Cough sets in and the sputum can be seen to be watery, profuse, bloodstained and containing white flecks of almost pure *Y. pestis*. The patient is usually very vague. The lungs can be heard to be severely affected and the breathing is fast. Delirium overcomes the patient and he usually dies by the fourth or fifth day of the illness. This disease in rats and marmots tends to attack the intestine and its mucosa.

Finally, septicaemic plague about which we seem to know least. It is, like the pneumonic form, a great killer of men and women. The primary site of infection is the blood stream which becomes infected with enormous numbers of bacilli. The infection is so overwhelming that the patient dies before the infection of the lymph nodes develops into the visible bubo stage. The one visible consequence is the frequent appearance of the skin haemorrhages showing as black or dusky patches on the skin surface. These, to be sure, also occur in the bubonic form of the disease but are more frequent, early and prominent in the septicaemic form as one would expect from the greater dispersion of bacilli consequent upon a blood infection. MacArthur (1926) has pointed out that these dark blotches are the 'tokens' of Shakespeare. Septicaemic plague is transmitted by the human flea.

The usual version of events in septicaemic plague is not entirely acceptable. The main event is an overwhelming infection of the blood. It seems then that this would have to be a constant character of the variant of *Y. pestis* involved as, while we may believe that a heavy infection of the blood may be necessary to set up an infection in a human flea, there is no reason to believe that the infected human flea delivers more than the usual number of bacilli. If only a usual number of bacilli are delivered, how is the overwhelming blood infection to be achieved in a short space of time in the new human host, which may be assumed to occur as there is evidence of areas where the usual infection is a septicaemic one? One satisfactory explanation would be for a strain of *Y. pestis* to exist which multiplies at an abnormally high rate and does so preferentially in the blood stream. Such a strain would be peculiar to septicaemic plague and would not be subject to the dying out phenomena of pneumonic plague. If such a strain, however, was slow enough in its development as to allow the appearance of buboes, we could have the situation of a killer strain of septicaemic plague which nonetheless produced some buboes, though not always in the classic places.

The belief that very large numbers of bacilli had to be present in the blood in order to infect a human flea comes from MacArthur (1926) in a simple anecdotal experience using twentieth-century bacilli. Blanc and Baltazard using a strain of *Y. pestis* known to produce septicaemic plague had no difficulty in infecting human fleas. The human flea in question is *Pulex irritans*.

Two anecdotes may not be out of place here. The specific name *irritans* brings to mind a story noted by Shipley; the great lady of the French court who was heard to observe: 'Quant à moi, ce n'est pas la moursure, c'est la promenade' ('For my part, it's not the bite, it's the crawling'). The one person who was less than thrilled with Albert Camus' brilliant novel *La Peste*, which purported to describe an ineptly handled outbreak of plague in what was obviously Oran, was the eminent French doctor-scientist Georges Blanc. Blanc was in charge of public health in Oran and maintained that no epidemic of plague could ever have broken through its defences, let alone rage undetected for days.

Septicaemic plague today usually displays no enlargement of the lymph glands (buboes) during the life of the patient. The patient is prostrated immediately the disease is apparent. The patient becomes pale with the loss of blood cells and is apathetic. The fever is quite low. Delirium, weakness, nervous reactions, stupor and coma ensue and the patient is dead quickly even, sometimes, on the very day of the first symptoms or by the third day anyway. Skin haemorrhages are common. All these symptoms and signs for all the disease forms are drawn from experience with the modern plague epidemic.

The epidemiology of these various forms of plague can be left until it becomes important to the argument or to history. One point has to be made for the sake of subsequent clarity. There is a strong tendency (probably found here as well) to describe the whole series of plague outbreaks between 542 and the eighth-century as Justinian's plague and the similar series between 1357 and the fifteenth-century as the Black Death. Strictly speaking only the first two or three years of the pandemic series (that is the first waves) should claim those titles.

The knowledge of Justinian's plague comes largely from Procopius, secretary to Belisarius, with some additional information from Evagrius Scholasticus and John of Ephesus discussed by Allen. Here is Procopius writing about this plague:

During these times (AD 542) there was a pestilence, by which the whole human race came near to being annihilated, . . . it did not come in a part of the world, nor upset certain men, nor did it confine itself to any season of the year. . . but it embraced the whole of the world, and blighted the lives of all men, though differing one from another in the most marked degree, respecting neither sex nor age. . . . I shall proceed to tell where this disease originated and the manner in which it destroyed men. It started from the Egyptians who dwell in Pelusium. Then it divided and moved in one direction towards Alexandria and the rest of Egypt and in another direction it came to Palestine on the borders of Egypt; and from there it spread over the whole world, always moving forward and travelling at times favourable to it. For it seemed to move by fixed arrangement, and to tarry for a specified time in each country. . . . It left neither island or cave or mountain ridge which had human inhabitants. . . . And this disease always took its start from the coast and from there went up into the interior. . . .

It reached Byzantium where it happened I was staying at the time. . . . Even in the sanctuaries, where they had fled for refuge, they were dying constantly. . . . But with the majority it came about that they were seized by the disease without becoming aware of what was coming. They had a sudden fever. . . .The body showed no change from its previous colour, nor was it hot. . . nor did any inflammation set in. . . . But on the same day, in some cases, in others on the following day, and in the rest not many days after, a bubonic swelling developed; and this took place not only in the particular part of the body which is called the 'boubon', that is below the abdomen, but also inside the armpit, and in some cases also beside the ears and at different points on the thigh. . . . For there ensued with some a deep coma, with others violent delirium. . . for neither physicians nor other persons were found to contract this malady through contact with the sick or with the dead, for many were constantly engaged in burying or attending those in no way connected with them. . . . With some the body broke out in black pustules about as large as a lentil and these did not survive even one day, but all succumbed immediately. With many also a vomiting of blood ensued without visible cause and straightway brought death. . . in some cases when the swelling rose to an unusual size and discharge of pus had set in, it came about that they escaped from the disease and survived.

Procopius was no Thucydides, even if he was somewhat more amusing as his scandalous and libellous 'Anecdotes' attest. However he does provide a great deal of information if not quite so dispassionately. The sum of what he has to tell can be listed thus:

1. The plague came near to annihilating the human race as he knew it.
2. It did not affect the whole of the world that Procopius knew.
3. It did not strike everyone.
4. It attacked male and female; old and young alike.
5. It struck at all times of the year, including winter.
6. It started in Pelusium in Egypt, then moved on to Alexandria and Palestine. It reached Constantinople in 542.
7. It moved at no special speed, sometimes slowly, sometimes fast, but it reached everywhere in the scope of its spread.
8. It always commenced at a seaport and moved inland from there.
9. People had no warning of the onset of the disease.
10. The fever came about suddenly, the skin did not change colour or become inflamed.
11. Shortly a bubo appeared, commonly in the groin or in the armpit, less commonly in the neck or on the thigh.
12. This was followed by coma or delirium.
13. It cannot be transmitted directly to those caring for the patient.
14. Sometimes the patient developed black marks on the skin which was a sign of impending death.
15. If the bubo grew large and burst with the release of pus the patient might recover.
16. There was an occasional vomiting of blood.

This is an excellent description of a disease and is easily recognised as the bubonic plague which struck the Far East in the late 1890s with, however, significant differences. These are the times of the year of the outbreak, as it includes winter, and the occasional fast movement of the pandemic.

So the Eastern Roman Empire (it is not intended to enter the controversy about when the Eastern Roman Empire ceased and the Byzantine Empire commenced) was visited in 542 by a disastrous pandemic which was characterised by buboes in the groin and armpit, which commenced at the ports and proceeded inland, in which there was an element of bloody effusions from the mouth after which a quick death was the usual sequel. This is classical bubonic plague with, apparently, a pneumonic element (though the lack of contagion to those close to the patient is puzzling). Procopius went on to say that the disease lasted only four months in Constantinople with the first three months being the worst. The plague killed 5,000 people a day in the city. Nearly all the towers erected as fortifications in the walls were filled with the dead and the city stank. Justinian, himself, contracted the plague and had a bubo in his groin. He was one of the lucky ones and recovered. The disease did not confine itself to the subjects of Justinian but attacked the Persians as well and stopped a Persian invasion in its tracks when Chrosroes, the Persian Great King, retreated to Assyria where there was said to be no plague. The pandemic also struck the barbarians.

Procopius was in an excellent position to comment on all these events of the time as he was secretary to Belisarius, Justinian's brilliant general, who was charged by the Emperor with the responsibility of recovering all the lands of the old Roman Empire. This task was to take Belisarius and his secretary over much of Asia Minor and the Mediterranean world. What had been the Roman Empire now consisted of the Roman Empire of the East under Justinian, the old North African provinces now under a Vandal king, the Spanish provinces under Visigoth role and the Italian mainland and Illyrian provinces now under the rule of Theodoric. Gaul was divided between Franks, Burgundians and Visigoths and finally Britain was divided between various Celtic and Teutonic kingdoms.

These barbarian kingdoms all had their troubles. The Vandals were fighting among themselves, the Visigoths were under pressure from the Franks to the north and the Ostrogoths could not make up their minds whether they were barbarians bent on loot or the natural successors to the Romans imparting enlightenment and *Pax Romana.* Justinian saw in all this confusion the opportunity to reinstate the Roman Empire of old but centred on Christian Constantinople. He trumped up a charge against the Vandal king in North Africa and sent Belisarius to right the supposed wrong. Due to internal divisions among the Vandals their conquest was surprisingly easy. Belisarius moved on into Sicily, where he met none of the disasters of his predecessors, and he moved up into the toe of Italy. Belisarius swept all before him and his progress up the Peninsula was triumphant. He was greatly assisted by internal divisions among the Ostrogoths and by his indomitable wife Antonia, of whom Gibbon writes: 'and if Antonia disdained the merit of conjugal fidelity, she expressed a manly friendship to Belisarius, whom she accompanied with undaunted resolution in all the hardships and dangers of a military life.'

Belisarius took Rome itself and the Ostrogoths fell back on Ravenna under the formidable Vitigis, whence they attempted to retake Rome, but on failing (due to disease?) retreated again to Ravenna. But now the ever present envy of Belisarius in Constantinople gained in strength and he was recalled, ostensibly because the remnants of the Ostrogoths hardly required such a general to deal with them. During the temporary eclipse of Belisarius the Empire suffered a Vandal rebellion followed by a Moorish rebellion. Encouraged, the Ostrogoths revived under Totila. This last was too much and Belisarius was recalled to the eagles, but now the plague had intervened and he was short of men, money, horses and arms and this consequence of the plague must be assessed.

At the time of the commencement of Belisarius' victories the Roman Empire of the East was at its zenith. Though Justinian was looking west, he had to protect his back from the implacable enemy of Greece and Rome – Persia. By a single stroke he bought 'perpetual peace' with Persia for a sum so small that his strength must have been such as to give the Persians considerable pause anyway. Josiah Russell (1968), the great American demographer, puts the situation thus:

> The increasing population of those areas (Asia Minor and the Balkans) in 395-476 helped to save the eastern half of the Empire when the western half fell to the Germans. With probably sixteen million persons (perhaps two thirds of the eastern half of the Empire) they were the chief source of strength. Several hints point to a rising population there just before the plague. In the Balkans the city of Strobi was prosperous and increasing in the period, and the province of Istria was exporting grain to Ravenna. Greece to the south of the Balkans was enjoying a prosperous era.

There are records of the ruins of many prosperous villages in the area east of Antioch, now desert, all having been built in the fifth and sixth centuries.

Russell goes on to say that there seemed to be no evidence of poor conditions in the eastern Empire prior to the pandemic (here, Russell may be forearming himself against a possible argument that decline commenced before the plague as was the case when he ascribed the population decline in Europe in the fourteenth and fifteenth centuries to plague). He writes:

> Given the low population even in the east by 400 almost any prosperity would have resulted in an increase of population. This general prosperity was apparently reflected in the increasing population of Egypt, which seems to have been largely dependent on its export trade in grain and other commodities of the Mediterranean; the expansion of its cultivated area was marked in this period. North Africa, not much disturbed by war even during the Vandal invasion, was in good condition. Under the relatively stable government of the Visigoths, Spain was probably increasing its population; it was prosperous even after the plague started. The Italian provinces of Venice, Liguria and Istria were supplying grain to Ravenna and the Campagna was sending grain to Rome. In the fifth-century Toulouse extended its walls and Marseilles was prosperous, indicative of good conditions in southern Gaul. Further north the Germans were pouring into England while the Britons were moving over into northern Gaul.
>
> The result of the prosperity and probably of the population increase was an improvement in government finances. . . no real indication of financial strain appeared before the plague. . . . The burden of taxation itself was reduced.

Other careful observers of Justinian's plague and its effects are Biraben and Le

Goff, Dols, Allen, and Conrad. Biraben and Le Goff spend some time in defining the biology of plague, then confine themselves to an excellent account of the pandemic as seen by Procopius and Gregory of Tours. They provide an indispensable chronology of the pandemic's progress in the years following its outbreak in 542. As to the effects of the plague, they tend to concentrate on the psychological effects and its overall death. They do ascribe a decline in the power of the eastern Empire to the pandemic. Their most startling suggestion is that the plague led to the conquests of Mahommet and the Arabs on the one hand and Charlemagne and the Franks on the other, the latter partly because the north of Europe including northern Gaul, Germany and Britain (?) escaped the plague.

Dols (1977), a scholar of the Muslim and pre-Muslim Middle East, is less ready to accept all of Russell's views. Dols (1) writes:

> Josiah Russell has also investigated the Plague of Justinian within the scope of his pioneering work on medieval demographic history; however there is a need for caution toward many of the author's hazardous assertions. At least for Middle Eastern demography, many statements are not based on primary sources but rely heavily on very questionable comparisons with European populations.

Only in another work does Dols (1977) put forward a demographic view of his own. He states that there is no agreement on the pattern of Mediterranean populations before 541, but goes on to say:

> Nonetheless there is little doubt that the period following the first pandemic (the latter half of the sixth-century and the seventh-century) marks the lowest level of Mediterranean population since the rise of the Roman Empire. The Plague of Justinian must be considered an important factory of this demographic decline.

These contradictory views will receive further attention.

In order to consider demography and other factors possibly involved in change it is necessary to have the geography of the pandemic firmly fixed [Map I]. Procopius states that the pandemic started at Pelusium, a seaport on the north Egyptian coast near present-day Port Said. There is, however, a blanket criticism which can be levelled at most of the chroniclers of this time. They had all read Thucydides, the master, and all too often repeated his style and even his very words, as if all history repeated itself literally. Procopius is sometimes accused of describing some of the effects and distribution of the Plague of Justinian in the terms which Thucydides had used to describe the Plague of Athens. In defence of Procopius it should be stressed that on the question of the origin of Justinian's plague he does not parrot Thucydides but strikes out on his own, unlike Evagrius, who states that it commenced in Ethiopia, a fairly direct copy of Thucydides, just as the Aurelian plague was said to have started in Ethiopia.

Modern opinion on the origin of this sixth-century pandemic is vague. Wu (1926) states that it commenced in the ancient focus in Western Arabia (the Hejaz and the Yemen) but this opinion gathers more from Wu's desire to date plague as early as possible as from any real information. Conrad puts the first mention of plague in these areas as 1157 which rules out this area as a source of Justinian's pandemic. There is a shaky hypothesis favouring a start in the area of the northeastern shores of Lake Victoria-Nyanza, where there is an endemic focus of bubonic plague, which is thought by some, on very dubious grounds, to be of considerable antiquity. The hypothesis is accepted by Conrad which lends it a little respectability. Thence it is assumed to have travelled up the Nile to the major port of Pelusium. This theory has the virtue of making everyone right if one accepts that all places to the south and east of the Nile, unknown to the Mediterranean world, as Ethiopia.

The summer of 542 saw the plague in upper Egypt, Nubia and Kush (in modern terms the southern Mediterranean seaboard, the southern Red Seaboard and inland from both covering Egypt, Sudan and Ethiopia). The early winter found it in Pelusium poised to invade the Mediterranean. From Egypt the course of the pandemic is well known from the writings of Procopius, Agathius and others. It moved north and west until in encompassed the whole of the Mediterranean world; east to Syria and Persia and north from Marseilles through France to Ireland – whether it reached England or not was in dispute but there can be no real doubt that it did. It reached the homelands of the barbarians. Constantinople suffered particularly, partly because it was a port and the crowded capital city of the civilised and organised Eastern Empire, but, partly and seemingly, no doubt, because it was the home of the historian and the source of all news and gossip. Biraben and Le Goff have found descriptions in Marseilles, Lyons, Bourges, Chalons-sur-Seine, Dijon, Ciermont, Viviers and Avignon in France, and in Ravenna, Istra, Gradof, Liguria, Naples and all southern Italy.

It was seen in Ireland and though MacArthur (1926) has stated that there was no record of plague in Britain of the time he felt that it must have reached the shores of Britain. He believed that the yellow plague of 550-3 was relapsing fever and that the plague recorded by Bede for 664 does not allow for a diagnosis. This is a curious mistake for one of MacArthur's standing and learning, for there is in Bede's 'Life of Cuthbert' a mention of an abbot with a swelling in his thigh and a severe disease. This can be read as a fair description of bubonic plague, and MacArthur was to agree later that bubonic plague did reach Britain in 664. Bonser was in no position to argue as MacArthur wrote the medical appendix to Bonser's paper and he does not affirm or deny the presence of plague in Britain. Bonser, however, does quote the well-known phrase of Geoffrey of Monmouth about the 'Plague of Cadwallader' (Cadwallader was a Celtic King of North Wales at the time and died of the plague) that such a multitude died of this plague 'that the living were not enough to bury the dead.' MacArthur (1926) had noted that the characterisation by Bede of the 664 plague as the Yellow Plague (= relapsing fever?) was probably a mistaken transcription at some later date.

Outside of Europe the plague reached Alexandria (Procopius), Antioch on a number of occasions (Evagrius), Jerusalem, Thrace (John of Ephesus) and the whole of Syria. Its distribution to the east of Syria is something of a puzzle. It would seem that the Arabs did not bring the plague back to the Hejaz, as Conrad says that the first mention of it there was in the twelfth-century. Equally it would seem that the Arabs did not carry the plague to Afghanistan, the Indus, Ferghana and Transcaucasia and thus into the Indian subcontinent and China, as all observers have the plague ceasing at about the present western border of Iran and at the Caucasus. Whether it penetrated Africa south of Egypt is anyone's guess.

CHAPTER 4
Plague
Justinian's Plague (part 2)

The triple scourge of war, pestilence and famine afflicted the subjects of Justinian; and his reign is disgraced by a visible decrease in the human species, which has never been repaired in some of the fairest countries of the globe.

Gibbon
The History of the Decline and Fall of the Roman Empire

What was the effect of this pandemic on this wider stage including the Mediterranean and the soon to become Muslim Middle East? We have heard of some of the views of Biraben and Le Goff and of Russell (1968). Dols (1977) is only willing to commit himself to the statement that: 'The plague of Justinian may have played a role in the history of the early Middle Ages.' He claims that the investigation into the demographic data has been too meagre to sustain the dramatic speculation that the pandemic and the recurrent epidemics which followed it were, as Russell claimed: 'the solvents of classic Mediterranean civilisation and were responsible for the formation of new political, social and economic patterns characteristic of the European Middle Ages.'

Staying for a moment with the Mediterranean and deferring consideration of the Middle East until later, it is necessary to first examine the more headlong views of Josiah Russell. He believed that Justinian's plague, in its first attack, killed 20–25% of the Euro-Mediterranean population and with its subsequent recurrences eventually reduced this population to 40–50% of its former level. That is to say that he believes that this pandemic killed and combined with a loss of confidence causing a drop in the birth-rate so as to reduce the population by up to half its number in southern Europe and this is greater than the usual percentage estimates for the Black Death. The consequences of such a demographic collapse he finds in the inroads made by the more loosely organised nomadic and semi-nomadic tribes through the frontiers of the Eastern Empire. For instance the Avars on the northern Balkan frontiers settled into what was to become Hungary, having been driven from the Asian steppes by the Celestial Turks (1). The Lombards, though allies against the Ostrogoths for a time, were not Roman citizens but settled nonetheless in northern Italy. Persia, the other settled power, bought off by Justinian, came under furious attack from the extraordinary expansion of Islam, and it is worth noting that the plague did not prevent the emergence of a major power in the Middle East, across the Near East, North Africa and into Spain and west to the Indus – the Arabs.

Russell (1968) notes that, during the successful years of conquest in the west by Belisarius' troops, the proportion of barbarians among the troops had dropped; so Justinian's prospects looked good with a rising population supplying his army's needs in manpower, food and taxes. Russell believes that a demographic collapse of the order he suggests, must bring in its wake the inevitable consequences of a shortage of manpower, money and food. He sees the evidence of these consequences in a flight from the land by the peasant classes, which, in his estimation, reduced the land under cultivation by 50% in 50 years, though less in the less productive areas. He sees evidence of a great depression, readjustments of the social and ethnic composition of the population and the creation of 'conditions which were sensitive to accidents.'

He believes that such a drop in numbers alone would affect society adversely, basing himself (a little shakily) on evidence from animal population studies. He says: 'with regard to art, the period 610–717 is the darkest epoch in the entire history of the Empire.' He finds the Empire's prosperity hard hit. Its army, estimated in the fifth-century by the *Notitia Dignitatum* to be 350,000 strong, was estimated in 565 to be 150,000 by Agathias. Local army strengths had been reduced from 25,000–30,000 to barely 10,000 by the time that the Arabs were threatening. It must be said that despite this Belisarius' successor Narses continued to defeat and hold the Ostrogoths, a point which will be taken up again later.

Russell notes that despite all this the Empire survived, land was settled by organisations of soldiers and free peasants; small holders took over many of the great estates of the past. Finally the Empire survived the greatest threat of all – Islam. To be sure the Empire survived at a much reduced level but the Mediterranean did not become Mahommedan. Russell (1968) concludes:

> The plague by its sheer power moulded the sixth and seventh-century society into a new demographic and social pattern. . . . The Byzantine area became more hellenistic and oriental. . . . In the West, Romania persisted under the leadership of the German rulers. . . . In the whole Mediterranean/European complex, neither Charlemagne nor Harun nor the great Isaurian and Macedonian dynasties (of Byzantium) could break up the pattern set up by the flea, the rat and the bacillus.

Later Russell (1985) was to conclude:

> The plague had two types of result: an immediate one upon the region where it occurred and an indirect one upon the world at large through differential mortality of differing regions. Within regions it simplified life merely by declining numbers. Cities were smaller and thus the industrial and commercial life was reduced and less diverse. The number of surplus men also declined and reduced the base for military expansion. In the west the English ceased to try to conquer Scotland and even Ireland. The Franks ended their adventures in Iberia and Italy. The differential mortality was naturally to the advantage of the drier and hotter land, principally the great desert and semi-desert areas. Islamic areas, for example, developed at this

time, about 610–732, at the expense of their neighbours. In the west it meant Islamic expansion first into North Africa and then into Iberia in 711. If the pandemic had any share in the power of Charlemagne, it was probably because of the impetus created by the rise of the population after the pandemic. More likely Charlemagne was the beneficiary of one of the most amazing series of one-man-one son (or successor) in history.

Russell might have been a little more explicatory about the infertility of the desert areas for plague. On the face of it they should be more hospitable than the colder areas for the transmitting agent is the *tropical* rat flea which could flourish in the hotter drier areas. The principal reason for the advantage the desert areas had over warm but moister areas was the sparsity of human population making it difficult for an epidemic to take hold.

Finally Russell (1985) asks two questions which he feels still require answers. The first is whether the house rat, *Rattus rattus*, was the only important carrier in the early medieval plague. The second is whether the early medieval plague, like the modern one, attacked only about one person in the household. The answer to both questions must be in the negative. The modern plague (1897 to the present) is a good model for the two earlier plagues but there are factors in the two earlier ones which are not present in that of today's. This last plague does seem to have been largely bubonic (except for the Manchurian outbreaks) and therefore zoonotic, that is to say transmitted from the rodent to man by the rat flea, and that seems only possible if the population of both man and rats is so dense that a zoonosis can become an epidemic. It is arguable that the populations of either mammal in the Mediterranean in the sixth-century and Europe in the fourteenth-century were sufficiently dense to support an epidemic which was exclusively zoonotic. It follows therefore that the two earlier plagues must have had some supporting means of direct transmission after reaching the ports as bubonic plague.

This would involve either pneumonic or septicaemic plague as we know of no other means of person-to-person transmission, that is not involving rodents. It would also mean that these two forms of plague would have to have allowed a certain number of their victims to develop buboes as these are so constant a feature of the contemporary descriptions of the disease. This would apply more to septicaemic plague than the pneumonic form and equally imply that the septicaemic form was a great deal more common than anyone else has allowed for except perhaps Ell (1979). If one is to believe the figures of thousands dying daily, one hundred million dead, and 50% of the population disappearing then more than one person per household would have to have come under attack. Again it is only possible to theorise. One per household is a typical zoonotic disease figure, usually one per occasional household, as there is no inter-human transmission and only one person at a time enters the eco-system of the reservoir host and the transmitting agent. In the case, for instance, of zoonotic sleeping sickness transmitted normally between bushbuck and the tse-tse fly it is only the male hunter or honey-gatherer who ventures deep into the bush and who makes contact with the enzootic and it is only he who contracts zoonotic sleeping sickness. He does not transmit onwards in his family as no constantly man-biting tse-tse fly is present in the village.

Plague transmitted directly person to person by droplets or the human flea without recourse to the rat would spell whole households attacked, and make Russell's question about the involvement of other rodents irrelevant. So it is concluded that many of the contemporary death toll figures in the Plague of Justinian and subsequent plague epidemics are more or less true and, therefore, the plague must have had a strong element of non-zoonotic epidemiology. A lesser element in the death figures may have been in the immuno-depressive effects of plague, which while not proven, seems likely. This would mean that those who had the disease, but who were destined to recover might be more susceptible to the concomitant diseases present and fall victim to them so reinforcing an already high death toll.

It should be said that there was one notable and distinguished social survivor of the Plague of Justinian. That is the Code, the Pandecs and the Institutes (*Corpus Iuris Civilis*) of Justinian. These form the basis of the legal systems of all the countries of western Europe except Britain. Without them, as Bray points out, there would have been no Roman law as it would have disappeared in the mists of time and no firm foundation for the laws of Western Europe as we know them today.

It is now necessary to examine the views of other modern experts on the Plague of Justinian (2), leaving aside the commentators of a previous age such as Gibbon, Niebuhr, Shrewsbury and even MacArthur. First their opinion on the actual population loss, remembering that two of the commentators, Dols (1974) and Conrad, were concerned primarily with the Middle East. Dols agrees that the plague did bring about the lowest level of Mediterranean population since the rise of the Roman Empire; however, as already noted he believes that the proposed consequences of that loss outrun the evidence for the population decline. Those consequences as outlined by Russell and others are:

1. Political power shifted from the Mediterranean to northern Europe (as maritime effort moved, in fright, to the North Sea and the Baltic).
2. Justinian's grand strategy to resurrect the old Roman Empire was in ruins due to lack of manpower and supplies and the eastern Empire was unable to resist the incursions of the barbarians. The Slavs moved into the Balkans; the Lombards into northern Italy; the Berbers into the north African littoral. All settled unmolested by dreams of a resurgent Roman Empire, and the ethnic map of Europe was ineradicably altered.

Dols writes that it is central to Russell's thesis that the nomadic and semi-nomadic peoples, being less concentrated were less prone to plague and so escaped the crippling ravages of the pandemic. Dols (1974) felt that, in the face of such an all-embracing hypothesis, and historian must establish the history of the pandemic in the Middle East and assess its effects upon the other great zone of civilisation now emerging outside the Mediterranean – Islam. Procopius had claimed that the pandemic engulfed the lands and the peoples of the known world, that being the eastern Empire (3), the rest of Europe, Persia where he had campaigned with Belisarius and the barbarian hinterland. He noted that Asia Minor and Egypt suffered greatly.

In the Middle East Dols (1974) chronicled six major epidemics of plague in the period 541–717:

1. The Plague of Sharawayh, 627–8, at Ctesiphon, the Sassanian capital. It killed

the Sassanian king.

2. The Plague of Yezdigird, 634–42, in the reign of Yezdigird the Third, 'The Great King' of Persia. Among the presents taken by Yezdigerd's embassy to China in 638 was an animal which could catch rats in their holes.

3. At the same time in Syria, the Plague of Amwas (or 'Umwas or Amawas) was raging. It struck twice. Dols uses this epidemic to develop his discussion about the propriety of fleeing an act of God. Conrad has a great deal more to say about this plague and disagrees with Dols about the religiosity argument.

4. The Plague of Al-Jarif or the Violent Plague, 688–9, swept through Basra and was said to have killed 70,000, 71,000 and 73,000 on successive days. It attacked even the sparsely distributed Bedouin.

5. The Plague of the Maidens, 706, which killed mostly young women in Basra.

6. The Plague of the Notables, 716–17, which killed the son of the Caliph, then the Caliph.

In the west Biriben and Le Goff reported seven epidemics of any great size though opinion differs on what may be considered a major outbreak. For instance eight major outbreaks have been claimed for the Middle East.

Dols spends much of his consideration on the psychological, mental and religious reactions of the population to the plague, and makes the point that the Muslim reaction of 'Insh Allah' in more or less sophisticated form was, much less damaging to the psyche than the Christian reaction of guilt. He also spends some time on the dubious medico-historical event of Abrahah and the 'Elephant War'. This, thought by many to be an early record of smallpox, keeps entering this narrative and will be discussed in the chapter on smallpox. He points out that the Plague of Amwas occurred in winter and so was probably pneumonic plague. Dols believes that only pneumonic or septicaemic plague will cause the death toll which could lead to a demographic collapse. He also notes the diminution of the plague on the ascent of the Abbasids to the Caliphate which they moved to Baghdad in the place of the 'Umayyads of Damascus. Dols feels that the plague in its first strike and subsequent recurrences in the heartland of the Islamic world (or what was to become its heartland) must have struck the Arabs with all the force that it exerted on the Byzantine Empire and the Sassanians. He writes:

> The recurrences of the plague have thus continually retarded natural population growth and served as a major factor in debilitating 'Umayyad strength.

He points out that plague tended to follow commercial routes both in the Mediterranean and in the Middle East, reflecting the probable dissemination by rats carried on board ship by sea or in forage for pack animals on land. The more directly transmitted diseases, which are inter-human, will always travel along man's lines of communication. With Dols' overriding interest in the psychological effects of the plague he notes, as two consequences of the plague, an increased interest in the medical texts of Hippocrates and Galen (a new slant on the reputation of the Arabs for keeping alight the flame of medical learning) and the stimulation the plague lent to theological learning. Both, of course, in the hope of a cure. At the end of one of his papers Dols offers a sting in the tail when he gives as his opinion that not all of the so-called recurrences of plague were necessarily *Yersinia* plague. This is a favourite disclaimer of historians, apparently afeared of making a direct medical statement, and desirous of a *caveat*. Not surprisingly when one considers the medical equivocation over the Plague of Athens and that of the Antonines. Important as it may be as a matter of fact it does not alter the central thesis set forth here where any infectious disease is grist to the mill.

Dols (1977) has a little more to say later. He contents himself with the statement quoted before that the population loss in the Middle East was due in large part to the pandemic. He quotes Russell's view that the plague contributed to the ability of the Arabs to expand at the phenomenal rate which they achieved, but then offers no comment of his own. He attributes the death of the three Companions of the Prophet to the plague and notes that their death elevated Mu'awiyah ibn Sufyan to the governorship of Syria thereby establishing 'Umayyad power.

Afterwards, during the 'Umayyad caliphate both the Syrian and the Mesopotamian populations suffered particularly badly from the plague, the governing classes as badly as the commoners. The plague season was the summer and at this time the 'Umayyad Caliphs and their court left Damascus for the countryside and their desert palaces. The Arabs also moved their troops out of the towns, which would lend colour to the theory that the original conquering Arabs were loosely collected and later became more organised and massed together, frequently in the towns they had conquered, which in the semi-desert of much of the Middle East, were the centres of plague.

While plague outbreaks continued to occur after the Abbasid takeover they were much abated. Dols recounts the story of the Abbasid supporter who tried to enlist the interest of the Damascenes by claiming Abbasid responsibility for the decline of the plague and received his quittance from a voice in the crowd which declaimed: 'God is more just than to give you power over us and the plague at the same time.'

The Arabs continually infiltrated into the Tigris–Euphrates valley which seems to have been relatively free from the plague except at its mouth (Basra). Dols makes an important medico-historical observation when he quotes ar-Razi as writing that Ahrun the Priest, an Alexandrian, living at the time of the birth of Islam (600), noted the spitting of blood during plague outbreaks. Dols claims that this is the first record of pneumonic plague in early medieval plague, which can only mean that he does not accept Procopius' description of vomiting blood as a description of pneumonic plague. This seems a little over-severe in its definition of pneumonic plague and blood-stained sputum. There is no record of haemorrhage of the oesophagus or stomach in plague and it was certainly plague that Procopius was describing, so I believe we must accept vomiting blood as the equivalent of blood-stained sputum. Alas, others are silent on the subject.

Allen is a little more forthcoming, though even he does not mention Procopius' statement and only mentions Evagrius' description of the very contagious nature of the infection, which might indicate an element of direct transmission. It does though deny Procopius' contention that the plague was not very contagious (to those who attended the sick), probably with justice. Allen, on the other hand, says that none of the chroniclers mentions a tightness of the chest or rapid and shallow respiration, which he claims are pathognomic of

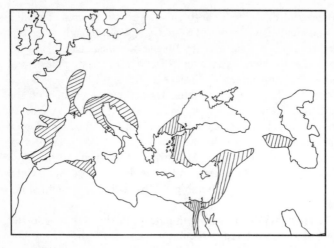

I. Known extent of the first wave of Justinian's Plague.
1. Pelusium,
2. Alexandria
3. Constantinople
4. Antioch
5. Carthage
6. Rome
7.Marseilles
(after Biraben & Le Goff, 1969)

pneumonic plague. It should be remembered that those who got close enough to make such a diagnosis in pneumonic plague would not have filled an insurance actuary with confidence and *Manson's Tropical Diseases* notes of the pneumonic plague victim, 'that by the time definite involvement of the lungs can be demonstrated, he generally dies'.

Allen's statement does raise problems, given Dols'(1974) insistence that only the highly infectious forms of plague can give rise to significant decline in population. This statement would strike at the heart of Russell's (1968) hypothesis, unless a large element of very mortal and swiftly transmitted plague can be said to be present. Indeed, Dols (1977) does believe that a significant demographic collapse did occur in the Middle East at the time of the Black Death and argues strongly for a large contribution from pneumonic plague in that collapse. That pneumonic plague occurred during the early medieval plague outbreaks seems proven both in the West and in the Middle East. This leaves us with Procopius' 'black pustules as large as lentils and these did not survive even one day.'

Here we meet with a familiar problem. When the physician says something happened on the third day he usually means the third day of symptoms. When the epidemiologist says it he usually means the third day after infection which if there is an incubation period of two weeks can be two very different times. When does Procopius mean? It seems accepted that the haemorrhagic black or purple spots, which can appear in plague victims, arrive after death in bubonic plague but occur during the illness in septicaemic plague and are more conspicuous in the latter. It would appear that, as Procopius' patients were still alive but died within twenty-four hours after the appearance of the large black haemorrhages, he was describing septicaemic plague which occurred often enough to be worthy of mention. So it is contended here that all three major forms of plague stalked the lands of Justinian and the 'Umayyads. Further discussion on this point arises when the question of immunity to plague has to be considered.

CHAPTER 5
Plague
Justinian's Plague (part 3)

Visium oculoram superabundant cadavera morturoram.
Paulus Diacamus (Paul the Deacon)
De gestis Longbardum, II, 26

The time has come to consider Conrad, a most important commentator on this
scene and the effects of plague on the advance of Islam (1). In his abstract of the
contents of his book he writes that the effects of the plague:

> contributed to most of the social, economic and political changes evident in
> the early mediaeval period. Just as the history of the fourteenth and fifteenth
> centuries cannot be understood in isolation from the Black Death, so also
> the history of the early Byzantine and Arab empires cannot be understood
> without considering the effects of two centuries of recurrent plague outbreaks
> in the heartlands of imperial power.

In his first part he gives an account of the life-cycle of the plague organism, its
transmission and its epidemiology. He lays stress on the role of the human flea,
quoting Martin, an eminent scholar working on plague, whose view it was that
the human flea and septicaemic plague played a prominent role in the medieval
plagues. Conrad goes on to discuss immunity to plague and the views of Russell
(1968) and Dols (1974). He had noted that the sources of the time, mention
repeatedly that the plague took off, in particular, foreigners, including slaves
and Marmelukes (in Egypt), and the children. He ascribes this mortality
distribution to immunity, foreigners and children not having had time to acquire
immunity by survival from attack. The argument is, in a sense, self-defeating
since if children do not survive there can be no subsequent population with any
immunity to provide a differential mortality. But this is an argument of despair
and there were those who did survive the plague, as many as 30% from bubonic
plague. But did they become immune?

As for foreigners, nearly all of the evidence before us points to a lack of
protective immunity being acquired by those who survived the plague, though
that evidence is somewhat contradictory. There are many records of the plague
being acquired more than once, even several times, by the same person and still
death followed his/her last attack. This is not the pattern of a disease which

prompts the acquisition of an effective protective immunity. Conrad finds Dols (1974) more cautious in his assessment but refuses to rule out (quite correctly) the possibility of the acquisition of an effective immunity. After all, we cannot know of those who failed to acquire the disease on being infected. However, the literature of most diseases shows that the knowledge of an acquired immunity is quickly acknowledged. It was known very early on that smallpox conferred lifelong immunity and Thucydides mentions the immunity to the Plague of Athens in the only description of the disease. No such immunity was noted for plague.

Dols (1974) raises another great red herring of all these discussions when he claims that certain susceptibles in the population: 'were particularly vulnerable to the recurrent plague epidemics due to a lack of immunity or poor health.

There is no evidence that either putative acquired immunity or poor health have any direct effect whatsoever on susceptibility to plague after being bitten by an infective flea. Susceptibility to subsequent disease may be affected by past experience with that disease but the question is in dispute in the case of plague as we will see later. There is no evidence that poor health predisposes a person to the development of plague once bitten by an infective flea or exposed to the sputum of a pneumonic plague patient. It is true that some immuno-depressive diseases may predispose people to certain other diseases but the question is very complicated and is not known to apply to plague.

On the other hand there may be indirect ways in which poor health could predispose people to plague: the lack of the ability to feed, for instance is the most obvious. It may well be that such elements as poor health, poverty, starvation, malnutrition, cold, heat, inability to bathe, lack of sleep may bring about those surrounding conditions necessary for the transmission of any particular infectious disease, such as over-crowding, greater reception of infective doses due to inanition, housing susceptible to insect invasion or the nesting of house rats, coughing due to oedema of the lung. . . the list is endless, but none has been shown to make a subject more innately susceptible to a particular disease through the lack of natural or acquired immunity.

To come back to Conrad, he makes the case strongly that, where the original sources stress a death-rate among some particular group there is usually an internal reason for the stress, such as a particular concern with that group and so having no means of comparison with other groups. He points out, too, that if plague immunity played a role in the severity of the plague among certain groups, how did plague continue to cause high death rates among the Egyptian populations during its recurrences.

When considering Russell (1968), Conrad finds it necessary to plunge into modern immunology, and, alas, here his sure touch deserts him somewhat, not that he is to be blamed, as whatever is said here and now will be out of date before the word-processor has time to print out the version. He says that it is not usual for an infectious disease to confer permanent immunity upon those who contract it and survive. While there is some truth in that statement, it requires a great many exceptions to be made before it would be acceptable. Indeed, the normal assumption is that all infectious diseases confer effective immunity and when they do not the scientist is spurred into action to find out what went wrong. In fact, virtually all infectious diseases confer some immunity, varying from partial to complete and taking varying times to do it and to lose it. Some medium-term immunity to plague is apparently conferred by vaccination as evidenced by the lack of plague among the vaccinated American troops during the Viet-Nam war, this is discussed by Butler and Cavanaugh, though there were to arise many doubts about that vaccine as it failed to protect the indigenous Viet-Namese. Other rat-flea-borne diseases among the American troops attested to the ability of Viet-Namese rat-fleas to bite American troops.

It also has to be said that, in general, a form of immunity can, in certain diseases, be donated to the offspring by an immune mother, in the form of immunoglobulin G, an antibody, which can pass across the placenta to the foetus. If that form of the immune reaction is the effective one, the donated immunoglobulin will protect the offspring for a period before the infant destroys the donated immunoglobulin. If this protection is operating still when the infant receives its first infection with that disease and if its own immune system is in good working order it will survive that first attack and gain valuable immunity of its own. This must not be thought of as a means of transmitting immunity to a new generation on a permanent basis as it lasts only for a few months in the new-born infant and is then lost. The only way future generations can inherit immunity as a group to a disease prevalent in the previous generation is by the inheritance of genes acquired as a protection or acquired otherwise which prove to be protective against that disease. For instance the gene for sickle cell anaemia inherited from one of the parents will protect against malaria due to *Plasmodium falciparum*, a deadly form of the disease. If both parents pass on the gene to an offspring it will develop full-blown sickle cell anaemia and eventually die of it. The singly donated gene is such a powerful protector against a deadly disease that the gene, which, being potentially lethal, should have died out in the population many years ago, is preserved for the advantage it confers to some African tribes living in the shadow of *P. falciparum* malaria.

It is frequently convenient to think of herd immunity being available in this way so that we can believe that pandemics die out because the race has become naturally immune due to inherited genes for protection. While it is certainly true that there are genes for resistance and genes for susceptibility we know very little about them in humans as yet and we certainly do not know whether they were acquired or selected as a direct response to disease stimuli.

Finally, any faith put in this method or ridding us of our harmful micro-organisms must face the fact that the diseases are still with us and must face the 'gene for gene theory', which states that for every gene developed by the host which limits the growth of an unwelcome visitor, that visitor develops a gene for increasing its ability to grow in the host and negate the host's genetic efforts. Taken together these points convince one that nature does not distinguish between the human and his/her invading parasites in their ability to manipulate the human's immune system. For the moment, microbes are just as good immunologists as humans. While most believe that *Homo sapiens* will eventually outstrip microbes in this ability, it has not happened yet and, as Conrad suspected, an acquired genetic resistance to plague does not exist as far as we know. So, no racial acquired immunity and little or no individually acquired immunity to plague exist.

Some acquired immunity can be made to exist as both mice and people can be immunised – this is discussed by Wake et. al. and Hurtrel et. al. – though the antibody based immunity acquired by experience with the disease or following vaccination is very short-lived. The effective and long-lasting immunity is cell-mediated (a special form of immunity based on the actions of the T lymphocyte) and probably based on the ability of the macrophage cell, stimulated by a T lymphocyte, to destroy *Y. pestis*.

Hurtrel et al. and Korobova et al have shown that a measure of the existence of this form of immunity is the delayed skin hypersensitivity test and this is positive in successfully vaccinated people. Donated immunity to the infant is also unlikely as the antibody-based immunity in the mother is short-lived and it is this form of immunity, as immunoglobulin G, which can be passed from mother to child as far as we know; the high death rate among children would go some way towards confirming this.

This high death-rate among children has been denied recently for some plague outbreaks as part of a more general argument which ascribes a role for iron deficiency in the inability of population groups to mount a successful response to plague. The argument is very dubious. It is entirely inferential and relies on a few experiments done with *Y. enterocolitica,* an organism claimed to be closely related to *Y. pestis. Y. pseudotuberculosis* would have been a more suitable subject as it has a 90% genetic homology with *Y. pestis* even though it differs from it widely in epidemiology and symptomatology. On the other hand according to both Bercovier et al and Moore and Brubaker *Y. enterocolitica,* shows less than 48% homology with *Y. pestis.* The general argument that effective immune responses have an absolute requirement for iron is incorrect.

We are faced, as was Conrad, with the apparent anomaly of a disease which confers little or no effective immunity to those who recover from it; yet which can be prevented by vaccination as shown by Butler and Cavanaugh et al. There is even an apparent exception to the statement that plague gives little or no effective immunity to those who recover. This is the work of Blanc and Baltazard who, in experiments concerning the infection of human fleas with a strain of plague bacilli from North Africa known to be at least partially septicaemic used recovered patients as a source of human blood for the maintenance of infected fleas. This would have been extraordinarily unethical, despite the availability of sulphonamides and anti-plague serum, unless they had the best of reasons for believing that recovered patients were solidly immune to the plague.

The only explanations that can be offered for the apparent anomaly of a disease which confers an immunity only reluctantly, if at all, would be the phenomenon of antigenic variation which occurs with influenza, sleeping sickness and, notably, AIDS; or the presence among the organisms causing the disease of many mutants or variants. In the first case the organism has the ability to change the nature of its surface coat that is in contact with the immune processes of the host so that those defences elaborated against it are no longer effective and the host has to start all over again only to find the organism repeating its evasive tactics. If one of these variants is transmitted to a person who had recovered by making an immune response to the first surface coat of the organism he/she will not be immune to the newly elaborated transmitted organism.

In the second case with the elimination of the first wave of the organism a new mutant can be selected from the variants present which will not now be susceptible to the immune defence. The overwhelming problem with the first of these explanations is that we know of no cases where antigenic variation is effective as a defence against cell-mediated immunity, the effective form of immunity in plague, though there is no theoretical reason why it should not occur. In the case of the second explanation which is only a variation on the first theme, Burroughs and Bacon show that there is good evidence for the presence of mutants of differing virulence and with differing responses to elicited immunity among plague bacilli. We may have to return to this question of acquired immunity as it seems more a subject for hope than study among some historians.

Conrad is rather harsh with Russell (1968) and claims that with the collapse of any immunological theory leading to an increased death-rate among children, so do Russell's theories about a catastrophic demographic decline collapse as they were dependent upon a high and long-term child mortality. It is not true to say that such a mortality did not happen simply because Josiah Russell is not an immunologist. There are ecological reasons why a high death rate among children could have occurred, as many of Conrad's primary sources have claimed. Children playing out of doors, whether in the dirt, in the street, in the cellar or the attic may have been in more intimate contact with the domestic infected rat and its fleas or with other patients with pneumonic and septicaemic plague. Children may be more tolerant of flea bites and thus receive a greater inoculum of *Y. pestis*. It is accepted these days that blood-sucking insects and arthropods are more likely to attack certain individual hosts than others. It is possible that children as a group are more attractive to fleas than adults for both intrinsic and extrinsic reasons. All the foregoing is to say that there are more reasons than just immunity for a differential death rate from plague between groupings among a whole population; if, indeed, this is true of children and children were a special target of the plague in many of its recurrences, then Russell's argument stands.

Conrad gives us an authoritative and fascinating critique of the 'Elephant War' story and though the story belongs in the chapter on smallpox, it is appropriate to say here that he is fully convincing in his conclusion that the disease which wiped out Abraha's Abyssinians was not plague. Conrad agrees with Dols (1974) that there were six great incidents of plague in the Middle East. He lists another important outbreak and a number of smaller ones. He spends a good deal of time on what he considers to have been the most important and damaging of these waves of plague, as it held up the advance of Islam; this was the Plague of 'Amwas (or 'Umwas). He records serious loss of life in Syria including most of the Arab commanders and many 'Companions of the Prophet' during the campaigning in Syria. This, as he points, out, cleared the way for the advancement of Mu'awiya ibn Abi Sufyan, the founder of the 'Umayyid dynasty, to the governorship of Damascus.

He gives even greater importance to the need, on the part of the Arabs, to repopulate Syria by settling themselves on the land instead of merely garrisoning it as they did in Mesopotamia, though he claims that this view is only tentative. Conrad, in general, does not believe that individual plague outbreaks were 'pivotal factors in the course of concurrent developments.' He finds that the effects of the pandemic were long-term rather than immediate. He does concede that in the case of the Plague of 'Amwas critical decisions were made under pressure from the plague which were to have long-term consequences. He believes that the plague of 'Amwas may have had a decisive impact on the way the advent of Arab rule affected Syrian society and administration.' The Arab high command lost the Commander-in-Chief, Abu 'Ubayda, his two chief subordinates and his successor Abi Sufyan. Indeed, Abu 'Ubayda was a strong contender as the successor to 'Umar as the head of all Islam. 'Umar was left to rely on inexperienced leaders, including Mu'awiya ibn Abi Sufyan who was able to make his way into the caliphate via the governorship of Damascus.

The other great consequence, according to Conrad, was the penetration of Syrian society by the Arabs, something they had not done in Iraq, except insofar as their garrison towns became thriving centres. The critical point was that there had been an extensive loss of the Syrian population, which was claimed, by some, to have been the result of a cruel policy of 'no quarter' which claimed the lives of so many that chaos reigned and further emigration ensued. Conrad agrees that there was a great loss of population, but challenges the view that the flight of the Syrian population was due to Arab cruelty. He feels that the contact between the peasantry and the invaders was not intimate and only intermittent. He is suspicious of the Christian sources of information as they had both religious and political axes to grind. He finds that Arabic sources show a general acceptance of the new rulers, who were more competent to deal with incursions from without the territory than had been the weaker and more remote Byzantines.

The Monophysite Church was not troubled and freedom of worship was assured, which had not been the case under the Byzantine Emperors, plagued by the Christological upheavals of the Early Medieval Church. So the Syrians did not flee from these new rulers. They died from and they fled from, the plague, with the consequence of a greater penetration of Syrian life by the Arabs than had been their intention. Their interest was the poll-tax and this could not be collected from a deserted countryside. Conrad concludes that the consequence of the Plague of 'Amwas (commencing in the spring of 17AH/638AD and ending about late 18AH/639AD) was a mortality which forced the conquering Arabs to cope with a declining population, particularly on the land, by a penetration of Syrian society aided and controlled by the new 'Umayyid dynasty.

A major plague struck Syria and the 'Ummayyids in 743 during the reign of Hisham ibn al-Malik, the last great 'Ummayyid caliph. It was during this outbreak that the 'Ummayyid caliphate fell. This particular manifestation of the plague was the worst since the plague of Amwas and resembled it in intensity. In fact during the reign of Hisham there were many outbreaks of plague in Syria; so many that Hisham was in the habit of withdrawing during the epidemics from Damascus to retreats in the Syrian steppes. At the beginning of this 743 outbreak Hisham died. The weather was bitterly cold and dry that winter, crops failed and plague (presumably pneumonic) broke forth in northern Mesopotamia and in the next year it spread north and east, so Syria was next. The new caliph fled for a retreat in the steppes, but he died in that year, possibly from plague. He was succeeded by his brother who died within a few months. From then on, pestilence ruled the 'Umayyid lands each summer. Disease led to famine. This pestilence moved west to Egypt and eventually Greece and Constantinople in

746 when it was identified as plague. Conrad writes:

> by the time this series of the plague was over the 'Umayyids had irretrievably lost control of their eastern provinces, and it is tempting to view the interminable plagues of the last years of the dynasty as an important factory in the victory of the Abbasid revolution. As long as the point is not pushed too far I believe there is a case for this.

The Abbasids had the enormous advantage of a cessation of the plague recrudescences on the advent of their rule and a little later Harun al-Rashid is praised for winning the favour of Allah, who then lifted the plague (cf Gregory the Great). To return to the nature of Justinian's plague, Conrad is confident that all three forms of plague were present in the early medieval Middle East and that bubonic plague was more virulent than it is today. These two contentions are probably interconnected. The more pathogenic the strain of *Y. pestis*, the greater its reproduction in the host. The greater the numbers of the infecting organism in the host the greater the likelihood of them reaching the lungs in sufficient numbers both to cause a cough and to give to that cough a lethal load of bacteria for transmission. Equally the greater numbers of the bacilli in the host the more likely they are to reach the blood-stream in numbers sufficient to infect *P. irritans,* the ubiquitous human flea. If one goes on from there and claims that the medieval plagues (Justinian's and the Black Death) were caused by a strain of *Y. pestis* which has since sunk into obscurity, then one can ascribe to this strain characteristics which give a better fit with such facts as we have than does the strain of *Y. pestis* which is with us at present.

This will seem to many a deceptively easy way out for a lazy man and provide too simple a solution of our problems for our puritan souls. The fact remains that it is increasingly obvious to the medical biologist that each characteristic of a strain or variant of a species of a micro-organism does not fit exactly with a supposedly same species expressing itself in a different ecology. The old idea of a fixed and immutable species, all behaving in the same way wherever they occur and all having the same appearance is dying fast under the assault of newer knowledge about variation within the species. It is uncomfortable to have the ground shift thus beneath one's feet but in our case it is convenient. It could therefore be the modern view of the medieval plague bacillus that it would be, almost inevitably, different from the modern plague bacillus in at least some respects. That is to say that the variant of *Y. pestis* selected by the medieval environment was not the same as that selected by late-nineteenth and twentieth-century environments.

One of the ways in which today we identify such variations is to identify minor differences in the enzymes of the organism; these are the chemicals which act to break down and rebuild the organism's chemicals and are fundamental to many of the functions of the organism including its virulence. Minor differences, therefore, may spell the difference between killing the host or giving it a headache. Indeed the virulence of *Y. pestis* is predicted by the presence or absence of two molecules which are prepared using an enzyme (2). There is, in short, nothing inherently disreputable in ascribing differing pathogenicities to strains of *Y. pestis* from the two mediaeval plagues and the modern one, nor would the assumption of antigenic variation obviate the theory provided that the antigenic variants do not spell a concomitant variation in the virulence as they do not in sleeping sickness (though they may in influenza). There is good evidence of mutation occurring to molecules in the plague bacillus which bring about greater or lesser pathogenicity (3). Such mutants could be selected by the environment.

After that divergence into medical biology we must return to Conrad who has much to say of great cogency about urbanisation, civilisation and infectious disease. They are thoughts which were adumbrated earlier, though not in such detail. One of the conclusions reached is that the desert rural Arabs were not greatly afflicted with plague, nor did they spread it until they settled into towns as they did in Syria. No case can be made for the notion that the conquering Arabs were great disseminators of the plague, though a case can be made for the plague easing the path of the desert-living plague-free Arabs.

There is some confusion of thought here and plague is treated as a disease carried by man only, whereas bubonic plague, which is probably the form in which plague moved any great distances, is carried by rats and fleas, animals which could be carried by Arabs in their forage as well as any other people (did camels need less portable forage than horses?) So it would have to be assumed that the desert way of life picked up fewer rats and fleas as fellow travellers. Conrad is adamant about the presence of rats in the Middle East from time immemorial and there are certainly many references to them in the pre-and post-Islamic periods, though one suspects that a number of Conrad's anecdotes refer to field rodents rather than *R. rattus*. Conrad is also convincing on the evidence for fleas and it is significant that the Bedouin complained of fleas in the towns. Conrad concludes that: 'the population of the early medieval Near East lived in deadly peril during the entire plague pandemic, and there was not a thing they could have done about it to protect themselves.'

On the subject of mortality due to the plague Conrad, picking his way through a mass of evidence, much of which is fragmentary and exaggerated, finds that Procopius, Severus of Antioch and al-Mada'ini have figures which stay within the bounds of belief. He says that, while some sources speak of 70,000 deaths a day or hundreds of thousands dying in a single epidemic in a single city, the three authors above have similar death-rates only for the first outbreak, which was certainly the most devastating.

Conrad quotes Hollingworth and Bailey and the application of mathematical modelling to the question of the population of Constantinople in 542 and the mortality due to the plague. The estimate made is close to others made using different methods and figures. This arrived at a figure of a population of about 508,000 with a mortality during the pandemic of 244,000, a death-rate of 48%. These figures would certainly argue an epidemic which was transmitted without any undue delay and causing a very high death rate, which does not chime with a purely bubonic plague outbreak which necessitates that each case must come from a rat flea which has had the infection from a dying rat. An element of droplet transmission, or the involvement of the human flea, appears essential.

Conrad goes on to consider each of the plague outbreaks in the Near East. Unreliable as all sources are in exact statistical demographic terms, he concludes:

It is so staggering to the imagination to even conceive of an urban population suddenly being halved by a plague, or even reduced by 25%, that such a

notion cannot but be regarded with suspicion. But let us recall that we are
dealing with an extremely deadly epidemic disease, the deadliest known to
mankind, spreading in sanitary and general urban conditions perfectly suited
to the maximum levels of carnage. The devastation is stressed over and
over again in the sources, where our contemporary observers speak of
deserted streets, the complete collapse of social order, and people dying so
fast and in such great numbers that, even with the vast common graves in
use, decomposing corpses still litter the streets and public places. In the
final analysis Bailey's model does no more than express in statistical form
what the medieval sources have been saying all along.

On the reaction of religion to the plague Conrad differs from Dols. Both agree
that Christianity and its forbear Judaism taught that pestilences were punishments
sent by the Divine Being to chastise whoever was felt at the time to be
transgressing. Hence the clinging aura of sin and guilt in the Christian reaction
to the plague. Dols thinks that the Muslim attitude was essentially that of 'Insh
Allah' relative to a divinely sent plague intended to kill unbelievers and send
the good Muslim to his reward, the justly acquired delights of Paradise.

Conrad, however, feels that is it impermissible to visit upon the thinly spread
Arab Muslims of the early medieval period, the beliefs and dogma they were to
acquire later. So he believes that, while Dols is correct in his views of the impact
of the late medieval plague in the fourteenth-century on Islam, these views cannot,
with justice, be wished upon early medieval Islam. He holds that the early
Muslims held to views of the plague which closely resembled those of the
Christians and the Jews, which were largely conditioned by the Bible and the
glosses put on it by the Qur'an. So the dominant theme of the reactions was a
belief in the divine source of the outbreak and the consequent uselessness of
resistance to it . It was not however a fatalistic resignation and it was permitted
to flee from it without the inevitability of the later Islamic Nemesis tradition,
exampled by the story of Death at Samarra, where Death finds his target despite
flight. The Syrians fled in numbers, which Conrad finds extraordinary, as it was
entirely alien to the nature of the sedentary Syrian.

This evacuation led the people to abandon crops, homes, factories, crafts,
offices, families and friends. Conrad says they were ill-prepared to do so and
counts it as one of the great measures of the impact of the plague. The flight
must have usually been to the lands of the Bedu who, living in the desert on the
fringes of the farming population, in the steppes and in small groups, largely
escaped the ravages of the plague. This group, then, free of the plague, cannot
have received the plagued fugitives with anything approaching enthusiasm,
indeed they would have avoided them 'like the plague'. All this would have left
the nomads in a position of great advantage, which was accepted, one assumes,
with glee. Disused farmland, the irrigation systems in disarray, was taken for
grazing land for the nomad stock and its possible return later to grain production
would be a matter of fierce resistance.

There was a known decline of agriculture in Syria in the years 542–749 and
it would be too great a coincidence for this to have had nothing to do with the
repeated epidemics of plague which swept over the area. Plague, then, halved
city populations, led to the complete disappearance of villages, sent the land

into non-production but did not reduce the tax expected from each unit of population, which for individuals went up and up as the population declined. These population units then collapsed as units within an ordered society, as, in Conrad's striking simile, 'a machine – which could not be expected to operate at 70% efficiency because only 30% of its parts had been removed.' Conrad notes that there is no information on the degree to which the 'Umayyid governments brought in outsiders to make up the population losses, as did the Byzantine Emperors. He writes that Constantine V transferred large groups of Armenians, Greeks and Syrians to Constantinople, even though these areas were also depopulated by the plague. It was at this time that Greece was said to have been 'slavonicised' and thus 'barbarous'. Conrad's final statement reads:

> But most important of all, the plague was a recurrent calamity which denied the populations in the areas it struck the opportunity to avail themselves of their enormous human potential for adapting to adverse circumstances. It is this aspect of the pandemic which in the long term accounts for the disease's importance. By maintaining constant pressure on Near Eastern civilisation and the institutions upon which it was based, the plague became more than another unique vicissitude to be endured and accommodated, but rather transcended this to become a force capable of eroding the foundation of sedentary life itself.

Another author to be considered is Allen, whose express desire it is to bring to notice the writings of John of Ephesus and to examine how his contributions affect the general view of Justinian's plague. John of Ephesus draws attention, as does Procopius, to the black pustules occurring on the skin of plague victims, He also confirms that bubonic plague was not always lethal, he had it himself and recovered. Allen judges from the writings of Procopius and Evagrius that Justinian's plague was mainly bubonic but particularly prone to complications and goes on to say: 'From Evagrius' description it seems that the plague was often transmitted directly from person to person, which indicates a strong penumonic element.'

As for the 'vomiting of blood' of Procopius, Allen will have it as an effect of plague on the digestive tract and the disclaimer has already been placed on this point. Allen also argues for the appearance of septicaemic plague in the 542 outbreak. He notes also that the estimates of the death rate in Constantinople made by Hollingsworth, were made in ignorance of the figures from John of Ephesus. Using those figures Allen arrives at an estimate of a 57% death rate for the capital of the Empire of the East. His overall death rate for all areas affected is one-third. John of Ephesus claimed that from Syria to Thrace there was no one to harvest the fields and that the public ways were deserted. Allen ascribes the ease with which the Persians penetrated to the coast in 573 to the depopulation of those areas by the plague, as much as to the inefficiency of the Byzantine army. Allen is outspoken in his belief that it was the plague and the consequent famines which brought the Mediterranean population to its unprecedented low in 600.

Teall concentrated on the effect of the plague on Justinian's army and argues strongly for a critically weakening role for the plague leading to the eventual defeats suffered by the Eastern Roman forces. He believes that the plague was the principle cause of the manpower shortages critical to the contraction of the Empire and its inability to recover. There are echoes of Boak in his arguments.

A number of other authors have put forward their views in the course of larger reviews. It was Cartwright's (1972) view that this plague was the worst pandemic that man was ever to know. Goodall thought that the plague spread to India, but this is not supported by the Indian historians, including Jaggi. There are those such as Henchen who have all plague coming out of the Chinese hinterland, but this is authoritatively denied by Pollitzer (1951). Pollitzer has his worries about the distribution of the black rat at the time, as it was believed, at that time, to have arrived into Europe after the Crusades, (see Colnat and Shrewsbury (1970)) and he wonders if domestic mice could have been involved, but other work has shown that the black rat has been present in the area from palaeolithic times (*pace* Twigg). Hare (1954) does not believe that the nature of plague has changed over the 1500 years we have known it, he also theorises that the periodicity of the plague epidemics (presumably not the pandemics) may be due to the periodicity among rodent /hosts (4).

Twigg, whose major concern it is to show that the Black Death may not have been bubonic plague, largely because he believes that the black rat (*R. rattus*) was not present in Western Europe in sufficient numbers to cause a major pandemic of bubonic plague, admits that Justinian's plague was bubonic. This does his argument no good as he has to agree that the black rat was present in Europe in the sixth-century and in numbers, and not therefore imported into Europe by the Crusaders. MacArthur (1957) has joined the argument about the presence of black rats in Europe in either the sixth or the fourteenth centuries and cites an Etruscan votive offering, now in Florence, which depicts a rat chewing on a ship's rope. Another rat is depicted on a Roman tomb of 100–150 in Rheims. He also draws attentions to the *Book of Kells* (850) which shows two rats eating the Eucharist bread with two cats nearby with rats on their backs. Davis believes that the *Book of Kells* rats are the field rodent *Arvicola,* though why he should feel that is more likely that a field rodent would be indoors eating eucharist bread than a domestic rodent, is not vouchsafed. Rackham has shown that a rat has been found in a Roman wall in Skeldergate near York, and that it was identified by the British Museum of Natural History to be *R. rattus* and its skull dated to pre-800. He says also that there is other evidence for the presence of the domestic rat in Europe since the Pleistocene and that Hinton was in possession of rats which were first-century AD. Bodenheimer lists a rat as one of the animals depicted on ancient Egyptian monuments. It has to be said however that there is no record of rats dying during an epidemic until the time of Avicenna in the eleventh-century.

There is a recurrent theme which states that the first medieval plague ushered in the Dark Ages and the second medieval plague brought them to an end; as an argument it is too general for accuracy. Biraben and Le Goff have a series of excellent maps showing the progress of the sixth and seventh century plague through western Europe and the Near East, except that they omit Britain.

Two high kings of Erin prayed most earnestly to God to: 'remove by some species of pestilence the burthersome multitudes of inferior people.' A perilous exercise as the hand of the Almighty was not known to be gentle in the matter of pestilences and there died in the subsequent plague both kings, Blathmac and Diomaid, Faeland of the Laigin, Cu cen Mathan in Cashel, Feichen of Fore, Aileran the Wise, Manchan of Lemanaghan, bishops and abbots without number and one third of the population. An unknown cleric did suggest praying for a good harvest, but was given short shrift.

Gregory of Tours tells the story (and I use the word advisedly) of Gregory the Great, made Pope in 590 during a major outbreak of the plague in Rome. He organised a great procession of penitence through Rome to appease the God who had visited this pestilence upon his people. Gregory the Great led the procession in person, with great attention to detail, different groups of penitents were to go to different churches and eventually all were to pray continually at the basilica of the Virgin Mary. This was in April and the plague had started in January. When the procession reached the bridge over the Tiber, with Hadrian's Mausoleum before it, an archangel appeared on top of the dome of the Mausoleum with a flaming sword which was then sheathed before the eyes of the penitents as a sign of the end of the epidemic. Alas for the story, Gregory and hagiology, *Y. pestis* is not known to recognise the authority of archangels and the brothers Limbourg, the illustrators of the *Très Riches Heures du Duc de Berri*, who display greater faith in *Y. pestis* than in archangels of tales, show the plague as killing penitents during the procession. Gregory is always given, in legend, hegemony over the plague, and Hadrian's Mausoleum became the Castel Sant'Angelo with the statue of an archangel sheathing his sword on its apex.

Gregory of Tours was far from being a mere hagiographer and he had important things to say about the plague and other diseases of the time. He noted the delay between the arrival of a plague ship and the outbreak in the port such as at Marseilles in 588; that is the time taken for the organism to get established among the local rats and set up the zoonosis by killing them and releasing their infected fleas.

Devignat has some maps of the spread of the early mediaeval plague and some rather fanciful ideas about the origin of the pandemic and the antiquity of the strains of *Y. pestis* from different foci. The means of identifying the strains are too crude to allow of any great confidence in the findings; these contain internal contradictions according to Pollitzer (1951). One known strain hails from Lake Victoria Nyanza and was described by Roberts who thought it to be of great age.

Fiennes notes that Justinian had won back most of the former Roman Empire despite the plague. This refers obviously to the continuing operations of Belisarius' successor, the remarkably successful eunuch Narses, after 542. These were largely mopping up operations against isolated Ostrogoths, equally affected by the plague. Narses also had the assistance of the Lombards of the Hungarian plains. Indeed, Narses was the instrument of the occupation of north Italy by the Lombards as he invited them there in justifiable anger at the nature of his dismissal by Justinian's successor Justin II and the slight suffered from Justin's wife Sophia, who sent him a spinning wheel and an instruction to join the women's quarters where he belonged. The Italian conquests could not be consolidated after the victories of Belisarius and Narses, due to the lack of manpower. It has been said by Bury that Witiges' Gothic army attempting to regain Rome from

Belisarius was weakened by disease and famine and had to sue for peace. It would be interesting to know what the disease was as it is too early for the plague pandemic.

There have been those such as McNeill who have hinted at the role of the waves of horsemen out of the Siberian steppes in bringing pandemics with them, while others such as Thorndyke who have scorned equivocation claim that the early mediaeval plague was brought to Europe by the Huns and the late mediaeval plague by the Mongols. Though I doubt this convenient explanation it would be fascinating to know whether disease played any role in the various decisions to quit the central Asian plateau. The Huns had a rather bad press, for apart from spitting babies on spears they were thought by the Chinese to have brought smallpox to China, though there is some confusion about the real culprit, the Hsiung-nu or the Huns, separate peoples. Biraben (1975) repeats his chronology of the early medieval plague. A study made by Laiou-Thomadikis, of the peasantry of the later Byzantine Empire makes no mention of any role for the plague of the earlier Empire in the state of their existence later.

So what can one conclude about the effects of Justinian's plague on the world stage? First it has to be said that it seems to have been confined to the Mediterranean, Europe north to England and the Near East to the eastern borders of present-day Iran. The great civilisations of the Far East appear to have escaped it. Within that area its effect was profound. It may be difficult to imagine the loss of a quarter to a half of your friends, family and neighbours but it would be difficult to maintain that it made no difference. Cipollo (1974), writing about troughs of mortality, puts it thus:

But much more frequently they were the result of epidemics and famines that wiped out a good part of the existing population. Reference is often made to the famous Black Death as if it were an exceptional disaster. Admittedly this unfortunate case deserves some special mention, for all Europe was struck more or less at the same time. But one has to remember that the sudden disappearance of a fifth of the population, or a third, or a half even was every once in a while, a recurrent catastrophe of local experience.

Justinian's dream of reconquering and reuniting the original Roman Empire, so near realisation, foundered on the tidal wave of the plague. The first headlong rush of the plague-free Arabs broke upon a plague-depressed population. As the plague established itself all affected areas disallowed any great enterprises as the manpower was not available. As the settled peoples contracted the relatively plague-free nomads and barbarians moved in to settle or graze the land. The Mediterranean came under commercial suspicion as a great vector of the plague and commerce started to move away to plague-free areas. Enormous areas: Iraq, Syria, Palestine, Egypt, the North African littoral, southern Spain, became Islamicised. Letters and art in Europe entered the Dark Ages, monastic life took a stranglehold on the intellectual mainstream of the Christian world. New boundaries were set up, many of which have persisted to today. The plague had all of the disrupting influence and more, that the waves of Asian peoples were to exert in Europe.

Can anyone doubt the profound effect of the plague as it rang down the curtain on the classical period of Mediterranean culture?

CHAPTER 6
The Black Death (part 1)

'The greatest calamity that has befallen the human race.'
MacArthur[2]

The Black Death struck Europe in 1348 with devastating fury. Once again it was *Yersinia pestis* on the rampage. It is not to be supposed that disease did not affect events between the two medieval plagues; in fact many enterprises were greatly influenced by outbreaks of infectious disease during this period, not least during the crusades when the Western European crusaders suffered terribly particularly from dysentery. Equally the enterprises of the German Emperors in Italy were dogged by disease. However it is the intention of this work to examine the effect of pandemics on history and no pandemic visited the known world in the six centuries between the two great plagues.

First it is necessary to try to determine what form the Black Death strain of *Y. pestis* took and where it came from, before we examine its effect upon mankind. The most famous description we have of this plague comes from the pen of Boccaccio:

> In the year 1348. . . that most beautiful of Italian cities, noble Florence, was attacked by a deadly plague. It started in the East either through the influence of heavenly bodies or because God's just anger with our wicked deeds sent it as a punishment to mortal men; and in a few years killed an innumerable quantity of people. Ceaselessly passing from place to place, it extended its miserable length over the West. Against this plague all human wisdom and foresight were in vain. Orders were given to cleanse the city of filth, the entry of any sick person was forbidden, much advice was given for keeping healthy; at the same time humble supplications were made to God by pious persons in processions and otherwise. And yet, at the beginning in the spring of the year mentioned, its horrible results began to appear, and in a miraculous manner. The symptoms were not the same as in the East, where a gush of blood from the nose was the plain sign of inevitable death; but it began in both men and women with certain swellings in the groin or under the armpit. They grew in size to a small apple or an egg, more or less, and were vulgarly called tumours. In a short space of time the tumours spread from the two parts named all over the body. Soon after this the symptoms changed and

black and purple spots appeared on the arms or thighs or other parts of the body, sometimes a few large ones, sometimes many little ones. These spots were a certain sign of death, just as the original tumour had been and remained.

No doctor's advice, no medicine could overcome or alleviate this disease. An enormous number of ignorant men and women set up as doctors in addition to those who were trained. Either the disease was such that no treatment was possible or the doctors were so ignorant that they did not know what caused it, and consequently could not administer the proper remedy. In any case very few recovered, most people died within about three days of the appearance of the tumours described above, most of them without any fever or any other symptoms. The violence of this disease was such that the sick communicated it to the healthy who came near them, just as a fire catches anything dry or oily near it. And it went even further. To speak to or go near the sick brought the infection and a common death to the living; and moreover to touch the clothes or anything else the sick person had touched or wore gave the disease to the person touching.

What I am about to tell you now is a marvellous thing to hear; and if I and others had not seen it with our own eyes I would not dare to write it, however much I was willing to believe and whatever the good faith of the people from whom I heard it. So violent was the malignancy of this plague that it was communicated, not only from one man to another, but from the garments of the sick or dead man to animals of another species, which caught the disease in that way and very quickly died of it. One day among other occasions I saw with my own eyes (as I said just now) the rags left lying in the street of a poor man who had died of the plague; two pigs came along and, as their habit is, turned the clothes over with their snouts and then munched on them, with the result that they both fell dead almost at once on the rags, as if they had been poisoned.

From these and similar and greater occurrences, such fear and fanciful notions took possession of the living that almost all of them adopted the same cruel policy, which was to entirely avoid the sick and everything belonging to them. By so doing, each thought he could secure his own safety. [Some led sober lives in separate groups; others took to dissolute pleasures but avoided the sick.]

In this suffering and misery of our city, the authority of human and divine laws almost disappeared for, like other men, the ministers and executors of law were all dead or sick or shut up with their families, so that no duties were carried out. Every man was therefore able to do as he pleased. [Many took a middle course living moderately, going abroad but carrying scented herbs and flowers as a comfort against the stench of decomposing bodies. Others fled to the countryside, believing that it was the city which was the centre of infection.]

Not everyone who adopted these various opinions died, nor did all escape. Some when they were still healthy had set the example of avoiding the sick, and falling ill themselves, died untended. [The disease broke up families, the sick were left without care. Servants profited from their master's misery, charging exorbitant amounts to tend the sick, but usually dying themselves before they could use the money. The dying received no attention and enormous numbers died. Many ancient customs were lost or altered. Wakes were no longer held, few dead were accompanied to the church by more than a small number of mourners. A bier might carry several bodies. The dead were buried in any grave which could be found. The lower and most of the middle classes were not buried at all but left in the street or houses. There were so many bodies that the cemeteries ran out of consecrated ground and had to use mass graves.]

Not to pry any further into all the details of all the miseries which afflicted our city, I shall add that the surrounding countryside was spared nothing of what befell Florence. The villages on a smaller scale were like the city; in the fields and isolated farms the poor wretched peasants and their families were without doctors and any assistance, and perished in the highways, in their fields and houses, night and day, more like beasts than men. Just as the towns became dissolute and indifferent to their work and property, so the peasants, when they saw that death was upon them, entirely neglected the fruits of their past labours both from the earth and from cattle, and thought only of enjoying what they had. Thus it happened that cows, asses, sheep, goats, pigs, fowls and even dogs, those faithful companions of man, left the farms and wandered at their will through the fields, where the wheat crops stood abandoned, unreaped and ungarnered. Many of these animals seemed endowed with reason, for after they had pastured all day, they returned to the farm for the night of their own free will, without being driven.

Returning from the countryside to the city, it may be said that such was the cruelty of heaven, and perhaps in part of men, that between March and April more than one hundred thousand persons died within the walls of Florence, what between the violence of the plague and the abandonment in which the sick were left by the cowardice of the healthy. And before the plague the city was not thought to hold so many people.

[Buildings were left empty. Famous names disappeared for ever. Men, women and youths in perfect health at midday were dead by nightfall. The churches had no congregations, the city was empty. Boccaccio goes on with an apology for leaving the city and then the famous tales commence.]

What can we learn from this description? First it should be said that Boccaccio was something of an hypocrite. His strictures on those who fled, his apparent disapproval of those who chose a light-hearted approach to the epidemic, his remarks on the peasants who deserted their work, his sorrow at the desertion of the sick, these sit ill with the merry tales of sexual misbehaviour which follow. These tales are told among a group, including himself, who had fled the city. But should this reduce his reliability as a witness? – surely not. The major items for consideration are Boccaccio's description of the disease in man and the death of those animals which came in contact with the disease.

His description of the terminal symptom in the East of gushing of blood from the nose is difficult to interpret as we do not know if he is talking about the Black Death in the Black Sea area, where it occurred before it did in Florence, or some totally different disease prevalent in the East and known to the Italians through someone such as Marco Polo or the Franciscans or the medical writings of the Arab physicians such as Al Rhazi or Avicenna. The descriptions of buboes is unmistakable. The appearance of the black or purple spots, following the buboes and just prior to death, would imply a greater involvement of the blood than is the case with the present modern plague pandemic. This, in turn, and including the description of the buboes spreading all over the body, would spell a greater likelihood of septicaemic plague commencing from the bubonic form as a greater blood involvement would make it easier to infect the human flea. This is supported by Boccaccio's insistence on the great contagiousness of the Black Death in Florence.

Death among domestic animals in contact with a human disease is not a feature of any of the diseases dealt with in this book, none is transmitted from man to animals to any significant degree, let alone kill them. Such descriptions, as in Thucydides and Boccaccio, have been a thorn in the side of medical historians, and have given impetus to alternative theories about the nature of the disease causing the epidemic in fifth-century-BC Athens and that of fourteenth-century Eurasia. It has been suggested, by Twigg, for instance, that the Black Death may have been anthrax, so accommodating the concomitant death of animals. The problem with such suggestions is that they raise more problems than they solve (1).

There are two choices before one in the question of the death of animals in the Black Death. The first is that Boccaccio was wrong. To support this is the fact that few other reliable observers mention it, though there are those who parrot Thucydides. Contemporary prints frequently show live animals among people dead or dying of the Black Death and Boccaccio himself seems to forget about it when discussing farm animals, including dogs and pigs, who return to the farm in which their masters and mistresses had died of the plague. It is the only passage in Boccaccio's description of the plague where he feels he has to reassure his reader repeatedly that he has seen the phenomenon himself and that it is vouched for by reliable witnesses.

There is no reason to believe that there was a concomitant murrain attacking animals at the same time as the Black Death in Florence was attacking man as no mention was made of it at the time, though there was one a little later. If Boccaccio was right then the strain of *Y. pestis,* for the disease of man was bubonic plague, must have had the ability to infect a wide variety of animals, kill them and do so in matter of hours if not minutes. This is too much to swallow. Even if the strain of *Y. pestis* existed that could infect all sorts of animals, there is no disease, including anthrax, which kills animals in hours (and certainly not minutes) after infection. A toxin might do it, but how would that impregnate a rag of clothing? No, it is all beyond the bounds of imagination and it seems that Boccaccio was being 'economical with the truth' and using his imagination on this occasion just as a thriller writer is able to summon to his help the instant anaesthetic in a drink or some deadly poison unknown to science to heighten his story, so I think Boccaccio was doing a little embroidery. After all, Boccaccio was a story-teller.

To summarise from the various descriptions of the Black Death. It was *Y. pestis* again, despite the doubts of some, including Twigg. It is highly unlikely to have infected animals and killed them. We have the word of the most acute medical observer of the Black Death of the day – Gui de Chauliac – that pneumonic plague played a considerable role in Avignon and the rest of France. He has the support of no lesser person than the Emperor Ionnes Cantacuzenos (John VI) of Byzantium who noted pneumonic plague in Byzantium. Ibn Khatimah, an Arab physician of Spain, practising at the time, mentions the spitting of blood and the extreme contagiousness of the disease. It must be remembered that the Black Death reached the Mediterranean in winter.

We have many mentions, both during the Black Death and subsequent outbreaks of the 'tokens', the blackened skin haemorrhages of septicaemic plague. It seems safe to assume that the variant of *Y. pestis* present in the fourteenth- and fifteenth-centuries plagues of Europe and the Middle East was capable of infecting the lungs easily and could achieve a heavy infection quickly so that the blood often became infected and was a site of overwhelming multiplication of the organism, capable of infecting the human flea, *P. irritans*. The organism could maintain itself in the rat flea for some weeks and on infecting man could then develop into pneumonic or septicaemic plague as well before or after producing buboes.

There would seem to be little doubt that the original entrance of the organism into a fresh part of the Mediterranean or the Middle East was as bubonic plague, involving the house or ship rat (*R. rattus*) and the tropical rat flea, *X. cheopis*, and only after that would plague appear sporadically as pneumonic or septicaemic plague. Entomologists feel that the tropical rat flea, that they know today, could not have survived the northern European climates. So, either the tropical rat flea of the fourteenth-century was a much hardier beast (it has been pointed out that this may have been so as it is a fur flea and not a nest flea; for an excellent discussion on this and the general points concerning the spread of plague in Nordic countries of Europe see (2)), or plague was carried to northern Europe by the direct transmission methods resulting in pneumonic or septicaemic plague. The problem facing us is that the descriptions of plague from Russia and Scandinavia leave no doubt that bubonic plague was present with buboes. Another alternative is to assume that the northern epidemic was supported by fleas and rodents other than *X. cheopis* and *R. rattus*, which is quite possible (see the involvement of marmots and hares in the chapter on the Bombay plague, as detailed by Zwanberg.)

It would seem we must assume that, if septicaemic plague was relatively common, then some of the septicaemic cases showed buboes (which is only a question of time and Boccaccio says the tumours commenced to spread out all over the body) as these are such a constant feature of the contemporary descriptions of the patients. In this case buboes would show as a general lymphadenopathy (swelling of lymph glands) and not be confined to the groin and armpits, though these would remain the prime and perhaps the first sites. We must assume, also, that the organism could move from one state to another with ease and a human flea, on leaving a dead human could feed upon and infect the local house rat and set up the bubonic plague zoonosis again in a new area.

In defence of all this manufactured epidemiology it can be claimed, with justice, that *Y. pestis* does exist today as a number of strains of varying virulence and that the virulence is governed by genes and plasmids capable of frequent change by mutation (3). Many observers believe that the penumonic element of plague is especially a winter phenomenon, while the variant of *Y pestis*, proposed here for the Black Death, would be able to cause pneumonic plague of itself and maintain it, though there is no doubt that it would flourish even more strongly in winter and in northern Europe. One can imagine pneumonic plague, tuberculosis, influenza and the common cold marching hand in hand.

For the distribution of the Black Death in Europe one cannot do better than consult the maps of Elizabeth Carpentier [1]. It will be noticed that there is a large quantum of movement from December 1347 to June 1348, and a lesser jump in the second half of the year. There is, once more, a large jump in distribution in the first half of 1349. The period of these large jumps includes the winter months of a time still in the grip, to some degree, of the little ice age. There is movement into Scandinavia and Russia in 1350 which would seem to presage an epidemiology well able to withstand cold weather and this for an epidemiology said, using evidence from the present pandemic, to require warm or temperate climates.

Many observers and chroniclers noted that the Black Death moved along the lines of human communication, sometimes quickly. One must ask oneself the question: how does a zoonosis do that? The answer, of course, is only if the reservoir animal and the transmitting agent travel with man, which usually means that the reservoir host is a domestic animal either carrying the vector or using a ubiquitous vector. The only other way would be the existence of a long-lived infected vector accompanying the travelling people. The black house rat has been/ called domestic but peridomestic would be a better term. Its tie is to the occupied house rather than to man, it tends to be sedentary and is unlikely to wish to accompany people on their travels. It has been suggested that it did so in the fodder necessary for the horses. This seems a very precarious way to maintain a moving pandemic of the proportions of the Black Death, when the life of a plague-infected rat flea is limited. It seems that a much more likely and sure manner would be for the disease to travel along man's lines of communication in the people themselves or in their ectoparasites such as their very own personal fleas. This spells septicaemic or pneumonic plague as the major travelling form.

The objection, of course, is the limiting factor of the early death of the engine of travel for the bacillus. This very early death in either septicaemic or pneumonic plague is counted, of course, from the time of first symptoms. For the purposes of epidemiology, the period of time in which the transporter of the infection may live is longer than that. The patient is infective from the time that he can infect a human flea or cough up infective droplets. While this is going to be no very long time, it could be, at least, days. When the patient dies either he will have already passed on the infection or he will be about to do so. The event of his death is likely to have spurred his companions to greater speed so as to escape the contagion which was thought to be in the air.

Ell [2] examined 300 medieval texts with mention of the late medieval plague and concluded that, on the basis of the patterns of the household foci, seasonality, clinical presentation, rat mortality and contact risk, the general pattern was one of a human flea-borne disease, or at least, a disease with a strong inter-human transmission element. Jorge, who could be said to belong to the North African school of plague experts where septicaemic plague was relatively common, is emphatic that the Black Death was frequently transmitted by the human flea. The point about patterns of household foci is that the modern plague pandemic frequently infected only one person in a household and moved on as might be expected of a zoonosis, while large numbers of cases in a single household spells a contagious disease being transmitted directly from man to man.

Others (4) have expressed a strong belief in the existence of both pneumonic and septicaemic plague in the Black Death and subsequent epidemics. Gottfried [2] argues for the presence of both man-to-man diseases by means of an equilibrium theory about the age of the relationship between man and *Y. pestis* and the pathogenicity of the organism. The theory is, however, dubious and probably misleading.

So it is concluded here that during the Black Death and at least some of its subsequent recrudescences, while the importation of plague to sea-ports was in the form of rat-borne zoonotic bubonic plague, the strain in man, once established, took on a strong element of both pneumonic and septicaemic behaviour so the epidemic became, to a considerable degree, inter-human and spread with far greater speed than would be possible for a zoonosis. The organism could and did return to its zoonotic mode at will and become rat-borne, rat flea transmitted and zoonotic as this epizootic would continue anyway. It could probably return to the rat from the pneumonic or septicaemic patient as well.

Where did it come from and is that epidemiologically important? There is a good deal of argument about the origins of the Black Death. For a long time the views of Heckert held sway, his stated belief that the Far East had been in the grip of a series of terrible disasters, first the floods, earthquakes and subterranean rumblings then a plague of devastating fury, was the accepted viewpoint. In the words of Hecker: 'India was depopulated,, Tartary, Mesopotamia, Syria, Armenia were covered with dead bodies; the Kurds fled in vain to the mountains. In Caramania and Caesaria none were left alive. . . .'

Alas for such stirring prose, all of this seems to have been pure fancy and none of it has survived modern scholarship. Jaggi finds no mention of plague in India before the days of the Moghuls, unless one believes that the pestilence which struck the army of Muhammed Tughlak in about 1332 was plague, and there is no convincing evidence for such a belief. Chinese sources such as Wong & Wu, and Ho, make no mention of any particularly devastating plague in China at the time, though there is a 1726 Chinese dictionary which is claimed, very dubiously, to have a definition of plague. There were epidemics of some nature in China at the time as there always were in most years (5). Creighton, the greatest of British medical historians, says there was no history of plague in China in the days of Kubla Khan.

The American historian McNeill believes that the 1348 pandemic started in the Far East, particularly as he is anxious to involve the Mongols in its spread as part of some greater philosophy of pandemics which will be discussed later. Biochemistry is against him, as the present strain in the Middle East ferments glycine but that of China, India and Burma does not. This is not the sort of evidence, however, on which to obtain a conviction of man or theory. Most authorities today believe that the Black Death originated in Central Asia, which gives a fairly large margin of error. The Gobi desert has been suggested by Gottfried as a sort of compromise between McNeill and the rest.

Norris a more precise observer believes it to have arisen west of the Caspian in the Kipchak Khanate, as he does not believe that the sparsely populated Asian trade routes would support the swift spread of plague. This belief incorporates the conviction that Justinian's plague settled down in the upper Middle East as an enzootic and stayed there until the fourteenth-century. A Spanish Islamic authority is quoted as giving the source as the 'Land of the Khiti' which it is claimed was the Kara Khiti who ruled the area east of the Aral Sea. One of the problems with much of this thinking is that behind it there tends to be the conviction that human plague must derive from human plague and this, of course, is not true of a zoonosis. Plague sprang from animals in the first place and may have done so again after any of the periods of its quiescence. The source of the plague, which turned up in the Crimea in 1346/7, is claimed to be from the area of modern Iraq and Kurdistan. This is a long way from the Khiti in Turkmenistan, Kazakstan and Uzbekistan. This whole theory has been brought into question by Dols because of the distances involved and the fact that the Spanish Islamic source stands on its own and is unsupported by other Islamic evidence. We are left with the rather vague opinion that the Black Death arose somewhere in that vast area – Central Asia – with a slight leaning to the Alma Ata area which has some flimsy evidence of mass deaths from Christian graves there.

We know a great deal more about how it reached the Mediterranean. It turned up west of the Caspian Sea among the Tartars. Understandably cross, they searched for a scapegoat and found to hand an outpost of Genoese traders in Tana (= Azov, on the Don near its mouth) whose headquarters were at Caffa (= Feyodosiya, on the south-east coast of the Crimean peninsula). They picked a fight with the Genoese and forced them back behind the walls of Caffa where they besieged them. By now the plague had a grip on the Tartars and it forced them to raise the siege. As a last gesture they tried a little crude bacterial warfare and chucked their bodies, dead of plague, over the city walls to infect the Genoese.

This shows a greater belief in the contagious nature of disease than is thought to be current at the time, but shows no great grasp of the zoonotic nature of bubonic plague, unless they threw the dead rats over the walls as well. Or were the Tartars better epidemiologists than we think, and had recognised the contagious nature of a human flea-ridden body dead of septicaemic plague? Be that as it may, and one must remember that the miasmatic theory of disease transmission, current at the time, would probably allow for infection to be set up by the miasma arising from a dead body, the story as we have it comes from the quill of one Gabriel de Mussis, who would have us believe that he travelled with the plague-ridden Genoese from the Crimea to the Mediterranean. Alas for romance, a literal-minded Italian scholar has shown that de Mussis did not stir from his fireside during that time.

I give a truncated version of this story here, largely drawn from the excellent account of the Black Death by Ziegler. The Genoese fled the plague in Caffa in the winter of 1347/8, taking ship to Constantinople then out into the Sea of Marmara and on to the Mediterranean, accompanied by the plague, presumably among the ship rats. Ziegler thinks that, while this is one way in which the Black Death reached the Mediterranean, it was probably not the only route. It may have come also via the Tigris on the spice and silk routes and thence to the Crimea and the Levant both. Certainly ibn Battuta saw it in Syria early in 1348 (this begs the question of what form the plague took in order to travel overland).

The Genoese ships arrived, some at Constantinople, others at Messina, Sardinia, Genoa and Marseilles, with, it was said, the crew lying dead at the oars. The inhabitants of the sea-ports, when they realised the danger, drove the ships away, thereby hastening the spread of the pandemic and tried to institute a makeshift quarantine. Then, in Ziegler's words: 'But by the time the Genoese authorities reacted, it was too late. The infection was ashore and nothing was to stop it. By the spring of 1348 the Black Death had taken a firm grasp in Italy and on the mainland.'

CHAPTER 7
The Black Death (part 2)

En mil trois cent quarante huit,
A Nuits de cent resterent huit.
En mil trois cent quarante neuf,
A Beaune de cent resterent neuf.

Anon

The Black Death was to strike Europe already in trouble from the famines consequent upon the 'Little Ice Age'. The population was probably already declining or, at least, static; the European feudal society was beginning to decay. Now came the pandemic of plague we know as the Black Death, which killed on an unprecedented scale. Of those who contracted the disease not less than 70% died. Most estimates agree that Europe eventually lost one-third or more of its peoples, some 25,000,000 dead in the years 1348-50. It swept through Italy to Spain, France, Switzerland and Yugoslavia in the first six months. It moved on inexorably to Britain, Austria, Hungary and Germany, then on to Ireland, Scandinavia and Russia.

Its effects were catastrophic. Governments, medicine and the Church were powerless to check it. People were overwhelmed both physically and mentally. One writer has likened the reaction to that which manifested itself in response to the atomic bomb at Hiroshima. Another has drawn a parallel between the aftermath of the First World War; neither comparison begins to be adequate. There are a number of excellent accounts of the Black Death, its spread and its nature (1). There are further valuable accounts of its occurrence in particular localities (2). There is an excellent summary of these by Elizabeth Carpentier (1962B). As the interest here is in the lasting effects of the Black Death and its recurrences, specific epidemics and their spread and mortality will be referred to only as they affect human society and its institutions permanently.

First it is necessary to say something of the state of Europe and the Middle East in 1348. Britain was in the political state given it by William the Conqueror, that is feudalism, by then only slightly modified by the Magna Carta. The Viking invasions had ceased and feudal anarchy was passing as royal authority (re-asserting itself under the Plantagenets and the King, sanctified by religious support), took the high ground as the head of a feudal system. France and the Christian portions of the Iberian peninsula were in a similar state. The king was the liege lord to whom the tenants-in-chief, the barons and the hereditary aristocracy rendered service, largely war service as they were the fighting men of the land. Elective monarchy had been replaced by hereditary monarchy, so relieving the electors of their power. This system in France had been reinforced and centralised by Philip Augustus and Louis IX, reversing the tendency to fission due to the power of some of the great landed feuditories and the practice of *appanage*. The system became the law of the land.

The feudal system in Germany was weakened by the great quarrel between Empire and Papacy, the eventual collapse of the Hohenstaufen followed by the 'Great Interregnum'. Rivalry between Saxony, Swabia and Bavaria ensured no central overriding authority by the thirteenth and fourteenth centuries, though each large province operated a feudal system. In Italy authority had devolved to the Papacy and to the jealously guarded administrations of the city states in the north, divided the one from the other by the Guelf-Ghibelline struggles, and to Norman-style feudalism in the south.

The leaders in all this were the newcomers – the Normans – searching for a system to ensure the constancy of their power within a state of almost constant war. The natural state of these leaders was war and the system was built around this. War required money and men, the king became the chief tax-gatherer and using the feudal system recruited his men from his tenants and landowners. At the beginning of the fourteenth-century the kings were close to overreaching themselves. Edward I of England had failed to subdue the Scots and Philip IV had failed similarly in Flanders. Indeed, France had just suffered the reigns of the 'Rois Maudits', a disastrous time. Successful war paid, to some degree, for itself in treasure, arms and men, but failure over-stretched the system. The use of mercenaries only managed to substitute a shortage of money for a shortage of men. The aristocrats of the system began to assert a counter-pressure to the theory of kingship. Within this system was the everyday form of feudalism, the relation between the landlord and the peasant. This centred around the *demesne*.

The villein or serf was tied in law to the land of the lord or monastery and worked that land (the *demesne*) as a service prior to working what land was allowed to him for himself. This peasant supported the aristocracy and the clergy and was not allowed to move from the *demesne*. The serf 'owed' the lord his labour and even extra work at harvest time . He owed the lord rent for any other land aside from the *demesne* that he might cultivate. The lord owed the serfs his protection in war and the clergy looked after their spiritual needs. Wealth was rural, and came from this system. Such merchants and manufacturing classes as existed were small and emergent.

In the period between the twelfth and fourteenth centuries the peasants had done very well and increased considerably in numbers. The motive force was the colonisation of new land as forests, marshes and hills came under the plough. New crops were available and the system of three field planting had come into use. All this had brought prosperity, which in turn had increased the birth-rate and the population had increased. This meant that more land was required, but the system had nearly reached its limit as the fourteenth-century began, and fresh arable land was becoming scarce.

This feudal system as outlined for Britain did not, however, hold entirely true for Germany and Italy. In Germany the central power of the Holy Roman Emperor was spent. The struggles between Emperor and Pope had exhausted both Empire and Papacy, but continued to bedevil northern Italy. Power in Germany was invested in feudal prices and dukes while in Italy the city-state was the power base in much of northern Italy, chiefly Florence, Milan, Genoa and Venice. The papal states were squeezed between these city-states and the Norman/Angevin feudal states in southern Italy. Such as it was Papal power was debilitated by a split, when, at the behest of France, a rival pope was set up in Avignon in confrontation with the Pope at Rome in 1305. Two Popes was nothing new, but this time it involved the pretensions of a newly emerging power – centralised France. The Hohenstaufens had collapsed in Germany, defeated in the south of Italy by the Angevins who in turn foundered in the face of the Sicilian revolt for ever remembered as the 'Sicilian Vespers'. Here was a power vacuum which was to tear at Italy's vitals for two hundred years.

The situation in Europe was unstable. Disastrous crop failures had occurred, particularly between 1315 and 1317 in the larger part of Europe and a number of more local crop failures had occurred since the 1270s. The failures had been due to a change of climate. After the period of the 'early medieval warm', an intense cold and wet period had settled on Europe – the so-called 'Little Ice Age'. The Alpine glaciers had increased in extent. Iceland lost its ability to grow cereals and England its vines. Northern Europe lost much of its wheat areas and the highlands of Europe produced greatly reduced crops. There was a widespread famine with a considerable number of deaths, said by Lucas to be due to starvation and disease. The primary cause of death was probably enteric diseases. Today, when famine strikes, one of our first fears is an outbreak of typhoid fever, and 1315 was only different in scale.

The feudal system was under various, forms of attack. The famines had destabilised the land-tenure system and led to increased movement among the peasantry. According to Coulton to keep their labour force, the lords of the *demesne* had started to experiment with commutation (release from service) combined with the letting of the land to free yeomen for cash. In England and France external commerce no longer expanded and exploration ceased. A number of Italian banks collapsed. The Hundred Years War had begun to devastate France and impoverish England. Civil war was tearing Italy apart, Germany was in anarchy, as detailed by Pirenne. The population appears to have remained steady or even increased which, as the food was decreasing, was leading to a classical Malthusian crisis for Europe. Europe was poor and needed a drastic remedy which would reduce the population. It got one!

On to this unstable stage stepped the Black Death to alter the whole way of life for all time. Sometimes this was to complete what had already commenced, sometimes society was set off on an entirely new path. The first subject requiring discussion is the demographic one. This has been a major point of contention among demographers and historians alike, as upon the estimate of the number of dead of the Black Death and its subsequent relapses rests all future opinions of the effect of the late medieval pandemic and epidemics of plague. There is nothing new which I can add to the discussions which have gone before other than to give a consensus.

Russell (1971) (3) was the first to apply modern demographic techniques to the problem and then only to England. He argued that the 1315-17 famine and accompanying pestilences halted the population growth in England which had reached a high point of 3,700,000; this was not a condition of over-population and England was prosperous. By 1377 he believed that the population had declined to 2,300,000, a loss of 1,400,000 or nearly 38%. These figures have been criticised as being too low. In among these figures, two separate arguments were developing. The first was on the figures themselves and the other on whether the continuing decline in the population over the rest of the fourteenth-century and persisting to the later half of the fifteenth-century was due to continuing outbreaks of disease or to simple Malthusian causes – population outrunning food supplies.

The death toll of the Black Death obviously differed from country to country. In England estimates vary from the 90% of some of the contemporary chroniclers to the 5% of Shrewsbury (1970). This last estimate need not delay us for long. Professor Shrewsbury kept his ability for being cantankerously wrong to the end. Morris swept his arguments to oblivion. There is a consensus on the death toll in England in the first Black Death pandemic (1348-50), which is between 25% and 35% of the population. It is usually expressed for simplicity's sake as one-third and it puts Russell's (1948) figure of 25% as too low and Pollitzer's (1951) figure of one half to two-thirds as too high except as a total figure for 1348-1720.

In France Gottfried (1983) estimates that the towns lost about 50% and the rural areas lost about 30% of their inhabitants. Vallin, in a more general work, sees a drop in the population of France from 1348 to 1450 of 16%. Duby, one of the more conservative of French historians, a group who have never accepted any great role for plague in history, puts famine in first place as a cause of population drop of the time without giving a figure for the drop. Carpentier, (1962B) looking at Savoie parishes finds a death-rate of 50%. The accepted figures for France seem to be those of Renouard, which had it varying from two-thirds to one-eighth of the population dead of the Black Death depending on locality.

In Italy we have estimates for individual towns and their environs which are thought to represent the death rate for the whole country. Carpentier (1962) found a death rate of 50% in Orvieto. Carmichael (1986) found a little less than 50% in Florence. Herlihy (1967) gives a death toll of two thirds for Bologna and Bowsky (1964) found a 50-58% death rate in other Italian cities. In Spain Verlinden (1971) found no profound effect of the pandemic. Ziegler, basing himself upon the Arab physician Ibn Khatima, says that Almeria suffered 780 deaths a day among a total population of 20,000 at the peak of the Black Death, no very great toll compared to Italy or France.

Germany suffered severely, attacked from the west from France, from the south from Italy and probably from the south-east from the Balkans. Ziegler gives the best overall account, though his concern is, to a large degree, with the recording of the excesses of the flagellants and the persecution of the Jews. He quotes Eubel as estimating that 35% of the higher clergy died and Reincke as estimating that between one half and two thirds of the population of Hamburg perished. Gottfried (1983) gives the death tolls as varying between 10% and 30% in Germany though Carpentier (1962B) gives us figures of 50% for Magdeburg, between 50% and 60% for Hamburg, 70% for Bremen but only 25% for Lubeck. Ziegler concludes that although Germany, Russia, Bohemia and Austria suffered badly their suffering was less than that of Italy and France.

The pandemic moved on to Scandinavia and the Baltic, reaching Russia in 1351 and even Archangel, Iceland and Greenland according to. The advent of the plague in these last areas is a major reason for doubting the wholly zoonotic nature of the Black Death. A zoonosis based on the black house rat and the tropical rat flea in Greenland stretches the imagination beyond its limits unless the lemmings and their fleas became infected. The Black Death wiped out the settlements on Greenland, according to Henschen. When such a statement is made it must be remembered that emigration and lowered birth-rates will have played a part. Denmark, Norway and Sweden suffered heavily, up to 64% in Norway, probably more than Germany for unknown reasons. Ziegler says the Balkans were severely affected as one would imagine from their proximity to Constantinople, a great centre of dissemination, though Yugoslavia is said to have received its epidemic from Italy and the wolves were said to have gloried in the unexpected windfall of fresh meat from which they did *not* die. Cyprus and the islands of the Aegean were struck exceptionally heavily. The general consensus is that Europe lost between twenty-four and twenty-five million people from a population of about one hundred million; that is a loss directly from the Black Death of about 24% in the years 1348 to 1355. After this, of course, a drastically lowered birth rate would begin to have an effect.

Our guide to the progress and consequences of the Black Death in the Near and Middle East is Dols (1979). He finds that the great collecting places and centres of dissemination were Constantinople and Alexandria. He believes that some plague in Egypt must have come from the Lake Victoria-Nyanza focus. It is hard to believe that it waited until the time that plague had reached Europe from a different source. In Cairo the plague came with the khamsin wind in spring (some excuse for thinking it to have been miasma-borne). It was usually over by June. This refers mostly to outbreaks subsequent to the Black Death itself. Plague also came in the autumn and winter when, Dols believes, it was in the form of pneumonic plague. Dols is a great advocate for a considerable portion of pneumonic plague in both the Black Death and subsequent outbreaks in the Middle East. However, he ignores septicaemic plague to too great a degree.

As in Europe change in the Middle East was already in progress. In Egypt the Mamelukes, previously powerful enough to have inflicted a decisive defeat on the all-conquering Mongols at Ain Jalut in 1250, were under stress from continuing civil wars, consequent on the break-up of the former dynasty of the Fatimids, whose successors they were. In the desert about the strip of cultivated land along the Nile lurked the Bedouin, always ready to make trouble and inroads into more civilised and agriculturally advanced parts. Plague struck, then, a partially unstable situation in Mameluke Egypt and its provinces of Palestine, Syria and the Hejaz. Other changes were in evidence after the disturbed ants' nest caused by the arrival of the Mongols and Timur. Islam had split with two centres, one in Egypt and one in Persia as the Tigris/Euphrates basin grew less important, following the Mongol destruction of Baghdad and the Abbasid caliphate succeeded by the disruption of much of the agriculture as Timur destroyed the irrigation canals. Egypt was to become the repository of Muslim law, religion and mysticism. Persia, with its ancient traditions and language, gave Islam its poetry and much of its secular learning. It is a curious fact that at the time of the Black Death the two great religions of the area were suffering a split, Christianity with a pope in Rome and another in Avignon, Islam with a centre in Egypt and another in Persia.

In the Middle East reliable data on death-rates is difficult to come by in the fourteenth and fifteenth centuries. Dols finds it impossible to be precise. He is, however, in no doubt that a major demographic collapse followed the Black death in the Middle East and that, as in Europe, this collapse persisted for nearly two centuries.

What then were the consequences of this frightful toll in lives? These need to be examined as two separate strands, the one on the political and social institutions of the day and the other on the prevailing thought of the time. It is also necessary to consider not just the Black Death alone but the cumulative effect of the subsequent outbreaks, some of them rivalling even the Black Death itself locally. There is an argument as to whether all these subsequent outbreaks, were plague and only plague. The answer is irrelevant to the central thesis of this book as, whatever the nature of the disease during these outbreaks it was infectious disease. The argument, therefore, will be ignored, fascinating though it is. In the same vein there is an argument about the effect of the 1315-17 crop failure and consequent famine upon the demographic collapse of the fourteenth-century in Europe, some putting the famine almost as high as the Black Death as a progenitor of the demographic decline (Malthusian doctrine v. losses due to disease), even as the prime cause over time. The argument relies on a high death- rate and so the argument comes down to which caused the greater number of deaths.

Starvation alone causes relatively few deaths and, whatever one's views on the relation between malnutrition and disease, it is disease which performs the *coup de grâce* during famine. It follows, therefore, that even if one believes that the famine was more important than the Black Death in the fourteenth-century demographic collapse it is still disease which is taking the lion's share of lives and it still needs to be identified. It is most unlikely, however, that famine and its usual consequent disease would have killed on the order of the infectious Black Death or brought about the number of deaths necessary to precipitate a demographic collapse of the severity of that of the fourteenth-century.

Saltmarsh believed that the more local epidemics of the later part of the fourteenth and fifteenth centuries maintained the impetus of the population decline and denied any regeneration of the population until the late fifteenth-century. There is no doubt that Europe's population did reach a nadir in 1450-70 and did not recover for a hundred years and this requires explanation. There are those who claim that many of the epidemics subsequent to the Black Death were not pure plague and that large elements of smallpox and typhus were present. Certainly the 'sweating sickness' struck with great virulence in this period and the experts are still arguing over the precise nature of this disease. It would be entirely reasonable to suppose that typhus had stepped on to the stage of Europe by this time but one would have wished for more written evidence of such an obvious disease as smallpox. Be that as it may, these epidemics were infectious disease and for the purposes of this book it is only the argument whether the continuing demographic crisis was due to continuing disease whatever that might be (and it is known that many of the outbreaks were, at least, predominantly plague), or due to war, to class struggle, and famine, which need to concern us here. Saltmarsh believed that the continuing epidemics were cumulatively more damaging in their prevention of population recovery than the original pandemic itself, if only in the sense of the duration of time in which they acted.

Bean opposes this view. He believes that the subsequent plague outbreaks did not make any catastrophic contribution to the population decline after the one-third death-rate in 1348-51. He believes, as do many, that it was the inter-human transmitted forms of plague which were the major killers and are necessary to explain the death rate of the Black Death. On the other hand he does not believe that pneumonic plague was evident in the subsequent outbreaks and he finds that plague became more and more bubonic and urban. He also appears to believe that some form of herd immunity was beginning to operate to reduce the amount and severity of plague present. I have already tried to explain why this belief is most unlikely. Later Bean (1982) stresses the importance of the Black Death as a critical event. He puts it on a par with the fall of Rome as a turning point in European history.

Robert reminds us that bubonic plague was present in England for three hundred and seventeen years, from 1348 to 1665 (up to 1720 in France) and that even in the seventeenth-century there were major outbreaks in England, in 1603, 1625 and 1655. During all that time the population was, at least, checked, the modern increase in the expectation of life did not commence until about 1660. He argues that the Black Death struck an England already in crisis and it could only have become epidemic because of the crisis, though by what biological mechanism he does not tell us. He claims that the existing crisis was Malthusian, that is the population had outrun its ability to feed itself. War, too, was contributing to this crisis. Robert believes that an epidemic like the Black Death can only take root if there is fertile ground for it, citing its failure to arrive before as proof of this. This sort of vague idea is unhelpful in being far too imprecise in its cause and anyway organisms have their own logic and priorities which bear little or no relation to those of man and this is even more true of those organisms involved in zoonoses. The question is far too complicated to go into here. Diseases have their own patterns of behaviour, which bear only a tangential relation to man's circumstances. Robert, while discounting the effects of the Black Death itself, does agree with Saltmarsh that the continuing epidemics were damaging in that they contributed to the check on population recovery.

Postan, with the powerful support of Titow and of Glascock favoured the Malthusian view of the demographic collapse of Europe in the fourteenth and fifteenth centuries, believing that the epidemics subsequent to the Black Death did not contribute sufficiently to the population loss to have halted so disastrously the potential increase in population, nor that they could have maintained the momentum of the population decline set off by the Black Death. Postan held to the Malthusian viewpoint that population declines of the magnitude and longevity as those which occurred in the period under discussion could only be the consequence of the failure of resources, in this case agriculture and food, coupled with the abnormally high population increases of the eleventh to the thirteenth centuries. This view omits sufficient consideration of the loss of consumers which accompanies any grave loss of providers.

Herlihy (1971) disagrees completely with Postan and basing himself upon his studies of fourteenth-century Pistoia, concludes that the Black Death was the cause of the lowered birth rate in 1349 and that subsequent plagues were the cause of the inability or lack of desire of the population to recover its normal growth rate. It would be especially interesting to discover from such studies as Herlihy's in Pistoia and Carpentier's (1962A) in Orvieto whether a lowered birth rate, caused by later marriages following the Black Death, was maintained through the period of the continuing plagues.

This is a delicate point; in some societies plagues and a general sense of doom lower the birth rate at least for a time, while in others the loss of a child to disease spells the immediate production of another. It could be that we are looking at the difference between an epidemic disease striking suddenly and universally and an endemic disease with a steady if unremarkable toll of human life. The first with its load of guilt, doom and hopelessness gives pause to the desire to introduce children to the plague-ridden world, while the other is an everyday affair and replenishment is the order of the day.

Hatcher also disagrees with Postan. He finds that over the period 1348-1520 the English population dropped by 60% and the later falls in population were not correlated with failures in the harvest. He believes that living standards were improving when the Black Death struck. Delatouche also disagrees with Postan and believes that there was, in fact, no Malthusian crisis prior to the Black Death and the population had not outrun its resources. Delatouche is inclined to ascribe the fourteenth-century crisis to a moral decline.

In an important paper, Bridbury agrees with Postan in the point asserting that the facts to be explained are not how population was lost in England during the Black Death in 1348-50 but how the impetus of the decline was maintained through the apparently disastrous years of the 1370s. Should anyone believe the question to be simple (owing to a lack of facts?) Bridbury's highly complicated and densely reasoned paper will convince them otherwise, and they will be easily disabused by a perusal of this paper in the original. Some of the admiration for this paper springs from an inability to encompass the whole of the argument. Russell (1966) has it that the third plague of 1369 killed 13.1% of the population of England and the fourth plague of 1375 killed 12.7% of the population; Bridbury does not deny these figures and one must wonder why he feels them insufficient to have maintained a decline in the English population in the 1370s.

So the demographic argument is not so much about the overall death toll as about whether diseases or population outrunning resources maintained the population decline or stagnation. There is little argument on the point that the Black Death started the decline in the population of England, though the diseases accompanying the famine of 1315-17 may have given the population rise of the twelfth and thirteenth centuries a check prior to the Black Death. Gottfried (1978) calls this argument Biology v. Malthus. Biologists tend to believe that population checks can occur independently of resources, through the agency of disease, which, while independent directly of resources, is dependent on such factors as vectors, reservoirs, virulence, immunity of the host, proximity and a whole host of factors described as the web of causation of a disease. Vectors such as mosquitoes are often peridomestic and are thus affected by prosperity in many ways such as the existence of mosquito nets or air-conditioning, the provision of breeding places such as irrigation canals or upturned cans, and so on.

Famine has classically caused overcrowding as it still does in refugee camps and this provides the conditions for the passage of lice, the lack of waste disposal and the increased quantum of droplets in the air between individuals. The biologist claims that the failure of a resource, of itself, has only mild effects on population levels, it is only disease, often secondarily connected to a resource failure, which can bring about the conditions of a population check and collapse. All this, of course, raises as many questions as it answers and the demographers continue to argue as they must to arrive at an approximation of the truth.

What is the main agent of population rise and fall beyond the simple facts of the ratio of the death-rate to the birth-rate? Which of these two is the more important? Does a population fall only because a large section of it dies or because there is a failure to breed fast enough or, as is most likely, a mixture of both? More specifically, can disease affect the birth-rate for any reasonable length of time or do humans and their birth-rate bounce back before the danger has past? These are questions for the demographers and in the case of the Black Death for those historian/demographers studying small local communities. The more we have of such studies the closer we will come to the truth.

It will be understood from the central thesis of this book that here the biologist's point of view is expressed with the belief that population declines and checks are almost always the result of disease epidemics and that the ability to separate disease from resource failure has been imperfect in the past. Chambers, a demographer, says that the Black Death serves as a classic case of the action of an autonomous death-rate. It follows from this belief that the massive population decline and the continuing trough of the fourteenth and fifteenth centuries were the consequence of the Black Death and the subsequent disease outbreaks most of which were plague or plague-associated. In the argument between those who believe the famine years of 1315-17 to be more important and those who believe the Black Death to have been the prime mover as a cause of the fourteenth-century crisis the case of Bruges is enlightening. Bruges was

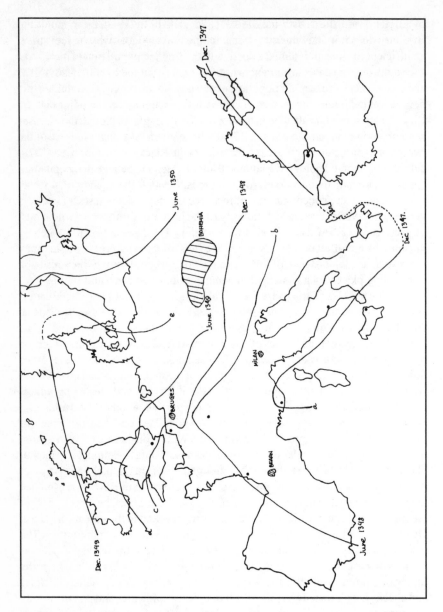

II. The spread of the Black Death in Europe. a. end 1347, b. mid 1348, c. end 1348, d. mid 1349, e. end 1349, f. mid 1350. (after Elisabeth Carpentier, 1962. Ann Econ So Civil. 17, 1062-92.)

an important commercial centre in Flanders with the importation of goods as a major activity. It suffered the poor harvests of 1315-17 just as did Ypres nearby where 10% of the population perished. Bruges was, however, spared the worst of the Black death for unknown reasons and it quickly recovered its prosperity.

One last view should be mentioned and that is the Marxist one. This would state that as no class struggle is involved in disease, it cannot be a force driving

social, political and institutional change. This view of the Black Death finds its
advocate in Kosminskii who finds the Black Death caused no European disaster
in the fourteenth-century, only some depression in England, while in Italy normal
life was quickly restored. Actual stagnation occurred only in France and it was
devastated by the Hundred Years War and the consequent economic depression.
While England did suffer some economic depression it was minor. Kosminskii
doubts every adduced fact which disagrees with his hypothesis but believes all
views and facts which support him. His view of other historians parallels this
attitude. His views suffer from the cardinal sin of choosing and squeezing the
facts to fit the hypothesis instead of allowing the hypothesis to grow out of all of
the facts.

CHAPTER 8
The Black Death (part 3)

The closest a parasite got to eradicating *Homo sapiens*
Hare

The time has come to consider the consequences of the population collapse. It is taken as a fact here that the motor of most major social and institutional change in the fourteenth and fifteenth centuries was the deprivation of population. This commenced with the loss of the labour to till and harvest the land, for the whole feudal system depended on the abundance of farm labourers supplying a surplus of labour and thus keeping the system stable. Mullet shows that the *demesne* consisted of the lord's land which was mixed in with the tenants' holdings each large enough to support a family and for which dues were paid and with common land used by the tenants but still owned by the lord. Aside from the lord all who lived on the *demesne* (or cour) were serfs or quasi-serfs and owed the lord service as soldiers, servants or labourers, though with new land in use in the thirteenth-century, the lord, who took rents from it, was less and less dependent on the forced labour of serfs.

Always when one speaks of a 'lord' one can also mean a monastery, the other great landowners. When this labour force, upon which this whole system depended, declined in numbers, the amount of land under cultivation began to contract all over Europe. The lord ceased to gather high rents and had far fewer labourers. The peasants who were left had all the good land they could manage and they became more mobile, moving on if they became dissatisfied with the lord. Society changed from a labour-intensive system to a land-intensive system. The lord became a rentier. The peasant was the major item in the population and without his demand markets collapsed. As the peasants died so labour had to be hired and money rather than service became common currency. With these changes the lord lost prestige and power and started to fail to maintain law and order. With this weakening of the grip of the lord the links of serf to the land of the lord grew weaker. Food prices rose as harvests were not gathered, wages went up steeply as too few labourers were available for the work which was needed to be done.

The clergy and the lords attempted to cut wages but the peasants' newly found mobility defeated such attempts. Laws were introduced to attempt to tie the peasant to the land of the lord but these too failed. The combination of high wages and low prices ruined many a lord but only benefited the remaining peasants, thus reversing the previous roles. The rich peasant, or yeoman, arose. Enfranchisement and commutation were for sale and even whole villages bought their freedom. With the contraction of both the population and the land under cultivation whole villages disappeared from the English countryside. The peasants drifted to the cities and a class of urban proletariat began to appear. It was difficult to effect repairs to existing buildings and equipment and these fell into disrepair. Lack of labour brought other means of power into prominence and the use of water-power became common. In Mullet's words the Black Death: 'disrupted the medieval synthesis'. The proceeding picture is largely one of England, as that is where the best records were kept.

The picture remains more or less true of France except that France had even more to contend with during the Hundred Years War which was fought on French soil. Emery has shown that Perpignan suffered a long disruption of economic life though not of social life. In the first two weeks of the Black Death all business ceased but after four weeks the scribes were at work again and thereafter the usual business of justice and municipal work recommenced, so that, despite panic and terror, the organisation of the town stayed in place. Carpentier (1962B) places herself firmly in the camp that believes that plague was the main cause of the fourteenth-century crisis in Europe and that it was the continuing outbreaks which broke the camel's back with these words: 'Il [the plague] s'aggissait d'un mal durable, solidement enraciné et reparaissant tous les dix ou quinze ans avec une obstination implacable. Ici est le véritable drame qui a marqué tout le bas Moyen Age.' (It appeared to be a long-lived sickness, well rooted and reappearing every ten or fifteen years with absolute certitude. This then is the real crisis that affected the whole of the later Middle Ages).

In Italy, a different system reacted somewhat differently. In the north the authorities tended to be city-states ruled in a variety of ways. These cities held sway over differing sizes of hinterland. Already aspects of later city life were apparent. Florence, half-way between a city democracy and a signorie, had its banks and its guilds. Venice, ruled by an elected doge and a council had its merchants. Milan, a signorie ruled by the powerful Visconti family, was a commercial centre. Rome was the centre of the Christian world even if it rarely behaved in a Christian manner, and it remained the never-to-be-forgotten dream of centrally administrated peace, though the supremacy of Rome in the Christian world had just suffered the blow of a divided papacy and anyway ignored the claims of the orthodox faith of Byzantium. All suffered terribly though variably from the Black Death and subsequent epidemics.

A curious aspect of this situation and indeed of others was that the Black Death seemed to have had little effect on mankind's desire to make war. In Carpentier's (1962B) words, 'la guerre sevit a l'état endemique.' The Black Death, though striking at the very heart of the Hundred Years War, hardly delayed it more than half a year and 1349 found Edward III of England searching for the men and treasure necessary for the continued prosecution of the war with France. In Italy the squabbles for and within the country continued only a little abated by the Black Death.

In Milan and Mantua a minatory approach was made towards prevention of the pandemic, entry into the city was forbidden and the citizens were not allowed to visit other areas. In Milan the house of a plague suspect was walled up with all of the inhabitants inside. Milan was spared the worst of the Black Death though probably not because of its draconian approach to public health. In Pistoia a famine in 1339-40 accompanied by a pestilence had carried off a quarter of the population. The Black Death then struck and according to one contemporary observer 'hardly a person was left alive.' Herlihy (1967) finds himself unable to believe that bubonic plague could sweep through a town as the Black Death did in Pistoia, he feels it would have required an army of rats and a legion of fleas. He adds that a death rate of 60% claimed for bubonic plague victims could not result in the death-rate of one half to two-thirds of the population as happened in Pistoia. As the Black Death took its toll in march and April in Pistoia and in September in the parts of Tuscany, he feels that pneumonic plague may not be the answer to this excessive death rate, leaving the reader with the assumption that septicaemic plague was present. In Pistoia the plague took off the very old and the very young and so at first it did not upset the financial equilibrium.

The major demographic reaction in Pistoia was to increase the birth rate and so population levels rose back to normal quite quickly, which demonstrates the difficulty in predicting human social behaviour. In Orvieto Carpentier (1962B) also found relatively little institutional change despite the demographic catastrophe. The town's rulers attempted to stay in charge of events (unlike Florence, according to Boccaccio), enacting a price rise in 1348 and another in 1350 to try to keep on top of the financial crisis. The manoeuvre did not work as the crisis had a momentum of its own and prices were not the only factor operating in the agricultural decline. Peasants continued to leave the land, labour continued to be in short supply and the economy continued on its downward slide. All this increased tensions between classes and groups. Carpentier (1962B) makes the same point as Bowsky (1971), that is that the plague destroys people not institutions and if the institutions are powerful enough or supple enough they will survive the plague (the argument has ominous overtones for our generation faced with the neutron bomb). So, in Orvieto, the institutional framework survived as it adapted, producing new legislation with new regulatory powers. This also says something about the ability to bend with the wind of the city-state system as compared to the more rigid feudal system.

In Siena, Bowsky (1971) had found that the institutions had also survived the demographic collapse consequent on the Black Death and commerce had continued with only a temporary dislocation. Repopulation of the land and the city had brought in foreign labour for the land and some for the city. The now less numerous but richer peasants had their feet on the social ladder and attempts were made to arrest their climb by means of stricter sumptuary laws (it appears ridiculous to us today that class was defined, at least in part, by a regulated form of dressing), and by new marriage laws. By the end of 1349, however, the new rich were powerful enough to challenge the magnates and the oligarchy of the city council by undermining the monopoly of banking, which was the fulcrum of power for the magnates. Monks were in short supply, so laymen began to enter the clerical work of the banks.

A new class of notaries arose in the place of the churchmen. Pressure on the ruling XI stopped the taking of bribes and the self-election practices, causing the threat, at least, of an enlarged franchise and the prohibition of bankers occupying seats on the XI. Indeed, one of the XI was actually brought to trial for mismanagement of funds. Eventually the XI fell. From these examples it can be seen that the city-based system of government and economy of Italy was more resilient in the face of the pandemic than the feudal and land-based systems of England and France and suffered less permanent damage or change.

Carpentier (1971) insists, nonetheless, that the subsequent plagues had their effect in Italy as well and they explain the slow and painful climb back to the Renaissance. As late as 1630-31 one and a half million were computed by Spooner to have died of plague in Italy, largely in Lombardy.

Reports had it that Padua lost 40% of its population, Verona 49%, Parma 50% and Cremona 60%. In 1656 Genoa and Naples were said to have lost half their population. In 1630 Milan lost 86,000 people and Venice 500,000, which according to Castiglione contributed to the decline of the latter city. Venice's population in 1563 was estimated at 168,000. It suffered two disastrous plagues, one in 1576-77 and another in 1630. In 1576, just before the plague, the population was 175,000; by 1581 it was down to 124,000 and by 1633 to 102,243. The losses were put at 51,000 in 1576-77 and 46,490 in 1630. With such losses can one doubt the continuing contribution of disease to the population losses, even if it was only a check?

Germany was in the limbo of the great interregnum, and the Hapsburgs were emerging as a power in Austria. Confusion and anarchy were the rule. In Germany, as in Italy, the effect of the Black Death was modified. The point is made again by Lutge that the Black Death destroyed people not property in Germany, so the means of production remained, unlike France which was much damaged by the Hundred Years War. Germany lacked the strong central power that existed in France and England and the power had devolved to the princes and princelings and it was they who wielded the feudal power. In Germany the towns were the hardest hit and their loss was made up by a drift from the countryside. This, combined with the losses in the rural areas themselves, led to a loss of labour for agriculture and some of the changes as described for England. The birth-rate dropped and the number of consumers diminished, though production remained relatively high, despite the loss of land in production. Agricultural prices dropped (for 100 years).

Cereals continued to be produced by forced labour, sending down prices further as consumption was far below former levels. At the same time the price of manufactured goods rose so the whole situation became highly unfavourable to agriculture. Property changed hands and wealth was redistributed leading to a drop in man-hours worked and to a drop in output. Incomes therefore rose and the towns became the centres of effort and wealth. The craftworker began to reach a status equivalent to the merchants and the guilds sprang up and commenced to rule the cities. The landed aristocracy sank to the position of rentiers and their position as the military elite declined. All this brought into being the basis of the modern German state.

Plague, as well as typhus, took a greater toll in the Thirty Years War than battle, according to Colnat. An epidemic of plague took off 300,000 in Prussia as late as 1709. To the east and south of Germany, Bohemia, Poland and Hungary had all taken advantage of German anarchy to establish with the help of German and Flemish settlers fleeing the plague, new and solid kingdoms, which entered the European culture. Dushan founded the fragile Serbian Empire. All these countries, with the curious exception of Bohemia, were ravaged by the Black Death. The memorials to the passage of the subsequent plagues dot these countrysides and also chart the progress of these plagues, showing that in all countries of central Europe the plague continued to strike well into the eighteenth-century. These later plagues made up for the mistake of the Black Death in omitting Bohemia.

In Sweden, according to Henschen trade ceased, agriculture collapsed and famine ensued; families were dispersed and morality disappeared. In Spain, despite Verlinden's (1971) dismissal of the importance of the Black Death to the progress of Spain, Spooner has found evidence in the later attacks of plague for the cessation of the upsurge in Castille after the 1599 epidemic, which carried off half a million people and had all the usual consequences of a shortage of labour on the land and a collapse of the urban industries. Less gold and silver were coming in from the New World to further destabilise the situation. Other epidemics in 1647 and 1649 added their force; the latter carried off one half of the population of Seville. There was famine and a further decline of the population (typhus was now adding its weight), the Spanish sought peace with the Dutch. With the Peace of Munster, Spain lost any dominance in Europe and Castille died, in Spooner's words: 'as it lived, a victim of its own illusions. a Quixote to the last.'

The Low Countries were affected like all the others except for a peculiar little pocket of relative freedom from the Black Death, though not from the subsequent plague outbreaks. This pocket consisted of most of the eastern part of present-day Belgium. Apart from this, the Low Countries suffered in much the same manner as did France, not unexpectedly when one considers the major ports involved such as Bruges, Ghent and Antwerp (the first two had just undergone a change of power from burgher oligarchies to bourgeois movements.)

Ziegler writes: 'It would be tedious and probably unprofitable to trace the Black Death in any detail through the remaining countries of Europe. For one thing the great majority of the more important chroniclers lived in Italy, France, Germany or England and most of the significant research has been done in these countries. For another the remarkably similar course which the Black Death took in each country it visited makes extensive treatment unnecessary.'

It should be noted, just the same, that this plague may have reached the New World in 1616, if we assume, as Cook did, that the epidemic of 1616-19 in Massachusetts was plague (it was more likely to have been smallpox). It devastated the Indians of the coast from Maine to Narragansett Bay.

Another aspect of the Black Death in Europe was its effect upon warfare. Although the habit of using mercenaries had commenced in Europe by the fourteenth-century, the main way to raise an army remained the summoning of the feudal levies. The labour shortage consequent upon the Black Death changed that and gave great impetus to the formation of mercenary companies until they became the mainstay of any army. This destroyed the standing of the aristocracy as the war class and led to the formation of such infamous groups as the 'White Company', which had none of the attractive romantic nature lent it by Conan Doyle's historical novel. Companies such as this roamed the countryside pillaging, looting and holding whole areas to ransom. The Routiers roamed France; the Condottieri roamed Italy; the Landsknecht roamed Germany and according to Wise, their true colours are best seen in the brutal Thirty Years War.

In the Middle East the major discernible effect of the Black Death and its subsequent outbreaks seems to have been in the Mameluke lands of Egypt, Palestine and Syria. Neustadt found that the Mameluke army (the source of its power) had been in steady decline from the time of the Black Death to the time of the Ottoman conquest of the Mamlukes in 1517. Neustadt lists the reasons as:

1. The Mamelukes had been too greedy too quickly and the resources were running short.
2. The army was ceasing to be a disciplined group as more and more soldiers played politics until it became the daily life of the army.
3. The recruiting grounds of the Circassian Mamelukes in the Caucasus and southern Russia had suffered badly in the Black Death (it was its reputed homeland) with a decreased population there leading to a manpower shortage among the Mamelukes.

In the fourteenth-century the Black Death had destroyed a large proportion of the Egyptian population including members of the army. Continuing outbreaks, all fourteen of them, were of lesser severity but still produced a significant mortality and had a disastrous cumulative effect on the army. It was never able to recover from the demographic effect of the last plague before another descended upon them. This cumulative drain spelt their end when they succumbed to the Ottomans, then on the rise, despite a previous visit from Timur.

Udovitch says that it is accepted that the fourteenth-century decline in Egypt and the surrounding territories was due to the appearance of the Mamelukes as the ruling class. They had prolonged the civil unrest by their presence, caused innumerable local dissensions with consequent weakness. The Bedouin encroached on to any land not firmly held, so agriculture was in decline and losing its labour. Land was thus returning to desert and the trade routes were interrupted. The towns had begun to suffer leading to higher taxation, forced purchases and similar abuses propagated by the greedy Mamelukes to maintain their fortunes and power. Inflation set in and town life began to deteriorate. Udovitch finds the moral decline of the Mamelukes to be an inadequate explanation for the crisis and the general decline of the Mameluke Empire in the fourteenth-century.

Although the Bedouin encroachment commenced in the 1330s, the long-term disastrous consequences did not begin until a little later. The oppressive taxes were not new and had not led to such a disaster before. There was no evidence for famine or starvation. He believes that, although the population decline, which was central to the material decline, had begun earlier, it was the Black Death which so accelerated it that, with the subsequent outbreaks, it became irreversible.

Dols (1977) dates the crisis time for the decline of Mameluke Egypt as the last decade of the fourteenth-century and is in no doubt that the primary cause of the decline was the loss of manpower. He points out that the Mamelukes had never managed to stamp out the civil wars following on the break-up of the Fatimid dynasty, their predecessors. As a purely military caste they abused the delicate relationship between the sword and the plough which had been the Arab strength in the Middle East. So in the fourteenth-century civil war was disrupting communications and the Bedouin were harassing the agriculturists, when into this arena trod *Yersinia pestis*, to a large degree, Dols insists, in the form of pneumonic plague.

Now the peasants began to flee the land, incomes fell which led to a financial crisis. Trades and crafts suffered from a lack of money. Irrigation, the life-blood of agriculture, was not maintained and fell into disrepair and disuse. None of these calamities was addressed by the weak central government, itself affected by depopulation. Although things improved in the period 1420-70 the depopulation persisted. The army was short of men and the Turcomen began to advance south into Mameluke Syria. Timur was exerting pressure from the east and the pastorialists were on the move. The Christians were raiding from the sea. The financial collapse had led to high urban wages while the rural poor remained poor and continued to exist under laws which tied them to the land and forced them to render service for their little land just as they had before the Black Death.

Dols believes that the supine reaction to the crisis may have had its genesis in the Muslim reaction to the Black Death, an attitude which will be discussed in the next section where the intellectual, psychological and religious response to the plague will be examined. Dols (1979) lists twenty major outbreaks of plague in Egypt in the period from 1344 to the Ottoman conquest in 1517 and these occurred in sixty out of the one hundred and seven years involved. He records a further eighteen in Syria and Palestine in the same period. Plague continued in these areas up until 1894, meeting as it were, the next pandemic of plague. Napoleon, it will be remembered, met with the plague during his ill-fated expedition to the Near East at the beginning of the nineteenth-century.

There is one aspect which must be discussed before we leave the subject of the physical effects of the Black Death and its subsequent outbreaks. This is the degree to which the uprisings of the fourteenth-century can be ascribed to the Black Death. There were three main eruptions of this sort: the Jacquerie in France, the Chiompi in Florence, and the Peasants' Revolt in England. The Jacquerie and the Peasants' Revolt were both, in part at least, rural though some urban admixture occurred in both. The Chiompi was purely urban. It is held by some, such as Holmes and Cowie, that the peasants' revolt both in England and France was the direct consequence of trying to hold down wages or increase taxes and that these measures were a direct consequence of the Black Death. Others, such as Henneman, find so many strands in the causation of these events that any particular cause is lost in the crowd.

The Chiompi revolt of 1378 or the revolt of the 'little people' was a revolt of the Florentine urban lesser guild workers. Though the Black Death may have been one of many strands in the causation of this uprising, it seems to have been largely political and stands as monument to medieval Italian quarrelsomeness. In Florence, in earlier years, Guelf fought Ghibelline with success and Florence became a Guelf city. With the danger of peace and quiet and the cessation of brawling in the streets, the Guelfs promptly divided into Black and White Guelfs and carried on brawling (1). The emerging large and prosperous guilds began to join the aristocracy, leaving the lesser guilds out in the cold. They revolted, with the surprising sympathy of the Medici, against the larger guilds and the nobles who ran the city, taking up the Guelf cry; just as today any political group terms itself a democratic institution whether it bears any political relationship to democracy or no. It must be concluded that the fourteenth-century revolts had too many strands to them for anyone, not wholly biased by political dogma, to say that any one particular strand was dominant. The only rôle it would be safe to ascribe to the Black Death would be to say that was frequently the force that tipped an explosive situation, which might have been building up for years, into mayhem.

The other main aspect of the changes wrought by the Black Death and its relapses is the psychological one – the changes it brought about in man's behaviour, knowledge, beliefs and desire to breed. First it is easy to agree with Gottfried (1983) when he claims that an important effect was the birth of modern medicine. It is a recurring theme of this aspect of the plague that disillusion with the prevailing view came first, to be followed by an intellectual stirring and questioning, followed finally with a different set of conclusions about the world around man. Medieval medicine was totally unable to cope with the Black Death and people became wholly untrusting of the medical profession and its knowledge and explanations. On reading the chroniclers of the time it is easy to see the concept of direct contagion being born and of it becoming a part of man's everyday beliefs before Frascatorius was to give it medical respectability in the sixteenth-century.

Medicine was a question of interpreting Hippocrates, Galen or Celsus, depending on taste. Medicine was therefore over a thousand years old in its knowledge and concepts. No new facts were elicited, no new ideas were elucidated, no attempt was made towards empirical medicine. The pharmacopoeia was entirely vegetarian and in case that should be thought to be the wisdom of the ages it should be remembered that men, women and children died in their millions at an early age. The surgeons were merely craftsmen, doing the bleeding, attending to wounds, applying poultices. As experience began to supersede an intellectual reliance on the past so the role of the surgeon improved. He started to do *post-mortems*, and gain first-hand experience and empirical knowledge which did not accord with Galen. The language of medicine changed to the vernacular and the patient began to know what was going on and thus hasten the process of change. Hospitals made an appearance. Quarantine was introduced in Ragusa then Venice, and health boards devoted to the plague appeared in Lombardy and Tuscany (2).

For the effect of the plague upon literature and art one has to go no further than Crawfurd's delightful book. He points to the rise of the cult of St Sebastian, whose likeness by Veronese hangs in the church of San Sebastiano, itself a memorial to the deliverance of Venice from the plague and the burial place of

Veronese. Sodoma's St Sebastian in the Ufizi in Florence was a plague banner from Siena and on its reverse side is a portrait of St. Roch, the patron saint of the Black Death and the plague. Roch, a young nobleman of Montpellier, caught the plague as a young man during the Black Death; he recovered and gave up everything to nurse the plague victims of Montpellier. The memorials celebrating St Roch are too numerous to detail as a statue or memorial was erected to him whenever the plague left a district temporarily. Churches, statues, memorial erections and paintings devoted to St. Roch abound all over Europe. Titian has a painting of him in the plague church of Santa Maria della Salute in Venice.

The Venetians dedicated the church of San Rocco to a delivery from the plague and had it decorated with paintings by Tintoretto. The Capella di Piazza attached to the Palazzo Publico in Siena, commenced in 1352, and finished twenty years later, was a celebration of the passing of the Black Death.

The Pestsaule and Karlskirke in Vienna are both dedicated to the passing of the plague. Europe is dotted with lesser churches and shrines devoted to the plague sometimes erected at an altitude in the mountains which spelt the upper limit of the plague. In art the emphasis changed from the hope of salvation to the gloom of certain death. Instead of the heavenly host, the virgin mother and the saviour child we find Christ as a man of sorrows, on the cross and grieved for by the mother. Meiss shows that death in various guises, bodies, coffins, funeral processions and bones became suitable subjects for the painters under the sentence of the Black Death. The best examples are the burial scenes from various illustrated manuscripts and murals of the time and the 'Dance of Death' from Basel. Holbein, who died of the plague, painted a 'Dance of Death' on a wall of the Palace of Whitehall which has not survived.

Thanks for the passing of the plague was the subject of innumerable painters including Titian, Corregio, Reni and Raphael. Benvenuto Cellini contracted plague and lived to describe it, but it killed Titian, Titian's son and Georgione. There are a number of paintings and etchings with plague as the main proponent, such as Manzoni's 'Plague of Milan', Poussin's 'Plague of Rome', Spandara's 'Plague of Naples' and Gros' 'Les Pestifières de Jafa'. Meiss notes the 'Triumph of Death' by Traini and the 'Tortures of Hell' in Florence, both immediately post-Black Death.

In literature we have *The Decameron* as a memorial of the Black Death in Florence, and Petrarch's heart-aching memory of his Laura, dead of the Black Death (3). Chaucer's *Pardoner's Tale* is about death which is equated with the contemporary plague. Plague in London in 1665 gave us Defoe's rather suspect *A Journal of the Plague Year*, an account of the great plague of London, 'written by a citizen who continued all the while in London'; and so he may have done, but he was only five years old in 1665,. It is very good anecdotal journalism and fairly reliable on the geography of the disease in London, but less so in other areas. Pepys did stay in London throughout the 1665 plague and 'made merry'.

The universities have been shown to have suffered badly during the Black Death as discussed by D'Irsay. Four English university colleges were lost. Plague tractates and miniatures almost became an art form (4).

Though Jahanjir's memoirs, the *Tuzk-e-Jahanjiri* could hardly be said to have their genesis in plague, that would be too ungracious to Nur Jehan, an act, which in her lifetime, would find you at the bottom of a pit leading to the Munana river; the memoirs do mention plague for the first time in India when it struck their beloved Kashmir in 1618. The daughter of a member of Jahanjir's household was said to have seen a mouse rising and falling in a distracted state. A cat grabbed but dropped it in disgust; next day the cat was nearly dead but recovered. The girl, however, died with a bubo and others also died in her house.

According to Hankin (1930-31) *The Pied Piper* of Hamlyn may be a memory of the 1362 plague outbreak which was known as the *Pestis Pueroram* as it carried off mostly children. It is held by some that the response of 'Santé!' following a sneeze dates from the Black Death in Avignon in its pneumonic phase. If you sneezed you were suspect of pneumonic plague and the response was to wish you good health (5). Language was affected by the Black Death as the clergy were heavily affected and died in such numbers that there was a shortage of monks as teachers. Translation from Latin to French was abandoned in Britain and Ziegler writes that English became the common language of all transactions.

This brings us to the Church and to religion. Both suffered directly and indirectly. They suffered directly as the clergy lost numbers disproportionately large as compared to their flocks, at least in England, which would appear to mean that they stayed at the side of their suffering parishioners and probably nursed them or delivered the last unction at the most dangerous time in pneumonic or septicaemic plague. At the same time the monasteries also lost a disproportionately large number. Both these events may have been due to the greater accuracy of the records of the dioceses and monasteries. Whatever the truth of it the Church was left poorly served in terms of parish priest and in terms of monks, the sole learned group in the land.

The stranglehold of the monks is hard to understand in these days of universal education. In medieval times most people and sometimes even the king could not read or write. In the hands of the monks was not only most of the writing and, therefore, much of the legal documents, wills, laws, business arrangements, marriage settlements and the like, but also a number of other essential skills. They were the architects and builders; they were the minters of money, they were skilled in agriculture and pisciculture. Their monasteries were the repositories of the nation's knowledge and archives, the churches held the sacred relics. In France the great monastic orders of Cluny and Citeaux, though by 1348 only a shadow of their twelfth-century greatness, remained the main exponents of ideas and teaching, and it has to be said, of dictatorial repression of others' views as heresy. The loss of this group from society, which was never full made up, spelt the passage of these skills to new classes and the new men arose; the lawyers, the scribes, the architects, the masons, the mint-masters, the metal workers and the universities.

Perhaps most important of all, education progressively passed into the hands of the layman. This gradual breaking of the absolute power of the clergy in so much of daily life is one of the most important effects initiated or continued by the Black Death. The loss of the parish priests combined with their inability to arrest the progress of the Black Death brought into being a general dissatisfaction with them priesthood and the form of religion they taught. Guilt was the major emotion felt ion Christendom after terror in response to the Black death. This was hardly surprising as the Church in Europe told the diseased populace that the plague was an instrument of divine justice punishing a sinful mankind. The priests as a class were classically there to prevent or ameliorate divine wrath. This Church also taught the remission of sins on confession and taught a merciful Trinity. The people confessed and believed in the mercy of God, but the Black Death went on its murderous way unchecked. Little wonder that the spectre of scepticism arose in the Christian flock.

The poor parish priest came under local attack, which was rather harsh if, indeed, he had stayed by the side of his flock when he could have fled, so much so that Ziegler suggests that he may have performed his duties grudgingly and timidly. Here, perhaps, was no lion of God roaring defiance at the miasma attacking the multitude, but rather a priest as puzzled and frightened as the rest. This scepticism gave rise to the discontented philosophy of Wyclif and his followers who suggested a greater humility in the Church might be appropriate.

A new spirit of enquiry was abroad untrammelled by superstition. Gasquet, in the spirit of the Church rampant, feels that Wyclif would have been better employed helping the sick and suffering rather than whining about the Church's role, but then Gasquet, being a cardinal of the Church of Rome, could hardly be expected to look upon a reformer such as Wyclif with any favour. Guilt also gave rise to some very unsavoury activity. Blame of the Church without loss of belief brought its dilemmas. This usually gave rise to some notion of cleansing of the Church and the usual number of righteous, with their lien on all truth and goodness, came forward to plague Church and people alike.

The Fraticelli, furious Franciscans, dissident and mendicant, preached a poverty-based Church and foretold Savonarola. Fraternities sprang up in all religious centres each with its share of the only truth. Though frequently they eschewed the flesh and the devil they had an uncomfortable habit of wanting everyone else to do so as well and in their way only. The thunderers had something to thunder about as one of the responses of the now richer inheritors of the population loss was a certain hedonism, which Boccaccio was to capture so brilliantly. Looseness of morals was, as ever, a favourite revivalist theme and served to confirm the need for God to have sent a punishment. Such declamatory effusion suited those classes, who were losing influence hastened by the plague's exacerbation of class differences, and who wished a return to the *status quo.*

Guilt brought forth a particularly unattractive confraternity, mostly in Germany, known as the 'Brethren of the Cross' or the Flagellants. Pious fanaticism is always an unlovely sight, if for no further reason than the juxtaposition of a belief in the mercy of whatever God, is being invoked and a murderous and maiming conduct towards fellow creatures. The Flagellants were no exception and have been very adequately dealt with by Ziegler, who made them a special study. He also chronicled the other activity which seems to seize Europe whenever it is faced with phenomena for which there is no explanation or no cure. They search for a scapegoat upon which to vent their sense of agrievement and usually start to persecute the Jews.

In 1348-51 the Europeans massacred the Jews in their thousands; they walled them up, they confined them in ghettos the more easily to persecute them. They said that the Jews had poisoned the wells or desecrated the Host so causing the Black Death, showing all of the logic normally present on such occasions. The fact that the Black Death was killing Jew and Gentile alike had no influence on these irrational beings, though the fact that they were getting rid of some troublesome creditors might have introduced a little logic into the pogroms. Germany and Switzerland were the worse offenders and there is a Ph.D. thesis to be written on the root causes of this type of murderous hysteria in Central Europe. Be that as it may the Jews moved in their thousands to Eastern Europe, particularly Poland where Casimir the Great had promised them sanctuary, thereby confirming and extending the Ashkenazy strand of the Diaspora east of Germany.

The affect on the population level of the lack of faith in the future and the consequent lowering of the birth rate will be discussed elsewhere.

Langer, the distinguished American medical historian, has urged that the next task for the historian of the Black Death is to examine it with the tools and techniques of clinical psychiatry. Ziegler ends his treatise on the Black Death with the words of Jusserand writing at the end of the last century:

> 'Faith disappeared, or was transformed; men became at once sceptical and intolerant. It is not at all the modern, serenely cold, and imperturbable scepticism; it is a violent movement of the whole nature which feels itself impelled to burn what it adores; but man is uncertain in his doubt, and his burst of laughter stuns him; he has passed, as it were, through an orgy, when the white light of the morning comes he will have an attack of despair; profound anguish with tears and perhaps a vow of pilgrimage and a conspicuous conversion.'

Ziegler goes on to comment:

> 'Jusserand's classic description of the European in the second half of the fourteenth-century captures admirably the twin elements of scepticism and timorous uncertainty. The generation that survived the plague could not believe but did not dare deny. It groped myopically towards the future, with one nervous eye peering over its shoulder towards the past. Mediaeval man during the Black Death, had seemed as if silhouetted against a background of Wagnerian tempest. All around him loomed inchoate shapes redolent of menace. Thunder crashed, lightning blazed, hail cascaded; evil forces were at work, bent on his destruction. He was no Siegfried, no Brunhilda heroically to defy the elements. Rather, it was as if he had wandered in from another play: an Edgar crying plaintively, 'Poor Tom's a-cold; poor Tom's a-cold!' and seeking what shelter he could against the elements. Poor Tom survived, but he was never to be the same again.'

In the Middle East Dols (1977) has a very different picture to convey. Here we have a Muslim people being taught that the Black Death was certainly a visitation from Allah, but a mercy as the fulfilment of a promise to the faithful, who would ascend to a paradise full of houris, a reward for faith. This same visitation was a punishment to the infidel, particularly the Christian, who could not hope to ascend to Paradise and was cast into hell. Whether one believed this or not you were not invited to eat the bread of guilt as the Black Death was a reward! Thus according to Dols the major reaction of the Muslim citizen on the

Middle East was their equivalent of 'Insh 'Allah', that is to say 'if God wills' spoken as a term of resignation.

This was not the only response. The rich of the Muslim world fled the plague, giving rise to some nice points in Mahommedan law – can you flee a gift of Allah? As one might expect, there was also some scepticism, despite which the Muslim religion stayed in place, untried and untroubled by reform or heresy, and as law as also religion this essential structure remained unshaken. Where in the West there had been claimed the usual manifestations of the Anti-Christ, in the Muslim world the Black Death was never seen in apocalyptic terms and no Mahdi was seen, claimed or expected. The Sunni (the prominent sect of the time) have no expectation of a millennium or a Book of Revelations about which the credulous can become hysterical.

Did the Black Death and its succession of plague outbreaks (or, if insisted, outbreaks of unknown diseases) have the effect of breaking a rhythm of history? Most authors, no matter what reservations they may express about detail, agree that the Black Death was a turning point in history in both Europe and the Middle East. Most authors also agree that the Black Death not merely marks the turning point but is of itself the generator of change. There is no doubt that it was cataclysmic and that it produced profound effects upon the minds of men, but more than that, it unalterably changed the mediaeval system of feudal organisation in Britain and France, though it has to be said that a number of institutions in France had to await 1789 for final change to occur. In Spain we must await further research into local effects to be sure of the changes wrought.

In Germany centralisation was given further impetus and wealth shifted critically in society. In Italy the Black Death brought into being new structures to regulate the city-states' societies and unalterably moved populations between cities and between city and hinterland; new classes moved into positions of power. New techniques appeared and water-power arrived to stay. It must be admitted that it is above all England which has supplied the material for scholarship and it is England which has been shown to have exhibited the most profound changes, possibly because most is known about England (6).

CHAPTER 9
Plague
The Bombay Plague

Dead rats in the East.
Dead rats in the West.
As if they were tigers.
Indeed are the people scared.
Few days following the death of the rats
Men pass away like the falling walls.
While three men are walking together
Two drop dead within three steps.

Shih Tao-nan.

The world was to see one further pandemic of plague, from 1894 to the present, which though it visited all of its old haunts of 542 and 1348 and many new ones, it, curiously, did not take a hold on the northern shores of the Mediterranean, despite two major wars on the continent of Europe. The naming of these plagues tends to the arbitrary and this last one has been named the Yunnan plague, the Hong Kong plague, the modern plague, the present plague and the Bombay plague. I have chosen to call it the Bombay plague because it was in Bombay where much of the epidemiological detective work was done.

This time *Yersinia pestis* appeared in man and black rats in the province of Yunnan in southern China in man and in tarabagans (Siberian marmots) in Manchuria and Mongolia and in man and a number of other rodents or near-rodents in many other parts of the world. This time also *Yersinia pestis* was unmasked by students of Pasteur and Koch. The plague in Hong Kong was shown to be caused by *Y. pestis* by Yersin and Kitasato (1) both in 1894, the organism was found in the black rat also by Lowson and to be transmitted by the tropical rat flea by Simond.

Later Wu (1926) showed that the Manchurian outbreak commenced from tarabagans. Wu believed that the tarabagans in Manchuria were infected with bubonic plague from rats imported from the south. The plague in Yunnan was largely bubonic, while the Manchurian outbreaks were pneumonic, so if Wu was right then the modern plague organism could move from being bubonic to being pneumonic without difficulty.

It is customary to refer to these three great pandemics of plague as separate, despite McNeill's belief that the second and third pandemics are one and the same. He writes correctly that the second visitation of the plague did persist in India in the twin foci of Gharwal and Kuamon in the southern Himalayan foothills, where it was recorded by Hutcheson in 1891–4. Seal agrees that this focus may have been a relict of the seventeenth-century Indian plague. McNeill tells us that the eastern limit of this focus in the 1850s was at the Salween river in Burma some 1500 km to the east of Kuamon without citing any authority for this surprising piece of zoogeography. Most authors believe that India was largely free of plague in 1886.

The plague, starting in Yunnan, was to spread over the Indian subcontinent, Burma, South-east Asia and China and to reach out to the Americas, Australia, Europe, Africa and the Middle East as recorded by Hirst. The Manchurian pneumonic (with some septicaemic) outbreak was confined largely to Manchuria though it did stretch into north China and the far east of Soviet Asia. The plague from Yunnan occasionally showed a pneumonic element as in Hong Kong early on and in Assam, the Punjab and China. Pneumonic plague also turned up very briefly in widely scattered outbreaks in locations as diverse as Queensland, Australia and on the Essex and Suffolk border in England (2).

Apart from these essentially local outbreaks the third pandemic was bubonic plague, one is tempted to say classical bubonic plague but as most of our knowledge of the epidemiology and symptomatology of plague comes from this last and present plague it can hardly be called 'classical'. It is this fact, in my opinion, that has bedevilled our understanding of earlier events, as the knowledge of this last plague pandemic has always tended to be applied uncritically to the little factual knowledge that we have of the epidemiology and bacteriology of the first two plague pandemics. *Y. pestis*, as it is studied in the world's laboratories today, is the variety which caused the Yunnan outbreak, or indeed, as often as not, the variety which continues to cause plague in the USA or South-east Asia; the disease it causes is bubonic plague.

We know its virulence, at least for mice and guinea pigs, is governed by the absence of two protein molecules in the outer membrane of the organism. Their presence or their mutation back from a non-functional variation would spell a dramatic loss of virulence (3). It is here, I believe, that we can find the answer to the problem that has bothered so many historians including Appleby – the reason for the disappearance of the Black Death well before the displacement of the black rat by the brown rat, also debated by Gale and Loosjes. I think that just as the *Y. pestis* which caused the Black Death was a mutant expressing great virulence with the ability to invade blood and lungs with ease, so, somewhere in the eighteenth-century in Europe, a mutation occurred which caused the loss of virulence and the associated characters in western Europe, probably by a change in the nature of the governing plasmid.

This changed plasmid would take time to seep through the population of *Y. pestis* hence the delay in the change of virulence reaching the remoter parts of Europe and east of Europe. This scenario was adumbrated by Robert. It follows from this that a direct interpretation of the effects of the sixth and fourteenth-century plague pandemics by extrapolation from the third plague pandemic would be an error. It has been said elsewhere in this book that zoonoses are usually sporadic and do not become epidemic unless a more direct means of transmission between man and man intervenes. The last plague was, it seems, from all the epidemiological evidence to have been zoonotic bubonic plague, however it did move inland from Bombay slowly, with the characteristic of usually infecting one person in a household before moving on. Above all, in the areas where it was most prevalent, it moved through very densely populated land. It seems that plague, alone of the zoonoses, can behave as a pandemic if the population density is sufficient. Small epidemics of zoonotic diseases in cities are known under very special conditions.

From whence did this third pandemic come? Hankin (1905) felt very strongly that the great Bombay plague sprang from the Kuamon and Gharwal foci and has a long circumstantial account of its spread based upon the movements of the Gharwali fakirs and their presence at all outbreaks of plague at such places as the Pali festival in 1836. Hankin, however, does not accept that the plague was transmitted by the rat flea and his epidemiological conclusions are based upon an incorrect biology. Leaving aside the McNeill and Hankin theories of a direct link between the late medieval plague and the late nineteenth-century plague via the Himalayan foothills, we are left with the general consensus, which agrees with Hirst, that the last plague pandemic arose in north Burma (Kachin) somewhere along the headwaters of the Salween and moved from there to the province of Yunnan in southern China.

In 1871 Yunnan was known to be under attack by plague and by a Panthay Mahommedan rebellion, though any connection between the two is unproven. In Yunnan-fu city (now Kunming) rats started to appear in the houses, running around wildly and then falling down dead. Shih Tao-nan had written his poem in Yunnan about the dying rats and the plague quoted above as early as 1792. So it seems that plague was at least endemic in Yunnan throughout the eighteenth-century, but Yunnan was, according to Wu and his colleagues and Pollitzer, (1951) too prosperous to be the subject of epidemic plague. This seems to be a most dubious proposition but the evidence is too hazy for a definite conclusion.

In the second half of the nineteenth-century the plague moved very slowly from Yunnan eastwards and did not reach the Pacific coast until 1894, though it may have been there before from the Burma focus. It reached the coast at Pakhoi, a small treaty port, about 500 km east-south-east of Gwangchou (= Canton). Still, at this point, it was not a serious outbreak. Later in 1894, due to a change in river transport dues, Yunnan's trade was switched from Pakhoi to Gwangchou and the plague reached Gwangchou; the possibility of a major epidemic became likely as Gwangchou handled much of China's trade with the surrounding countries and with Europe.

The first cases in Gwangchou were mild, though dying rats were noticed. Three months later the epidemic gathered speed (and probably virulence) and it was becoming obvious that a pandemic of plague was a possibility. A hundred thousand deaths occurred in Gwangchou, but, as in the houseboats on the Thames in 1655, none died in the boats on the Pearl River. Four months later the plague was in Hong Kong and the fat was in the fire. Hong Kong was the great entrepot of the Far East and handled shipping from all over the world and so the possibility of a pandemic was fast approaching a certainty.

The West woke up and sprang into action. With the terrible lessons of the Asiatic cholera still fresh in their minds, and the confidence, lent by Pasteur and Koch, in their ability to handle the great epidemic diseases, they showered Hong Kong with medical commissions. The French Commission included Yersin, a pupil of Pasteur's laboratory. The Japanese Commission included Kitasato, a pupil of Koch's. The British, the Germans, the Italians, the Austrians had all weighed in. The British sent troops to assist (?). As it happens the organism of plague was very easy of isolation and identification. It was abundant in the bodies of its victims and grew happily on the simplest of bacteriological media; it was easy to stain and examine and it infected guinea pigs, fulfilling those of Koch's postulates, which were safe to pursue, with flying colours (4).

So now the aetiological agent was known the epidemiology did not long remain in shadow. In 1894/5 Yersin and Lowson in Hong Kong showed that the organism of plague occurred in the rats and in the fleas on the rats. Later that year Simond incriminated the rat flea as the vector of *Y. pestis*, a theory already put forward by Ogata who was not universally believed. From this time a large number of other species of rodents, their predators and even members of the rabbit family with an equally large number of species of fleas from them have been incriminated in one epidemic or another. It is not to the purpose here to list all of these species as the plague they carried remained more or less the same and as the taxonomists have not yet made a final decision on the names of them all. The geographical spread of this plague is to the purpose. The plague was in Hong Kong in 1894 and now its spread was swift partly because it was by ship and partly because its virulence allowed it to build up quickly. The spread was particularly along the commercial routes of the grain trade, adding to the suspicion that bubonic plague might travel best in grain and fodder.

The pandemic reached Bombay and its most exuberant growth in 1896; there was said to be plague in India in 1895–6 and that this was probably a flare-up from the old foci in the Himalayan foothills by Seal. Bombay, another great entrepot, reinforced the pandemic and it spread now to Manilla, San Francisco, Sydney, Capetown, Buenos Aires, Oporto, Honolulu, Glasgow, Mauritius, Auckland and of course the ports of Burma, Thailand, Indo-China, Java, China and Japan.

There are excellent studies of its spread and impact (5). In Australia and England the plague merely touched the coast but never took hold even though the visitation was sometimes pneumonic. In South Africa and the USA the plague settled down and cases are still seen sporadically. *The Times* of London recently reported a small outbreak of plague in Tanzania. Plague has persisted in South-east Asia particularly Viet-Nam. In India the pandemic was a major disaster.

Its arrival in Bombay is vividly described by Liston thus:

About the sixth or seventh of April (1896) rats began to die in large numbers in a *chawl* or block of tenement houses. Suddenly the death among the rats ceased, and on April the eleventh the people became troubled by fleas. The fleas became so numerous that they had to quit their rooms and sleep on the verandahs. While living in the verandah on April the seventeenth one of the inhabitants. . . became infected with plague. Another case occurred on the same day in a room adjoining.

So plague came to Bombay; in a few months it was epidemic. The population began to flee the city for the hinterland carrying the disease with them (as fleas?) Eventually one half of the population of Bombay fled. They had greatly resented the draconian search and identify methods of finding plague cases used by the British Army according to Dodwell, and this resentment led to some insurrection and an upsurge of Peshwar/Maratha nationalism led by Bal Gangadhur Tilak with his story that the great Maratha hero had only been sleeping and was about to awake and evict the upstart British. As the hot weather started the fury of the plague died down, only to commence again over wider and wider areas, moving to Ahmedabad, to Karachi, to Poona. Again the people fled carrying the plague through the Punjab, through the Uttar Pradesh to the whole of India, reaching Calcutta after two years.

By 1903 the annual deaths in India from plague were over one million. From 1903 to 1905 the death toll from plague was 1,300,000 per annum, the Punjab suffering the most. In all India was said to have lost over twelve and a half million souls to this pandemic from 1896 to 1948. As Butler and Vilmorovic show, nowhere else suffered on this scale, though China must have lost hundreds of thousands and the disease persists to this day in Viet-Nam killing hundreds and occasionally thousands yearly.

The Manchurian outbreak of pneumonic plague had two waves and our guide is the great Chinese plague fighter Wu Lien-Teh. In Transbakailia and Mongolia the tarabagan (*Arctomys bobac*) was infected with *Y. pestis* but was hunted for its skin. The local Buriats and Mongols knew very well the dangers of handling these animals. They always shot the animals and never handled a sick or weak animal. They warned each other of any incidence of sick animals and tended to leave the area of any such reports. In 1910, however, there was a large increase in the demand for tarabagan skins and the price went from 0.3 to 1.2 roubles a skin; the number exported increased from seven hundred thousand in 1908 to two and a half million in 1910. The increase in numbers exported was due to an large influx of amateur inexperienced get-rich-quick Chinese in 1910.

They trapped the animals in snares by hand and congratulated themselves when they found sluggish animals as these were easier to catch. They skinned such animals inexpertly, allowing the blood of the tarabagans to enter cuts in their own hands. Subsequently they huddled together in underground dwellings at night. Tarabagan skins piled up at Hailar further down the line from the railhead at Manchouli on the Chinese Eastern Railway. As is often the case with the variety of *Y. pestis* to be found in the wild in reservoir rodents, this strain of the organism tended to invade the lungs and gave the tarabagans pneumonic plague as well as the buboes in the mesenteric membranes of the intestine where *Yersinia* would spill out on inexpert dissection of the animal.

These inexperienced hunters were infected with a disease they did not know and in a form most likely to be transmitted in the cold and crowded conditions of the underground inns they used at night. The epidemic started slowly in such sparsely populated areas as Inner Mongolia and Transbakailia and it was ignored until it reached the railhead. Still the epidemic was recognised only slowly as, in the past, plague had been the rat-associated bubonic form coming from the south. Now they were faced with an epidemic based on the tarabagan hunting areas around the Ugunor lakes and the rivers Emengol and Mergen, an area avoided by the very people who knew anything about the disease – the Mongols and Buriats – as they had recognised the area as unhealthy earlier in the year. By the autumn of 1910 pneumonic plague was well established in Manchouli and was beginning to spread west into Siberia and south-west into China.

Travelling on the railroad it established itself in Harbin astride the crossroads of the railway with forks leading from Manchouli and Hailar to Vladivostok on the Chinese Eastern Railway to the east and to Mukden and Tsingtao on the South Manchurian Railway to the south. The plague had travelled over 2,700 km in seven months and reached Vladivostok, Tientsin and Chefoo, all important ports on the Pacific. It killed sixty thousand people. Then it died out and by April of 1911 it was gone as might be predicted by the observations of Pollitzer and Li who showed that the twentieth-century pneumonic strain could not maintain itself as pneumonic plague alone and would always require to be fed from another source of the organism if it was to survive more than one winter.

In this epidemic there was some septicaemic plague which developed so quickly that the organism did not have time to reach the lungs before the patient was dead. The tarabagan skins were disinfected at the railhead and the store at Hailar, from this one can deduce that Wu and his team had arrived to undertake the control of the disease. There was a brief outbreak of pneumonic plague in 1917. The experience of Wu's team with these outbreaks was to stand them in good stead when pneumonic plague broke out again in the same area in 1920 and the second great Manchurian pneumonic epidemic commenced. In both cases the epidemics were confined to Manchuria with only small overspills into neighbouring countries.

On this second occasion the environmental cause seems to have been a civil war which brought about a critical overcrowding on the stations of the Manchurian railway. In April 1920 it was reported that the tarabagan of Transbakailia were leaving their burrows despite the cold and the Buriats and the Mongols began to see more and more tarabagan dying. In September three soldiers, who had been hunting tarabagan by snare, died of bubonic plague. More isolated cases turned up, all west of Manchouli. In October plague turned up in the local fur factory to the east at Hailar among the workers; two of these cases were septicaemic. Nine contacts were identified and isolated but they decided to run away to the mines of Dalainor (= Kulun Nor) to the south of Manchouli. Here in the underground passages inevitably they infected others with what had become pneumonic plague. One thousand of the four thousand miners died and the rest fled the mines to Manchouli where a further four thousand and forty-one died.

Others reached Tsitsigar where they infected more people and a further one thousand seven hundred and thirty-four died. Inevitably the epidemic progressed to Harbin and the division of the railway. In Harbin another three thousand one hundred and twenty-five were garnered by the plague. Though the epidemic proceeded to Vladivostok it was losing impetus and by late spring it had gone. This time the plague had claimed only a modest nine thousand and three hundred dead.

What effect did this pandemic have on the stage of history? Remarkably little it has to be said. Although it was in Hong Kong that the black rat *Rattus rattus* was found to be the major and dangerous reservoir of human plague, it was in Australia during a very minor invasion of the disease that it was shown that plague could be prevented by strict rat control. Australia's outbreak was mild because the Australian authorities were successful with a quarantine and a ship-rat prevention campaign which was obeyed and maintained and the bacillus did not get into the local rodent population as it did in the USA. As a boy in Adelaide, I can remember being shown the rat guards on the ropes mooring the ships to the wharf in the Outer Harbour and having it explained to me in terms of great earnestness the reasons for the precaution. Australia-wide there were only one thousand two hundred and twelve cases of plague with about a 40% death rate. So the world learnt how to prevent plague, but why did India continue to suffer so greatly from the plague?

The painful lesson, to be learnt anew during the attempts to eradicate malaria in the 1950s and 1960s, is that effective disease prevention and control programmes require an infrastructure of considerable medical, economic and institutional sophistication to maintain them, particularly as the programmes begin to bite and remove the immediate dangers. Such sophistication is not available in all countries of the world even today. In India of the early 1900s it must be admitted the education of the people, the sophistication of the institutions and the spread of the medical and public health services were not such that could initiate, maintain and oversee a public health programme of internal quarantine and local rat and flea control. Despite this the world, or at least western Europe, felt justified in that late nineteenth-century optimism that all could and would yield to rational thought and to the practice of the science within their grasp. Had they not stripped an ancient enemy of his disguises and laid bare his designs? Admittedly cure lay in the future, but it was a cure confidently expected. The great allies in the battle against disease; engineering, public health and sanitation were now to be given the chance they desired against mankind's greatest enemy – plague – the disease which took its name from all epidemic disease. In this expectation our fathers and grandfathers were largely right. We do have plague under control at present and reasonable hopes of keeping it there.

This optimism may have been misplaced with other diseases as we will see, but here at least mankind does seem to have won its battle and we see the reverse of the doubt and hopelessness of the fourteenth-century. Some of that reverse is due to the conquest of an ancient enemy.

The other lesson is that a country such as India could lose nearly thirteen million dead in the 1900s and shake off the loss. In Amritsar city in the Punjab the population in 1891 was 173,769; in 1901 it was 201,719 and in 1911 it was 182,917. In Maharashtra state, which includes Bombay, the population was 3,220,570 in 1891, 3,217,202 in 1901, 3,243,989 in 1911 and 5,665,111 in 1941. Mitra and Sachdev show that for Bombay itself the figures are 851,550 in 1891, 812,912 in 1901 and 1,018,388 in 1911. The population of the Indian subcontinent has shown a smooth progression upwards (with hiccups no doubt). It has been claimed to have been 100,000,000 over two millennia ago; 120,000,000 in medieval times; 154,000,000 in 1800; 189,000,000 in 1850 and 237,000,000 in 1900. It can be seen that while there is a pause in the upward movement of the population figures in the plague period of 1896 to 1901 it is no more than a hiccup in the smooth upward progression of India's population rise.

There must have been a labour shortage on the land in the first five years of the twentieth-century though there seems to have been little flow of people from the land to the cities. Ho, in his study of the Chinese population from 1368 to 1953 AD, has nothing to say about the effect of plague on the Chinese population in the late 1890s or early 1900s and seems largely concerned with natural disasters and famines as regulators of population.

CHAPTER 10
Malaria (part 1)

The tertian fevers were more common than causus and more troublesome. The quartan fevers showed, in many cases, their quartan nature from the start. There were many cases of quotidian, nocturnal and irregular fever. The worst, most protracted and painful of all the diseases then occurring were the continued fevers.

Epidemics, Book I, Hippocratic Writings.

Malaria is the great fever disease. Whenever, in the older records, one sees mention of fever the first disease to come to the mind of the unobsessed observer is malaria, not least because of its distribution over much of the world's surface until recently. Malaria, in the earlier part of this century, was recognised as man's worst enemy even worse than man himself. Morbidity and mortality due to malaria world-wide were greater than any other disease, even though malaria is not primarily a killing disease nor is it usually epidemic. It is thus the great chronic endemic disease, causing debilitating and incapacitating illness. This means we must change our language a little; we are no longer talking about a pandemic in the sense of an epidemic which infects more than one continent but a world-wide endemic of enormous proportions, infecting millions on millions daily.

Malaria of man is caused by protozoan parasites of the genus *Plasmodium*, transmitted by mosquitoes of the genus *Anopheles*. There are four species of *Plasmodium* which infect man regularly, though there are a few species of *Plasmodium* from monkeys which can infect man but they are of no epidemiological importance. The four species are *P. malariae, P. vivax, P. ovale* and *P. falciparum*. With the exception of *P. ovale* they have been with man from the time that man separated from the great apes. No doubt *P. ovale* came on the scene shortly after that variety of man arose which lacked the molecule on its red cell that allows the penetration and development of *P. vivax*, to take the place of *P. vivax* in that human variation.

The genus *Plasmodium* finds a home in most orders of vertebrates including the anthropoid apes, monkeys, rats, porcupines, bats, antelope, birds of all sorts, lizards and snakes. A parasite of catholic tastes! The species infecting one animal usually will not infect other animals except closely related species. In man an infected mosquito injects along with its saliva a form of the parasite called a sporozoite from its salivary glands. The sporozoite leaves the blood stream of man and enters the cells of the liver and grows and multiplies there for 5–16 days depending on the species. It then breaks out of the liver in its thousands of daughter parasites. These invade the red blood cells and cause the disease in man known as malaria. At some time in the red cells the parasite develops sexual forms which when taken up by a blood-sucking anopheles mosquito are fertilised and grow and multiply on the mosquito's stomach wall. The daughter parasites of this stage of growth are the sporozoites which collect in the salivary glands of the mosquito ready to be injected into the next person.

P. malariae causes the disease in man known as quartan malaria, that is the fevers peak every four days counting as did the Romans with the first day as day 1. So the fevers were every three days and it is typical of malaria to have recurrent fevers. The reason for this is that when the parasite has grown in the red cell for a predestined time it bursts releasing daughter parasites which invade new red cells. At the same time it releases its excretion products which give man a high temperature, as high as 106°F or over 41° C. The periods of growth of all the parasites in the blood is remarkably synchronised and in the case of P. malariae takes 72 hours and so fever occurs every 72 hours. Quartan malaria today is a disease largely of the tropics though there is reason to believe it was common in more temperate areas in earlier times. It is a relatively mild form of malaria, though that is a highly objective and clinical view; no attack of this disease is other than extremely unpleasant. P. malariae is remarkable for its ability to remain in man for tens of years. The chimpanzee and probably the gorilla share P. malariae with man.

P. vivax in man causes the disease known as benign tertian malaria. That is to say that the blood cycle is of 48 hours duration and the fevers occur every two days and it is benign compared to the malaria caused by P. falciparum. Like P. malariae it is not a killer. Indeed the malaria-free day can appear almost pleasant in comparison to the days of fever. Benign tertian malaria is a disease of the sub-tropics and the temperate zones and is very widespread. This was the common form of malaria in Europe in days gone by. Benign tertian malaria has the ability to relapse which it achieves by persisting at the liver stage. A relapse is where an infection acquired in the summer will eventually self-cure but reappear again in the same patient without reinfection in the spring of the next year ready for the reappearance of the Anopheles mosquitoes, which transmit it and which have been inactive over the winter months. Despite this the parasite normally dies out in a patient in two to three years (and tales to the contrary require laboratory confirmation prior to acceptance). Malaria parasites have a number of strategies to ensure their presence in the right form when the mosquito bites and the regular blood cycles are probably a mechanism for ensuring pick-up and transmission at night.

P. ovale is also capable of relapsing and is also tertian. It is the least important of the malaria parasites of man, causing a relatively rare and mild disease. It is a parasite of West Africa, where P. vivax cannot thrive as the West African generally lacks the particular receptor molecule on his/her red cell surface which P. vivax requires to enter that cell. No doubt P. ovale evolved, probably from P. vivax to fill this empty niche. P. ovale is said to cause a milder disease than P. vivax. It seemed to me that the difference could be summed up as a residue of the desire to live with *P. ovale* and a desire for a quick end with *P. vivax*.

P. falciparum causes malignant tertian malaria in humans. Though its blood cycle is 48 hours long the disease usually starts with a quotidian fever, that is every 24 hours. This is apparently because *P. falciparum* takes longer for all of its parasites in the blood to settle down to a synchronised 48 hour cycle. As *falciparum* malaria is cured today as soon as possible the fever is frequently seen as quotidian for the whole period of observation. This confusion of periodicity makes many of the older reports of disease which are identified by fever patterns difficult to diagnose. In the absence of drug cure this disease is usually completely self-cured in about six months (it does not relapse) or the patient is dead.

P. falciparum is the killer among the malaria parasites of man. During the blood cycle *P. falciparum* retires into the inner organs of the body to complete much of its developmental cycle. The older forms of this malaria parasite in the blood have the capacity of making the surface of the red cell, which they occupy, sticky and these infected red cells will then cling to the walls of the smaller vessels of critical organs such as the brain. This impedes the blood flow, even stopping it so, in the brain, causing coma and death from cerebral malaria. Other organs, such as the heart, the kidneys, the liver and the intestine may be starved of the oxygen and nutriments carried by the blood and so be critically damaged. Unless this parasite is involved malaria will not have a profound effect on the demography of any particular area. Immunity to malaria is acquired slowly and painfully and there is no effective vaccine as yet.

The African (or the South Eastern Asian or the New Guinean) living in the most intensely malarious (due to *P. falciparum*) areas commences to suffer numerous life-threatening episodes of malaria from the age of about six months to one year, being bitten by an infective mosquito about once every month. It is not until he or she is about four years old that the ability to control the severity of the disease is acquired and it is not until the child is eight or nine years old that the number of parasites in the body comes under some sort of control. The African adult has a relatively effective immunity and rarely suffers from malaria attacks though he may have the parasite in the blood and be passing it on. It has been argued, not always convincingly, that the other malarias will have an effect on birth rates and, more convincingly, on the ability to till the land and maintain the institutions of society. Such effects are probably confined to the occasions when malaria becomes epidemic, usually when an ecological accident has greatly increased the number of transmitting mosquitoes. All malaria has the effect of enlarging the spleen, the organ charged with the duty of removing live and dead parasites out of the circulation.

Malaria is at its most dangerous to a people when it is epidemic and attacks the adults with little or no previous experience of the disease. Such occasions in more recent years have been when forests are cleared and conditions established for the ad lib breeding of the local malaria-carrying *Anopheles*; when the water expanse or the water table is altered so as to encourage the breeding of *Anopheles*, as happens when dams are built or the rainfall is exceptional; when certain types of labour aggregations occur, such as the importation of Indian labour to Mauritius or for the building of the Mombasa-Nairobi railroad. A major epidemic occurred in Brazil in the 1930s when the extremely dangerous African malaria vector,

Anopheles gambiae was imported accidentally and flourished along the Brazilian rivers. The campaign to control and eradicate it was one of the great victories of the Rockefeller Foundation. Finally mini-outbreaks can occur in areas of *P. vivax* infestation when all patients infected in the previous year suffer the spring relapse. Despite this warning about epidemic malaria it is the day to day damage done by uninhibited malaria in such zones of intense malaria as Africa south of the Sahara, south-east Asia and Papua-New Guinea, due to *P. falciparum* which takes the real toll of life but relatively slowly if surely.

In Africa alone the World Health Organisation believes a million infants a year are lost to malaria. In total some two million people are thought to die each year from malaria. So in fifteen years malaria kills more people than the Black Death or outbreaks of smallpox or the 1918–19 outbreak of influenza but it does it gradually over time. Malaria deaths are not concentrated in time as are those caused by plague or smallpox and today malaria acts on a far larger population than did the Black Death or smallpox in the Americas. This is a much truncated view of malaria and those interested in a fuller picture are recommended to a recent compilation entitled *Malaria, Principles and Practice of Malariology* edited by MacGregor and Wernsdorfer.

While one assumes on internal evidence that malaria is as old as man we do not have records of it before 3000 BC. In approximately 2700 BC the Chinese classic medical script Nei Ching records the enlargement of the spleen in association with fevers. China also described malaria as the disease of the three demons: the demon of chills with a bucket of icy water; the demon of fever with a brazier and the demon of the headache with its hammers. This leads in neatly to our description of the symptoms of malaria. It commences with vague symptoms of malaise with some headache, some general unease, possibly vomiting, possibly some confusion. The real attack starts with feeling of great cold and an intense shivering fit, the teeth chatter and the body is convulsed with shivering and shuddering. The temperature of the body then begins to mount and the fever begins, temperatures of as high as 106°F or 40.5°C may be reached at the height of the disease. The body feels intensely hot, there is a great thirst and the headache commences. After about six hours the fever breaks with a copious sweating and a feeling of considerable relief. In 48 or 72 hours it will all start again. In the absence of any drug the fevers will go on for two to three weeks reaching a climax after about a week or so then becoming less and less severe until the patient is better.

The Indians in their Ayur Veda grant a whole book to the 'Fever', giving a good description of malaria some hundreds of years before the classic descriptions of the Hippocratic writings. The Ebers papyrus of about 1570 BC contains a recognisable description of malaria. Halawani and Shawarby argue that an inscription in the Temple at Dendera which describes intermittent fevers after the Nile flood refers to malaria, but this attribution is discounted by de Zulueta (1987). Paul Russell in his excellent book, *Man's Mastery of Malaria*, perhaps overambitiously entitled, thinks that the disease of the Shulamite boy cured by Elisha of a coma (II Kings, IV, 35) may have been cerebral malaria. Also from the Bible we have Christ rebuking the great fever of the mother of Simon's wife (Luke, IV, 39). The library of Ashurbanipal containing the Sumerian tablets renders nothing recognisable as malaria, which would not surprise de Zulueta who argues cogently that severe malaria did not become a problem in the Tigris/Euphrates basin until later.

An important controversy arises over Greece, as there are those such as Jones (1) with the weighty support of Ronald Ross himself, who would have us believe that malaria was instrumental in bringing down ancient Greece. Homer, writing (or more correctly singing) in the sixth or seventh centuries BC, mentions a disease associated with the dog-star Sirius, seen typically in the autumn. Many believe that an autumn fever defines aestivo-autumnal fever, that is malignant tertian malaria due to *P. falciparum*. De Zulueta argues that this is most unlikely as the necessary *Anopheles* mosquitoes were not present in Greece or Asia Minor at the time for the transmission of *P. falciparum*. On the other hand the nearly contemporaneous mystic poems frequently attributed to Orpheus do have a description which Lividas is sure serves to delineate both the tertian and quartan varieties of malaria thus:

> If a blazing chill comes to a man on alternate days or a fever with chill get a hold of him, he will not be able to use his limbs. But if he is afflicted by the slow misery of a four day fever it will remain with him for a long time as this is not cured by the noble agate-stone.

This description is so good it must be admitted that it places both *P. vivax* and *P. malariae* in Greece in the sixth-century BC which should not bother de Zulueta whose thesis it is that the mosquitoes were present in the north Mediterranean shores which could transmit these two parasites in pre-Periclean times but the heightened transmission of them both and the transmission of *P. falciparum* had to await the invasion and multiplication of better transmitters.

Lividas, who is an enthusiast for malaria and would like to see it enthroned in any contest for age of mention, quotes Kardamantis as believing that the killing of the Lernean many-headed Hydra by the hero Heracles (Hercules) is an example of the attempts to rid the Argos plain of malaria by the draining of many-headed delta of the Lerna river which was a swamp by stopping up the underground river which fed it. This resembles the story about Empedocles (504 BC) in Sicily, who is said to be the first malaria engineer, as it is claimed that he drained swamps about Agrigentum, so ridding the town of a pestilence. He prevented the sea from entering the river mouth which was building up the water (2). If the Lerna mouth was also tidal, (3) then it is possible that an *Anopheles* was present in both places which could breed in brackish water and transmit malaria.

Kardamantis, not content with making Heracles into an anti-malaria worker has him at work in the nearby lake and swamp of Stymphalia killing the Stymphalian birds (identified with fevers and rigours), this time as an examplar of excavating the underground sink-holes which fed a local river thus draining the swamp. I suppose we can be thankful that the Nemean lion did not turn out to be *Anopheles sacharovi*. More seriously we come to the pure gold of the fifth-century BC Greece and the Thucydides plague, no-one has suggested it was malaria. This is the age of the Hippocratic writings and it remains an eternal mystery as to why they did not mention the Thucydides plague. But we do find excellent descriptions of malaria so it must have been present in some of its forms in fourth and fifth-century BC Greece. No doubt it added to the burdens of the Peloponnesian War.

It is de Zulueta's convincing argument that the dangerous *Anopheles* such as *A sacharovi* and *A. labranchiae* did not arrive in sufficient numbers north of the Mediterranean to allow a dangerous amount of malaria or allow any breeding of *Anopheles* sufficient to transmit enough *P. falciparum* to have a demographic effect. However the indigenous mosquitoes such as *A. atroparvus* (which, *pace* de Zulueta, can transmit *P. falciparum*, see Shortt et al) were present and transmitting a low incidence of malaria. This argument effectively eliminates malaria as a significant agent in history north of the Mediterranean until well into the first millenium AD.

As has been said it was Jones, with the powerful support of Sir Ronald Ross, the discoverer of the mosquito transmission of malaria, who put forward the belief that malaria could not have been active in the Greece of the fifth-century BC or the years before that because the glorious century of Athenian Greece could not have arisen in the face of malaria as Ross saw it in Boetia and around Lake Copias in 1905/6. Jones thus meets de Zulueta coming in the same direction but by a different track. Jones puts a great deal of reliance on malarial cachexia, a rather vague term meaning generalised weakness, as the main feature of the disease, a symptom which he blames for causing social and institutional disruption.

While it is true that epidemic malaria, due even to the malarial parasites of lesser virulence, does seem to be able to bring the normal activities of a rural population to a halt as has been seen in India, and noted by Christophers, it remains very doubtful if malaria was ever epidemic in the Greece of Pericles or the fourth-century BC, or whether *P. falciparum* was present in sufficient amounts to affect the demography of the Greek population. It is difficult to be convinced that endemic malaria, due to the malaria parasites of lesser virulence, of itself can bring a nation of the calibre of Periclean Greece or its successors to its knees, as Jones would seem to be claiming in the centuries immediately following the fifth-century BC.

Nor is it possible to be any the more tolerant of the notion that any great, powerful and expanding peoples can be extinguished by an endemic disease. Weakened by disease they can be, but their response to such a weakening or an epidemic seems to be governed by laws that can be only dimly comprehended. It would seem that, if expanding, the population recovers itself, if declining, the population may be irreversibly altered by the event. In sum it is impossible to follow Jones in his belief that malaria had a critical role in the decline of Greece from the peak of the Periclean Age. To believe that Greece was in decline from the fifth-century due to malaria leaves the emergence of Macedonia under Philip and Alexander to be explained.

In the remainder of the Mediterranean there can be no doubt that Carthage suffered from malaria, including *P. falciparum* as well as its less virulent cousins, as Hanno the Navigator would have brought it and its mosquitoes back from Sierra Leone in the early sixth or late fifth centuries BC. Despite this, and the disastrous defeat at sea near Himera in Sicily by Gelo the tyrant of Syracuse in 480 BC, Carthage prospered and went on to its most glorious period, and later was able to challenge Rome in the second-century BC in Rome's own backyard. We have already looked at the defeat of Hippocrates and Himilco before Syracuse in 396 BC which brought Carthaginian pretensions in Sicily to a temporary end and destroyed the Magonid dynasty of Carthage.

The other great power of the Mediterranean now arose to be greatest and grandest of them all and was to maintain a grasp on the imagination of man for well over a millenium despite its decline and fall – Rome.

CHAPTER 11
Malaria (part 2)

'The green and stagnant waters lick his Feet,
And from their filmy irredescent scum
Clouds of mosquitoes gauzy in the heat,
Rise with his gifts: Death and Delerium'

Lawrence Hope,
Malaria
in *Songs from the Garden of Kama.*

Hackett has said that Aeneas himself had been warned of the general insalubriousness of the area around Rome, though Dryden seems to have ignored that section of the *Aeneid*, unless 'greater ills' are all he vouchsafed to us, and only translated the strictures on the climate and diseases of Crete and Creusa's guide-book praise of Latium's shores. Even the most cursory reading of Livy leaves the reader wondering how the infant Rome ever survived the endless epidemics. Malaria is not forgotten and we hear of quartan malaria among the troops being recruited in Sicily in 174 BC.

It is curious how often one reads of quartan malaria in the older records as today it is much less common than the tertian forms of the disease. Either it was indeed more prevalent in those areas of earlier recorded history such as the north Mediterranean littoral (which would lend oblique support to de Zulueta) or its longevity in man and its distinct periodicity made it more conspicuous. Livy notwithstanding, Rome, in its younger days, does seem to have been a less malarious place than it was to become. We have seen already de Zulueta's explanation for that; there is another. This lies in the remarkable system of underground tunnels built by the Etruscans to drain the land in and around Rome before the city's greatness. Grant (1980) believes that the mouth of the Arno was relieved of malaria by the construction of such tunnels by the local Etruscans. Other Etruscans built their cities (e.g. Vulci, Volterra) on a height, a sure sign in other parts of the world of the presence of malaria. Grant believes that malaria depopulated the Maremma (the area around the lake of Bolseno), even in Etruscan times.

Pallotinno believes that the Etruscan civilisation could not have reached the heights it did without the drainage system which kept malaria at bay. He points to the civilisation in the lower reaches of the Po and in the Maremma. It has been made clear the doubts which must cling to such statements. While the Etruscan drainage system did undoubtedly keep out malaria to a considerable degree it is impossible to agree that, if malaria had been present at the time, it would have prevented an expanding peoples from further expansion. The drainage system probably controlled only a fairly minor problem as the dangerous mosquitoes were not in the Italian peninsula of the years well before Christ in sufficient numbers to cause significant amounts of malaria. Malaria in Rome has a distinguished biographer in Celli one of the brightest lights in the illustrious constellation of Italian malariologists. His *The History of Malaria in the Roman Campagna* is a milestone in the historical treatment of malaria (1).

Celli believed most firmly with Pliny that *Latifundia Italium perdidere* (Malaria has and is ruining Italy). He saw the hand of malaria in most major happenings on the Italian mainland. Brunt would disagree. He is careful to explain why the old Latin stocks failed to reproduce themselves in the period from the third-century BC to the time of Augustus and why the Italian population of the Principate did not provide soldiers in the last two centuries of the Republic. This period coincides with time of low or static population increase and the time of Hannibal's invasion of Italy, which according to Jones brought malaria to the Italian mainland. Brunt does not accept Jones' (1907) arguments because of internal contradictions and Jones' *argumentum e silentio*. It is true that Jones does not prove his case that malaria was critical in either the downfall of Greece or Rome.

Brunt does not believe that malaria constituted a new factor on the Roman scene late in the third-century BC and so is an inadequate explanation for the demographic decline in the area around Rome from 225 BC. He believes that the Campagna was malarious in the third and second centuries BC, while Celli thinks that malaria was not a major factor in the middle Republican years (due to adequate drainage) and it only gained a grip in the first-century BC.

Any reading of this situation must take into account de Zulueta's ideas about the advance of dangerous malaria bearing mosquitoes into the northern Mediterranean. That is to say that in the Europe of the aftermath of the ice ages only *Anopheles atroparvus, A. messeae, A. maculipennis* group and probably *A. plumbeus* would have been present. None of these mosquitoes bite man frequently enough to be dangerous vectors of malaria and they probably did not transmit the *P. falciparum* of the day. Only the late arrivals, *A. sacharovi* and *A. labranchiae* could have set up a dangerous malaria situation.

So decisions as to when malaria comes into the picture as an influence on the history of Europe comes down to when these two malaria vectors rose to sufficient numbers to be dangerous in the northern Mediterranean. De Zulueta argues persuasively that this was not until the zenith of Roman expansion in the times of Julius and Augustus Caesar when deforestation assisted the establishment and breeding of the two new species. He argues that previous to that the minor amounts of benign tertian and quartan malaria had little or no effect upon the great initiatives of the classical Mediterranean.

Inter alia he points to a similar situation in the Tigris/Euphrates basin and Anatolia, submitting the remarkable good health of Xenophon's 'Ten Thousand' throughout their march as evidence. It has been argued that neither Julius Caesar and Pompey at Dyrrachium nor Antony and Octavian at Actium further down the Adriatic coast could have fought such battles in the early twentieth-century in the presence of malaria. An unlimited faith in the ability of man to wage useless war under almost any conditions disinclines one to be convinced by such arguments. The argument is based on the experiences of the French and the British at Salonika in the First World War. The French had 120,000 men under arms but in 1916 could put only 20,000 in the field, at the same time the British had 30,000 men in hospital and by 1917 this figure had risen to 70,000. Two million service days were lost to malaria. But put men in the field they did and they fought a war of sorts despite malaria.

The conclusion has to be that malaria had little or no influence upon the decline of Periclean Athens and it was not a major cause of the demographic decline during the Roman Republic. The question of its effect upon the Roman Empire is rather more open. It has been argued already that disease was a primary contributor to the decline and fall of the Western Roman Empire because of the demographic collapse between the years 193 and 235. It has been said, by Jones, (1909) that due to the presence of the two more dangerous vectors of malaria it would have been a dominant disease problem in the Empire as whole by the time of its collapse. This, of course, does not state that it was a major cause of that collapse but it is difficult to escape the conclusion that it played its part.

Celli believed that malaria was no great problem in the Roman area when Rome had been expanding in the first three centuries BC and agrees with North that it is inconceivable that a people could build up a civilisation, as did Rome, in the face of malaria as it was to be known later in the Campagna, the Maremma and Latium. The conclusion of both is that malaria did not exist then in the form to be known in those areas later. While the conclusion may well be correct, the means of reaching the conclusion are dubious.

It is constantly reiterated that this or that civilisation could not have arisen in the face of one disease or another. Taking malaria as a case in point, Sri Lanka saw the rise and fall of two great civilisations in the face of epidemic malaria of far greater severity than Italy was to see. The whole great Khmer Empire was built on the Great Lake, one of the worst malarious areas known to us today and unlikely to have been any different then.

The clinching argument belongs in Africa, that hotbed of the very worst of malaria where the Empires of Ghana, Bornu, Mali and Songhai were built and lost in the period between the eighth and nineteenth centuries. In these areas the great European powers of the nineteenth-century could not fight, conquer and rule without the assistance of local levies.

So, *pace* Celli and North, malaria, though of importance on where not to site your farm in Latium, was not a disease to shape the fate of nations in the time of the Roman Republic in the north Mediterranean littoral. It was certainly a disease of sufficient importance to receive magisterial descriptions of its symptoms from Galen and Celcus in the first centuries after Christ. From the Augustan age onwards it assumed greater and greater importance to the inhabitants of Rome and the market gardeners supplying the city from the *Agro Pontino*, where the Volscians had flourished. Hackett expresses surprise that the greatest city of its time was: 'a metropolis set in a malarious desert', though he admits that urbanisation would have drastically reduced the breeding of *Anopheles*.

At some time in this period the means of malaria control, accidental or inherited from the Etruscans began to fail Rome, though perhaps the final blow to those factors partially controlling malaria did not fall until the sack of Rome by the Goths early in the fifth-century. The Goths were to stay only six days in Rome because, some think, the city was so unhealthy. If so their next port of call to the south of the city would have given them a nasty surprise as it was the notoriously malarial Pontine Marshes. It was now that Alaric died, some say of malaria. This area has been the especial study of Ilvento in relation to malaria. It contained the *Via Appia* paved by the Romans in 310–313 BC. It would seem that in the middle of the first-century BC the *Agro Pontino* was not unhealthy and at least partially drained even though Horace found the noise of the mosquitoes annoying.

It was difficult to drain as there was little or no gradient. The wars between Marius and Sulla in 88–86 BC saw the area sacked but the drainage systems seem to have been kept in some sort of repair. Nero then Domitian in the first-century AD both lived in the midst of the area with all the appearances of enjoyment. Later both Nerva and Trajan attempted to drain the marshes, so it would seem that what was later to become notoriously malarious, was relatively salubrious up to the early second-century, with periods of neglect and unhealthiness. After this time the birth rate fell, the agricultural labourers on the estates tended to be slaves rather than local inhabitants and the district became underpopulated, even the slaves became fewer and fewer, one must assume from attrition rather than from emigration due to the soft hearts of their masters.

The *Agro Pontino* became a desert, the water was no longer controlled and the marshes took over. One of the great food producing areas of the Roman hinterland went out of production. From then on the history is a doomed tale of constant attempts to reclaim the land by Goths, by Popes, even by Napoleon. The discovery of the malaria parasite and its transmission gave new impetus to clean up and colonise the *Agro Pontino* and it was finally achieved by the government of Mussolini. It was settled again in 1930, though even then 80% of the population had enlarged spleens. We have in the *Agro Pontino* an undoubted instance of how malaria can denude an area of people, agriculture and life itself. There is another lesson not so palatable. It may require governmental influence of a nature unloved by democrats and civil libertarians to put in place effective disease control measures and maintain them in the face of improved health. The history of disease control is also a history of disobedience of all and any disease control restrictions. One must not confine one's study of the vast Roman Empire to a small sector around Rome. Although McNeill and Cartwright (1972) ascribe a role to malaria in the decline and fall of the Roman Empire this must be guesswork as descriptions of malaria in situations where disease could reasonably be claimed to have a major influence upon a critical social or institutional change are difficult to find. Of course malaria may have reinforced other influences.

As we are with the Italian peninsula it would seem sensible to stay with it. By the ninth-century Rome had been sacked by Ostrogoths, Visigoths, Lombards and Saracens. Such drainage systems as had survived the first of the conquests had vanished by the time of the last. These ravishers were followed by Hungarians, Normans, Germans and French; the Campagna was reduced to a desert occupied only by occasional shepherds. Malaria even played a part in protecting Rome by repelling Henry II's army in 1022. The Pontine marshes became part of the papal states and various Popes tried to restore it to its former fruitfulness without any permanent success.

Elsewhere any development of Sicily or Sardinia was doomed by malaria and Sardinia was the first target for an insecticide-based anti-malaria programme after the Second World War. The valley and particularly the mouth of the Po were thought to be highly malarious though this has been doubted by Bruce-Chwatt because of the extent of the exploitation of the land in these areas. Despite this exploitation it is said that the downfall of the Gonzagas at Mantua was due to malaria and certainly Napoleon's armies suffered from malaria before Mantua, this is discussed by Chevalier.

The history of the city of Venice on its lagoons which was to become a state with its *terra firma* on the mainland which included land with rivers full of malaria is replete with stories of malaria and many doges were said to have died of the disease. One of the few romantic tales from that unromantic and sometimes sinister commercialism concerns Bianco Cappello and her love affair with Francesco de' Medici. In a truly Shakespearean end he was believed to have taken poison destined by Bianco for her brother-in-law Cardinal Fernando. In her horror at the mistake she grasped a piece of the poisoned tart and swallowed it herself. It is now believed that they both died of malaria.

Venice was in danger in her early days from Charlemagne's son Pepin, who attempted to attack the city from the *terra firma*, not unreasonably, as the Venetians had invited him to occupy the city then refused him. Pepin's army camped on the *terra firma* opposite the city for six months unable to penetrate the city's lagoon defences. According to Norwich malaria took its toll and Pepin's army had to retreat an in a few weeks Pepin was dead. Carmichael (1962B) has shown that tertian and quartan malaria were present in Florence in the fourteenth-century to add their weight to the miseries of the Black Death.

In England malaria made occasional appearances and was endemic in the Kent and East Anglian marshes due to the relatively innocuous *A. atroparvus.* MacArthur (1951) has chronicled its unimportant history. It is mentioned here only to say that, while it may have contributed to the continuing demographic decline in fifteenth-century Italy, it could not have done so in England, by any stretch of the imagination, as claimed by Russell (1985). Only *P. falciparum* could bring about the devastation he claims for malaria and that form of malaria was not present in Britain then or later.

Runicman writes that malaria took its toll of the Crusading armies in the newly conquered Kingdom of Jerusalem of 1100, though other diseases such as dysentery and scurvy were probably more severe. Sterns finds that malaria was a major component of the diseases of sick knights in hospital in Palestine during the Crusades; it seems to have been little more than an irritant.

CHAPTER 12
Malaria (part 3)

As burning fevers, agues pale and faint,
Life-poisoning pestilence and frenzies wood,
The marrow-eating sickness, whose attaint
Disorder breeds by heating of the blood.
Shakespeare, *Venus and Adonis*

It is outside Europe that one must search for the profound effects of malaria. The greatest amount of research on the effects of malaria on the economy of a country was done by the British in India between the two World Wars. Sinton in a major study entitled 'What malaria costs India, nationally, socially and economically', estimated that the cost of malaria was about £80,000,000 annually in the 1930s and concluded that, if India was to feed itself and employ its growing population, it must control malaria. The flaw in this argument lies with the second of the needs. India's population was growing and continues to grow, probably because new farming techniques were being introduced and new land was being cultivated. Deplorable as this must be to the Malthusians and the population controllers, it does not denote a population or a state in decline, even if it may predict it. Not only that, India's population continues to grow today and take advantage of a 'green revolution' despite the return of malaria to the sub-continent.

Sinton's conclusion was that malaria was the greatest single cause of population retardation from a normal increase due to retarded conception and interrupted pregnancy. He estimated that malaria caused one million deaths a year directly and a further one million indirectly. This all has a slightly hollow ring to it when one considers the phenomenal population increase in the period from the 1930s to the present with the contribution of malaria control being effective in the 1960s only (1). Christophers, in the same series of enquiries on the damage done by malaria to India showed what epidemic malaria can do to an area, taking the Punjab in 1908 AD as his text. He found that in a population of about two million, malaria killed about a quarter of a million or a death rate of between three and four hundred per thousand, mostly malaria directly with some malaria related. In 1921 64% of deaths were due to 'fever', but the population of the Punjab went up and up despite even epidemic malaria.

It has to be said that Sinton would have been greeted with much scepticism today if he were to claim that malaria causes a lower birth-rate and interrupts pregnancy as his figures and conclusions were inferential rather than factual. Today we do not know of any direct mechanism by which malaria would lower the birth rate and while it is possible that epidemic malaria may depress the number of early marriages it is unlikely to be a more lasting phenomenon than epidemic malaria itself which always blows over.

Indeed, in Africa, in endemic malaria areas an infant death due to malaria earlier than the normal next pregnancy usually brings about a new pregnancy immediately to replace the death, so raising the number of live births. It should be remembered that malaria is a major cause of infant deaths in Africa. Similarly today we do not believe that malaria interrupts pregnancy, though it does cause some interuterine starvation leading to underweight babies who may continue not to thrive as they should.

It has been claimed none the less by Viswanathan, that malaria in Maharashtra state reduced the birth-rate, though as we noted in the chapter on the Bombay plague, according to Mitra and Sachdev, the population of this state rose steadily in the period 1891-1941. While it has been said by Dutt et. al., that epidemic malaria, in such places as the north India plain, where 3% of the population was laid low by malaria, and Sri Lanka, where there were 60-80,000 deaths, can devastate districts, bringing agriculture to a halt and famine to the area, these epidemic events are the exception to the normal rhythm of the years and do not permanently interrupt the inexorable rise in the population of these areas. Such epidemics are the consequence of exceptional rainfall bringing about conditions for the breeding of malaria vectors well above normal. Curiously this is due to excessive rainfall in the north India plain raising the water table and bringing into being large tracts of shallow water, but in Sri Lanka it is due to a comparative drought which, in the areas of heavy rainfall, also brings about tracts of shallow water. China, today, has malaria in the Yangtze basin and in the south of the country especially the island of Hainan. From about 750 to 1250 the Chinese population grew rapidly in the south; in the Yangtze valley population increases of from 100% to 1000% occurred, partly due to immigration but partly due to prosperity.

It would not seem that malaria played any depressive role on the population of the malarious areas of China.

In the Americas a major effect of malaria can be seen in its role, in association with yellow fever, in holding up the development of the Panama Canal. This will be dealt with in the chapter on yellow fever. During the American civil war malaria took its toll but it cannot be claimed to have influenced events. In World War Two in the Pacific the US had a half a million cases of malaria among its troops and Japan had similar numbers, but it would be a brave man who claimed that the effort on either side was in any way half-hearted.

It is tempting to ascribe the disappearance of both the highland and the lowland Mayas to a disease outbreak but there is no evidence for such a proposal despite the fact that there was a major disease outbreak among the Mayas prior to the invasion of Mexico by Cortez. The disease was called mayacimil (= maya death) and, though the two American discoverers of many of the Maya cities in the nineteenth-century, Stephen and Catherwood both contracted malaria in Maya country, there is no evidence to connect mayacimil with malaria. It seems that the Mayas, like some of the Peruvian coastal tribes, were in the end victims of an agricultural failure.

In Africa, south of the Sahara, where malaria is both endemic and intense or in the language of the epidemiologist holoendemic or at least hyperendemic, the story is different. Here we are in the homeland of *P. falciparum* and we do find evidence of retardation of society, institutions and even tools. Here the connection to malaria seems plainer though mixed with a whole number of other retarding influences such as the slave trade, poor soil and tribalism. Africa is said to lose one million children a year to malaria and this has an inevitable effect on population. Whole areas of West Africa had, in the time before and after the Second World War, stable or declining population. The decline was usually due to an emigration to the towns. The towns did not share this population loss and generally showed an increase in populations, sometimes dramatically so. This was due to the combination of emigration from the rural areas and the easier control of malaria and other diseases in towns, both accidental and deliberate.

The economic loss to a society of a high death rate among the non-working element of the population is notoriously difficult to assess, and it has not been attempted with any conviction in Africa with reference to malaria and the child death-rate. The demography of malaria eradication programmes has been examined by Prothero but this is not to our purpose as these examinations have been directed at the *modus operandi* of malaria eradication and the effect of the movement of peoples on the results of eradication measures. In Africa south of the Sahara it can be said with certitude that malaria has drastically retarded the growth of population, industry and governmental institutions. With the failure of malaria eradication in Africa and now the arrival in that continent of *P. falciparum* malaria resistant to chloroquine, the most powerful drug in the malariologist's armamentarium, the outlook for Africa is anything but rosy. Add to this situation rampant AIDS and one can only predict the most grim future for Africa for the next decades.

It can reasonably be asked how (or even why) the European powers in the nineteenth-century conquered and held vast areas of this diseased continent. First it must be admitted that they did so in the teeth of malaria. The most cursory perusal of the annals of European exploration of West and Central Africa in particular leaves the reader in wonderment at the sheer recklessness of such people as Mungo Park, Livingstone, Clapperton, Lander and Laing among the British; Rene Cillie, de Brazza, du Chaillu and Marché among the French; Heinrich Barth and Schweinfurth among the Germans, who in the late eighteenth and nineteenth centuries traversed the most malarious areas of a notoriously malarious continent without the aid of any anti-malarial prophylaxis. Their companions died of yellow fever, typhoid fever and above all malarial fever. Yet they went back to certain death of some sort and a surprisingly large proportion of them died at the hands of the naturally hostile locals. The fate of so many of them from one fever or another, usually malaria, was shared by the traders, missionaries and soldiers who followed in their wake to the haunts of the *Anopheles*.

Mungo Park and his brother-in-law set out from the Gambia River for the Niger in 1805 with forty Europeans in the rainy (malarious) season, they arrived at the Niger only eleven strong; Park wrote to his wife not to worry. He died on the Niger and his servant and companion Lander went back again, also to die. Boyle recorded cerebral malaria as well as typhoid fever and ordinary malaria among the sailors of his ship in The Gambia in the wet season. In the early nineteenth-century the death rate for Europeans in The Gambia was 150 per annum, but the native levies remained largely healthy. Carlson believes that fever prevented European penetration of West Africa despite the lure of slaves and gold. He notes that between 33% and 56% of all British individuals going to the West Coast of Africa died in their first few years there of fever or dysentery.

Of the crew of a trading ship investigating the mouth of the Niger in the 1830s forty out of forty nine were dead before they retreated from the fever. In the next expedition to the same area M'William reports that sixty three out of one hundred and forty five Europeans were dead in the first five weeks and again they retreated with most of them sick. Truly it was a case of 'Beware, beware the Bight of Benin, Where none come out but many go in'. Then Alexander Bryson, a naval surgeon, demonstrated the efficacy of prophylactic quinine and Dr. William Baike went up the Niger to the confluence of the Benue and set up farm there, surviving on quinine and so changing the commercial situation of West Africa.

Gore notes that almost every attempt to wage war in West Africa had been unsuccessful owing to disease. In the 1850s, while Europeans died like flies, native levies or 'acclimatised West Indian blacks' had only a 0.3% death-rate though a 22% hospitalisation rate. During the Ashanti campaign among British troops 511 died or were invalided out due to disease while only 202 were killed or wounded in battle.

Quinine (or powdered bark) was not always successful in preventing malaria. Gelfand recalls that Royal Navy expedition went up the Zambesi in 1823 taking bark as a prophylactic; the three Europeans died but the two Africans survived.

Aubrey states that during the French campaigns in Madagascar as late as 1895 the French lost 5,731 out of 5,756 of their own troops to disease, mostly malaria. Despite this the French conquered and held Madagascar. There is little doubt then that malaria held up the European exploration and exploitation of Africa south of the Sahara. This hold-up also spelt an arrest of the development of modern states in Africa, unpalatable as that might be to liberal thought. However powerful indigenous states did arise in Africa and did so in the teeth of malaria. The question is did they decline due to malaria? It is impossible to answer this question with any hope of accuracy but it should be borne in mind that malaria is a killer of infants in Africa and adults are largely free of it, so if it was the adults that built up states in malarious Africa it is unlikely that malaria brought them down.

On the other hand it is a fact that over most of holoendemic and hyperendemic malaria areas of Africa not even the wheel had been developed by the indigenous African and the tendentious question is whether such a lack of development was due to the diseases they suffered, the chief of which was malaria. The answer, in my opinion, has to be – No. Malaria is not a significant disease of the African adult in the most malarious areas because of the developed immunity to it and it is the adult who experiences the pressure needed for the invention of such aids to civilisation as the wheel.

Supporters of the belief in a decisive role for malaria in the retardation of African development will ask, can a lifetime of malaria so sap the will to invent and develop, or the intellectual capacity to do so, so that progress in the Western sense is not achieved? These are unanswerable questions and are answered more often from prejudice than from reason, but if we accept that the advances of which we speak spring from the adult suffering the insults of permanent endemic malaria and so developing immunity then we must accept that the influence of malaria has been minimal. The most that can be said with safety is that Africa has been held back by malaria because the disease held back the penetration of the continent by the technologically advanced and politically sophisticated European powers.

The other areas of intense malaria are south and south-east Asia, Indonesia and Papua New Guinea. Nicholls and Lividas both believe that the great Sri Lankan civilisations based on Anuradhapura in the millennium before Christ and on Pollonnaruwa in the millennium after Christ were the victims of malaria. Unless much more information becomes available this must remain guesswork, though it is true that these civilisations did rely, as so many did in Asia, on large amounts of impounded water for assured rice growing.

It might be assumed that such conditions would be just right for explosive mosquito breeding but it would be preferable to have the views of a competent mosquito entomologist before being committed to such a view, as in the 1930s dangerous levels of mosquito breeding in Sri Lanka were a feature of drought conditions rather than flooding from impounded water supplies or the creation of artificial lakes.

The other fascinating area for speculation is the rise and fall of the Khmer civilisation as chronicled by Groslier and Arthaud. This was based on a large and unfailing supply of water for rice cultivation and fish protein. The Khmers were an Indianised people in the south of Cambodia and Viet Nam. They moved up the Mekong River from its delta to the middle river reclaiming the land for rice cultivation. At the beginning of the ninth-century Jayvarman returned from exile in Indonesia to unify these people and bring into being the Khmer people based on Angkor. They settled around the Tonle Sap or Great Lake.

This remarkable geographical feature is a lake, which in the dry season is a shallow collection of muddy pools, but which begins to fill up in July as the monsoons start. It fills from a back-wash of the Mekong to which it is connected by a tributary. The force of the flow down the Mekong in the monsoon is so great that water is forced up its tributaries. The water recedes from the Great Lake in October trapping millions of fish. These floods and the water trapped by them with the assistance of reservoirs built by the Khmers allowed three to four crops of rice to be gathered each year and it was on this and the bounty of fish that the prosperity of the Khmers relied.

The civilisation fell despite its advantages. Briggs believes it fell because of: 1. Overbuilding. 2. Thai incursions into the lands of nearby peoples, so robbing the Khmers of slaves 3. Conversion to Hinayana Buddhism. 4. Finally the sack of Angkor Wat by the Siamese.

It is inevitable that a medically-minded person should wonder about the role of malaria in this downfall given the reliance on standing impounded water and the breeding of *Anopheles* (2). Are there any other clues as to the importance of malaria to the Khmer civilisation? The Naga figure (the cobra) is very common in all Indianised religions and is frequently represented as many-headed (3–6), as can be seen in the Naga balustrades at Bakong Preah Vihar and Beng Mealea, but particularly at Angkor Wat. The question arises whether the many headed Naga figure represents the seven deltaed Mekong River, the source of Khmer prosperity and the source of its malaria.

The cobra is worshipped both as evil and good. It can kill but it also protected the Buddha from the elements when he was still gaining wisdom. The central myth of the worship of the Khmers was the 'churning of the sea of milk', where the cobra Vasuki is pulled at one end by the gods and at the other end by demons with Vishnu in the middle.

The thrashing of Vasuki causes a foam out of which asparas are born. If the cobra heads/river delta represent malaria then the cobra has good and evil at either end (it would be advisable to know if the demons are always at the delta and poisonous end) with Vishnu holding the ring, though mounted on the snake-killing bird Garuda. This is not really any more far-fetched than Heracles' conquest of the Hydra being represented as the draining of the delta of the river Lerna but no more believable for that, indeed Krishna (the Indian Heracles), the son or atavar of Vishnu, is reputed to have killed Naraka, the King of the serpents. If this particular flight of fancy has any merit then the 'taming' of the cobra by snake charmers could represent relief from or cure of malaria.

To end on a lighter note (as if the Naga story was not light enough) there was an Arab physician who treated a case of tertian fever and succeeded only in converting it to a semi-tertian (and more dangerous) fever. He claimed half his fee. Perhaps he should have listened to Marco Polo who commended the earth from the grave of St Thomas at Trincomallee as a specific for malaria.

CHAPTER 13
Yellow Fever

aka. Yellow Jack.   **aka. Vomito Negro.**

Yellow fever is a notorious companion of malaria and like malaria is transmitted by a mosquito. Yellow fever, however, is caused by a virus, known as an arbor virus because it is arthropod-borne. Arthropod is an awkward term made necessary by the need to include the mites and ticks in the definition as both transmit viruses but are acarids and not strictly insects (members of the Insecta).

The yellow fever virus belongs to the group of viruses known as the flavoviruses; it is about 20–60 nanometers wide, (1 nanometer = 1/1,000,000,000 of a metre or 10 Angstrom units) so can only be seen by the electron microscope. It causes disease by invading the human liver. The disease commences some 3–6 days after the bite of an infective mosquito with mild influenza-like symptoms; chills, some fever and headache for a few days, at which stage it may resolve spontaneously having caused no more discomfort than a backache, loss of appetite and some prostration. It may progress to a fulminating fever of 103° F (39.5°C) or more. The fever is always accompanied by severe long-bone ache and intense headache. Albuminurea (albumin in the urine) follows with continuing fever. Jaundice sets in, to give the disease its name and there is some bleeding under the skin. The pulse rate increases, but may be followed by a period of calm when the pulse rate drops. The patient starts to vomit and the vomit may be tinged with blood progressively until old blood gives the vomit the characteristic black colour. This is due to bleeding into the intestine particularly the stomach. Spontaneous bleeding may occur anywhere both internally and externally. At this stage the patient is near death. If the patient recovers he is immune to a second attack for life.

The epidemiology of yellow fever is complicated. It is a zoonosis, the virus being transmitted from animals to man by mosquitoes but after that the disease may become epidemic when it is transmitted by mosquitoes directly from man to man. The true home of the virus is in the monkeys of the forests of South and Central America, the Caribbean and Africa south of the Sahara. From this enzootic base it has broken out to man in these areas and then occasionally becoming epidemic and spreading to ports and river systems within the limits of the latitudes of 40 N and 35 S in North America and Europe as well as causing epidemics in its areas of origin.

It has never spread to Asia, which is something of a puzzle, as suitable mosquitoes and susceptible monkeys are present in Asia for the spread of the disease. One explanation has it that other arbor viruses akin to the yellow fever virus are present and common in Asia and these cross-react immunologically with the yellow fever virus and prevent it taking hold.

In order to found an epidemic the virus is first set up as an enzootic among the forest monkeys in the forest canopy where the mosquitoes which transmit the virus live and bite. These mosquitoes are species of the genus *Haemogogus* in South America and *Aedes simpsoni* among others in Africa. From time to time this enzootic among the monkeys becomes epizootic for poorly understood reasons and may in that form enter a village and man either because the monkeys encroach on the village and the infection is picked up by the mosquitoes which bite man or because man encroaches on the monkey habitat and is bitten accidentally by an infected mosquito carrying this newly virulent virus.

Once the epizootic virus enters the village there are present in the village the ubiquitous *Aedes*, which is a notorious vector of yellow fever and a constant companion of man in South American and African 'bush' villages. This mosquito is able to breed in very small expanses of water such as discarded bowls or tin cans. Carter and Strode show that unlike *Anopheles*, the vectors of malaria, which bite at night, *Aedes*, vectors of yellow fever, bite during the day the most common of these *Aedes* vectors is *Aedes aegypti*, the yellow fever vector *par excellence*.

Like all zoonoses the epidemiology of yellow fever is endlessly interesting with its permutations and combinations of animal and human behaviour necessary to bring the virus and host together in such a manner that disease results. It is not possible here to discuss these problems in the depth they deserve, but it can be said that the virus may be relatively harmless to its monkey hosts but on other occasions it may kill monkeys on a large scale, particularly in South America.

In man in Africa it is obviously possible for the virus to give man a mild disease as antibodies to yellow fever can be found among villagers with no memory of a yellow fever-like disease. Usually, however, it is highly pathogenic during epidemics. Man with yellow fever is infective to mosquitoes in the first few days of the disease and the mosquito incubates the virus for about ten days before becoming infective.

The control of yellow fever in South America was one of the great achievements of the Rockefeller Foundation who used the elimination of *Aedes aegypti* as the main means of control and the viscerotomy service as the main epidemiological tool for the discovery of outbreaks. This service was based on an instrument which took a sample of liver from all dead people at post-mortem compulsorily by law, in a manner which did not give offence to the bereaved relatives. It was possible to diagnose yellow fever from the piece of liver taken. Finally the instrument for the world-wide control of yellow fever has been vaccination, after the workers at the Rockefeller Institute modified the Asibi strain of yellow fever virus to produce the 17D strain which was sufficiently innocuous, while still infecting man, to be used as a live vaccine.

There is a theory that the yellow fever virus came originally from Africa. Carter gives us a scholarly account of the disease which struck the Mayas, a few years before the arrival of Cortez. In the Maya records there are two descriptions of diseases (other than dysentery), one called *mayacimil* (= maya death) and the other called *xekik* (= blood vomit). He points out that the black vomit of yellow fever cannot usually be recognised as being caused by blood. Corlett, rather puzzlingly, ascribes black vomit to plague and *vomito negro* to yellow fever. Carter notes that Finlay believed that a later Mayan epidemic was yellow fever and that the Mayas did know yellow fever. We are always talking about the lowland Mayas. Carter is doubtful though he does accept that *mayacimil* might have been yellow fever but finds no evidence for knowledge by the Mayas of yellow fever before the outbreak of *mayacimil* (see also under smallpox).

The epidemic which occurred in the Yucatan just after the Conquest is not accepted as yellow fever by Carter, though he does accept the 1648 outbreak in Maya country as described by Lopez de Cogolludo as yellow fever. He worries about the great gap in time between the *mayacimil* and this outbreak. Major believes that this 1648 outbreak was yellow fever and it destroyed the Yucatan Mayas. He dates yellow fever from much earlier among the Mayas than does Carter.

From 1648 onwards yellow fever became a well-known disease and one greatly feared by the mariners of the Caribbean, the merchants of southern and eastern North American sea-board and the Spaniards of the Americas. Yellow fever is suspected as the disease which brought Drake's crew low after their little chase of the Spaniards over the island of St Jago in 1585, though the timing and the persistence is a little suspect unless infected *Aedes* were shipped as well. By the late eighteenth-century the dread of disease had shifted from plague to yellow fever as epidemic after epidemic swept through the young United States of America and its fingers brushed Europe's western ports. Yellow fever was malaria's right hand in Africa and did almost as much as malaria to block European advance into that continent. We have, however, no records which lead us to believe that yellow fever, or indeed malaria, debilitated the efforts of the African peoples to develop as nations as did epidemic sleeping sickness within the medical memory of the Europeans.

There is no record of the disappearance of whole peoples or kingdoms due to the twin mosquito-borne diseases as there is for the damage done by sleeping sickness to the Kissi people in West Africa by the decimation of their population, or to the tribes of the northern and north-east shores of Lake Victoria-Nyanza, moving, as it did, whole peoples away to seek safer dwellings inland. The two mosquito-borne diseases were more insidious in Africa but if both were in full operation they must have played their part in retarding the aspirations of any emerging or emergent nation in Africa, perhaps yellow fever even more so as it is epidemic and does affect adults.

In the Americas Moll tells us that yellow fever was the possible cause of the failure of the first three towns to be built in Jamaica, and early attempts to colonise Puerto Rico by Ponce de Leon were frustrated by the disease. That the cause was yellow fever is doubtful as it did not seem to be properly established as an epidemic disease until the seventeenth-century. Moll does ascribe two disease outbreaks in the West Indies to yellow fever in 1635 and 1640 and gives this disease a contributory role in the drying up of Spanish immigration to the Americas in the seventeenth-century. Napoleon's dreams of a Caribbean Empire broke on the scourge of yellow fever when seven eighths of the 25,000 French soldiers sent to reconquer Haiti died, largely from a yellow fever epidemic.

This disease was to act as a great deterrent to would-be invaders of the Spanish Main and it repelled attacks by the British against Cartagena in 1741 (see *Roderick Random* by Tobias Smollett) and against Havana in 1762. It was even called the patriotic disease in South America as it attacked invaders rather than locals. It remained a major scourge in the West Indies killing up to 85% of the infected population at times. Between 1853 and 1900 it killed 36,000 in Havana alone, nearly half of them in the outbreak which lasted from 1870 to 1879. Even when the US troops ousted the Spanish in 1898, yellow fever showed its mettle and attacked the US troops severely, stinging the USA into doing the research, brilliantly carried out by Walter Reed and his team, which led to the discovery of the role of the mosquito in the epidemiology of the disease and eventually to the vaccine. Yellow fever took its toll of both sides in Bolivar's struggle to rid South America of its Spanish overlords. Yellow fever's most famous victory and its greatest defeat took place in Panama, to which we will return later.

In the USA and Canada yellow fever struck Halifax, Boston, New York, Baltimore, Philadelphia, Norfolk, Savannah (which lost one third of its population in 1817–20), Charleston and above all New Orleans, causing dismay a havoc wherever it struck. Powell describe the outbreak of 1793 in Philadelphia, a town which contained at the time Washington, Jefferson, John Adams and Alexander Hamilton. The disease caused a constitutional crisis over where the capital of the thirteen states should be sited. It was this outbreak which made the reputation of one of the greatest of the USA's physicians – Benjamin Rush. Winslow reckons that yellow fever visited the eastern and southern sea-boards of the USA thirty five times between 1702 and 1800 and then attacked every year except for two years.

Philadelphia, for instance, suffered epidemics in 1699, 1741, 1747 and 1762, then came the 1793 epidemic which removed one-tenth of the population. Duffy (1966), however, plays down the effect of these outbreaks upon the colonists as yellow fever was the exception rather than the rule in the everyday diseases. He believes that malaria and dysentery did more harm than yellow fever and smallpox. Note, however, that he refers only to the colonists and not the red Indian. Duffy records the 1853 epidemic in New Orleans where 40% of the city was sick and 10% died. In New Orleans in 1878 on July 24 four people died of yellow fever and on July 28 the up-river towns commenced a quarantine of river boats from New Orleans. Despite these precautions an epidemic of yellow fever swept up the Mississippi and by the time the epidemic was over 100,000 had been sick and 20,000 died. As with plague those who could, fled the river. The epidemic reached Ohio before it petered out.

The *John D. Parker* was towing barges and went up river from New Orleans in mid-July. By the time it reached Ohio it had lost 23 men dead and spread yellow fever up half of the Mississippi and nearly the whole length of the Ohio rivers. According to Duffy (1971) there was an epidemic of yellow fever in New Orleans as late as 1902. All these epidemics were, in fact, pandemics arising from South or Central America or the Caribbean. Yellow fever was attacking a young, emergent and vigorous nation in the United States and it did no permanent damage to that nation's emergence. A useful chronology of the USA's epidemics can be found in Marks and Beatty, while Moll has a complete account of all epidemics and pandemics in the New World.

Ships sailing from the New World or Africa to Europe carried fresh water in barrels, a situation made for the breeding of *Aedes· aegypti*, so the long sea voyages did not see the demise of the virus and the disease was kept going by the ship's own tame *Aedes*. So yellow fever reached the shores of Europe, particularly Spain and Portugal. Cloudesley-Thompson believes that many Europeans must have died of yellow fever during the slaving journeys from West Africa to the Americas though many of the Africans would have survived as they could be immune. He places yellow fever at San Domingo in 1502 when many Spanish immigrants died including their leader Ovanda. He puts further yellow fever epidemics in San Domingo in 1554, 1560, 1567, 1583 and 1588, much of which was due to the slave trade. Ackerknecht (1965) tends to agree with Carter but puts the first recognisable outbreak as late as 1620 in Cuba despite the presence of the slave trade being there for some years. Cloudesley-Thompson has a chronology of yellow fever in the Caribbean.

Inevitably yellow fever arrived into the European ports, the only question was whether it could take a hold. It attacked Spain, Portugal and Italy, arriving at Cadiz in 1701 and 1731, Lisbon in 1723 where it took off 6,000 dead and Malaga in 1741. In 1810, a critical time for Spain as Wellington's Peninsula war was raging against Napoleon's marshals, Prinzing discusses yellow fever which played havoc in Cadiz, Cartegena and Gibraltar. The last outbreak was at Madrid in 1878. Coleman tells us that in the meantime it had got as far as the Atlantic ports of France, such as St Nazaire in 1861, and according to Smith and Gibson even to Swansea in 1865, though at such places there were no indigenous *Aedes aegypti* to keep the yellow fever going for any length of time in comparison with Spain where it is obvious that some indigenously propagated yellow fever did occur. It should be stressed that the *Buide Connail* or yellow plague of sixth-century Ireland was not yellow fever but probably relapsing fever.

In Africa yellow fever has been an important disease among other important diseases. It has already been pointed out that it was the companion of malaria in slowing the penetration of Africa by the European powers. It is fashionable today especially in Africa itself to decry the effects of this penetration but the fact remains that it was this very penetration which put and pushed Africa on the road of progress towards a better life for its inhabitants. Life in Africa remains still incredibly poor and its institutions fragile and weak. There is no doubt that progress towards better health, education and industrialisation would have been poorer and slower without the European powers and one does not have to be illiberal to say so. Yellow fever remains a force to be reckoned with in Africa even today as recent epidemics in The Gambia, Mali and Burkino Fasso have shown (1).

The Ethiopian epidemic of the early 1960s was particularly vicious, though luckily confined to a sparsely populated area. It killed 5,000 just the same. Gore noted yellow fever as endemic in the Senegal and The Gambia in the 1870s with epidemics every seven years or so. It is not much better today. There were epidemics in the Senegal in 1740 and Sierra Leone in 1764 and another epidemic at St Louis in the Senegal in 1780. Pym found yellow fever in the Cape Verde islands, Sierra Leone, the rest of the west coast and Spain in mid-nineteenth-century and noted that the disease was destroyed by the cold. Singer and Underwood say that the legend of both the 'Flying Dutchman' and Coleridge's *Rime of the Ancient Mariner* were about ships struck by yellow fever.

The rise and fall of yellow fever is epitomised in the building of the Panama Canal. De Lesseps, flushed with his victory over the Sinai desert and the construction of the Suez Canal, arrived in Panama with 86,000 French workers to cut the isthmus and build the Panama Canal. Not long after he had started 52,000 were sick and 22,000 had died of yellow fever and malaria. Panama was said to have two seasons, the wet, when you died in two to three days of yellow fever and the dry when you died in one to two days from malaria. A gloomy view which owes more to desperation than clinical accuracy. A penny-pinching administration refused to continue to pay de Lesseps and he retreated to France. In Havana a sanitarian called Gorgas had shown great energy and skill in cleaning up the city and preventing the breeding of *Aedes aegypti* and *Anopheles* and thus controlling both yellow fever and malaria.

Walter Reed's group had just demonstrated the *Aedes* transmission of yellow fever and Ross' discovery of the mosquito transmission of malaria had been known for some years. Gorgas, with enormous tact and energy, destroyed the breeding places of the mosquitoes and by the time he had finished there were few mosquitoes to be found in Havana. In 1904 there was a disastrous epidemic of yellow fever in the Panama Canal Zone and the authorities decided to call in Gorgas. He launched an immense programme of attack against the domestic breeding places of *Aedes aegypti* combined with the killing of any adult mosquitoes seen near the breeding places. New breeding places were prepared as traps for the adults. It was all too expensive for the Scrooges at the headquarters of the canal organisation and they called a halt.

They had mistaken their man and Gorgas fought. Eventually an independent report from the American Medical Association was sought. It was touch and go but Gorgas was vindicated. He went on and even the redoubtable *Aedes aegypti* had to give him best defeated by its very aspect of danger, the ability to breed domestically. Yellow fever had been brought under control with quite surprising ease and speed (7 months). Malaria was a tougher opponent but it too eventually yielded. Gorgas was not universally thanked, as Coleman shows, the Far East thought that the ease with which shipping now passed into the Pacific Ocean would bring yellow fever to a previously free Asia. The USA and Britain did honour him and he was created Knight Commander of the Order of St Michael and St George and was given a state funeral in both Washington and London.

Yellow fever is said to have ruled the Spanish Main for two and a half centuries, defeating the attempts of the European powers to become dominant in the region as Spain's grasp weakened (2). Yellow fever is said to have inhibited much needed emigration from Portugal and Spain to South America and the Caribbean. Yellow fever sent the victorious de Lesseps of Suez packing from Panama. Yellow fever scared the living daylights out of the citizens of the south and east coasts of the USA, until cholera came along to give them something else about which to worry. The Atlantic sea-board of Europe was no less worried. Yellow fever arm-in-arm with malaria held back African development both indigenous and imported. Though yellow fever was said to have diverted trade from New Orleans to other ports in the USA, it seems to have caused not even a stutter in the progress of all parts of the USA and finally as a whole to world power status, indeed some believe that the failure of France to acquire and hold Haiti led directly to the Louisiana Purchase.

CHAPTER 14
Smallpox (part 1)

Where are you going my pretty maid?
I'm going a-milking, Sir, she said.
What's your fortune my pretty maid?
My face is my fortune, Sir, she said
Anon

It is curious that one of the great infectious diseases of mankind should be called small. It was an accident of naming that gave smallpox the prefix of small; it was done at the time of great concern, among those that did the naming, with syphilis – the great pox. With smallpox we are dealing again with a virus disease. This time the virus is a little bigger – about 200 nanometers – though it causes changes in the cell which it occupies visible with a normal microscope as they are up to ten microns (or ten millionths of a metre) in width. Transmission is by droplet infection not contact as one might expect from a disease where a major manifestation of the disease is to be seen on the skin. The disease is in fact transmitted from human lung to human lung. The disease may kill when the virus concerned is *Variola major*, however an attenuated form exists, generally called V*ariola minor* (though this is in dispute), which causes a less dangerous disease known as alastrim. This is a Portuguese word meaning fast-spreading. Smallpox kills about 25% of those who contract the dangerous form of the disease (or up to 100% of cases of haemorrhagic, purpuric or confluent smallpox) and it is normally epidemic. According to Torres alastrim kills less than 1% of its victims. We will concern ourselves with smallpox only.

Smallpox is less contagious than chicken-pox or influenza (both lung to lung virus diseases) as the virus tends to be deeper in the bronchi and so less available to the sputum and droplets on coughing or sneezing. The patient is not infectious when the disease is developing early on and only becomes so when lesions (as pustules) exuding virus appear in the mouth and pharynx. It is when these pustules burst to shed virus (a brief period) that the patient is most infectious. Other material such as bed-linen may be infectious as well as the virus can live quite a long time outside the body. The disease starts after about 15 days of incubation and starts with a toxaemic phase (a blood poisoned phase) which is when the virus is spreading via the blood. This produces a rash in the same areas as that in which *Y. pestis* produces buboes. The toxaemia produces classical virus disease symptoms with high fever on the first day.

On the second day the rash appears where the smallpox pustules are going to appear. The pustules (pocks) appear on about the third day and the pocks are found focally around a central area, usually the forehead or mouth and cheek area, on the back of the wrists and on the back of the hands. This eruption spreads over the face, to the trunk and to the arms and legs. To begin with these spots are bright red. They become papules then vesicles with a head. At the time of the appearance of the rash the temperature goes down until about the eighth day of the disease when the temperature rises again and the skin becomes itchy and painful. On about the tenth day the pustules start to burst and then commence to scab. After about four weeks these leave behind the characteristic pitting of the skin of a person recovered from smallpox, which was a most desirable sign in a servant of the eighteenth-century. At the time of the breakdown of the pocks they may coalesce and so become confluent smallpox, a more severe form of the disease which shows much fever, rapid pulse and delirium.

The most severe form of the disease is haemorrhagic smallpox, often called black or purpuric smallpox in one manifestation or haemorrhagic pustular smallpox depending on where or when the haemorrhages occur. Death from smallpox is due to the multiple haemorrhages and is frequently complicated by broncho-pneumonia. Eye involvement is also common and a frequent sequel to smallpox is blindness. The joints may be affected and lead to permanent damage. If a person has been vaccinated he or she may suffer a modified form of the disease of lesser or aborted pathology called varioloid. Smallpox has to be distinguished from chicken pox, but differs from it by being more common on the face and favouring exposed surfaces. The lesions are all of the same size and are deeper in the skin tissue.

Thanks to Jenner this dangerous disease has disappeared from the world, at least for the moment. It must be remembered that smallpox came from somewhere in the first place, as cow-pox from cows, or as monkey-pox from monkeys for instance, and these viruses are still about, (it was cow-pox which immunised the milk-maid of the poem so keeping her complexion clear). The cost of freedom from smallpox will remain constant vigilance. It had, in its day, a simple epidemiology, cases always commenced with a focal distribution around a primary case. The transmission was simple droplet infection with virus coughed up in the sputum from the mouth, larynx and bronchi. It required only that sufficient virus was present for the recipient to receive an infecting dose. Immunity to the disease among those who had recovered was complete and absolute, and this formed the major basis of the success of vaccination and the world-wide eradication campaign of the WHO based on it.

There were other assisting factors such as a lack of an animal reservoir, the lack of relapses, the availability of large amounts of heat-stable and effective vaccine and the obviousness of the disease – discussion of this can be found in Fenner and Kaplan – and finally the ability of the vaccine to protect against all of the strains of virus in the world. Whatever the reasons for the success of the global eradication of smallpox it remains man's greatest achievement in the field of public health. For, make no mistake, this was a disease of the first rank which had ravaged humans for millennia and had brought down whole peoples. It appears to have been with man for some considerable time.

There are those who think that it was smallpox which destroyed the Hittite Empire late in the second millennium BC and that it had infected the Pharaoh Ramses V in about 1160 BC. Hopkins believes that there is enough evidence to accept that smallpox had affected other Egyptian mummies as well. Adamson thinks that an Accadian tablet describes smallpox so putting its existence back into the second millennium BC. Though the story of the destruction of the Hittites by smallpox has found favour with those who would wish smallpox on to all period of history and have found what they believe to be records of the disease in India in about 400 BC, including Hopkins. Lehmann, however, states: 'We are as ignorant of how the Hittites lost their supremacy as how they acquired it.' One knowledgeable observer doubts if smallpox appeared in man prior to the first-century AD.

Hopkins is a major historian of smallpox but tends to be overenthusiastic in his recognition of smallpox in every disputed historical instance. He wonders if Alexander's army on the Indus had contracted smallpox and plumps for smallpox for the Athenian plague. He is happy to place smallpox in China, brought in by the Huns, in about 250 AD, though this is in dispute among medical historians. He finds that the disease of the Carthaginians before Syracuse in 395 BC was smallpox with the same certainty as it has been ascribed to influenza by others. He is content to accept that the disease of Abraha's Abyssinian army besieging Mecca during the so-called 'Elephant War' in 569–70 was smallpox, a belief which is examined below. He is a little more cautious about the Antonine plague but mentions the important fact that Rhazes thought that Galen was diagnosing smallpox. I am of the opinion that in none of these cases can a diagnosis be made with this degree of certainty.

A case in point is the 'Elephant War'. Abraha was the envoy of the Negus of Abyssinia to the Yemen and therefore a Monophysite Christian. He built a cathedral in an attempt to atone for his multifarious sins and invited some Arab leaders to worship in it (this is prior to the rise of Islam). An Arab chief from Mecca defiled the cathedral by defecating in it. Abraha collected an Abyssinian army, with an elephant to lead it, to lay siege to Mecca and punish it for the crime of its chief. The inhabitants of Mecca prayed to Allah (? according to later glosses by Islam) to protect his holy shrine. The elephant is said to have refused to advance on Mecca and instead knelt before it. Allah sent birds like swallows and starlings from the sea, each bird carrying a stone, the size of a lentil, one in its beak and one in each of its claws. These they dropped on Abraha's host. All 60,000 who were hit died, the Abyssinians fled and many died on the route. Abraha himself was smitten and progressively lost his fingers; he died and his heart burst from his body (1).

The story takes on some importance as Mahommed is said to have been born on the day of the defeat of Abraha and so the day gains hagiological significance. It is all very doubtful indeed. It is difficult to see why smallpox was read into this description except that many believed it to be the first description of a disease which became obvious in later records, and there is reason to believe that smallpox was already present in the Arabian peninsula at about the time of the 'Elephant War'. Conrad disputes the chronology and puts the event before 555, rather than at 570, thus disconnecting it from the birth of the Prophet. Kister agrees and puts the date even earlier at 552. Conrad grants the underlying truth of the legend and points out that no Arab historian mentions plague as a cause so disconnecting it from Justinian's plague. He grants therefore that the disease may have been smallpox if indeed it was a disease.

Conrad complains of many accretions which the story has gathered and notes that smallpox was already known in Arabia. Kaplan puts smallpox as epidemic in Arabia by the end of the sixth-century. Kister equates the elephant expedition with the events recorded in the inscription 'Ry 506' which describes an expedition of Abraha's against the Ma'add whom he defeated handsomely. Kister also records another diverging tradition that Abraha's grandson was attacked by men from Mecca and Mecca was attacked in revenge. It can be seen that there is little firm ground under one's feet in the study of this legend, apart from anything else it has strong affinity with the mythology surrounding the trials of Prince Gautama when becoming the Buddha. He was in the jungles when the prince of Darkness gathered an army including elephants to overawe and defeat Gautama; instead the elephants all fell on their knees and worshipped the future Buddha. Asoka, the great Mauryan emperor of India, on conversion to Buddhism, sent monks out all over the world, as far as Syria and Egypt, to proselytise. Did one reach Mecca and were the later commentators on the Koran doing a little myth-borrowing? The learned and ever-sceptical Elgood discounts the entire story as a piece of medical history. China also has early records of smallpox. Records of it have been put as early as 1000 BC (2), but this has been widely discounted. Another group have put it at 49 AD or just before (3). The consensus appears to be that the first truly recognisable accounts date from the third-century and that description is by Ko Hung. Rolleston, however, will only admit that this description is suggestive of smallpox. There has been a confused attempt to blame the Huns for the introduction of smallpox into China and the disease was called Hun-pox. The story is muddling as the war in 49 was against the Hsiung Nu, a possibly related but different people, and they too have been accused of introducing China to smallpox. The date of the introduction of the disease has been put as late as 317,by Gordon, when it was called *tien hang* (see Wong for a translation). Parker notes a sixth-century record of the disease in China. Just to confuse the story a magisterial view from Needham, the great Cambridge historian of Chinese science and medicine, puts the first mention of smallpox in China as 497. In India Jaggi declines to give a date to smallpox's first recognition but agrees that variolation has been practised for a long time in India.

It is necessary to define terms here. The practice of variolation is old (eleventh-century in China) and consists of giving children the actual disease usually by placing scabs of smallpox in the nostrils. Provided the child survived the disease, and most did, the child was immunised for life and spared the disfiguration of the face which accompanies normally acquired smallpox.

The practise of vaccination dates from Jenner and the late eighteenth-century AD; it involves the introduction of vaccinia by the light but skin-piercing jabs of a needle contaminated with the virus. Vaccinia virus is of obscure origin but was probably the cow-pox virus which cross-reacts with *Variola major*. The vaccinatee receives a very mild disease which merely raises a small papule but this immunises him or her from true smallpox though it had to be repeated about every three years or so to maintain its efficacy. Cooray puts the first description of smallpox in India at about 600 in the Susruta Samleita. Hopkins also believes that there is a description of the disease in the Sushruta Samhita in the 400 version but Jaggi finds no such recognisable reference.

In Europe, Gregory of Tours described an epidemic which swept through southern France in 580/1 (4), which Hopkins, among others (5) is convinced was smallpox, though I think it requires the eye of faith to believe it was not merely epidemic dysentery in some form. The disease described by Eusebius, Bishop of Caeseria in 302 is more convincingly named as smallpox as it includes spreading ulcers, loss of sight and many deaths. Needless to say Hopkins is certain that the Antonine and Aurelian plagues were smallpox. The first undisputed description of smallpox belongs in the Middle East and is that of Rhazes in the tenth-century and from now on we are on firm ground, and smallpox can be discussed in relation to the damage it was to do among the peoples of the world.

Smallpox has had its greatest effects in the New World, but before examining that, its effects in the Old World will be examined. Here the guide is Hopkins, though others have contributed important observations. Cartwright (1972) suggests that it is possible that it was smallpox which drove the Huns into migration from their trans-Baikal steppe home. The Huns beheaded the bishop of Rheims in 451 and this bishop, who, as St Nicaise, was to become the saint of smallpox apparently had had smallpox. This would seem to date smallpox in Europe before the advent of the Huns but one can see how the Huns got the reputation as smallpox-bearers among the Europeans as well as the Chinese.

Smallpox has a formidable record as a killer of rulers, though few or none of these deaths have been of earth-shaking importance. As by no means all of Hopkins' claims for the presence of smallpox can be accepted, so not all of the list he gives us of distinguished victims of smallpox died of necessity from that disease. For instance the death of Pericles can only be ascribed to smallpox if one accepts that the Athenian plague was smallpox, a proposition to which not many are yet ready to subscribe. The extinction of the Magonid dynasty can only be ascribed to smallpox if one accepts that that was the disease which laid low the Carthaginians before Syracuse in 396 BC was smallpox, another doubtful proposition.

The fourteenth-century was overshadowed by plague but smallpox was present and no doubt made its contribution to the epidemics which disallowed any recovery from the demographic effects of the Black Death. In the fifteenth-century as plague began to decline in importance, so the star of smallpox rose both in fact and in the consciousness of man. Hopkins says it killed 50,000 in Paris in 1438, though I can find no confirmation of this. By 1430 smallpox had attacked Iceland and the European settlements of Greenland and exterminated the latter according to Hopkins, with some help from unfriendly Esquimos. Others grant to plague the doubtful privilege of denuding Greenland.

In the sixteenth-century smallpox was endemic over most of Europe, occasionally becoming epidemic and reaching high points in the latter half of the century. In the seventeenth-century smallpox rose to challenge plague and typhus as Europe's most devastating epidemic disease. In 1614 a major epidemic swept over much of Europe and it may have been this epidemic which supplied the disease to the New World. In 1619 smallpox eliminated the Gonzaga family whose Mantua lands were already held in fief to malaria. The heir was subject to the French crown and Richelieu seized the opportunity to gain a foothold in a Hapsburg stronghold and added to the flames of the Thirty Years War.

In this war of the silly and incompetent Frederick against the bigoted Ferdinand, disease was given one of its greatest opportunities. Tilly, Mansfeld, Wallenstein and Gustaphus Adolphus and their lesser hangers-on marched and countermarched over Germany killing, robbing, maiming and starving the populace and carrying with them the germs of typhus, plague, smallpox and dysentery. The crowded military camps, the migration of hordes of homeless refugees all combined to give infectious disease one of its greatest periods. Disease, as discussed by Zinnser, accounted for far more lives than any of the futile battles.

Plague, typhus and smallpox rode with the mercenaries and were to reach first Russia then Siberia, where smallpox was to kill so many that the dead could not be buried. In 1691 another smallpox epidemic in Russia killed off whole towns, though it should be said that given smallpox's usual death rate it is doubtful if it ever killed off whole towns at one blow unless all suffered haemorrhagic smallpox. If indeed a whole town did disappear then it was likely to be the combined effect of smallpox and subsequent emigration. Also in 1691 Spain lost the heir to the throne and his rival in The Netherlands William II, who had tried to take over The Netherlands, and his wife died from smallpox in the mid-seventeenth-century. His son left the Netherlands, and contented himself with his wife's realm of England, though she too died of smallpox. The history of the Hapsburgs is riddled with smallpox as is that of their rivals the house of Bourbon.

Even the Sun-King suffered from smallpox though he very evidently recovered. Britain of the seventeenth-century suffered severely from smallpox and 5% of all deaths were registered in London as due to this disease. After the Great Fire of London which followed on the Great Plague, smallpox grimly fastened on the survivors. In the eighteenth-century smallpox was to take off a Queen of England, an Emperor of Austria, a King of Spain, a Tzar of Russia, a

Queen of Sweden and a King of France. Hopkins claims that the death of Joseph I of Austria from smallpox lost the Hapsburgs the Spanish succession. Louis XIV, having survived an attack of smallpox, lost his heir to it, however he felt reasonably sure of his succession as he had a grandson and a great-grandson. He lost both to smallpox, but the sole surviving great-grandson became Louis XV.

At the beginning of the eighteenth-century variolation was sweeping into Europe from the Middle East, which, in turn, had acquired it from India. By the end of the century smallpox was in retreat before Jenner and vaccination. Not that vaccination was immediately acceptable as the 1802 cartoon of Gilray portrays. Not before time either for in the period 1750 to 1800 Copenhagen alone lost 12,000 to the disease and Sweden lost 27,000 between 1779 and 1784. All this pales before the losses in Russia where one seventh of the children were said to have died of smallpox. In France a tenth of the rural population was said to have died from smallpox. Before vaccination was universally accepted in Europe smallpox continued to take its toll in the nineteenth-century when 800,000 Russians were lost to it. An epidemic of smallpox followed on the footsteps of famine and typhus after the Irish potato crop failure in 1848.

A major pandemic struck Europe in 1824–9, another in 1837–40, the latter killing 30,000 in the home of vaccination – England. The English replied with the Vaccination Act which made vaccination compulsory. The Franco-Prussian War brought not only defeat to France, but the indignity of a smallpox epidemic as well to the home of Pasteur. The negligent French army authorities had failed to vaccinate their recruits. The Prussians were more prescient. Troop movements of raw unvaccinated recruits spread smallpox among the only one third vaccinated French population and 60–90,000 died. French prisoners-of-war carried the disease deep into Germany where it killed 162,000.

Bismark wondered who had won the war. The answer was, as usual, up until very recently, disease! This epidemic spread over the rest of western Europe and to the New World. It was to differentiate sharply between those countries with compulsory vaccination and those without, with the negligent having three times the mortality. At the outbreak of the Franco-Prussian War the anti-vaccination lobby was still powerful, but the statistics defeated them. Despite this Russia was still reporting 400,000 cases of smallpox in the period 1900–10.

Mecca, which had been spared the worst of the plague acted as a great broadcaster of smallpox, an argument for the zoonotic nature of plague, which cannot be easily broadcast along man's lines of communication while smallpox and cholera are, as man-to-man diseases.

Hopkins tells us that the second attempt to introduce Buddhism into Japan from China introduced smallpox as well and was therefore condemned as an importer of disease. Buddhists were flogged and their images destroyed, however the epidemic persisted in spite of the anti-Buddhist activities and when an Emperor became infected it was assumed that this was a punishment for not having accepted the religion and Buddhism was made welcome. Farris shows that epidemic smallpox continued to plague Japan from the sixth to the tenth-century, infecting and often killing Emperors. According to Hopkins it was in

Japan at this time that the red light therapy of smallpox was born. Red cloth was always hung in the patient's room and the red light was said to be beneficial. This practice became strongly embedded in the mythology of smallpox and even in the 1956 edition of Manson's *Tropical Diseases* one can find the following statement: 'The treatment of smallpox with red light has been hallowed by time and custom and it is certainly true that the maturation of the spots is less when they are guarded from light.'.

The story of variolation in China has a period charm. It is said that a famous prime minister Wang Tan lost all of his children to smallpox and when later in his old age he was granted a son he wanted to assure the son's life. He consulted a Buddhist nun from Tibet who advised blowing the scabs of smallpox up the nostrils of the youth and he was thus protected. The Buddhist nun went back to her sacred mountain and became a goddess of mercy worshipped by women as the 'Goddess of Smallpox'. When the Manchus broke through the Great Wall in 1644 they were led by Manchu officers who had recovered from smallpox. The first Manchu Ch'ing Emperor died of smallpox and of his eight sons the third, who had had smallpox, was chosen to succeed him, and a very successful Emperor he proved to be, laying the foundations of the prosperous Ch'ing dynasty.

China was rich and expanding in the seventeenth-century despite smallpox. Hopkins has smallpox in the East Indies in the sixteenth-century and says that there is a part of the Bornean creation myth which tells of a cull of one half of the population every 40 years. He believes that the reaper was smallpox. In India smallpox has been present for a long time, though whether it was present in epidemic form at the Beas in Alexander's time must remain in doubt, despite the belief of some that it was smallpox which turned around his troops.

The Goddess *Shitala* or *Sitata*, who was worshipped as the Goddess of smallpox is said by Hopkins to have a representation in a ninth-century temple in Rajasthan, and to have been worshipped as a goddess of smallpox in the first millenium AD. Nicholas has made a special study of the goddess and her history and finds that, while the name is early, it was then associated with a mild disease and no serious disease is mentioned in association with *Sitata* until the seventh-century AD and was well established by the eighth-century *Sitata* worship was controlled by the Brahmins and became important in south-west Bengal when smallpox added to the tribulations of the disease-ridden Bengalis who were already under pressure from the British, the Maharattas and the Moghul Emperors. This epidemic was to take 3,000,000 lives and, not unnaturally, *Sitata* worship remained strong in these areas. Vaccination in Bengal gave rise to confrontation between the British public health authorities and the Brahmin heads of the Hindu religionists. The vaccine lymph was maintained in cows and the problem was whether a good and religious Hindu could be inoculated with material which was derived from a sacred animal – the cow. The matter was referred to the Hindu equivalent of the College of Cardinals and the decision, much to the relief of the medical authorities, was to say yes to the three main questions; 1. Can a Hindu receive lymph from a cow without sin? 2. Can a

Hindu inoculate cow lymph into a child without sin? 3. Can a Hindu inoculate lymph from one cow to another without sin? Even in 1963 some 26,360 people died of smallpox in India.

For Africa we do not have a great deal of reliable information about the disease in earlier times. Its presence in the millennia BC relies on the diagnosis of smallpox made on the mummy of Ramses V which Hopkins has seen and is certain was infected with smallpox, though others such as Smith and Rosenthal are far from certain. Hopkins, not content with this, claim three more mummies were smallpox sufferers and that the population along the Nile at the time as well as around Lake Victoria-Nyanza, around the Sahara and at Zimbabwe was sufficient to support smallpox. All this is pure hypothesis. Pankhurst found that in Ethiopia there was a belief that smallpox came into the country 1,500 years ago with the Axumite soldiers in 310 or with the soldiers defeated in the 'Elephant War' in 570. Ethiopian records do not allow of any precise dating. There are records of a great epidemic in 1811 and it was said that smallpox was a greater enemy than the locust. Ethiopia was the last bastion of smallpox to fall to the eradication scheme.

It seems that smallpox was carried into Spain by the 'Moors'. Mahommed led the Arab tribes 'inflamed with fanatic fury and contaminated with smallpox' accordinh to Moore. This would mean that it reached Spain from Africa in the seventh-century. Burckhardt, followed by Baker, the explorers of the Nile found smallpox to be common in the Sudan in the early nineteenth-century. Epidemics of smallpox occurred in the Sudan about every 7–8 years and every 16 years in Ethiopia as detailed by Harterig and Pankhurst. The Mahdiyyah period in the Sudan saw major smallpox epidemics in 1885, 1891 and 1895 and was associated with famine and major movements of peoples. Hopkins believes that smallpox arrived on the east coast of Africa in the thirteenth and fourteenth centuries, brought there from India by the Arab traders.

Smallpox played a part in protecting the Portuguese settlements from African attacks, the Portuguese being substantially immune from the disease. This would mean that the African was not immune which would make a nonsense of any claims that smallpox was epidemic in the Kenyan hinterland. Hopkins is sure that the Haj must have carried smallpox from Mecca to Songhai and Mali where the Niger River would have supported the populations necessary for epidemic smallpox. This seems a little elaborate as it could have come down more simply from the north African coast with ex-slaves or Arabs.

In Australia smallpox took a hold only on the aboriginal peoples and the first epidemic among them followed on the arrival of the first fleet with convicts on the east coast, an event not celebrated in the recent festivities. Crumston has shown that there was in fact a delay of one year between the arrival of the fleet and the epidemic among the aborigines which was puzzling. The whites had their worst epidemic in 1881/2 when 40 died, but a half of the aborigines in the area of Botany Bay were swept away. A similar, but far far more tragic story emerges from any study of the effects of smallpox on the indigenous populations of the New World.

CHAPTER 15
Smallpox (part 2)

Are not these thy steps I trace,
In the pure snow of her face?

Spilman, 1602

Borges, the Argentinian poet, opened the first story of his *A Universal History of Infamy* with these words:

> In 1517 the Spanish missionary Bartolome de las Cases, taking great pity on the Indians who were languishing in the hellish workpits of the Antillean gold mines, suggested to Charles V, King of Spain, a scheme for importing blacks, so that they might languish in the hellish workpits of the Antillean gold mines. To this odd philanthropic twist we owe, all up and down the Americas, endless things.

He goes on to list some of these endless things: W.C. Handy's blues, 500,000 dead in the US civil war, the verb 'to lynch' in a Spanish dictionary, the dungeon-ridden Napoleonism of Toussaint L'Overture, voodoo, the habanera. He forgot the most important of all – smallpox.

An English physician of the last century said: 'If America gave us, as people confidently say they did, the great pox, we more than returned the compliment by introducing to her acquaintance the smallpox.'

Smallpox arrived in the New World, as far as we know not long after Columbus landed. He despaired of using the Amerindians of the West Indies on the sugar plantations and he brought in West African slaves to do the work. This introduced the Amerindian to smallpox for the first time and it was almost to wipe him out. The first epidemic was in 1495 and, while it killed hundreds of Spanish soldiers after the battle of Vega Real, Moll says that it eliminated 75–80% of the local Indians on San Domingo. In 1515 another smallpox epidemic killed two thirds of the Indians of Puerto Rico while sparing the Spanish. Then came the Spanish Conquest of Mexico.

Already there had been a number of Spanish voyages of exploration along the coast of Yucatan and the New Mayan Empire (lowland) had been contacted. These Maya were to suffer a major epidemic in 1515 or 1516, which some, including Morley, think may have been smallpox contracted from one of the voyages sent by Velazquez, the Governor of Cuba, that of Valvida, or from the colony set up by Balboa in Panama (1). Velazquez, who had ambitions of becoming viceroy, had been impressed by the stories of gold seen in Maya country and was anxious that another expedition should venture to the Yucatan peninsula.

In 1518 he found the ideal leader in Hernando Cortez and a new expedition was built and equipped. Cortez led this expedition from Havana on February 10, 1519 and picked up a Mayan-speaking Spaniard who was a survivor of the Darien expedition. Cortez landed at Tabasco where he met with some resistance and twice he had to fight to impress his superiority on the Mayans. He gained in these battles the inestimable prize of Dona Marina (Malinche), his future constant companion, interpreter and adviser.

On April 17 Cortez landed at Cempoala (= Vera Cruz) and was quickly in touch with the Aztec King Montezuma. Cortez wanted to march immediately to Tenochtitlan, the Aztec capital on Lake Texcoco near present- day Mexico City. Montezuma refused permission, probably because his sister was in a coma. Cortez had to cool his heels in Vera Cruz for three months, which did not suit his temperament. He decided to march on Tenochtitlan anyway. En route he defeated the Tlaxcalans, later to become his allies, and reached the lakes within which the Aztec island capital lay joined to the mainland by a system of causeways. At this point Cortez learnt that Velazquez, fearing quite rightly that Cortez had no intention of handing over any conquered territory to him, had dispatched a small force under a Pamfilio de Narvaez to recall Cortez and take over from him.

Included in Narvaez' force, (according to Diaz) was the fateful figure of a smallpox-infected negro slave, who, according to one nineteenth-century American historian: 'bravely worked the smallpox for Cortez and the superior civilisation'. A more stupid remark it would be difficult to imagine. Others think that the infection may have come from the Yucatan outbreak but there is no agreement that this outbreak was smallpox. Whatever the truth of all this, in 1519 smallpox had landed on the coasts of the American continent, an event to be compared to the landing of Columbus himself. Cortez, in the meantime, had enjoyed the hospitality of Montezuma and entered Tenochtitlan. He now had to leave in a hurry to outface this new menace to his intention to set up a viceregal territory in New Spain. He left 80 men in Tenochtitlan under his lieutenant Alvarado and dashed for the coast, cannily sending before him those who could bribe Narvaez' men to desert and join him.

He left with only 70 men but was joined by a further 360, who had been out in the countryside scavenging, By the time that he came up with Narvaez, half of Narvaez' force was his anyway. Thus he was able easily to defeat Narvaez and join this force to his own. He now had some 1,300 men and a number of Tlaxcalan allies, who resented the presence of the newly arrived and martial Aztecs. These Tlaxcalan allies began to fall sick with confluent smallpox. Back in Tenochtitlan Alvarado interfered with one of the Aztecs' rituals and they rose against him. By the time that Cortez reached Tenochtitlan again Montezuma had managed to assuage the wrath of his peoples and he was able to welcome Cortez, whom he admired greatly, once again to his peaceful capital. Cortez returned this hospitality by imprisoning Montezuma in the palace of Lord Face of Water. Cortez was trapped too in this palace in a city surrounded by water and by Aztecs wanting their King back. The Spaniards caused Montezuma to be killed.

The Aztec throne now devolved to Montezuma's brother Cuitlahuac, a far cry from the self-tortured peaceful Montezuma, and he attacked Cortez immediately. Cortez had to try to fight his way out of the city along one of the causeways, but without success. Cortez was losing men he could not afford with such a small force at his disposal and he was running out of powder and shot, so furious and continuous were the Aztec attacks. Eventually he broke out at night over a temporary bridge. He got half his force over to comparative safety before the Aztecs cut the bridge. He got 500 men to safety and turned back with some cavalry to rescue the rest but was driven back. Cortez now found himself in a hostile and aroused countryside and in imminent danger of being swamped by Cuitlahuac's warriors from the city. But they did not materialise in any numbers.

They were engaged in an even more deadly battle with Cortez' main ally, – smallpox. There have been other explanations of the failure of the Aztecs to wipe out Cortez there and then. It has been suggested that the Aztecs may have had to pause to sacrifice to their War God, Humming Bird, though without much conviction. Prescott, himself, who barely mentions smallpox, believes that the Aztecs were too busy cleaning up the dead bodies from the streets to pursue Cortez. He puts the fear of putrefaction of the dead bodies and consequent pestilence as the explanation for the desire of the Aztecs to clean up the streets. It is not a notion which need keep us for long. The Aztec knowledge of infectious disease is unlikely to have included any such sophisticated idea, and they must have been used to bits and pieces of dead bodies in their city. It is impossible to believe that a war-like people, who had fought their way to the top of the Mexican tree and who practised human sacrifice on a grand scale, would put off the final defeat of a formidable enemy in 1519 because of some unlikely notion of public health.

The inescapable conclusion is that the disease which had commenced to ravage Cortez' allies, the Tlaxcalans had entered the city and found there the ideal breeding ground of a crowded virgin population with no immunity whatsoever.

Cortez retired and marched around the lake to the north, eventually to Otumba, which a considerable number of Aztec soldiers had also reached. Cortez attacked them and killed their leader Serpent Woman. The Aztecs fled convinced that Montezuma had been right and that Cortez was a god and equally convinced of the invincibility of horsemen and guns and the immunity of Spanish to smallpox. Cortez force reached the city of his allies, the Tlaxcalans. In Tlaxcala he was received with kindness though he had brought the smallpox to them as well as the Aztecs. He now had only 440 men, 20 horses, a few cross-bows and fewer muskets. He needed to lick his wounds and stayed five and a half months in Tlaxcala leaving smallpox to do his work for him in Tenochtitlan. It was in the nature of this man that he should make a further attempt on the capital and he would know that the capital was in the grip of a terrible epidemic and that his force was more or less immune.

By now thousands of Aztecs, including Cuitlahuac himself, had died of smallpox. Supplies of powder and shot reached Cortez, men and horses arrived from the coast and he set about building some thirteen sloops to cope with the defences of the water-girt city. Cortez marched for the lake, meeting no resistance on the way even though some of the mountain passes were easily defendable. The Aztecs, wholly preoccupied with smallpox, had hoped that Cortez would quit the country and when he advanced they offered peace and the occupation of the city as a delaying tactic. Cortez cleared the valley to the east of the city of Aztec forces and launched his sloops. When they were in place he gave his answer to the peace proposals by attacking the city. Although the Aztecs defended themselves, they made no sorties despite their originally superior numbers and interior lines of communication. Cortez had launched his attack at the end of the month of May 1521, and landed from the sloops at the junction of two of the causeways, from there he slowly fought his way into the main city. Twice he reached the city proper but could not maintain himself there.

More Mexican allies joined him as the Aztecs were not locally popular and eventually he established himself in the capital, only to be thrown back once again. Cortez was nothing if not persistent and possessed a view of himself which Montezuma must have seen, that of the eventual ruler of the enormous and rich province of New Spain. He maintained the siege, bottling up the Aztecs in the north-east of the city, crowded together and allowing smallpox a field day. The Aztecs were short of food and dying like flies from rampant confluent smallpox. By now 50,000 Aztecs were said to have died, mostly from smallpox, and Bernal Diaz says: 'We could not walk without treading on the bodies and heads of dead Indians. The dry land was piled with corpses'. There was no longer any need to resort to warfare to capture the city. The besieged were now starved and stricken with disease. The city was a vast charnel house and pestilence had swept off far more than famine. Cortez suspended operations in the hope that the Aztecs would surrender, but most likely to rest his men and patch up his forces. He was now master of a foodless and diseased capital and a promising start had been made on the reduction of the population of Central America from 25,000,000 by 18,500,000 to a mere 6,500,000; a reduction of 74% in the space of ten years or so. Others have different figures but none of them fall below a loss of two thirds. Three million died in the first outbreak and subsequent epidemics kept up an irresistible demographic pressure. If this figure is thought unimaginable one has only to read on and realise the remainder of the tragic story of smallpox and the Amerindian to be able to encompass the extent of the tragedy. Even the Black Death removed only one third of Europe's population and that is often thought to be unimaginable to us today. Smallpox killed in the Americas on an even vaster scale and among a population of comparable size but lacking the chroniclers. It is instructive to recall some of the observations of those who have studied these events.

Duffy writes:

The courage and determination of small bands of Spaniards who pushed into the vast unknown and populous lands cannot be gainsaid, but the glorious victories attributed to Spanish arms would not have been possible without the devastation wrought by the Spanish diseases. Spanish arms performed a notable feat; but it was their most potent weapon, sickness, which made the Spanish-American Empire, and later, as an ally of the English and the French, was to subdue the Indians of North America.

Moll recalls that smallpox was called: 'the live coal that burned its way clear through Mexico'. McNeill writing of the effects of smallpox and the belief in its divine origin says: 'The extraordinary ease of Spanish conquests and the success of a few hundred men had in securing control of vast areas and millions of persons is unintelligible on any other basis'.

Crosby (1967) notes that Cortez and Pizzaro overthrew the two highest civilisations of the Americas in a few months and a few ill-armed Spanish defeated thousands of dedicated warriors with stone-age and early metal-age weapons. These societies had been built up through generations of fierce fighting and their organisation was military and yet they crumbled at the touch of the Conquistadors. To Crosby it seems nigh incredible, despite the superiority of steel over stone, cannon over slings, firearms over bows and cavalry over foot soldiery; despite confusing religious issues and lack of unity, while each factor was worth a hundred more soldiers to Cortez or Pizzaro and, of course, each kept his nerve. But it remains a matter of wonder until it is remembered that the Spaniards had a far more powerful ally waiting in the wings – smallpox.

It has been claimed that neither the Mayas or the Incas had any great epidemics of disease prior to the importation of infectious disease by the Spaniards but this is not strictly true as the Mayas had had an epidemic of some sort before the arrival of the Spaniards and Pizzaro was greeted by Oroya fever in the Andes. It should also be remembered that the conquest of the Incas by Pizzaro did not parallel exactly Cortez' conquest of the Aztecs. Pizzaro had the advantage of a smallpox (or measles) epidemic before his arrival which had weakened the Incas and killed their great Inca Huayna Capac and his heir. Whether this epidemic came from Spanish occupied Panama or La Plata it preceded Pizzaro, who arrived in Inca territory in time to take advantage of a civil dynastic war and the Inca equivalent of Montezuma, Atahuallpa was, in fact, a less than legitimate pretender. Dobyns points out that the Incas and the Andes in general did see a number of epidemics before the great 1720 epidemic (despite claims to the contrary), though the decline and disappearance of the Andean and littoral civilisations are attributed more to a Malthusian crisis than disease.

Crosby goes on to say that when Columbus joined the two halves of the world together he introduced the Amerindian to his deadliest foe – European epidemic diseases; to smallpox, to measles, to plague, to typhus, to malaria, to yellow fever, to tuberculosis, each and everyone a ravening killer meeting an

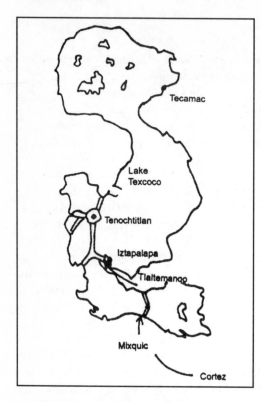

Tecamac

Lake
Texcoco

Tenochtitlan

Iztapalapa

Tlaltemanco

Mixquic

Cortez

III. Smallpox in South America

isolated and virgin population with no previous experience of these infections. The deadliest of these was smallpox. Parry points out that the demographic collapse of the American Indian occurred also in areas where the Spaniards had not penetrated so that the collapse could not be Spanish perpetrated persecution alone and had to be a cause which travelled – smallpox. Ashburn calls smallpox and measles the shock troops of the Spanish Conquest and points out that smallpox was usually confluent and so the more deadly.

It now becomes necessary to examine the scourge of smallpox in other areas of the twin continents. Moll tells us that in 1577 smallpox killed off one third of the population of Venezuela and in 1590–1610 disease headed by smallpox killed two million Indians in Bolivia, Argentina, Chile and Paraguay. Smallpox killed 90% of the Indians in Bogota in 1587–9 and the 1720 epidemic in Peru took off another million. In Peru in 1525 Pizzaro had found five million Indians still reasonably well organised following the rule of Huayna Capac; by 1821 there were only about 650,000 scattered Indians left. Two epidemics were said to have taken off 90% of the Indians from Colombia and tens of thousands from Ecuador in the seventeenth-century. Smallpox epidemics persisted in Mexico through the nineteenth-century. Russell sees a new meaning in the word decimation (not the loss of one tenth but the reduction to one tenth) in Mexico where the population fell from 25,000,000 in 1519 to 2,500,000 in 1608 and attributes the decline to smallpox. The Antilles had their smallpox early thanks to Columbus and lost up to 80% of their Indian inhabitants. Smallpox even defeated the fierce Caribs. Santo Domingo's Indians were reduced from one million to five hundred! by the mid-sixteenth-century. Moll has a chronology of disease outbreaks, including smallpox, in the Americas. The impressive thing about these figures is the size of the per cent dead. No civilisation can stand persistent 80–90% death rates in epidemics. More of such figures can be found in the *Cambridge History of Latin America* edited by Bethell.

CHAPTER 16
Smallpox (part 3)

Thirty million white men are struggling and scuffling for the goods and luxuries of life over the bones and ashes of twelve million red men, six million of them dead of smallpox. . . .

Catlin, 1876.

In North America our guides are Hopkins and Stearn and Stearn supported by many others (1). Smallpox seems to have got into North America by a multiplicity of routes. Canada was infected early and smallpox may have come from Canada into New England but elsewhere no one seems to know exactly where and when smallpox first set foot on the soil of any particular part of North America and the future USA. There is a report of a Dominican friar who tried to relieve the sufferings of the West Indians by resettling them which could have been one source. By the end of the sixteenth-century contact had been made between Europe and the whole of the east coast of North America as well as the Hudson Bay area and European settlements were set up in the following century with the French penetrating up the Mississippi drainage basin. These first explorers did not mention smallpox.

The first major epidemic of an European disease seems to have been in 1616-19 in the north-east of the USA of an unknown nature. Most observers assume that it was smallpox though it may have been plague. This epidemic nearly exterminated the Massachusset, a people of the Algonquin nation, and it swept Boston harbour clear ready for the arrival of the Pilgrim fathers in 1620, a clear case, if one was needed, of the hand of God working on the side of right, or at least righteous. The Puritans found a countryside almost depopulated, and thus New England was made easy to settle. Other Algonquin tribes were affected in their turn, the Wanpanoags, the Pawtuckets and the Abnakis. The Indian population dropped from 30,000 to 300 and the country was made safe for the white man. The population loss does sound like smallpox in the Americas.

In 1633 another outbreak struck and as the local Indians became disenchanted with the European interlopers, this epidemic was hailed by the non-conformist Christians as God's manifest judgement on the savages. God was on the side of the small battalions, or more accurately He was on the side of the small-pox. Because this epidemic was smallpox and it even claimed 20 of the Mayflower's complement; either these were sinners or it was another example of God's evenhandedness despite expert guidance from those in direct communication with Him. All the whites, at some time or another, employed a little discreet bacteriological warfare against the Indian. A trader presented the Indians with a keg of rum wrapped in a flag contaminated with smallpox crusts. Smallpox among the North American Indian was also confluent with a 90% death-rate among cases. The Europeans remained largely untouched, not entirely as smallpox does not work at the behest of man no matter how religious he may be, and the settlers suffered from the disease too though always to a lesser degree. Smallpox now had a remorseless grip on the Indian nations and it swept on west and north; it was only prevented from being even more deadly than it was by the relative sparseness of the population. It had become epidemic up and down the east coast. Boston saw epidemics in 1633-4, 1649, 1666, 1678, 1689, 1702, 1721, 1730, 1752 and 1764 after which variolation and later vaccination began to take effect.

Smallpox killed 700 of the Narraganesset and 1,000 of the Connecticut Indians. Still spreading west it drove the Dutch out of New York state. Dysentery and measles joined in and did nothing to improve the popularity of the Europeans with the original inhabitants. Dysentery led to accusations of poisoning. From 1633 to 1641 there was an almost unbroken sequence of epidemics in the area of the Great Lakes and the St Lawrence River. Here all Indians were attacked bringing normal life to a standstill. The Hurons infected the Algonquin, then the Petuns became infected. In 1669 the Quebec area was attacked again; the Iroquois, who stood astride the path of the disease in 1637 and seemed to have escaped it, now felt its full wrath, catching the disease from their own raiding parties who had been attacking the infected Huron. The Iroquois were the allies of the British in an intended attack on the French at Montreal but the smallpox among the Iroquois aborted the attack. In 1662 another epidemic killed off whole families of the Iroquois.

In 1699 the disease reached into the Mohawk nation who were engaged in a savage war with their neighbours to the north-east. They fought a decisive battle but smallpox ensured that there were no victors; the fur trade running through the area was severely affected for lack of trappers and traders. In 1679 the Five Nations (Iroquois) were again hard hit and again with awful timing the British attempted another attack upon the French, this time at Quebec with the help of the Mohicans and the Iroquois. Again the attack had to be called off as smallpox decimated the Mohicans and destroyed the cohesion of the Five, indeed the Mohicans attempted to join up with the Iroquois, who, scenting smallpox, packed up and went home

The French fur trade was dependent upon many of these Indian nations in the eastern end of the Great Lakes, particularly the Huron. Their destruction by smallpox caused the collapse of this fur trade. Towards the end of the seventeenth-century smallpox broke out in the north-east and penetrated west up the Illinois River attacking the Illinois people and then south into the Carolinas where the Quapaws on the Arkansas River were almost destroyed. Smallpox reached the

Gulf of Mexico and it destroyed the Tunica and the Indians in and around Biloxi Bay. Inexorably it moved on to infect the whole of the Mississippi River. The settlers attempted to quarantine their towns by forbidding the entry of Indians, who, if found in the town, were fined $5 and whipped until free of smallpox. Quite where that curious idea of therapy came from is not known but it does seem to connect smallpox to the notion of crime and punishment.

In the eighteenth-century the Indian resistance to the white invasion stiffened. Until that time the Indians had tended to be involved in wars between the whites and the Iroquois often held the ring in the Franco-British wars. The English, eventually victorious, decided to attack the Iroquois, who it has to be said, had attacked the English on occasion. A confederation of north-eastern peoples under Pontiac attempted to rid themselves of the bearers of smallpox and the struggle dragged on for some time. The Indians were suffering wave after wave of smallpox. In 1703 and 1708 smallpox epidemics entered every wigwam. The dead were buried in a cemetery in Quebec which was dug up in 1854 in order to lay some pipes; the result was a severe epidemic of smallpox, a testimonial to the longevity of the smallpox virus. In 1717 another epidemic broke out among the Five Nations.

These epidemics were said to be made worse by the Indian habit of sweat baths for all illnesses. A wigwam was sealed and steam led into it, the patient or patients sat unclothed in the consequent steam bath. This has generally been considered an excellent method of disseminating smallpox, though the belief owes too much to the popular idea that smallpox is transmitted by touch. Transmission, no doubt, did occur in the steam bath as long as the infected person was coughing and probably the life of the virus in the droplet may have been prolonged by the steam.

In 1731 the Seneca were infected and they fled the epidemic, to the west, thus spreading it far and wide among the Sioux, the Piegans and the Snakes. On the confluence of the White and the Mississippi Rivers the Quapaws were struck early in the eighteenth-century and then were struck again in 1721. In the second half of the eighteenth-century smallpox strengthened its grip on the south. The Cherokee had suffered an epidemic in 1738 and lost one-sixth of their warriors, in 1752 the disease reached the Miamis along the Ohio River and then it moved west to infect all of the Indian nations to the west of the Mississippi. In 1760 it broke out among the Dakotas and the Menominees. California was already infected but another epidemic occurred in 1763. In 1757 the garrison at Lake George at last surrendered to Montcalm, partly because they were riddled with smallpox. Montcalm's Indian allies butchered the survivors and contracted smallpox for their pains. Another epidemic occurred along the Ohio River among the Mingoes, the Delawares and the Shawnees. At the same time another outbreak was decimating the hostile (to the British) Indians in the north around Hudson's Bay.

By 1778 smallpox was in Louisiana and Texas and attacking the Cherokee to the north and east. Scottish traders had explored the north west by 1780 and the Indians resenting the intrusion were preparing to exterminate the intruders. A smallpox epidemic intervened and swept through the whole territory of the upper Missouri, the Saskatchewan and the Columbia Rivers as far north as the Great Slave Lake; the Cree and the Chipewyan suffering the most. In this outbreak the Gros Ventre had suffered too and when attacked by the Kennistenos, the Assiniboin and the Ojibways they were unable to resist and were scalped.

The scalps, of course, proved an excellent method of disseminating smallpox and when the attackers fled before the evidence of the disease they carried it with them in the prizes; only four made it back to the aptly named Dead River. That was sufficient, however, to infect their tribes. The Ojibways fled from the outbreak and carried the disease on to the Rainy Lake. The new hosts to the disease fled to new villages and so on; the epidemic spread along the Pigeon River to Lake Superior at Grand Portage and further to Fond du Lac and Sandy Lake. The Ojibways lost between 1,500 and 2,000.

In the south smallpox got in among the Indians of New Mexico and killed 5,000 (why not before?) In 1780-5 the Dakota were struck and the Cherokee revisited, which broke their last resistance to the expropriation of their lands. Smallpox returned to the east coast in the 1780s and in the north the Crees suffered again. In 1787 the Wyandots were struck then the Creeks in 1789. In 1799-1800 the Ottawas were halved. Now variolation, inefficient as it was could take a hand. Jefferson attempted to promote it among the Indians and later the USA government's treaties with the Indian nations included the supply of vaccine and money for its promotion. The nineteenth-century which brought a gleam of light, also brought to the new government of the USA the vast problem of the plains Indians whom they had pushed to the west of the Mississippi.

In 1801-2 the tribes along the Columbia and the Missouri Rivers contracted smallpox and, it is said, cholera, though this latter is impossible as cholera was not to reach the shores of the USA until 1832. The epidemic spread to the Omaha on Omaha Creek, who decided to die fighting. They formed a great war party and attacked first the Cheyenne and then the Ponca, the Pawnee and the Oto. The survivors went home leaving smallpox behind. The Omaha were reduced to one third of their former population and they lost their great chief Blackbird. The Ponca were reduced to impotence. This epidemic spread to the tribes of Texas in the south and the Missouri in the north.

In 1837 another epidemic hit the rivers but spared the vaccinated. It moved up the Missouri by the agency of the river-boat 'St Peter' and ruined the Mandan, the Arikaree, the Assiniboin, the Blackfoot, the Piegans, the Bloods and the Gros Ventre, killing 6,000 and going on to attack the Dakotas on the Little White River and the Iowa on the Missouri and the Mississippi. It progressed up the Oneota River and met the Crows who took it on to the Flatheads, the Semte'use, the Pend d'Oreilles and the Kalispe ending up with the Spokane and the Colville. A Pawnee war party took it down to the Kiowa, the Wichita and the Caddo. Later it reached the Chippewa and on into Washington and Oregon among the Chinook and the Nez Perce who had escaped earlier epidemics.

This 1837-40 epidemic struck a population of Indians who had been free of smallpox for some time, though the Pawnee had lost 10,000 to an epidemic in 1831. In this second great epidemic of the nineteenth-century the Omaha, the Oto and the Missouri were so few in numbers that they actually merged with the Pawnees so as to resist encroachment by other tribes. In this epidemic the other great plains tribes were hit, the Sioux, who surrounded and were the enemies of the Mandans, the Osage, the Konza and the Ponca all suffered and smallpox reached down to strike the New Mexico Indians again.

Generally it was not the US cavalry which breasted the hill to save the beleaguered settlers in their wagons, it was smallpox. The Sioux defeated the US cavalry at Little Big Horn, but never defeated smallpox. In 1838 smallpox struck the extreme north-west of the USA and the Cayuse Indians. It moved south to California and in the west it was said to have killed between 60,000 and 2-3,000,000 (dubious!) It devastated the Pawnee again and reduced the Osage by half. The Osage infected the Kiowa, the Chickasaw, the Choctaw and the rest of the peoples of the Arkansas River. Mortality figures reached a new high. In British Columbia the Blackfoots and the Kolosh suffered a 60-70% death rate. Smallpox reached for the Arctic and the Aleuts lost 2,000. In the far north the Esquimos also suffered and according to Hare (1954) were nearly wiped out.

The two massive epidemics of 1801-2 and 1837-40 have been said to have cost the Indian peoples 300,000 dead despite the entry of vaccination into the reckoning. The 1837-40 epidemic was said to have had a 98.3% death-rate among sufferers. This was genocide on a grand scale and fit to rank with dreams of Hitler and Himmler, though exceeding their execution. In 1844 a new epidemic struck California and in 1845 the Crows were the victims. The Walla-Walla on the Columbia River were infected. In 1848 the Iowa had their turn and in 1850 smallpox wiped out the Cour d'Alleyne; the Dakota and the Aleuts suffered yet again. In 1852 the Pueblo Indians were dying in their hundreds. In the north-west there was a new epidemic in 1852-4 among the Nitinats, the Nootkas and the Makahs. The Indians along the Columbia, Yakima and Klikitat Rivers were infected and their numbers were reduced from 6,000 to 500. In 1854 the Sioux and the Dakota were the subjects of yet another epidemic.

River ships continued to be the agents of dissemination of the disease, devastation and death. In 1836 the *Clara* brought the disease to the Arikaree, the Mandan and the Assiniboin killing about a quarter of the survivors of the last epidemic. The story seems never-ending as now in 1857 another epidemic sprang up among the Kickapos of Kansas moving on to the Yancton Sioux, the Winnebago and the Squaksins of Washington. Smallpox was now beginning to behave like measles, waiting for a susceptible population to grow up and be struck as well as those adults who remained non-immune. A population will have the greatest difficulty in withstanding such an attack by a killer disease lodged firmly in the terrain. The firm lodgement was ensured by constant importation by whites. The dismal story goes on with epidemics in 1861-2, 1865, 1867, 1869-70, 1872-3, 1876, 1877, 1878, 1882, 1883-4, 1898, 1901,

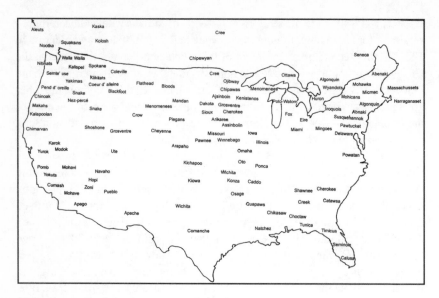

IV. Smallpox in North America.

1906-7, 1912-13, 1914-15 and 1917-18, by the last date quarantine and vaccination were reducing the epidemics to small beer and in the last two outbreaks there were no deaths.

This woeful story is owed largely to Stearn and Stearn and what has been put down here frequently has been copied directly from their account. They estimate that in America north of the Rio Grande there were about 1,150,000 Indians in the early sixteenth-century. By 1907 this figure was less than 400,000 (2). It cannot be claimed that the whole of this drop in population was brought about by smallpox alone, smallpox was assisted at times by measles, typhus, chicken pox and possibly plague. Nor can one claim that disease was the sole agent of devastation.

The Christian moralists of the nineteenth-century tend to blame the demon drink, an innate worthlessness and an inability for self-help for the decline of the north American Indian. Most of this is a pitiful attempt to shift any blame going onto the victims by representing them as unable to cope with life as it was unfolding, so the decline was no fault of the white man. This may well be true but for the inevitability of disease reaching the Indian from the white man. That portion of blame laid at the door of whisky pales into insignificance beside the role of disease. There is no doubt that like most peoples the Indians failed miserably to adapt to the new circumstances, continuing to fight among themselves when oblivion loomed over them. Many another people have done the same without virtually disappearing from the earth. It was disease which tolled the death-knell of the North American Indian and among those diseases smallpox reigned supreme. (3)

CHAPTER 17
Typhus (part 1)

The history of typhus is written in those dark pages of the world's story which tell of the grievous visitations of mankind by war, famine and misery of every kind.

Hirsch (1883)
Handbook of geographical and Historical Pathology

Epidemic typhus is the disease of war and famine and overcrowding. The outstanding fact about the epidemiology of epidemic typhus is that it is transmitted by the body louse (*Pediculus humanus)* and the louse abhors solitude, it likes to snuggle up to one and the only substitute it will accept, even for a moment, is another human being. One has to refer to 'louse-borne typhus' or 'epidemic typhus' when speaking about the pandemic disease as there are a number of other typhuses, transmitted by ticks or mites, which are usually endemic and zoonotic, and do not concern us here. Louse-borne typhus has or had a large number of psuedonyms: War Fever or Febris Militarius, Camp Fever, Gaol Fever, Spotted Fever, Epidemic Fever, Putrid Fever, Fourteen Day Fever, Malignant Fever, Petechial Fever, Spotted Ague, Ship Fever, Sharp Fever, Exanthematic Typhus, Hunger Typhus, Famine Fever, *Tarbadil* (Spanish), *Typhus Exanthematique* (French), *Morbis Hungaricus*, *Matlazahuatl* (Mexican Indian) and possibly *Citua* (Inca), (see Zinnser, for even more names). The names give some idea of its wide distribution, its epidemiology and its virulence.

The organism responsible for epidemic typhus is *Rickettsia prowazeki*, a name which commemorates two of the workers who uncovered its secrets and who were claimed by it. Both Ricketts and Prowazek died of typhus while working on the disease. The rickettsiae are organisms which are larger than viruses and smaller than bacteria, and may have a length of up to a filamentous 2 microns (= 2X 1/1,000,000th of a meter). It occurs in the blood of men and women of all ages in the first days of the infection and so is spread all over the body. The organism in man is infective to lice for the first 11 days after infection. In the louse it grows in the intestine and is passed out in the faeces and eventually kills the louse.

In man the disease has an incubation period of five to fourteen days between the infection by *Rickettsia prowazeki* and the first symptoms of the disease. The first manifestations of the disease are rigour (chills), fever, nausea, vomiting, violent headache and pain in the back and limbs. The breath is foetid and the body gives off a mouldy mouse-like smell according to MacArthur (1959) but a smell of a drying wet umbrella according to Hort. The rash appears after four or five days in a maculate form. It first appears on the wrists or the shoulders and trunk and on the skin folds of the armpit. The skin is flushed and livid, but not hot to the touch. The rash spreads to the extremities and the abdomen but not the face or neck. The maculate appearance of the rash progresses to a mottled irruptive appearance and as toxaemia sets in, the body becomes dusky in colour and the patient becomes stuporous and/or delerious, possibly deaf and usually mentally slow.

After 14 days the fever may disappear in uncomplicated cases and the patient may recover. The disease lasts about two to two and a half weeks and the crisis is usually at about 9 to 12 days after the first symptoms. Up to one third of those afflicted may die, particularly if pneumonia intervenes. An attack confers a reasonable amount of immunity and second attacks are rare and, if they occur, mild. Relapses may occur and are called Brill-Zinnser disease. The disease can be cured by chloramphenicol and a vaccine now exists.

The disease occurs in all parts of the world where the climate requires that clothes should be worn, as the body louse is shy and needs to hide its nakedness under a good layer of man's apparel. Thus the West African, living in a hot and humid climate sensibly wears the minimum of clothing and does not acquire epidemic typhus, but the Ethiopian living in Africa at 2–3,000 metres requires a certain minimum of clothing to protect himself from the cold and has both the louse and typhus. Louse-borne typhus is a disease of the temperate and cold areas of the world. Transmission of the disease is effected by the rickettsiae in the faeces of the infected body louse and is long-lived in those faeces. It continues to live even in the dry and powdered faeces.

The simplest form of transmission is the scratching into the skin of the faeces after an infected louse bite. The louse is a devilishly itchy companion and hard scratching is the order of the day, and thus the faeces may be scratched into a break in the skin. The louse was man's invariable companion in Europe from the sixteenth-century until ours (and no doubt from well before). The head louse sets up such an irritation that heads were shaven and thus the wig was born. Should an infected louse be crushed and the gut contents scratched in the result is the same.

Perhaps more insidiously dangerous is the dry, light, powdered and infected louse faeces which can carry live rickettsiae. This can be blown about and remain fairly concentrated in confined places. It can even infect other lice. If breathed in by man it can set up an infection, or it can possibly gain entry through the eye. This is why this disease is the disease above all of the doctor and the research worker, who are at risk to this form of transmission. The records of typhus are full of details saying all or a high proportion of the attending physicians died of the disease. The doctor, of course, does not have to be lousy to acquire the disease under such circumstances. In the inter-epidemic periods typhus may be kept going in rats transmitted by rat fleas.

From whence did it come? Our great expert in this case is Zinnser, the author of perhaps the best-known and widest-read of historical books written by a doctor and from the view of medicine – *Rats, Lice and History*. Zinnser, apart from being an amusing and sardonic medical historian, was an expert on typhus and was a member of Strong's American team which was responsible for bringing the great Serbian typhus epidemic in 1915 under control. Zinnser assumes that louse-borne typhus developed from a rat and rat-flea origin. He believes that such an infection in rats would occasionally jump over to man and set up dead-end infections which would not be transmitted onwards. When a large enough number of men settled together the body louse entered the scene and the conditions for epidemic disease would be set up and epidemic typhus could commence. Rat-tick-man-rickettsia would act as yet another link in this chain. Whatever the truth of the matter it is easy to see a link from simple rat-flea murine typhus to epidemic typhus of man (1). Leading on from this thought is the designation of the disease of Silenus in the Hippocratic writings (Epidemics, I, ii), which resembles typhus, as one of the cases of a murine typhus spilling over into man sporadically.

Apart from this Hippocratic description and leaving aside the contention that the Athenian Plague was typhus, there are no convincing descriptions of a disease which can, with confidence, be ascribed to epidemic typhus until the second millenium after Christ. That is not to say that attempts have not been made. Keil has pointed out that the louse was present in the Athens of Pericles and even before, tradition having it that the King Agesilaus of Sparta was bitten by a louse while sacrificing to Minerva in the eighth-century BC, so Zinnser's musings that the human body louse may be a recent adaption looses some of their appeal, unless one assumes that all early reports of lice refer to head-lice which do not transmit typhus. The first descriptions of a disease which is accepted as epidemic typhus in the second millenium depends on the medical historian one reads. They are listed in (2). Leaving aside once again the question of the Athenian plague, from this list it would seem that Europe's first experience of epidemic typhus was probably in the eleventh-century with intermittent small outbreaks in the next few centuries. The first major experience with the disease seems to have been in Spain in 1489 when the strain of *R. prowazeki* was brought in from the Eastern Mediterranean.

Epidemic typhus then moved on into Italy, while continuing to sweep through the Iberian Peninsula. Zinnser has translations of Villalaba, the Spanish medical historian on the presence of the disease in Spain at that time. Zinnser is interesting on the first occurence of typhus in the New World but his discussion is not to our purpose here. In Italy typhus decided the critical war between Charles V of Spain and the Holy Roman Empire and Francis I of France by causing the cessation of the siege of Naples by the French troops and allowing the Imperial troops to cut up the retreating French; retreating not from the weaker Imperial forces but from the forces of *R. prowazeki*.

From now on typhus was to play a controlling role in all European wars up to and including the First World War. Typhus moved into Hungary and the Balkans where it was the arbiter of the struggles of the Hungarians to hold back the victorious Crescent flag. Though Hunyardi was to defeat the advance of Mehemmed II with the aid of an epidemic in 1456, it turned on him and he was, himself, killed by the disease, be it plague or typhus. In that troubled area epidemic followed epidemic and typhus was among them, hence Morbus Hungaricus. In 1542 identifiable typhus struck when Joachim of Brandenburg led his Germans into Hungary and lost 30,000 to the disease.

The Germans appear to have been highly susceptible leading Zinnser to believe that at that time Germany was still clear of the disease which was a disease of the North Mediterranean littoral up to the Pyrenees, the Alps and the Danube. But it was spreading. The troops from Germany took it back with them. Typhus was not yet finished with the Turkish-Hungarian struggle and when Maximilian II led his Imperial troops into Hungary to protect his Eastern frontiers from the advance of the resurgent Ottoman Empire under Suleiman I, now free of the Shi'ite Persian threat, he was at first successful. Then typhus took a hand with such effect that Maximilian had to retire and conclude an unfavourable peace with Suleiman. Not only that but his troops dribbled typhus back through Germany, Italy, Bohemia, Austria and eventually France. From its epidemic centre in Hungary typhus spread East as well and took up permanent residence in Poland and Russia where it may well persist today.

Spared, so far, the ravages of war-borne typhus Britain saw it periodically at the famous Black Assizes about which Creighton is so eloquent, but they were minor events, though they do have one interesting sequel. From the fourteenth to the eighteenth centuries disease was thought to be a contagion existing in the air as an effluvium. A preventative was a bunch of sweet-smelling herbs or flowers. Hence the famous portrait of Cardinal Wolsey carrying a pomander of herbs. Today the idle visitor to London may, if present at the right time, come upon a procession of the Justices of the High Court carrying posies of dried flowers, a habit seemingly more appropriate to the female Justice than her associates. These posies were the traditional prophylactic against the typhus as gaol fever and a memory of the Black Assizes where judges died like flies.

In 1538 the Ottoman Empire was to have its last great year, even threatening the Portuguese in Gujerat. From then in the last two decades of the reign of Suleiman and onwards the empire was in a slow decline. The Safavids on their Eastern borders were sapping their strength and manpower. In Hungary the constant battle against the Hapsburgs was not the usual string of successes. A few fortresses were gained but the man-power of the Empire had received a disastrous blood-letting. This blood-letting was, by no means, from enemy action alone, except insofar as typhus was an enemy. This loss of man-power combined with inflation and static frontiers produced a growing internal crisis in the Empire and a slow decline in influence.

The Christian West was eventually relieved of the Islamic threat, at least in part, by grace of typhus with plague at its heels. A new power to the north of the Ottoman Empire shifted its view of the world and the West breathed again. Not that the West had not been busy with other fracas. Incurably aggressive it had been occupied with one succession quarrel after another with the French trying to keep the Hapsburgs out of the major thrones of Europe. The great schism in Christianity did nothing to add to the stability.

The West embarked on the Thirty Years War in the first half of the seventeenth-century, which, in fact, consisted of a number of *causus belli,* each following on top of the last. They made a cockpit of Central Europe filled with marching and counter-marching armies and footloose and unemployed mercenaries. Prinzing, who gives a blow-by-blow account of typhus' ravages of Germany, says that from the start of the war in 1619 (leaving aside the squabble over the Duchy of Julich-Cleves-Berg) to 1630 typhus was dominant but after that it linked arms with plague and they ravaged step for step. In the words of Zinnser: 'The Thirty Years War was the most gigantic natural experiment in epidemiology to which mankind has ever been subjected.'

Hardly surprising when one recalls some of the more spectacular of the indignities to which man subjected man. Can one think of a more effective means of spreading bacilliary, amoebic, and viral dysenteries than the form of torture practised upon the local peasantry by the soldiery to force them to reveal the hiding places of food? Human and animal excrement was poured down their throats through a funnel. A very direct experiment in epidemiology.

Prinzing records the medical history of the Thirty Years War. The Habsburg Emperor, the pious, austere and very catholic Ferdinand II, determined to bring the German adherents of Luther and Calvin, headed by Frederick V of the Palatinate, back to the True Faith. He decided that killing them was the quickest way to do so. A quick victory in Bohemia by the army of the Catholic League under Tilly and the restoration of the only true faith in Bohemia and Moravia convinced him that war would soon bring the Protestant princes of Germany to their senses, and add to the glory and possessions of the Habsburgs. (There were numerous other reasons for these wars including a determined resistance to Habsburg hegemony, but religion was a useful rallying cry, even when the Catholic Majesty of Spain fought the Pope himself. Frederich points out, however, that religion was the core of politics in the seventeenth-century.)

The troops of the victorious Ferdinand drove the defeated Count Mansfeld (the 'Attila of Chrisendom' and the exemplar of Durer's mercenary knight) and his *landsknecht* (mercenaries) from Bohemia, where there was little typhus, and Mansfield retreated down the River Main to the Rhine and on into the Palatinate picking up typhus somewhere on the way. We are now dealing with a disease which travels directly with man and relies only on that man being lousy – a fairly universal state at the time – as Simplicius Simplicissimus frequently avers. Mansfield went through the Palatinate like the wrath of Jehovah, was defeated again on the Rhine and went down it into Alsace laying waste the countryside and seeding it with typhus. From now on wherever the soldier went typhus followed him and played havoc with town and country, such as during Mansfield's subsequent retirement north to east Freisland.

The Counter-Reformation seemed victorious and the unhappy Protestant German princelings lined up to recant and swear allegiance to Ferdinand but this was too much for Denmark and for France though Habsburg Spain rejoiced, both Wedgewood and Runciman discuss this. France felt squeezed between Habsburg Madrid and Habsburg Vienna and Denmark did not relish a Spanish navy regnant from the Mediterranean to the Baltic. Christian IV of Denmark, allied to Gustavus II Adolphus of Sweden, invaded the Empire to help the Protestant Princes but without substantial help from Gustavus Adolphus who was wholly engaged in a war with Sigismund of Poland.

Attacking south Christian was forced to halt short of Imperial Lower Saxony owing to inadequate support from the wavering Protestant Princes and the entry of a new Catholic army into the lists but he managed to riddle Saxony with typhus with help from Mansfield's mercenaries who had joined him. This was the time of spitting babies on the end of lances and the cutting off of women's breasts and by now typhus was taking such a toll along with the other depredations of the ungovernable, unpaid and unsupplied soldiery that princes who hired mercenaries tried to make sure they fought their battles in someone else's territory, (Durer's frequent drawings of a landsknecht shows what an all-pervading individual the mercenary was even a century before the Thirty Years War). In 1624/25 Christian lost various small skirmishes, then Tilly, the general (from Belgium), of the Catholic League was joined by the fateful figure of Wallenstein (3) with 24,000 men and all the armies became infected with typhus.

Count Albrecht von Wallenstein was a Czech adventurer who had volunteered to supply the Catholic league with 40,000 men paid for by himself so long as he could officer it himself. As he had taken virtually all of Bohemia for himself he was well able to afford this army. Wallenstein lured Mansfield away from the main Protestant strength and crushed him. Wallenstein's business was war and he had no desire to see an early conclusion to his source of income, in consequence he delayed before chasing Mansfield. This allowed typhus' great ally – Mansfield and his army of lousy mercenaries to spread the disease now joined with plague and dysentery through Silesia and Moravia.

In the meantime Tilly with some help from Wallenstein's troops had defeated Christian at Lutter-am-Barenberg in August 1626. Christian was forced to retire back to Holstein. Once again the Counter-Reformation cause was triumphant and all its lines of communication from northern Italy to the Spanish Netherlands open. Wallenstein now set out to scour the North and Baltic coasts of Protestantism. Tilly was wounded and the main command of the Catholic troops now devolved on to Wallenstein who carried war, typhus and destruction to the northern seas. He occupied and infected Denmark, Mecklenburg, Holstein and parts of Pomerania. Only one city – Stralsund – with help from Gustaphus II Adolphus held out, but that was enough for Wallenstein who arranged a peace treaty, despite again defeating Christian of Denmark, either from a desire to fight another day or from a genuine desire for peace and some form of catholic dominated tolerance.

Wallenstein with 125,000 men under arms was lord of all he surveyed but had to feed his soldiers. These he billeted wherever he could usually without asking permission and spreading typhus in Pomerania and Saxony. In this peace Christian got back most of what he had lost during Wallenstein's foray to the North except the health of his subjects, and the religious liberation of Germany from Rome.

Gustaphus II Adolphus now freed himself of the Polish war by means of a temporary truce and he viewed the presence of Wallenstein on the south Baltic coast with no enthusiasm whatsoever. Wallenstein, meanwhile, had fallen out with his master, whom he had converted willy-nilly into a near-puppet. Ferdinand II's view of Europe was of an austere almost inquisitional Catholic Europe cleared of heresy and Protestants. Wallenstein preferred loopholes, through which some tolerance could glimmer and Europe could combine against the Turk. Wallenstein retired to his tent and Ferdinand ordered all Church lands, alienated during Protestant rule, to be returned to Mother Church.

This was too much even for the vaccilating German princelings. France viewed a triumphant and assertive Habsburg Emperor with alarm. Richelieu found the excuse to attack the Hapsburgs over the succession at Mantua, (which we have examined in the chapter on malaria). The Pope joined in the attack on the Hapsburgs and, though Wallenstein might seem to have been vindicated, the intransigent Ferdinand dismissed him to pacify his enemies and probably with some very murky and double-dealing interventions from the arch-schemer of France – Richelieu. Wallenstein took his dismissal remarkably meekly.

Into this maelstrom strode the heroic figure of Gustaphus II Adolphus and his dream of a Protestant Europe, in its centre *Dominus Maris Baltici* and a capital in Stockholm. Gustaphus Adolphus was a very able general (compared by many to Alexander the Great) and he fell upon an Empire robbed of the genius of Wallenstein. Though Prinzing does not say so it seems possible that Gustaphus Adolphus' army may already have been infected with typhus from their Polish adventures which would have been infected in its turn by the *Morbis Hungaricus*. In any case as the Swedes swept south they were passing through typhus infected land, they would have slept in the hay or the beds of evicted peasants and acquired their lice infected with *Rickettsia prowazek*i.

The subsequent passage of lice between people is easily enough imagined if one has seen the mode of ridding a shirt of lice by shaking it vigorously in a crowded barracks. So Gustaphus Adolphus carried typhus south again as far as Bavaria. As he marched and counter-marched through Pomerania, Brandenburg and Saxony he left behind him a desert of man-made ravages, typhus and plague. He penetrated west to Magdeburg where he was held up by Tilly but whom he defeated at Breitenfeld in September 1631. He then continued his advance to the west marching through the Palatinate, Bamburg, Wurzburg and reaching Mainz. Eventually he reached the very centre of Imperial power at Frankfurt-am-Main. This cut the Empire's lines of communication with Habsburg Spain and the Spanish Netherlands. It was all getting a bit too successful. Richelieu wanted a neutralized Empire not a destroyed one and Gustaphus Adolphus looked set to bring about a Protestant federation under Swedish hegemony. He had destroyed another army collected under Tilly, who wounded, died a couple of weeks later. An alarmed Ferdinand recalled Wallenstein.

Fuller believes that it was Wallenstein's aim to establish a weakened Emperor at the head of a strong Empire with himself as the Mayor of the Palace (a curiously Merovingian notion) and as Gustaphus Adolphus moved into Bavaria, Wallenstein moved against his lines of communication with the North by entering Franconia and threatening Nuremburg.

Gustaphus turned north to face this threat but was unable to defeat Wallenstein, as many of his soldiers were now down with typhus and plague and he was forced to retreat north. Peace negotiations broke down but Wallenstein attacked Saxony which Gustaphus Adolphus felt forced to defend, despite the Saxon betrayal of the Swedes at Breitenfeld. The Swedes defeated Wallenstein at Lutzen, but Gustaphus II Adolphus was now dead. Wallenstein was discredited and turned on his master only to be assassinated in February 1634, leaving Europe as the playground of Richelieu's plotting. Despite this, the Catholic league was to defeat the Swedes decisively at Nordlingen in September 1634 and a peace was negotiated.

The Swedish troops divided up into battalions of hungry unpaid men and spread death, destruction, typhus, dysentery and plague on their retreat north. Ferdinand, too, was now dead, but the war was not. The war, never of the most chivalrous nature, now descended into sheer ferocity. France declared war on the Empire. The war was carried back and forth, raids reaching to Paris and in its path went typhus. Spain became more active on the Habsburg side. The Spanish forces were crushed at Rocroy by Enghein (Louis, Prince de Conde) and Turenne who went on to invade Bavaria before peace was again negotiated. This spelt the end of an era in European war as the Spanish pikeman, who had dominated Europe for a century and a half gave way to disease (there were too many of them), lack of money (the silver mines at Potosi were failing) and the musket (which required fewer men).

The reason for this rather long-winded account of a war has been to show the sheer amount of territory that was fought over and seeded with disease time and again. The worst devastated areas were Bohemia, Wurtemburg, Saxony and Thuringia, all in the very heart of Europe and where any epidemic disease was best poised to invade new areas. The toll in life was tremendous and the results in terms of religious objectives were nil. Sweden hung on to a bit of Pomerania, France got Alsace (and may have wished subsequently that it had not), Spain kept The Netherlands and the Franche-Comte.

If no great differences to the political map of Europe resulted there were other consequences. There are those who say there were not but a glance at the demographic figures, unreliable as these may be, points in a different direction. Lebrun shows a modest increase of the population of most countries in Europe for the period 1600–1700 except for Germany, Spain and the Italian states. He shows a loss of population in Germany from eighteen million to ten million. Clark says that the seventeenth-century saw a moderate increase in the population of the European countries with the exception of Hungary. Others have said that the German population was reduced by between one third and one half and even by 70% in some areas and this demographic loss was not made up until the second half of the eighteenth-century.

Prinzing claims that Germany lost one half of its population and in detail that Saxony lost 934,000; Bohemia 780,000; Bavaria 80,000 families; Wurtemburg 347,500 and Hesse one half of its population. Individual cities showed deaths well above normal. Leipzig lost between 1618 and 1648 24,450 when its normal death toll would have been 9,000; Dresden lost 26,375 as against a normal figure of 10,000; Breslau 51,843 as against a normal figure of 24,000; Augsburg lost 52,033 as against a normal figure of 16,000 and Frankfurt lost 41,108 as against a normal figure of 15,000.

That disease had spread far and wide is shown by the evidence from Basel which was not directly in the war but lost 14,927 at a time when it would have lost normally only 6,000. If the war persisted in an area that area lost more than half of its population. Given the usual casualty figures of those days of about one battle casualty to nine disease casualties and assuming that the civilian population did little better, then typhus aided by plague and dysentery, even by the most conservative estimate, must have accounted for not less than one half of these losses. Seventeenth-century war, then, as a broadcaster of disease alone was to bring enormous demographic pressure upon the population at the site of the war. Further to that the armies of the Thirty Years War were three to four times as large as those of the previous century and Kennedy makes the point strongly that the economic base for waging war needed therefore to be greatly increased. This could bear down on the poor and the peasants as always.

In Castille, where the major revenue source was the labouring class and where that class, according to Lynch, had come under furious attack from typhus and plague by the end of the sixteenth-century, it was seen that the whole class was slipping into a demographic decline which could only increase. This decline accelerated in the early seventeenth-century so providing less and less for the war ambitions of the Spanish Habsburgs. The demographic decline brought famine in its wake and war reaped its own harvest but the great garnerer of life all over Europe was disease with typhus at the head.

Whatever the reasons for the failure of the Habsburg's attempt to establish a hegemony over Europe, be it economic, military as Fuller believes, or the determination of other states, particularly France, to prevent Habsburg imperial ambitions and the consequent diffusion of Habsburg effort, which is the view of Councell, the demographic collapse of the two centres of Habsburg power – Spain and Austria – must have been contributory to put it at its least and may have been decisive. Wedgewood believes that the demographic and economic decline had commenced before the Thirty Years War, but does not deny that the wars would have accelerated the trend.

CHAPTER 18
Typhus (part 2)

She died of a fever And none could save her,
And that was the end of sweet Molly Malone;
But her ghost wheels her barrow
Through streets broad and narrow
Crying 'Cockles and Mussels alive, alive-o'.

Typhus went on to affect the outcome of every war on the European continent up until the Second World War when its one great threat was aborted by DDT. In the War of the Spanish Succession, Augsburg, which had suffered already, was almost wiped out by typhus in 1701–6 and typhus spread along the Rhine. Typhus broke out again on the Rhine as France and Germany were involved in the War of the Polish Succession. Southern Germany was to suffer outbreaks of typhus again during the War of the Austrian Succession and another outbreak almost wiped out a French army at Ingolstadt.

Typhus took its toll of both sides during the siege of Prague in 1742 with 30,000 dead. No wonder that Germany took time to recover demographically from these depredations. At the battle of Dettingen half the British army was prostrate with dysentery and typhus broke out in their hospital. In the seventeenth-century Ireland was becoming a new focus of dysentery and typhus was to ravage the troops of Cromwell in Ireland. In 1605 Mrs Montgomery wife of the newly appointed Bishop of Derry, Raphoe and Clogher wrote, 'Our Irish visitors sometimes lend us a louse which makes me many times remember my daughter Jane who told me that if I went to Ireland I should be full of lice.' Ominously typhus made an appearance in Londonderry where the Protestant supporters of William and Mary were under siege by the Catholics (with its unfortunate echoes still ringing today). The troops of William's general Schomberg at Dundalk were attacked by typhus and 16–17,000 died. In 1739 the potato crop in Ireland failed, dysentery, relapsing fever and smallpox broke out. Louse-borne relapsing fever is a harbinger of typhus according to Post, and sure enough typhus joined the other diseases in 1720 a forewarning of the tragedy to follow. Creighton notes several more typhus outbreaks of varying severity in Ireland before the disastrous outbreaks of the mid-nineteenth-century.

Immediately after the French Revolution of 1788 when Prussia was poised to invade France and crush the infant revolution it was essential for Brunswick's Prussians to first take the forts of Longwy, Montmedy, Sedan and Verdun. While bypassing Verdun, bombarding and taking Valmy the Prussians were attacked by dysentery and typhus and retired leaving their sick, who in turn infected the French. Later when Verdun was invested the besieging allies were again afflicted with typhus. It could be said that the French revolution's most potent ally at this time was typhus. With the continuation of the wars associated with the early days of the French Revolution typhus continued to enjoy the garnering of enormous numbers of victims. The outbreak in the west spread even as far as Brittany and the Royalist troops in the Vendée. It killed 10,000 in Nantes.

As Suvarof's early victories in northern Italy pushed the French back they infected Nice where one third of the population died. Fourteen thousand died in Genoa in 1799/80 as this epidemic spread. At Austerlitz, Napoleon's greatest battle and his answer to Trafalgar of the same year, 1805, typhus swept away the sick and wounded in enormous numbers from both sides. Austrian Silesia was infected and 100,000 died. Typhus took its toll in the Peninsula War of the early 1810s. Then came typhus' greatest victory.

The greatest invasion of typhus on to the European stage was during Napoleon's retreat from Moscow, an event which broke French power and the domination of Napoleon in Europe. Cartwright (1972) believes that this tremendous blood-letting which nearly wiped out all of Napoleon's veterans was largely the result not of Marshal Ney's General Winter and General Famine but General Typhus. Already typhus had done great execution as it was spread throughout Europe by Napoleon's armies. Hirsch claims this to have been typhus' apogee and Napoleon was the unwitting agent of spread in typhus' greatest epidemic.

Napoleon had scoured his Empire to amass over 600,000 men from France, Italy, Spain and Poland and poised them on the Niemen where the local Polish peasants were able to donate to the army a share of their typhus infected lice. This army, unprecedentally large for the time, heaved itself across the Niemen and reached the Dneiper where 655,000 troops crossed, the central Grand Armée group was 450,000 strong. Within a month 80,000 of this army was sick or dead and in six weeks one fifth of the army was down with disease, largely typhus. Napoleon was unable to bring the Russian army to battle and they kept disappearing in front of him as more and more of his army succumbed to disease.

After nine weeks his sick and bedraggled army stumbled into Smolensk where Napoleon paused to give his physicians time to patch up his disease-ridden army. Soubiran notes that the sanitation practised by Larrey and his army doctors did not include delousing, though they knew typhus well (1) and thought rightly that it was transmitted by the clothing. The death rate continued. Unless Napoleon could bring the elusive Russians to battle soon his troops would be too few and too weak to win him his decisive battle. So he decided to advance on his original target of Moscow and so he hoped, entice the Russian army to stand and defend their capital before he lost so many men that he would lose the battle.

As it was he had only 100,000 fit men for the battle he so desired and the Russians obliged him at Borodino. The battle was indecisive and both sides could claim a victory. Both sides were losing men fast to typhus but the Russians had interior lines of supply and recruitment. Napoleon staggered on to his goal and reached Moscow to find it deserted with no Russian army to be seen but known to lurk somewhere nearby. Some reinforcements brought Napoleon's army back up to 100,000 men but he was losing men to disease as fast as he was reinforced. He had lost seven out every ten of his men and had only one inconclusive battle to show for all his effort. He decided to evacuate and 95,000 men retreated from Moscow carrying what sick they could. These were left behind at Orel and Smolensk to die of typhus in Russian prison camps. On reaching the Dneiper he found he had lost at least another 40,000 men; Marshal Ney's heroic rearguard was down to 20 men. He came back with 93,000 only of his original 655,000, and only 25,000 of his 450,000 strong Grand Armée. These troops straggled back to their homes spreading typhus far and wide particularly in Germany.

Everywhere the French built a lazeret so they started a typhus epidemic. 7,051 died in Konigsberg, East Prussia lost 20,000. In Danzig 11,400 soldiers and 5,592 civilians died. Almost all due to typhus with some help from dysentery and pneumonia. Saxony was prostrated by typhus and in a demographic and economic collapse. Napoleon had collected a new army of young recruits non-immune to typhus and they marched across typhus-ridden Saxony to confront the invading typhus-ridden Russian army (they had lost 61,964 men to disease). Napoleon believed that only those who feared an epidemic disease got it. Typhus killed 21,090 of those new recruits in Dresden alone. Twenty thousand sick were dumped on Leipzig. Eighty thousand sickened and died in 1813. Typhus was bleeding France dry of men and Napoleon suffered a defeat at Leipzig. Zinser writes that he had lost 105,000 in battle and 219,000 from disease.

A hundred thousand starving, defeated and sick men retreated to the Main strewing corpses and typhus on the way pursued by the typhus-carrying Russians. The French army was in retreat and typhus was gaining its greatest heights as it spread throughout central Europe, eventually to the gates of Paris. About two million people contracted the disease in 1813/14 and some 250,000 died in Germany alone. The pleas to Napoleon to give up must have been clamorous and insistent for typhus was bleeding France to death (2).

Post concentrates on the period immediately after the final defeat of Napoleon in 1816–19 and is clear that neither starvation-death nor malnutrition as a cause of increased rates of infectious disease, play much part in increased death rates. He is emphatic that the change in social conditions is the major manner in which famine or want effect the transmission of infectious disease. He believes that the major rise in death rates in the period was in the north-west of Europe and that typhus and smallpox were the cause. There was a typhus epidemic in Europe in 1816–19 with a case fatality of 16–37% and deficiency diseases joined typhus as the famine deepened, all leading to high mortality rates in 1817. Plague now joined the ranks of death and consideration of typhus must give way to the greatest of the epidemic killers.

Typhus was never to have quite such a heyday again but it continued to ravage armies or impoverished countries right up until 1943 when it met its greatest defeat. It found itself face-to-face with DDT. The next step it took on to the world stage was in Ireland, a country which had been familiar with it probably for most of the second millennium after Christ. Woodham-Smith believes that the Irish term 'famine-fever' meant not only typhus but relapsing fever as well and Crawford would seem to wish, at least, to add pellagra to the score if not to replace them all with pellagra in the 1880 outbreak and possibly the 1847/9 outbreak. The general opinion is, however, that the fever which accompanied any wide-spread distress in Ireland in the nineteenth-century was largely typhus, though it has to be said that the descriptions of typhus by the accepted expert, General MacArthur, occasionally owe more to Thucydides and MacArthur' belief that the Athenian plague was typhus than to a sober clinical description of the disease (3).

In 1847 the potato crop was infected with a fungus and failed disastrously in Ireland. As the potato was the staple crop and indeed the only crop of the poor this spelt famine and famine was to strike a population living in filthy conditions where families were more numerous than houses. Over-crowding was the norm and a severe winter would cause even greater crowding together. The population was lousy. Many typhus infected and lousy beggars roamed the streets and country lanes. There was a common belief that starvation caused fever as typhus followed every famine (4).

No proper quarantine facilities existed. This was the situation when in March of 1847 it became obvious that a major epidemic of typhus was gathering force. All Ireland was affected and in some towns every house had a case of fever. A formerly dilatory government passed a Fever Bill in April, and some hospitals were set up. Inadequate as this Bill was and despite the provision of inadequate money the Bill and its provisions eventually bit and was to bring the epidemic under control. By September the dead were buried, the towns partially cleaned up, the hospitals built and quarantine of cases ensured. The Irish hated these quarantine hospitals and would not use them if they could avoid it, so true assessment of the effects of the epidemic are difficult to come by.

However Woodham-Smith believes that ten times as many died of fever as died of starvation and the mortality rates of the typhus cases were very high, 66% even among the better-off classes. The population was thought to have dropped by one quarter and emigration added immeasurably to that, as the people fled the disease and British rule taking typhus with them. Salaman says the population of Ireland in 1841 was 8,175,124 and in 1851 6,552,385, a loss of 1,622,739 this needs to have added to it the figure of natural increase for ten years so the total loss would be in the order of two and a half million in a country of less that ten million people.

Not all of this loss can be attributed to disease and famine, though Salaman believes some million of this figure can be attributed to disease and famine and, as famine does not kill in such numbers, that the majority was due to diseases of which typhus held pride of place. He has typhus death figures of 17,000 in 1846 57,000 in 1857, 46,000 in 1848, 40,000 in 1849 despite a successful potato harvest and 23,500 in 1850 AD and that represents less than half of the true figures. The 'accursed isle' was depopulated. Robert points out that typhus defeats itself by lowering over-crowding so that when good times return the lower numbers of peasants present frequently prevents typhus from taking a hold.

The Irish emigrated with hatred of the British in their hearts, the effects of which can still be seen in such organisations as Noraid. They went to the slums of Liverpool, Cardiff and Glasgow, to a miserable existence still harried by the typhus they brought with them. They went to the New World, to Boston and New York to add a whole new colour to those cities and to donate typhus to them, though the efficiencies forced by cholera on the health regulations of the eastern sea-board ports of the US were able to cope quickly with these importations of typhus.

These quarantine and emigration restrictions forced many a would-be immigrant north to the St Lawrence River where the pressure became so great that the quarantine regulations broke down and typhus entered Montreal and Quebec who both had epidemics though only Montreal suffered badly and more than 6,000 died. The disease-ridden Irish were not popular immigrants but the US rallied generously to their aid, as it continued to do so to the poor, the weary and the down-trodden and it must be said the sick. Proust notes that the Crimean War provided another opportunity for typhus to show its ability to profit from war. In the earlier part of the war in 1854/5 there was little typhus among the allied troops though the Russians were already suffering. In December 1855 to March 1856 The French army suffered severely from typhus and lost at least 7,000 men, over 5% of their army. As many as 17,515 has been claimed as the figure of typhus dead which would argue for 35,000 sick among an army of 130,000. Zinnser claims that among the French army of 309,000, 200,000 were in hospital; 50,000 for battle wounds and 150,000 for disease.

The English lost only 62 dead from typhus. The Russian death-rate is unknown but was greater than the French and included many civilians of the Crimea. The British troops brought it back to Great Britain where some thousands contracted it. The French displayed more energy and ran a strict and effective quarantine, particularly at the Isles d'Hyeres offshore from Toulon and the French civilian population were protected. Typhus, on this occasion, cannot be said to have influenced events, despite the contention of Henschen that typhus killed 900,000 in the Crimean War.

During the First World War typhus was again prominent. Not, however, for some incompletely understood reason, in the trenches of the Western Front where all the conditions for its explosive outbreak were present. Trench fever was present and was caused by another *Rickettsia*. It is said by some that there may have been a cross-immunity between these two *Rickettsia* and so trench fever kept out typhus. The Germans and the Austrians were understandably worried about typhus which was present in the east fronts and tried not to transfer troops from the east fronts to the west. Ackerknecht (1965) says that all nations at war with the Russians in the present millennium have contracted typhus except the Japanese, and the Russo-Japanese war of 1905 was the first to be waged in which the battle casualties of both sides exceeded the casualties due to disease. Hobson thinks that the West Front soldiers failed to become infected with typhus because they were better fed, a curiously old-fashioned view in the nineteen-sixties. Others held that quarantine and delousing held typhus at bay in the west. Whatever the reason the great attacks of typhus were confined from now on to the eastern European countries and the Balkans – to Serbia, Poland and Russia. Of the last, Lenin was to say of his revolution: 'Either socialism will defeat the louse or the louse will defeat socialism.'

In Serbia in 1914 the Austrians attacked Serbia repeatedly and cases of typhus began to appear in the Serbian army in late 1914, when the typhus-infected Austrian army retreated in December 1914 leaving behind them their sick with typhus. Among these prisoners-of-war typhus gained rapid ground and spread to the Serbian troops at Valjevo. The 60,000 typhus infected Austrian prisoners were distributed around Serbia and an epidemic of typhus got under way and increased in that winter of 1914/15 and by April there were 6,000 cases a day. Thus a very severe epidemic of typhus had commenced, the most severe the world has seen, according to Strong and the American team sent to help out (this team included Zinnser).

Serbia had not yet recovered from a war with the Turks and the Bulgars in 1912/13. before she was at war again with Austria and the Central Powers. Cholera had already stretched their medical apparatus in 1913 and Serbia was in no condition to withstand typhus with only a total of 350 doctors. She was to lose 126 of those doctors to the typhus epidemic, six out of seven doctors sick in one hospital and twelve out of fourteen in another of which six died. The death rate among typhus cases was high in this epidemic being 30–60%. The hospitals were hot-beds of infection and the prisoner-of-war camps were infinitely worse. One half of all Austrian prisoners-of-war died of typhus in these camps.

Combined Allied medical relief teams carried out extensive sanitary work based mostly on getting rid of the lice by hot baths and sterilisation by steam of all clothing for now it was known that typhus was transmitted by the louse. They also cleaned up housing, transport and public places, no hiding place of the louse was safe. Thus the epidemic came under control with steam-sterilisation of clothing and other non-human homes of the louse and its eggs holding pride-of-place as the most effective control measure.

Typhus had suspended all military activity by the Serbians for six months (Hare states that typhus killed one quarter of the Serbian army) and had impeded the advance of the Central powers and at its height 2,500 military cases were entering hospital daily accompanied by some 7,500 civilians. However it has to be said that Austria's quarrel with Serbia was not a central event in the First World War.

Further to the east and north another epidemic of typhus was to break out in Poland in 1919. Again an American team was sent to help and Cornebise tells the story. The Americans went in with four columns each containing a bath and one column with a steam steriliser as well. The winter of 1919/20 was too severe for much bathing so the epidemic was not halted. It is an almost impossible task to get people, who are not accustomed to bathing, to do so in cold conditions. They genuinely think you are doing them a fatal damage. The Americans were to find the older Poles preferred death by typhus to the undignified death by bathing. There was also a respect for those companions of a lifetime – the lice, who were held to have prophylactic properties of their own. Poland appears to have survived this epidemic without any permanent damage, but to the east it was more touch and go. From the Russian retreat in 1916 through the surrender and the revolution Russia was to suffer 30,000,000 cases of typhus with 3,000,000 fatalities, a staggering number. No wonder Lenin was apprehensive. But the revolution survived.

Typhus had not given up, it persisted during the inter-war years in North Africa and the horn of Africa and in Korea but it was not again to do the damage that it had wrought in the past. It was to turn up again during World War Two in the concentration camps and the prisoner-of-war camps(5). Stowman tells us that typhus was still present in Bessarabia, sub-Carpathia and Croatia just before the war so its spread into Germany via the displaced persons and slave labour is not surprising. Fiennes says typhus caused more deaths in the German prison camps than either starvation or massacres (?) Crew writing about Sandbostel concentration camp says 389 out of 893 sick died of typhus, a 43% death rate. Berben found that typhus broke out in Dachau in 1943/4 and the mortalities went up from eight a day to one hundred and sixty eight a day mostly in Block 30. They continued to die in Dachau from typhus after their liberation, 2,266 dying in May 1945.

Cloudsley-Thompson believes there were 20,000 cases in Germany between January and April 1945. The Eastern front and the countries over-run by the Russian army must have suffered even worse outbreaks of typhus. Hobson says that Irma Grese, the lady who made the tasteful lampshades from Jewish skin in Belsen, contracted typhus, which seems fair enough. She was nursed to health in order to be condemned to death. Typhus made a last-ditch attempt to become epidemic in the allied West in this war when it broke out in Naples in 1943/4 but this time man was ready for it.

It is difficult to explain the bliss which follows on the insertion of those nozzles up one's trouser legs and sleeves which delivered the DDT powder. The next day one is miraculously delivered from the creeping and crawling, from the vague itches and above all the feeling of uncleanliness. One's inseparable companions of months have all disappeared, no longer fed on German flea powder. No more bets on the race from fingertip to armpit, no more competitions on the ability to roast a louse in a candle flame without burning one's skin. None of this, of course, had any effect upon the progress of the Second World War or the peace but serves to remind us that typhus is not that far away.

In Asia we have much less information. It was known in Beijing in 1868 according to Gordon, and Hirsch claims there was an epidemic, possibly the same one, in north China and Beijing in 1864–6. If the Turks can be said to be Asian then they certainly were greatly afflicted in, for instance the Crimean War and again in the Turko-Russian war of 1877/8. In this latter war the Turks were to suffer from typhus less than the Russians but still lost many men to the disease. In India Jaggi says there is only a small focus of epidemic typhus in the North-West frontier area though zoonotic tick typhus is present in India.

The presence of these endemic forms of typhus in much of Asia may protect against epidemic typhus. It is said to linger in Korea and Hobson says there were 30,000 cases in Korea and Japan in 1945/6. Stowman (1945B) states that there was a very severe outbreak in Iran in 1943/4 which saw 3,000 cases a week at its peak. It is assumed to linger still in Siberia. Here again cross-immunities may play a part. The experimental cross-immunities between endemic tick typhus of Siberia, the tick typhus of North Africa, Rocky Mountain spotted fever and epidemic typhus are complicated but in the field it is possible that Siberian tick typhus may donate sufficient immunity to *Rickettsia prowazeki* to prevent an outbreak of the epidemic disease.

In Africa the great centres have been in North Africa including Egypt and the highlands of Ethiopia. Our knowledge is all confined to the twentieth-century. Barkhauss has noted the disease in the uplands of Ethiopia and I would be surprised if it had not been present in some of the camps established during the recent famines in Ethiopia or in the government camps established for resettlement there. It was still present in Burundi and Rwanda as well in 1981, according to Major. In North Africa there was a major outbreak of typhus in Egypt with 96,000 cases during the Second World War, a further 136,000 cases were recorded in French North Africa. The rest of Africa is seldom lousy.

In the New World we have already seen that the Irish outbreak was transported to Canada. Carter believes that *matlazahuatl* which spread through Mexico for the first time in 1545 was the Spanish *tabardillo* or typhus. Moll has it in Mexico in 1519 and wonders if the disease which struck down the Inca Huayna Capac and swept through Peru was typhus, though Dobyns obviously thinks not. Dobyns believes that the disease which struck Drake's men at Cartegena in 1586 and subsequently swept through South America may have been typhus. Zinnser, as one would expect, is most interesting on the origin of typhus in the New World. He is sure that the head louse was present in the Americas before the Conquest and so the body louse may have been too, though he argues elsewhere that the body louse is a late adaption of the louse family.

He believes that typhus would have had difficulty in surviving the several months of time it took the Spanish to cross the Atlantic, though again it has to be said that a dead infected louse may have continued in its old hiding place in clothing for a long time on people who certainly slept in their clothes on board ship and did not bathe. Such a dead louse could still be infective. Zinnser puts the first definite typhus outbreak in the New World as 1576 in Mexico but says that the 1545 outbreak may well have been typhus. Cook (1946) made a special study of disease among the Mexican tribes and concluded that, while the 1576 epidemic was probably typhus it is not wholly proven. He believes that the disease was not known in the New World before 1519. He finds only reference to gastro-intestinal disorders before the Conquest with little or no epidemic disease.

Moll believes that an epidemic in Guatemala in 1524 was typhus and wonders if the Inca *citua* which occurred every winter and caused 'Inca-death' was typhus. He finds that Buenos Aires had typhus outbreaks in 1621 and 1642, probably brought in by Russian immigrants. The natural disasters which brought enough people together to set off a typhus epidemic were the eruption of volcanoes as in Guatemala and Peru in 1687, 1746, 1773 and 1786. The 1773/4 outbreak in Guatemala brought into being a rudimentary health organisation of sorts. The nineteenth-century saw many outbreaks mostly in Mexico as in 1860, 1864/7, 1875/7, and 1884 and even in the twentieth-century Bolivia and Chile still had cases of typhus. Most often, one will note, in high altitude countries.

In North America the War of Independence saw a small outbreak of what was probably typhus among the New York army when over 8,000 soldiers were sick. Philadelphia had an outbreak in 1837 before the Irish emigration. Surprisingly the American Civil War saw no outbreak of typhus and no one, to my knowledge has provided an explanation for this surprising failure on the part of typhus to take advantage of such a fertile soil for its depredations. It can be said that apart from some possible help to smallpox in causing the tremendous demographic decline of the Amerindians in Mexico, typhus has had little effect upon the Americas.

Typhus, then, has exerted its effect upon history in its influence upon wars and their aftermath. The absence of typhus was one of the main causes for the remarkable fact that the Russo-Japanese war of 1906 was the first in history in which casualties on both sides from battle actually outnumbered those from disease and that only because the long sea journey of the Russian fleet had eradicated most of the infectious disease from those notably disease -prone peoples. The Japanese naval medical services were a model of their time.

It is a surprise to this author, at least, that whole histories can be written of battles without mention of the army's or the navy's sanitation systems or the casualties due to disease let alone any investigation into the nature of the disease which was such a much more efficient killer than the instruments of war. Fuller is able to say that the major causes of the end of the Middle Ages were the Black Death and the discovery and use of gunpowder. This sums up the view that the means of war were of equal importance as disease in the outcome of battle, a view which does not bear a moment's study of the casualty figures. One must also cast doubt on the simple act of war as a significant fact in the decline of populations, while this may be true of emigration on occasion, it is almost never true directly in terms of death-rates.

The demographic collapse in Central Europe in the seventeenth-century was only indirectly due to war. The true cause was disease with typhus dominant, despite what C.V. Wedgewood believes. It is usually claimed too that the desertion of the land was due to the depredations of the soldiers though the cause was surely more subtle. There was a constant demand for more soldiers caused by losses due largely to disease. The peasants who filled these gaps were themselves reduced in number by disease. We come back time and again to disease not to battle or even to licentious soldiery. C.V. Wedgewood feels able in 1938 to write her history of the Thirty Years War without listing a single disease in her index and referring, as she must continually, to all diseases as plague without indicating whether she is using the term specifically or generically. Lord Acton, in his acrid little essay on the same war sees no necessity to mention disease at all. Concannon's view seems more correct when he wrote: 'What is proposed is effectively a reassignment of priorities; and the first step in the discussion is to reconstruct the pallid skeleton of undisputed fact, and then to proceed to argue whether the bones should best be represented clad in the ruddy flesh of battling warriors and heated diplomats or in the blotched, fetid livery of plague and typhus.'

The contributions to history made by typhus were:

1. Typhus decided the war between the Spanish King Charles V and the French King Francis I and led to the confirmation of Charles V as Holy Roman Emperor, the arrival at a point of power of the Hapsburgs.
2. During the Thirty Years War Germany lost half of its population mostly to typhus and the consequent demographic collapse of Central Europe in the seventeenth-century delayed any substantial recovery from the decline already caused by the Black Death and postponed the recovery of Germany until the rise of Prussia. At the same time Hapsburg Spain spent itself in war and was unable to sustain the effort, due in part, to a demographic decline caused by disease of which typhus and plague were the main components.
3. An enormous contribution to the defeat of Napoleon on the road to and back from Moscow with its consequences of loss of man-power that put Napoleon on the slippery slope to final defeat.
4. In World War One it eliminated Serbia as a warring nation and held up the advance of the Austrians into the Balkans. These views are not universally accepted and McNeill, in particular, believes that typhus had no notable demographic significance for the peoples of Europe.

One could end with the words of Zinsser: 'Typhus is not dead. It will live on for centuries and it will continue to break out into the open whenever human stupidity or brutality give it a chance.' Thirty years ago it could have been said this was a counsel of despair dispersed by the magic of DDT. Now in the days of DDT-resistant lice and the continuing brutality shown by man to man in such places as Rwanda it seems as if Zinsser was more far-seeing than had been thought.

CHAPTER 19
Cholera (part 1)

'and thou shalt have great sickness by disease of the bowels,
until thy bowels fall out by reason of the sickness day by day.'
Chronicles, XXI, 15

With cholera we are dealing with a disease whose importance is found in social history and the advent of sanitary legislation. We are also dealing with a disease which is still in a pandemic state in the world today. The great pandemic outbreaks of cholera in the past were Asiatic cholera and were not seen outside Asia until 1829. Incidences of cholera-like disease had been noted before then in Europe and epidemic cholera was present in India before 1829 but it had not escaped out of India until that time. Recently the nature of epidemic cholera has changed and the present pandemic is mostly of the form called 'El Tor', which is milder, though in Bangladesh both the old Asiatic cholera and El Tor cholera exist side by side and the result is far from mild. In this chapter I intend to mention such outbreaks of dysentery (largely typhoid fever and some bacillary dysentery) as appear to have had some effect on important events.

Cholera is caused by a bacterium called a vibrio *(Vibrio cholera)*; typhoid fever of concern to us is caused by another bacterium called *Salmonella (S. typhi, S. Paratyphi A and S. paratyphi B)* and bacillary dysentery is caused by bacteria of the genus *Shigella* of which there are a number of species. First *Vibrio cholera*; it is a very active bacillus, shaped like a comma and about 1.5 to 2 microns in length (two millionths of a metre) with one or two flagella, which, lashing about, give the vibrio a violent spiralling movement and thus its name. The important fact about its spread is that it is passed out in the faeces and is transmitted by contamination, contamination of material entering the human body by the mouth, that is contamination particularly of water but also of uncooked food by means of dirty handling or by flies and by means of contaminated linen and clothing. It is an infection of man only and so is spread along his lines of communication.

It is typically acquired when large numbers of people share the same water for bathing, waste disposal, cooking and drinking. Such conditions obtain on the Ganges, when pilgrims practise their religious observances of mass communal bathing in and drinking of the holy Ganges water. The Brahmaputra and the Yangtse Kiang Rivers have also acted as great transmitters of cholera. Other great foci of spread have been the Haj at Mecca and the pilgrimages to Hardwar in India. The vibrio is susceptible to temperatures above 50°C and to the acidity of the gastric juices, though it is able to survive these if in sufficient numbers.

The disease in men and women is characterised by profuse purging and vomiting of watery, almost colourless material, along with the suppression of urine, muscle cramps, coldness of the skin and body, collapse and death. Symptoms may occur within hours of infection (the size of the infecting dose is critical) or they may be delayed for days. It may start as an ordinary diarrhoeal attack or as full-blown cholera. Besides diarrhoea there may be depression and tinnitus. The diarrhoea will proceed quickly to the profuse watery stools typical of the disease, only containing any amount of faecal matter in the first of the stools. The effusions pour out of the patient and become the characteristic rice water stools, that is like water with white floculi in it. Exceptionally the loss of water from diarrhoea and vomiting may be five litres a day. The passage of urine ceases. The diarrhoea is associated with stomach cramps. The vomiting is the same; some food in the vomit to start with, but rapidly becoming rice-water in appearance. Muscle cramps supervene as the water loss brings about an imbalance of the salts of the blood and body.

The patient goes swiftly into collapse, the skin becomes shrivelled and the softer parts of the body shrink and cave in on themselves. The pulse becomes weak, thready and may cease altogether. The body surface temperature drops several degrees and the blood pressure also drops. The patient becomes comatose after which the patient may recover remarkably quickly or he may die or he may go into a febrile state which can spell recovery. The passage of some urine is a sign of recovery. Death is from renal failure and circulatory collapse. The dangerous period is during the fluid loss, and if this can be counteracted and reversed by fluid replacement then the patient is saved.

While the organism is killed by suplhonamides and wide-spectrum antibiotics such treatment is commonly too late to prevent the deadly fluid loss as even after the organism is killed the effects of the infection go on and the fluid loss continues. So the really important treatment is to replace the correct amounts of fluid and salts in a manner that enables them to be absorbed quickly and usefully. While this can be done with oral replacement fluids in mild cases of diarrhoea, it is a slow method and there may be difficulties about the absorption of some salts through the intestine.

In cases of severe diarrhoea, as in severe cholera it will usually be necessary to administer the replacement fluids by intravenous injection using special sterile fluids. Such treatment if available promptly may turn a 50-70% death rate to one of 10% or less, even lower now as the less virulent 'El Tor' is treated and the fluids improve. There is a wholly unsatisfactory vaccine which requires multiple injections to achieve what is claimed most dubiously to be a satisfactory immunity, more discussion of this can be found in Levine.

On the other dysenteries, typhoid fever (enteric fever) is again the result in most cases of crowding, particularly among soldiers and dubious water supplies. The typhoid bacterium is passed out in the stools of an infected person and from there it must contaminate food, drinking water or other objects conveyed to the mouth in order to infect the next sufferer. Some people are able to remain infected and infective by continuing to void bacteria for years, Gordon notes Mary Mallon of New York ('Typhoid Mary') in particular, and if such a person is a food handler then the situation is made for a local outbreak of typhoid fever. Epidemics are generally the result of an acutely infected person passing out many bacteria and being in a position to contaminate material destined to be taken internally by others. The prophylactic measures of value are always measures of personal hygiene both among those at risk and those in a position to handle food and drink. An efficient waste disposal system is a *sine qua non*. Paratyphoid A is common in the East and Paratyphoid B is common in Europe. All three organisms *(S. typhi, S. paratyphi A and S. paratyphi B)* are small motile rod-shaped bacteria, about 2 to 4 microns in length and 0.5 microns in width with flagella.

All three organisms cause a similar disease. The constant and most prominent feature of the disease is fever which may occur suddenly or more insidiously and the fever may be high or low, with or without relief, and last for variable lengths of time. The major feature of the fever is that it is continuous with only slight fluctuations. For such a fever the pulse rate is surprisingly low. The fever is the result of the bacteria's invasion of the blood stream from across the gut wall. The bacteria's toxins are then produced directly in the blood giving a typical dull and heavy appearance to the skin of the patient with perspiration and flushing. At some time diarrhoea is likely to appear. It may follow after a period of constipation or it may appear immediately after the two week incubation period. On occasion there may be only constipation. There is some pain and unease in the intestine.

As in malaria the spleen will enlarge, though not to the same degree, but the enlargement is quicker and the spleen may therefore be a little tender. After a week the typical rose-coloured spots of typhoid fever appear. Final diagnosis is by the isolation of bacteria from the stools by culture and/or by detection of antibodies to the bacteria in the blood. Chloramphenicol (and the hands of St Paul, Acts, XXVIII, 8) is curative. Mortality is about 10% of cases. There is a vaccine which has to be administered about every six months. Recovery confers some immunity which if constantly renewed appears to confer a reasonably comprehensive immunity. In other words constant stays in typhoid areas seem to reduce the number of attacks.

The shigellas cause an epidemic dysentery which is the most likely candidate for any epidemic dysentery being of any influence in the history of man. Once again we are dealing with an organism which gains entry into man by contamination of his food and water. Epidemic dysentery is a disease of the rainy season in the tropics because, it is said, that in the rural areas the rain inhibits people from defaecating far from the dwellings, the organisms are not destroyed by desiccation and the waterlogged soil retains the organisms on its surface. Waste disposal is absent. It is probably a little more subtle than that. A light rain, as is seen early in the rainy season in the tropics, is ideal for the preservation of and contamination by the organism especially by toddlers. The heavy rain which follows may actually wash away the organisms and it is not until the heavy rains have ceased that the organism is able to lie around again, a menace to adults and children alike. The worst scenario is when the washed off organisms penetrate a standing water supply such as a well or a small reservoir. As before the important transmissions are contamination of food or drinking water or in some tropical countries direct transference of the bacteria from faeces to the mouth by toddlers. Contamination of food and drink may be by flies which can carry the bacteria on their feet or in their intestines or it may be by infected food handlers. In Europe a common medium of spread is milk and/or milk products, particularly ice-cream.

Though it would probably be unacceptable to a bacteriologist it is intended here to treat the shigellas as a group. They too are rod-shaped bacilli of about 1 to 3 microns and do not move of their own volition. The disease they cause is typified by diarrhoeas of varying severity, varying probably with the size of the infecting dose. There will be frequent passage of increasingly loose stools with griping and straining at the toilet. There may be blood in the stools in severe cases. Fever may or may not be present. Vomiting may occur early on or may not be present at all. In mild cases the whole incident may be over in a week. On the other hand, in fulminating dysentery, the temperature may shoot up, the stools become liquid and offensive, vascular collapse can intervene and the patient die. The patient may carry the organism for a long time and act as the starting point of an epidemic. Both sulphonamides and antibiotics are effective. Fluid replacement may be necessary. There appears to be an immunity, the newcomers to an area of contamination seem to suffer more and more often than old-timers.

Dealing first with cholera, transmission is by entry of the vibrio into the intestine of man via the food or drink, but particularly water. A patient may excrete as many as 100,000,000 vibrios at a time and up to 400,000,000,000 altogether. The most common form of transmission of cholera is the contamination by faecal material of rivers used as a water supply or for ritual bathing and drinking such as the Ganges. The second great source is the contamination of such sources of drinking water as wells and reservoirs. The most common time of transmission is the wet season when the water table is high, the loss of vibrios by absorption into the soil is low and the wash off of organisms into rivers is high. It is beginning to be shown that the vibrios may be kept alive and even allowed to multiply in river water by some sort of relationship with water plants. Though there is evidence, as we will see, that cholera in epidemic form was present in India long before the West knew it we have detailed evidence for only one major epidemic there before 1820, though no doubt that is due to lack of information rather than a reflection of a true state of affairs.

According to Wu, Dudgeon thought that cholera was old in China and had been recorded there as far back as 2,500 BC, but not in epidemic form. MacGowan, on the other hand, thinks that cholera was a new disease to China in its epidemic form. Macnamara says that Whang Chu Ho described cholera in the first millennium before Christ but not the epidemic form. Pollitzer (1954A) says that there is a Sanskrit work written in Tiunbet during the reign of T-Song De-Tsen (802-45 AD) which certainly describes cholera.

Wong and Wu place cholera in seventh-century China. Wu says it might have been present in the sixteenth-century and was certainly present in epidemic form in south-west China in 1817 and in Guangchou (Canton) in 1820 having been transported there by British troops from Burma. From Guangchou it moved to Wenchow and Ningpo where it was severe. The cholera stretched all over China in 1821. This was China's 'cholera year'. Macpherson points out that a Portuguese ship which called into China lost 70 men to a disease known as *Pesima Maladia di Flusso* which was thought to be cholera. His later records refer to India.

In India Jaggi says that cholera was well recognised in the Charaka Samhita. He believes that the army of the Zamorin of Calicut was destroyed by cholera as well as malaria and smallpox in 1503 and puts cholera in Goa in 1543. Macpherson has cholera as *mordexin* in India in general in 1599, but specifically in Goa in 1543 as severe epidemic cholera. He finds it in the Arakan Islands in 1602, in Bengal at Seopra in 1670 and in Sri Lanka in 1679. Macpherson records cholera as *mordexin* (Portuguese) in Amboyhna in 1690 and cholera as *bort* (Dutch) in Java in 1965-1712. The Dutch became well acquainted with *bort* which they equated with *mordexin* and it was epidemic in Java many times in the period up to 1817. All these outbreaks appear to have been epidemic cholera. It was prevalent in the Isle de Bourbon in 1716. Macnamara agrees that the army of the Zamorin of Calicut which was struck by malaria and smallpox was also probably subject to cholera as well. The disease had been described as a 'sudden disease which struck with a pain in the belly so that the man did not last out eight hours.'

Macnamara's *A History of Asiatic Cholera* is the great source for the early references to cholera and for the epidemiology of its early pandemics (1). Macnamara quotes Gaspar Correa's *Londras da India* for its mention of the defeat by disease of the Zamorin's army and the 1543 epidemic of cholera in Goa. The Portuguese, he says, called it *Moryxy* and the Arabic name was *Hachaiza* which was its name all over India. The disease caused vomiting, cramps, dimming of the eyes, blackening of the nails of the fingers and toes and an arching of the feet. The number of dead in Goa was so great that they could not be buried. A Dutchman seeing the disease in Goa in 1586-89 called in *mordexin*. This concentration of descriptions of the disease in Goa has no epidemiological significance and merely reflects the source of European records in India in the sixteenth and seventeenth centuries. By the seventeenth-century the records were stretching to the East Indies and this again only reflects the Dutch entry into the Far East. By now European records had cholera in Goa, Batavia and the Indian coast north of Goa as far as Surat.

In the east in Bengal there had been a long tradition of worship of a Goddess of Cholera, who rejoiced in the name of Oola Beebee according to Macnamara or Ola Devi according to Felsenfelt. A temple to the lady was still present in Calcutta in the late nineteenth-century. The story goes that this lady was wandering in the woods one day and stumbled over a large stone which turned out to be the symbol of cholera and worship of this stone was the only true prophylactic against the contraction of cholera. People came from all over Bengal to this forest to worship at the shine. In 1720 or thereabouts an English merchant built a temple for the stone and an idol of the lady, so worship was transferred to the new temple. The new idol was of a carcass on which a vulture is feeding, on the back of the vulture sits the goddess with four hands. On her right sits Munsha, the goddess of snakes and next to her sits Shiva the Destroyer. Next comes a suppliant woman praying to Shiva for the life of her husband who is depicted as dying of cholera. On the other side of the goddess are the idols of Sheetola (= Shitala of Felsenfelt; it will be remembered that she was the goddess of smallpox), the goddess of cholera, and then Shusthee, the goddess of children. A curious sidelight on the activities of the British 'moghuls'. It leaves one in no doubt that epidemic cholera was a feature of life in eighteenth-century Bengal, but did it ever burst out of India and the East Indies before the late eighteenth-century apart from the Isle de Bourbon?

Macnamara would seem to think not and he places it at Madras in 1774, endemic in the Amboo valley, in Arcot and throughout Travancore country in the 1770s. He finds it recorded in Ganmjam in 1781 and lapping up to Calcutta. In 1783 it is said to have killed 20,000 of the pilgrims to Hardwar. The Maharattas at war with Tippoo Sahib lost many to cholera. It was seen in Madras again in 1787 and in 1796 a Franciscan friar listed all of cholera's multifarious names in India. But it was in the 1780s that it first reached pandemic status. Pollitzer (1954A) of plague fame had become in the 1950s the WHO's favourite epidemiologist and was asked to write a treatise on cholera. He agreed with Macnamara that cholera must have been present and indeed prevalent in Bengal for a long time to have generated the rites and worship accorded to it. He believes that such rites could have arisen only in response to a violent and epidemic disease. He notes that it is claimed that there is a monolith in Gugarat dating from the days of Alexander the Great with an inscription reminiscent of cholera.

Pollitzer notes 64 records of outbreaks of cholera as seen by the Portuguese, the Dutch, the French and the British between 1503 and 1817. He also notes the existence of a so-called cholera in Europe in the seventeenth-century including a description by Sydenham himself in 1680 but Pollitzer says this incident did not spread and was not asiatic cholera but rather a form of bilious remittent fever. If cholera did extend its tentacles out of India in this period it was not to the West.

East, however, is another matter. Pollitzer notes that there is a word in China form cholera, *huolan*, which is old and dates back to the Neiching and other very old chronicles, but he claims that this was not true epidemic Asiatic cholera. Pollitzer records a report of cholera entering China from Malacca in 1669 and another of cholera reaching China from the Cormanadel coast epidemic of 1761 or thereabouts. The 1770s epidemic reached Burma, Java and probably Malaya.

This was cholera's first, uncertain toddling steps towards full pandemic status. In all this Pollitzer agrees with Macnamara whom we will now follow.

Macnamara traces the travels of the first great pandemic of cholera which started in Jessore in August 1817. It first showed as an epidemic in the bazaar of this dirty, insanitary and over-crowded town. Calcutta had rumbling cholera at the time and in fact all the towns of the Bengali delta of the Ganges had cholera in the humid wet season. The Jessore outbreak was, at first, thought to be the usual outbreak which could be expected in the humid monsoon and which would, in time, pass. This prediction was tragically wrong for the Jessore outbreak was the harbinger of something new and terrible. Cockburn believes that this is the first time true epidemic cholera occurred and as such was a new disease. De disagrees. It is true, however, that this time cholera was killing in hours and spread quickly out all over Bengal in three months. It went on to overrun Bundelkhand (Vindhya Pradesh) taking the army of the Marquis of Hastings in its path.

It then died down a little but came back in 1818 with renewed force. It occupied all of its usual haunts, then, swift and deadly, it spread to Nepal in the north, to Agra, Delhi, Bombay and Surat in the west and to Bangalore and Seringapatam in the south virtually, that is, the whole of India. Macnamara gives a careful tracing of this epidemic, one needs a detailed map of India to follow him through all the movements of cholera during this epidemic [see Maps V and VI].

Further than this, Asiatic cholera started its overseas travel. It moved on into Sri Lanka and Burma, the latter being involved both by the sea route and by land through Arakan. Shipping took it on to the East Indies where it killed 100,000 in Java alone. It got overland to China. In 1820 it had got to both the Philippines and China by sea and visited all the classic Chinese ports, mostly treaty ports such as Guangchou, Wenchow and Ning Po. It spread up the Yangtse valley. By 1822-4 it was reported well inland both in central and north China, including Beijing. From Beijing it joined the caravans *en route* to Russia. It got to Kyakta and the Chinese border with Russia. In 1822 it reached Japan at Nagasaki from the East Indies and exacted a tremendous toll in lives from the Japanese.

The British sent a small force of soldiers to the Oman in 1820 to assist the Sultan overcome a rebellion. A second group carried cholera from Bombay to the Persian Gulf, and from Oman it moved on to Muscat, Bahrain and then Bushire. It went inland to Shiraz. In the Gulf it reached Basra in 1821 and killed 15-18,000 in three weeks. It proceeded up the Tigris/Euphrates basin to Baghdad, where the Turks were fighting the Persians. The Persian army defeated the Turks near Erevan but were then themselves defeated by cholera. They retreated in terror, carrying cholera into Azerbaijan and Tabriz. From Tabriz it was carried, inevitably, to Teheran, then north to the Caspian and Tiflis; others carried it to Isfahan and back to Baghdad.

The Persian army was by now reduced to 10,000 men and of these, 5,000 then died of cholera. Cholera moved from Tiflis into Astrakhan, where the desperate Russians tried to stop it by quarantine. Cholera also turned west along the caravan routes to Aleppo, and soon to Alexandretta on the Mediterranean coast, also south towards Cairo to the consternation of the Egyptian government. The Egyptians enforced a strict quarantine and seemed to give the cholera pause. Then the weather intervened and in 1823-4 a severe winter stopped cholera in its tracks and it spread no further west from Alexandretta, no further south from Palestine and no further north from the Caspian during 1823. Also from Sri Lanka, by courtesy of HMS *Topaze,* cholera was carried to Mauritius and on to Zanzibar. Cholera did not spread inland from Zanzibar possible due to a lack of sufficient numbers of adjacent people. This was the first cholera pandemic and, though it broke back to and recurred in the Near East and the Caspian ports, it died down by the end of 1823 and stayed away from the world other than India in its epidemic form for six years.

The second pandemic seems to have sprung from the Caspian area and as such could be termed a recurrence of the first pandemic. However, its origins are in dispute according to Pollitzer. Macnamara points out that even in India, even in the Ganges delta itself cholera was quiescent, but not for long. In 1826 cholera started up again in its Bengali home. Macnamara insists and Jaggi agrees that it was from this epidemic that the great second pandemic of the 1830s arose and that it was Bengali cholera in origin that once more reached the Caspian to spread over much of the world. Others (e.g. McGrew) believe that cholera had never left the Astrakhan coasts of the Caspian and that the new pandemic arose from this persisting focus. Hare, (1954) Felsenfeld and Cartwright (1972) all connect the 1830s pandemic to the 1820s pandemic so as to make a continuous pandemic of cholera from 1817 to 1837 with a lull in the middle.

Macnamara has the cholera moving up the Ganges as before from an outbreak in the delta to Benares (Varanasi) then Hardwar (Haridwar) on through the Punjab and via the caravan routes through Afghanistan and Persia and so the Caspian. By 1829 Macnamara has cholera at Bokhara then Orienburg and here Macnamara joins other commentators (with the involvement of Bokhara there is even a theory that the cholera arrived overland from China via the silk route). By 1831 cholera was at the Baltic at Riga and inland at Warsaw. The Russians were in the midst of one of their interminable fights with the Poles and cholera took a terrible toll of the embattled soldiers. This war did a great deal to propagate cholera and help it on its way.

Meanwhile in its southern prong, cholera had reached another of its great allies: Mecca with, of course, disastrous results as the single ritualistic water source had become contaminated. Cholera that year killed about half of the pilgrims on the Haj and took off the governors of both Mecca and Medina. The Haj pilgrims broadcast the disease throughout the Muslim world. The pilgrim route took cholera (here again we have a disease of man only, which therefore travels man's communication routes at the pace of man) to Alexandria and Istamboul, both great entrepots, so infecting the whole north African littoral and Egypt. From Istamboul cholera crept into the Balkans and on to Hungary and the Danube.

In the north, war took cholera to Cracow and north into Russia even as, far as Archangel (2). Cholera swept on to Sweden. Cholera was now reaching out towards western Europe and western Europe was all too well aware of it. A London journal wrote: 'In Asia the fiend was contemplated by us with curiosity, in the wilds of Russia with suspicion, in Germany with alarm, but on English soil with TERROR.' For in 1832 cholera burst on to the European scene via Germany. No one believed it could be stopped, despite the hope Jenner was giving for the control of smallpox, and it awoke distant folk memories of the Black Death. The *Quarterly Review* in 1831 recorded: 'A new pestilence, which in the short space of fourteen years has desolated the fairest portions of the globe and swept off at least fifty million of our race.' The echoes of Gibbon and Justinian's plague are unmistakable. Western Europe had been free of plague for over one hundred years, smallpox was on the retreat and yellow fever was but an infrequent visitor. It was only the lesser races which suffered great epidemics in the opinion of nineteenth-century western Europe.

Cholera came as a very nasty surprise indeed and Europe was in thrall to it. It struck terror into the hearts of a civilisation which had thought that the external world was softening towards it. While the Industrial Revolution had created a hell on earth for the poor, its benefits combined with overseas empires had convinced the ruling classes of Britain, Spain, France, Russia and even in emerging Germany that a new prosperity had come to bless mankind in perpetuity. Cholera, by bringing a sense of hopelessness back into everyday life, dealt this complacency a rude blow. This pandemic also reached the New World where it caused no less panic and despair, though as Major notes, in this first wave it reached only North and Central America.

Creighton takes up the story of cholera's visitation on Britain. There is an eerie feeling about reading Creighton in this day and age, as he wrote his great history of British epidemics in 1891-4 and at the time was still able to reject all the modern theories of disease aetiologies. He would have none of the new-fangled ideas about disease being caused by microscopic organisms transmitted by drinking water or insects when it was well known and established for years that all disease had a cosmo-telluric/miasmatic origin except for a few curiosities like snakebite. Pasteur and Koch failed to convince him. So one stands in awe of Creighton's massive scholarship and meticulous tracing of epidemic disease, only to be set back on one's heels by his refusal to accept work such as that of Snow, who showed that cholera was transmitted by contaminated water in 1854. Snow started work on cholera in this second pandemic in the 1830s. Creighton will occasionally mislead because of this myopia but his chronicling of epidemic disease in Britain is impeccable.

As Longmate discusses, the first cases of cholera in Britain were in Sunderland: a 12 year-old girl called, appropriately enough, Isabella Hazard and a keel-man called Sproate, who had contracted the disease in October 1831. It spread to Scotland, then to Ireland. In 1832 it spread from Britain to France. The distribution of cholera in Britain seems to have been determined to some degree by the concentrations of population though considerable anomalies occurred. Birmingham, one of Britain's largest and most populous cities, remained relatively free of cholera. These exceptions were remarkably lucky for Britain as many of the major areas of potential class struggle and points of social explosion in the Midlands manufacturing centres and the Yorkshire mill towns were spared the worst excesses of the cholera. Someday it would be worth someone's time to examine the water supplies of those places in the 1830s to see if a lack of the opportunity to contaminate water supplies played a part in the relative immunity of these centres to cholera. The sea-ports suffered badly, partly, no doubt, due to reinfection from outside. Manchester, also a port, was severely hit, and as it contained many poor Irish immigrants they were especial sufferers.

Cholera was rapidly emerging in western Europe as a disease of the poor and insanitary, whose water supplies were most prone to contamination. McGrew (1960) believes that the fact that the Reform Bill appeared in the middle of a cholera epidemic was no accident, and we will return to the political aspects of cholera later. This pandemic reached far into Europe in 1832 and had enveloped the Low Countries. It had reached France too late to take any part in the curious revolution which replaced Charles X by Louis Philippe on the July 27-9: the 'Trois Glorieuses' of 1830. Cholera struck Paris the most severely of the French cities, though other cities such as Lille, Lyon, Marseilles and Bordeaux were infected. The Paris of the 1832 outbreak was the Paris of *Les Miserables*, filthy, insanitary and crowded with the poor. The cholera was most severe in the St Avoy area, the streets of which were choked with the dead. One hospital saw 500 patients a day (3). As elsewhere the disease greatly increased class tensions between workers and the bourgeoisie.

Cholera was typically a disease of the poor in France, as it was everywhere else in Europe and the USA. The working classes became convinced that the bourgeoisie combined with the authorities were trying to poison them. The distaste of the bourgeoisie for the poor was reinforced by their carriage of cholera (4). The barricades went up once more in Paris in June 1832 but to no avail and the attempted insurrection was easily snuffed out. Cholera appeared in Granada in the summer of 1833 and by 1834 6,000 were dead from among a population of 65,000, more details of this can be found by looking at Ocana's work. Cholera had visited Germany, Austria (though the mountainous areas were spared), Sweden, Poland and Russia before the spread to the west of the continent. Nowhere did quarantine restriction on movement, however enthusiastically enforced, impede its inexorable movement through the continent. In most of these places, as in France, the poor were convinced that the other classes were poisoning them for Malthusian reasons. Minor riots and rebellions occurred in Berlin, Hamburg and St Petersburg.

Cholera was bad in Europe in 1835 and it swept through Italy in 1835-7 eventually reaching Malta, though this would seem almost certainly to have been a second visit as it is unlikely that Malta would have escaped infection from Istamboul in 1831-2. In 1836 it was again in the Balkans and Vienna. It swept on north-west to Munich and east to Hungary. Continuing these moves it reappeared in Hamburg to the north and Prussia and Poland to the east. From Europe, especially via the poor Irish immigrants, cholera found its way to the North American eastern sea-board at the St Lawrence Seaway and at New York. The Irish, many of whom had already been buried at sea, landed into quarantine on Gros Island in the St Lawrence River about 30 miles downstream from Quebec. Between June 2 and June 23 1832 some thirty thousand immigrants arrived, seven thousand on one day. The quarantine broke down as the Irish, already apprehensive of authority, escaped off the island to Quebec. The first cases of cholera in Quebec were seen on June 8 and cholera was established in the New World. It went upstream to ravage Montreal. As usual there was much cautious delay before the sickness was labelled cholera.

Cholera now took the obvious route up river then down the rivers leading into New York State. This travel by river reflects the main means of transportation in the New World which was justly proud of its waterway system. It also possibly reflects the means of cholera transmission via river-supplied drinking water. In the path of southward advancing cholera, Albany declared a quarantine on traffic coming downstream from the north. Passengers promptly got off the boats to the immediate north of Albany, went west overland, and came into Albany on boats from the unprotected westward direction, according to Chambers. In Quebec and Montreal Bilson writes that the people blamed the government for cholera's visitation and its stability was threatened; cholera became an election issue in Montreal. The medical profession lost much of its prestige and reputation and the inadequacy of the public health administration was cruelly exposed by the non-existent hospital accommodation and the total failure of the quarantine measures.

In New York State cholera found a newly improved canal system ready to transport it all over the state, despite new quarantine laws, and it was by this route that Chambers feels that cholera reached the city of New York, that is from Canada rather than from Europe directly. The first case, however, was a poor Irish immigrant called Fitzgerald, who fell ill on June 26 1832, so the poor Irish immigrants got the blame for the epidemic anyway. It did not help that they were Catholic for the dominant Puritans were already thundering from the pulpit that cholera was born of sin inevitably linked with poverty. It was of no help to the poor that cholera was, indeed, a disease of poverty. Cholera was in Philadephia on July 5 to join the hangovers. By August this outbreak had died down but cholera had spread from Maine across to Wisconsin by means of the efficient canal system and the Great Lakes. All towns on the Erie suffered badly and Chicago was badly hit. By August cholera had appeared in the south.

Any infectious disease in New Orleans was bad news as the Mississippi valley lay open to infection from its mouth. It was wrong of the song to stigmatise 'ole man river' as 'done do nothing'; he carried disease with great efficiency! Sure enough, cholera appeared in St Louis, taking in Natchez, Vicksburg and Cairo on the way, but largely sparing Tennessee. From Cairo cholera went up the Ohio to Pittsburg but could not compete with Pittsburg's notorious weather. According to Chambers and Rosenberg, winter called a halt to cholera's march, but the disease reappeared in 1833 and 1834 before it disappeared for a period. In 1837 cholera got to Guatemala according to Henschen, and in the consequent difficulties the President was overthrown.

During all this time of cholera's sojourn away from its homeland it was quiescent in India. It became epidemic again in the period 1830 to 1845. In 1840 it was reported in Dacca which was to become its second home. Now the deltas of both the Ganges and the Brahmaputra were seeded with cholera. In that same year cholera became pandemic again, spreading from Bengal all over India and Sri Lanka, then east to the Philippines and China, north to Afghanistan in 1842. This pandemic was to travel on to Russia, Europe and the world. This was the second pandemic and will be described below. In Asia, China, Burma, the Philippines, the East Indies, Malaya, Indo-China and Japan (infected from Java) had all been visited by cholera in the first half of the first pandemic from 1817 to 1822 and it is thought by some that China was one of the sources of an epidemic in Russia in 1831. Maxwell says that the 1820-1 epidemic was the most severe in China. It affected mostly the south and he claims that it caused 'myriads of deaths'. Maxwell believes that cholera always started in the south in China but progressed rapidly north by sea and more slowly by land. When cholera reached the Yangtse it would move inland as well.

Maxwell believes also that the arrival of cholera to China was always by sea from the East Indies or from Indo-China. Wu, however, thought that China may have been infected by a land route from Bengal, though not via Burma. Asia, west of India, suffered greatly from the first pandemic. It has been noted that British troops took it to the Oman. From the Oman Persian traders took it all along the Persian Gulf whence the slave trade took it to the East African coast. Iran and Iraq were both severely affected. From infected Bushire cholera moved inland and at the same time moved up the gulf to Basra; from Basra it again moved inland. In the second half of this first pandemic the cholera in Basra had infected the troops of Said bin Sultan in 1827 and it progressed into Iraq, Iran and Arabia where it reached Mecca in epidemic form in 1831.

Macnamara believes that this second outbreak in Mecca may have been fed from an epidemic raging on the Malabar coast in 1833-4. The pilgrims from the Haj took the disease home into the Middle East and North and East Africa. East Africa had been visited briefly in the first part of the pandemic at Zanzibar when it had failed to establish itself. In North Africa cholera spread down the Nile as far as Ethiopia and the Sudan; it also spread along the north African coast to Tunisia in 1834 and again in 1835. Cholera proceeded on to Algeria where French troops were infected in 1834-5 and they may have transported it to Marseilles and Toulon.

Christie in his book on cholera in Africa is most interesting on the advent of cholera on the east coast of Africa and on the infectious possibilities of the Haj. He notes that a Haji may not kill a louse or a flea on his person, though he is allowed to kill kites, ravens, scorpions, mice and rabid dogs. The Haji pilgrim is, therefore, an ideal vector of plague, typhus and relapsing fever. All pilgrims desire a ration of the holy water of Zem Zem which seems apt to cause boils and

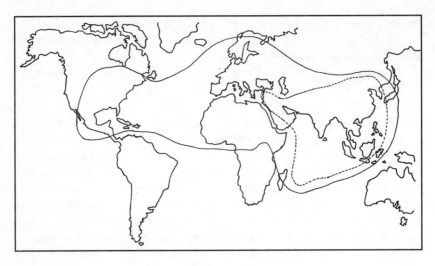

V. The first epidemics of Cholera out of India

diarrhoea possibly due to an over-concentration of Epsom salts in the water. Mecca was filthy and the privies, when they existed at all, were emptied into a hole in the road. Water was in two large cisterns and was rain water imported from far away and very expensive. The Ka'aba and the floors of its hall were washed daily with this water or Zem Zem water and the washings drunk by the devout. Cholera struck this gathering during almost every pandemic, not just once but frequently; Stock records 33 major cholera outbreaks originating from Mecca. It acted as the most potent of the broadcasting agencies of the disease. Australasia and Oceana were never visited by cholera. That was the first pandemic (or possibly the first and second pandemics).

CHAPTER 20
Cholera (part 2)

The inhabitants of Gateshead fell asleep on the 25th of December in perfect security and devoid of panic, but before the sun rose on the 26th fifty five individuals had been seized, thirty two of whom were destined not to see it set.

J. A. Lawrie, 1832

Cholera had become epidemic again in Bengal and the delta of the Brahmaputra in the period 1830-45. In 1840 cholera became pandemic again, spreading all over India and Sri Lanka then east to the Philippines and China, north to Afghanistan in 1842. In China it was reported in Shanghai in 1840 and China was to suffer one of her worst attacks of cholera. From China cholera turned south for Burma and it also joined the caravans of the silk route and moved to Bukhara. This pandemic was to travel on to Russia, Europe and the world. This was the second pandemic of cholera. It encompassed the Caspian, slid south into Iran and Afghanistan and was epidemic in Russia by 1847. At the same time the Middle east was invaded from Bombay and the Haj again became a centre of spread of cholera. Cholera proceeded inexorably into Europe. The infection was in Istamboul in late 1847. Winter now gave cholera some pause but by March 1848 it was again on the march, into the Balkans, reaching Great Britain, Spain and Norway, enveloping all the other countries of Europe on its way. From the Haj it moved again into Egypt, always fertile territory for it.

From western Europe cholera once more curled its cold fingers around North America. So this pandemic almost circled the globe, only Australasia, southern Africa, southern South America, a few scattered islands and central Africa, as far as we know, being spared the misery called cholera. In England some of the first attempts at medical statistics were made by Farr. He likened the visitation of cholera to an invasion by a foreign army; it had killed 53,293 of Britain's citizens during this visit. In France, where medical statistics were relatively advanced, 104,000 were recorded as cholera's toll. In Italy 24,000 were reported dead of cholera. It was this outbreak which allowed Snow to formulate his ideas on the transmission of cholera by contaminated drinking water.

New York became the cholera centre of the USA and this outbreak of cholera was stigmatised by Chambers as being the worst of the disease epidemics which had hit the country (this, given the ravages of smallpox among the Red Indians, has to be a white man's view). Cholera reached New Orleans and roved up the Mississippi valley and also into Texas. It joined the gold rush to California and infected the major towns at the start of the paths to the burgeoning west, St Louis and Cincinnati. Cholera reached down into Mexico in 1853 and on into South America, to Rio de Janeiro and then the Argentine, detailed discussion of this can be found in Moll's work.

In Africa, apart from Egypt, the infected pilgrims from Mecca brought cholera to Massawa on the Red Sea coast of Ethiopia in 1858 and to Lamu on the Kenya coast, then on to Zanzibar decimating Kilwa on the way. The people of Kilwa said that they did not know the disease, confirming the surprisingly confined nature of the first visit of cholera to the east coast of Africa during the first pandemic. Later cholera was to cross Burton's path and prevented his projected exploration of the Rufifi River south of Zanzibar according to Christie. This, then, was the second pandemic (second in the Eurocentric sense) of cholera, which lasted from 1840 to 1864. The third pandemic of cholera is put as starting in 1852 by some including Pollitzer and Macnamara but 1863/5 by others (1). It would take a bold man to differ with Pollitzer and Macnamara simultaneously on the subject of the history of cholera, but Pollitzer, cautious as ever, notes that the third pandemic contained many local recrudescences of what were pockets of the second pandemic and this makes a step by step reconstruction of the third pandemic impossible.

Macnamara and Pollitzer say that this pandemic, like the others, broke out from India, from the 1852 Indian epidemic to be specific, and it had infected Iraq and Iran by 1853. The pandemic moved on from the Middle East and into Europe again in 1853-4 and joined in with the Crimean War, though the source of the cholera of the Crimean War is in doubt as it may have come from the Balkans and southern Europe. The pandemic, as before, moved to the New World. It was present in Rio de Janeiro in 1855 and in the Guianas. There were four epidemics in Mauritius from 1834 to 1862. The pandemic on reaching Zanzibar stayed this time and moved inland as far as Uganda, south to Mozambique and Madagascar and north to Ethiopia.

There was an increase of cholera in Bengal in 1859 and from this increase cholera again invaded the Middle East, moved on into Russia where it became inextricably mixed up with an epidemic already raging. At this time cholera also pushed south in Europe to Spain and in the north invaded Germany, Scandinavia and The Netherlands, though whether this was due to the fresh impetus of a new strain of the vibrio or merely normal recrudescences medical science today is unable to tell us. From Spain cholera moved, once again, into North Africa. It lingered on there until 1864, but had disappeared from northern Europe by 1859.

The fourth pandemic began in 1863 in the Bengal and reached the Haj at

Mecca by unknown means, and, indeed, may have been there already. Whatever the case, maybe in May 1865 the Haj suffered an extremely violent outbreak of cholera which is said to have killed one third of all pilgrims. From Mecca the pilgrims, as always, carried the disease over the Muslim world, especially to Alexandria which was infected by June of 1865. Alexandria then broadcast the disease south into Egypt and via shipping all over the Mediterranean, to Istamboul, the Levant, Ancona and the Adriatic and to Marseilles. From these vantage points cholera moved up through the Balkans into Austria, up and down the Italian peninsula and into France.

This time the cholera was not very severe in France, Spain, Britain, Germany and Scandinavia and it died down in early 1865 only to flare up again in the spring of 1866, when it caused many deaths and great misery. Its spread and effects were abetted by the wars between Prussia and Austria and between Austria and Italy. In 1866-7 cholera killed more than 90,000 in Russia, though the reappearance there in 1867 did comparatively little damage. Russia remained, however, a major distribution point of the disease.

These epidemics treading on the toes of previous outbreaks must have been affected to some degree by acquired immunity among the survivors in the population, weak and uncertain as the immunity to cholera may be. From Russia in 1870-3 cholera spread into Finland and Sweden and on into Prussia, central Germany and Austria/Hungary. Hare (1954) says that this pandemic killed more than 1,177,455 people in Europe (which does not say very much for any putative immunity). The fourth pandemic reached the West Indies from Marseilles and reached New York in 1865-6, probably from Europe by ship, but failed to take a grip because of the severity of the winter, or may have reached the city by ship from Germany in the spring of 1866 just after which a severe outbreak occurred in New York in May 1866. By now the railroad had superseded the canal and river boat, and cholera could travel fast and by first class. From the great entrepôt of New York the railway network stretched out all over the USA. New Orleans became infected by ship but with the passing of the river boat did not act as the great broadcasting centre of disease it had once been. Troop movements greatly assisted the spread of cholera as the USA was in the middle of its civil war. This time cholera spared Canada but moved south to South America, particularly Brazil, in 1866-7.

This pandemic also did great and extensive damage in Africa where it reached Somaliland from India via Aden in 1864. It crossed and recrossed the Red Sea and penetrated Ethiopia progressing through Kenya to Tanzania. From here it crossed into Zaire and went south to Zanzibar, Mozambique and Madagascar. In the north of the continent the Mediterranean shores were invaded at many places and Algeria, Tunisia, Morocco and Libya were all affected in 1865-7. The Moroccan caravans carried cholera to Mauritania and Senegal whence it proceeded to The Gambia and Guinea Bissau.

The fourth pandemic stumbled along for a while before it could be said to have ceased. There were outbreaks of little importance in the period 1873-5 in

Northern Europe and the USA. The Middle East had minor epidemics in 1871-2 and Syria did have a serious epidemic in 1875, though the source of the epidemic remains a mystery. In China cholera was said to be severe and extensive in 1862. Cholera was thought by Hirsch to be active again in India in 1863 and this epidemic infected anew the East Indies, China (where it was mild) and Japan in 1863. If one assumes that the fifth pandemic started in 1881 then the 1879 cholera epidemic in Japan belongs to the fourth pandemic. This outbreak in Japan was very severe and caused 162,637 registered cases and killed 105,786, a 65% death-rate which seems high and, no doubt this is because the deaths recorded are more or less accurate while the case numbers were under-reported as stated by Yamamoto.

The fifth pandemic started in 1881, as usual in Bengal, and moved on to the Punjab which had a serious attack of cholera. The infection was carried to Mecca where cholera was present in the Haj of 1882 and that of 1883. In the latter year it appeared in Egypt and the following year in Toulon which experienced a sharp epidemic. Cholera reached Marseilles and Paris, but France suffered only 10,000 cases with about half of those dying. In Italy quarantine was enforced with its normal total lack of success and Italy suffered about the same number of cases and deaths as France. Spain was to suffer much more sadly in 1884 with about 160,000 cases and 60,000 deaths. Great Britain, though invaded, did not suffer any epidemics, as by now the knowledge that cholera was carried by contaminated drinking water had led to comparatively efficient waste disposal systems and the provision of clean drinking water. New York was again attacked by cholera arriving by a steamer from Marseille in 1887, but it was rapidly diagnosed and isolated. South America, not so well organised, had several severe outbreaks.

Cholera was explosively present in the eastern Middle East in 1892 and from there Russia was again invaded, where the authorities seemed incapable of cleaning up the living environment. In this year of 1892 a severe outbreak of cholera occurred on the Elbe where it was serious only in Hamburg, which had not cleaned up sufficiently its drinking water supply taken directly from the Elbe. Across the river Altona had installed a sedimentation filtering plant and, though using the same water, it escaped the epidemic. In Africa the northern littoral and Francophone West Africa suffered again, while in 1895 and 1896 Egypt saw cholera epidemics. None of these epidemics was, by past standards, severe, according to Barna and Burrows.

During this pandemic India continued to suffer considerable numbers of deaths from cholera and continued to infect its neighbours in Asia. Thus the East Indies and Malaya were stricken with cholera in the years from 1888 to 1896. China had a severe outbreak in 1881-3, then again in 1890 and 1895. Japan was attacked in 1881, 1882, 1885, 1886, 1890 and 1895.

The sixth cholera pandemic commenced, one assumes as always, in Bengal after an exacerbation of cholera there in 1889, and violent cholera epidemics were recorded from Calcutta and Bombay in 1900 to join hands in misery with the plague. Cholera moved westwards as usual into the eastern Middle East. By 1902 it was at Mecca and being broadcast over the Muslim world. It arrived in

Egypt but also via unknown means it moved north around the Caspian and on into Russia. In Russia the disease was slow to assert itself and it was not until 1908 that it spread to the large cities. By 1910 cholera was in full swing and killing more than 100,000.

This pandemic never reached the New World, and caused only occasional cases in western Europe. It was, however, epidemic in Austria/Hungary, northern Italy and the Balkans, usually transported there by Russian immigrants. Mecca was again infected in 1907 and 1911. It is a measure of the devotion to the sacred places of Islam that the pilgrims continued to make the Haj to this home of pestilence just as it is a measure of the inefficiency and fatalism of the Meccan officials that Mecca was to remain for so long a pest-hole of disease, not of course that Hinduism has any better record, and it would take some fine statistical work to establish which religion has contributed more to the spread of cholera. Perhaps it could be argued that the rituals on the Ganges, being more at the centre of the pandemics, were the more culpable.

In the Middle East the sixth pandemic continued to take its toll right up to 1923. Like its predecessors the sixth pandemic moved east from India, and Pollitzer (1954A) has an excellent table which shows the ravages of cholera in the Far East in the period from 1902 to 1922. A recent paper in a tropical medicine journal commences by saying: 'In the twenty five years since the present seventh cholera pandemic started in 1961, studies on cholera and its causative organism have revealed changes in the haemolytic property of El Tor vibrios.'

It is clear from this introduction that we are still enjoying the dubious benefits of the seventh cholera pandemic, but that we are now dealing with a new form of the causative vibrio while still suffering the presence of the old form of the vibrio. The new vibrio, know to science as the El Tor strain causing El Tor cholera, a less severe form of the disease even though it can cause 70% fatalities, arose in the Celebes and spread over much of the world as the seventh pandemic of cholera. It established itself in the Sinai peninsula at El Tor.

Classical epidemic cholera had remained epidemic in Bengal, killing 450,000 people in 1921 according to Christophers, and over 300,000 a year between 1927 and 1930 according to Henschen. In 1961 the El Tor vibrio got into the Ganges delta and supplanted the classical vibrio. The new vibrio proceeded along the same routes as the old vibrio, moving to the Middle East, Europe and Africa. There were severe outbreaks in Africa in 1971. Air transport might have been made for the spread of cholera and in 1974 Europe had several hundreds of cases of El Tor cholera. There is a good map of the spread of the seventh pandemic of El Tor cholera in the first chapter of *Cholera* edited by Barua and Burroughs.

The seventh pandemic killed 1,969 out of 12,917 cases (16%) in the Celebes in 1961. It moved on to the Asian mainland in 1963 or possibly earlier and then rapidly along all its old routes to the Caspian Sea. It is said to have been given pause by a vaccination programme in Iraq and Iran in 1966 and it certainly did appear to halt for a while at the Caspian, but in 1970 it broke out to cover all those areas of the world that previous pandemics had reached, plus another 24 countries. It moved into the whole of the West African coast for the first time (where it still exists as I write) and reached the Horn of Africa in the same year. The El Tor vibrio became established on the Brahmaputra delta in Bangladesh along with the old classical vibrio, where they both are studied intensively today.

Pollitzer said that it was impossible to estimate the final death toll due to cholera as percentage death-rates among cases fluctuate and emigration was considerable; however, the toll must have been in the tens of millions. This, then, is the unfinished story of cholera's visitations on earth, and it is now time to examine its effects upon mankind. Cholera on entering western Europe and the USA met the Industrial Revolution. This revolution was far from universal or evenly distributed but, in general, cholera in the burgeoning West met a population on the increase and a civilisation in the act of expansion. As has been said before, it seems that disease is unable to deal any disabling blow to such populations whether in terms of a stay in the increase in the population numbers or in terms of a pause in their territorial or financial expansion. The Industrial Revolution had provided, unevenly to be sure, the environment in which man felt he could safely increase his birth-rate and the population of western Europe and of the United States of America was in the middle of an explosive increase. Cholera, despite a death toll of at least a million and a half in Europe, made, no impression on the growing population of Europe.

In the Far East, where the death tolls were far, greater – for instance over one million in India alone in the years 1904-6 and so India must have lost tens of millions to cholera overall – cholera, like the nineteenth/twentieth-century plague, did not affect the upward growth of population. Here we must search for some different answer for the unaffected population increase as until recently the Industrial Revolution, has passed by the Far East, except as a victim of commercial exploitation by the West, with the obvious exception of Japan.

If one is to trace an effect of cholera on man's course in this vale of tears then one must look to man's early effective mass struggles against an infective disease. Quarantine had been introduced to combat the Black Death and the subsequent outbreaks of plague but it had no consistent success against plague and against cholera it proved to be a failure time and again. Jenner's vaccination had made the first break through in the fight against smallpox, its use was not envisaged as a global strategy in the nineteenth-century. From the moment of Snow's discovery of the role of drinking water in the transmission of cholera, nineteenth-century western man began attempts to provide sanitary conditions for his fellows on a national basis. Early attempts to control cholera were by no means always successful and tended to rely heavily on the discredited quarantine regulations, but it is not the success of control measures that we need to examine but the effects of the disease and the means of control on social behaviour and health legislation.

While it is true that the vibrio of cholera can be carried on cooled foodstuffs, soiled clothing, flies, night soil fertilised vegetables, by far the greatest agent of carriage is water used for drinking and such waters are usually standing surface waters such as canals, rivers, tanks and wells for those populations we are considering, that is rural populations and those of the world in the last century. The risk is considerably increased if the water is also used for bathing as outlined by Hrisch et al. So effective precautions rely almost entirely on safe disposal of human waste and on the protection of drinking water from faecal contamination. The provision of both these services was a matter for government, locally or nationally.

Before examining the legislation and engineering set in train in the nineteenth-century and the connection between these new developments and cholera, one should look briefly at cholera's intervention into war. Russell, the war correspondent of the London *Times* and one of the first of that glamorous breed, reported the Crimean War and, as is well known, took such note of the British Army's medical services as to make 'The Lady with the Lamp' a figure famous world-wide. Russell reported on the movements of the French First Division who reconnoitred in the direction of Dobrudscha on July 27 1854 from Varna (Bulgaria), mostly it is said to get them out of the camp at Varna in which cholera had appeared, brought by the French themselves from Toulon and Marseilles. On the first night of the march the French were struck violently by cholera. From midnight to eight in the morning of the July 28 1854 six hundred men died. The other two French divisions became involved and the French hospital at Constanta could not even bury the dead. The French lost 7,000 men and took cholera with them wherever they went.

On August 23 the British, who had avoided cholera up until then, were attacked. The light division suffered a sharp assault by cholera. They moved to Monastir. In Varna civilians were dying of cholera. It broke out in the fleets who promptly weighed anchor. The armies were now suffering severely and they decided to evacuate the infected Bulgarian coast. They boarded transports and headed for the Crimea. In the meantime cholera had entered the Russian army and was said to have killed 20,000 men. Cholera then abated only to break out again in the winter of 1854 at Balaklava. Russell says that the dying Turks made the city a cloaca and the sick tended the sick, the dying the dying. Cholera made its contribution to the 7,000 sick in the hospitals at the Bosphorus and at Scutari. The complaints of Florence Nightingale caused the British Army to look anew at its sanitary arrangements and to make the sanitary engineers a new branch of the army, though the lady herself remained unconvinced of the transmission of dysentery and cholera by the faecal contamination of food and water to her dying day in the early twentieth-century.

The French were less prescient and the Franco-Prussian War of 1876 was to catch their army unvaccinated against smallpox. As for other martial events, cholera seems to have had remarkably little effect on the British conquest of India which progressed with apparent smoothness in the midst of terrible cholera outbreaks in that home of cholera. In the, American Civil War Marx obviously thinks that the dysenteries, presumably both bacillary and typhoid, were the great medical enemies of both North and South, and he feels that dysentery lost Gettysburg for the South. Cholera seems to have had little impact.

CHAPTER 21
Cholera (part 3)

Non content d'affliger les peuples de l'Asie,
L'air pestilentiel du Gange et de l'Indus,
Traversant le Thibet vient par la Siberie
Apporter jusqu'à nous le cholera morbus.
Sapet, A. 1836.

In 1832 when cholera struck Europe, it found Great Britain in the political turmoil of the Reform Bill and France in the aftermath and after-excitement of the 1830 revolution, the eviction of Charles X and the ascension of Louis Phillipe. Revolution in France was viewed with a jaundiced eye by other European states who had internal rumblings to contend with without any encouragement to them from the volatile French, much given to exporting ideas and unrest. McGrew (1960) laments the lack of any mention of cholera in discussions by historians of the Reform Bill, the Paris revolution and the Polish troubles of 1830–1. He claims that cholera was vital to these events. The timing is not really with him. The Reform Bill had been formulated in March 1831 and was before the Houses of Parliament before cholera reached Sunderland. The bill stumbled at the first three hurdles and McGrew may have a point in that the presence of cholera and the dissatisfaction it caused with the government's handling of health affairs may have weighed in the balance in favour of the passage of the Reform Bill when it was finally passed in June 1832.

Though cholera exacerbated class hatred in Paris and a few barricades went up cholera was too late to have affected the 1830 events and their aftermath. French historians have not been receptive to the notion that disease may be a factor in the march of history. Neither at the time, (see Stern = Marie de Flavigny = Comtesse d'Agoult = Georges Sand), nor in the twentieth-century do they recognise the presence of cholera as an epidemic in 1832 or 1848, despite (or because of) the great events disrupting France at those times. Cholera gets passing mention in 1832, only because it carried off Casimir Perier, a prominent bourgeois politician. Apart from that the labouring classes were seen as suffering from tuberculosis, rickets and 'les pidémies physiques et morales', whatever that means.

The French historians are much more interested in ideas and the class struggle in the two revolutions of nineteenth-century France and in the leading role of French thought in the wider upheavals of continental Europe. Disease has no part in this thinking until the more detailed and localised historical studies of the 1960s. In Poland again cholera was coeval with an uprising and seems unlikely to have had much influence on events, though it may have fanned the flames, said by the French to be 'made in France'. As the material for study of the health reforms of the nineteenth-century is most easily at hand for the United Kingdom and the United States of America, it will be these countries which receive the lion's share of attention. These two countries were at the forefront of these advances and their contributions were a model for other countries (1). When, in 1832, cholera arrived in the United Kingdom, the Reform Bill was passing Parliament and Jeremy Bentham had just died but had left behind him a definition of a moral and philosophical climate which included legislative intervention into matters of social reform and public health. He also left behind a number of dedicated workers who were to penetrate the workings of government to promote his ideas, culminating in the work of Chadwick, in the Royal Commission's enquiry into the Poor Laws.

Chadwick was able to insert Farr into the system dealing with the Acts replacing the Poor Laws as the Registrar-General of those Acts and thus reliable figures arrived to fuel the fight for sanitary measures to relieve the misery of the poor. These moves were as much driven by the incidence of typhus as the advent of cholera and the central event in the influence of cholera was to wait for Snow's finding in 1849 that the cholera in Soho Square was due to the contaminated water supplies drawn from the Broad street pump. Even then acceptance was slow and often not forthcoming. Chadwick himself had thought, as did most authorities, that cholera and dysentery came from a miasma; even so some of the direction of his proposed measures were to the point as they attempted to clean out or abolish cess-pools and direct excreta down drains or sewers.

By the 1840s there was a Royal Commission on the Health of Towns and it reported in 1844 and 1845. These reports inflamed public opinion, as the parlous state of the living conditions of many of those citizens of the United Kingdom who lived in the towns was made evident, and in 1848 parliament and the people were ready for the somewhat delayed Public Health Act and a triumphant Chadwick was promoted to a place of power where he could work and achieve for himself without having to persuade others to act. This was just in time for, as the General Board of Health came into being with three members including Chadwick, cholera struck again. As Snow's discovery took a grip the Board was able to provide clean drinking water. Sir John Simon was created Inspector of Nuisances for London, a splendidly Victorian title, but had the powers and duties of a public health officer and he transformed the health of London, largely by public health engineering. A new Public Health Act came on to the statute book in 1875 which led via the National Health Insurance Act to the National Health Service of present-day Britain.

The important point to be stressed here is not the direct influence of cholera on the events of the day as advocated by McGrew (1960) but the effect of Snow's discovery of the role of contaminated water upon civic engineering and the immense and largely forgotten empire of the civil engineer under our feet. The view of McGrew (1960), however, should be stated. He feels that cholera is an inextricable part of the social unrest of its day. This theory has its being in the fact that cholera was a disease of the poor with their polluted drinking water supplies and the consequent resentment expressed by the haut bourgeoisie of the poorer sufferers and transmitters of cholera. On the other hand the resentful and oppressed labouring classes, noting that this new disease attacked mainly their own class, suspected and made abundantly clear, their suspicions that they were being poisoned by the authorities, the agents of the new rich.

McGrew does say that in the Great Britain the poor did not blame the rich, there was no class hatred and there were no demonstrations. In Great Britain this lack of class resentment was reinforced by the conscience of the non-conformist manufacturers and employers who were, to some degree, improving the lot of their workers. Elsewhere in Europe, McGrew feels that cholera inflamed all the tensions between classes and in Great Britain a desire for the reform of society, not merely parliament, was in the air also urged on by cholera. McGrew is convinced that it was cholera which provided the final goad which sent the Paris mob into action.

These arguments make cholera a part of the political process. Today many feel that the argument is taken too far and is not supported temporally by the events of the day. If the Carlists saw a connection between cholera and liberalism why is this not mentioned by the French historians occupied with French thought of the time? The point about the poisoning of relations between the new rich and the workers is well taken, though the very thought would send Marx spinning in his grave, but did it bring forth important consequences? It is difficult to believe it was any more than a bit of mud which stuck. At a time of tension anything will be believed and used to fuel the fire. If it raises the temperature so much the better.

One can appeal to the resentment felt by the English radicals at the powers taken by the government to combat disease and their consequent decision not to believe the new theory that cholera was transmitted by contaminated drinking water, another classic example of political theory overcoming fact and logic. McGrew has to admit that, despite this resentment which included dismay at the inability of anyone to do anything effective about the disease, the public never broke out into panic and total demoralisation in Britain as they had during the Black Death. Discontent was fanned, but no breakup of established institutions ensued in Britain.

A magisterial view comes from the pen of Asa Briggs. He supports McGrew in stating that cholera, wherever it appeared, reinforced social apprehension, tested municipal structures and their efficiency and threw into cruel relief the shortcomings in the administrative structures, political platforms and social mores. He notes that in the world's most advanced industrial area, – the cotton mill towns of Yorkshire and Lancashire – the incidence of cholera was much lower than other areas if not actually absent and the class conflict in these, the most industrialised towns, which might have resulted from severe cholera was not seen. Also Birmingham, the great centre of reform, had little cholera. So Great Britain was fortuitously spared some of the possible unrest consequent upon cholera. Briggs believes that a search for the political significance of cholera in the Great Britain requires a careful individual dissection, locality by locality, to build up a true picture. He points to the same need in France, where Lyons, a key industrial area, also had little cholera. This disease attacked in an unpredictable manner and a sufficient concentration of the disease to strike off the spark causing fear, anger and panic was not always present. Briggs does believe that cholera added another dimension to the political volatility of the Paris scene in 1832 by its inveterate inequality and attack of the poor. There is no doubt in Brigg's mind that it added an edge to social conflict (though Durey would disagree).

Briggs notes that in India it did not, however, add to the Indians' resentment of the rule of the British Raj. While in Paris and London the advent of cholera caused some anti-clericism, in other places it reinforced religious belief and the reliance on religion. It was, of course, convenient for some of the more ardent church-goers to believe that cholera, a disease of the poor, was God's judgement on sin and sinners, for who could doubt that Hogarth's gin-sodden outcasts were a just target for divine displeasure. In Paris the ejection of the last of the Bourbons in 1830 and the cessation of cholera were not thought to be disconnected with all the logic of enthusiasm. The end justified the means.

The Church of England leaned towards the divine displeasure theory in 1832 but did initiate charities and supported public health legisaltion. The Western world was a commercial one and the restriction of trade inevitably brought trouble with the mercantile class, so quarantines of any sort were highly unpopular with the very class upon whom Britain's prosperity depended. The propensity of the municipal authorities, in the grip of the merchants, was always to play down the existence of cholera or to flatly deny its presence. This in turn irritated the target of cholera, the working classes. So Briggs tends to label cholera as the disease of class hatred but warns that this was not universal and enjoyed peaks and troughs.

By 1848 the impetus to obey sanitation laws and various public protective measures was greater than in 1832 and the Public Health Act of 1849 had a fair wind from cholera and parliamentary business was conducted at an unwonten pace. On the whole the 1848 epidemic was much more democratic than the previous outbreak and tended to attack across a wider social spectrum so legislation and public health became a more important outcome of the cholera epidemic than the exacerbation of class differences which were a feature of the first epidemic. Despite this, sanitary improvements were slow to come, after all they cost money and Britain was trying to maintain a world-wide empire on a shoestring.

Neither the French nor the Germans, let alone the Spanish, the Italians, the Austrians and the Russians, were fully paid-up members of the Industrial Revolution as yet. Briggs points out that the revolution in public health legislation was not being fuelled by the masses but by a small intellectual minority, who saw man wresting his destiny from chance and fate. Durey notes the failure of the planned demonstration in London in March 1832, which was to attack the government and change it so as to cause the disappearance of cholera; he tends to discount the effect of cholera on the class struggles of the day in Britain.

Morris finds that cholera was all things to all men and was used as grist to whatever mill they were grinding at the time. The upper and middle classes saw it as a drag upon commerce; the working classes saw it as a direct threat to their lives and as a trick to deliver them either into the hands of the doctors or the ruling classes. The view of cholera as a knavish trick was common. Malthus was thought to have approved of the disease by his detractors. The collection of cadavers for anatomy schools somehow got into the argument, and hospitals were reviled by the poor as a place where you became an object of study not cure.

When isolation was introduced into hospitals the worst fears of the poor about the illiberality of hospitals were confirmed. In Glasgow an ambulance was attacked and a hospital stoned. Morris does not believe that cholera had any part in the passing of the Reform Bill or in the reform of the Poor Laws. In 1832, the people just wanted cholera to go away and did not believe anything useful could be done to prevent it, but in 1848 the people felt that the disease could be attacked and clamoured for governmental action. It was this change in belief which brought into being the Public Health Act. In 1832 cholera had, according to Morris, very little effect on public health measures and played no role in the subsequent ten years of the Factory Acts debates and those on the Poor Laws. Morris bases himself on the records of the debates themselves and so his view must be accepted despite the views of Longmate and McGrew.

It is Longmate who makes a point of saying that the lower classes of central Europe and Russia were convinced that cholera was a poison being spread by the rich, their social and political enemies, for Malthusian reasons. This belief gave rise to incidents in Hungary, Berlin and St Petersburg. Longmate also chronicles the development of public health legislation in Britain and reminds us that the conditions in the tenements was not improved by the lack of windows engendered by the government tax on windows. In 1832 a cholera bill was passed which attempted to put the cost of care of patients on to the persons affected and the responsibility for the arrest of the disease and the burial of victims on the Privy Council. As it was the poor who were affected the Radicals had a field day. The Government was forced to give way and pay for some of the anti-cholera measures and consequences of the disease. Longmate puts the losses due to cholera in 1832 as 21,882 dead in England, 9,592 in Scotland and 20,700 in Ireland.

So the United Kingdom had lost one in one hundred and thirty one of its population, while Russia had lost one in twenty, Austria one in thirty and Poland one in thirty two. It is obvious that this does not compare with the one in three of the Black Death. Longmate claims that, by 1833, reformers in Britain had the whip-hand and that as a consequence new acts such as the trail-blazing Reform Bill became the vogue and a whole series of reforming Bills followed including the Factories Acts, the Poor Laws, public education, reorganisation of local government and, as always when government becomes active, an increase in the collection of vital statistics including the central registration of marriages, births and deaths.

As we have heard from Morris this concern for reform does not appear to have been driven by the fear of and concern for cholera as far as can be ascertained from the records of parliamentary debates. Chadwick, with political cunning, pointed out that disease control prevented the sick and the poor becoming a financial burden on the privy purse and disease became a government concern. Though Longmate is convinced that this whole legislative activity was engendered by an atmosphere of fear of cholera, there are powerful voices, including La Berge (1988), who oppose his view and deny the role of cholera in most of this legislation and even deny cholera any real role in the progress of public health in general.

The Public Health Bill was reintroduced in 1848 after its failure to pass the houses in 1847. This time it was passed with, according to Longmate, the· powerful help of newly resurgent cholera. There were other powerful influences at work including the news of unrest from Paris, Berlin and Vienna. With this new law and the machinery set up by the new Poor Laws Britain was in a much better position to cope with the disaster that was cholera in 1848. Despite this the United Kingdom suffered 440,000 cases up until the time that cholera abated in 1849.

On the credit side Snow wrote *On the mode of communication of cholera*. Cholera was to return in 1853 and claimed a distinguished victim. Chadwick, hounded by the 'dirty party' and by a rather badly-behaved *Times*, (who put freedom for the wealthy higher than health for the poor), left the Board of Health. This outbreak was very severe in Britain and particularly violent in Soho, thus providing grist to Snow's mill. The infamous Broad Street pump was incriminated. Now Britain was on the high road to public health. Miss Nightingale's light shining from Scutari and Mr Russell's dispatches from the Crimea (*The Times* led back to paths of sanitary righteousness) fuelled the progress of the country towards a new sewer system and the regular supply of clean drinking water. The day of the sanitary engineer had arrived and Binnie, who chronicles their rise, points out that the advent of the whole water engineering complex in the United Kingdom is inextricably bound up with sanitation and that the driving force for that was cholera. Eversley concluded that, while the cholera outbreak of 1832 was of interest medically; politically and socially it marked the start of a new era. This view, which can be criticised chronologically, has come under increasing criticism for internal reasons of late and the arguments will be summarised when the overall effects of cholera are assessed.

The foregoing mirrors what happened in Europe at a lesser speed (2). The obscurantist attitudes which held back the development of public health in Britain applied with equal or greater force on much of the continent of Europe with the notable exception of France, who had shown the first glimmerings of an organised public health consciousness after the disappearance of Napoleon, probably due to the experiences of the Grand Armée in the field with typhus, plague, dysentery and smallpox (3). In Europe the ruling classes were at grips with the organising poor and their liberal supporters. They were disinclined to envisage any new radical legislation, particularly in commercial centres. Much of Europe lived under the shadow of steadfastly autocratic Russia.

For France Chevalier's book chronicles the events in a Paris under attack from cholera. He shows that, in demographic terms, cholera was very small beer indeed. The one in a thousand mortality caused a rise from a general average death toll annually of 46 to a figure of 56 per thousand in a cholera year, the figure dropped back immediately the cholera abated. This compares with figures of two hundred per thousand for plague. The 1832 cholera outbreak covered the last days of the Restoration, though Larrey had said that France was too civilised to contract cholera. It seems to have had little or no effect upon events though Delaporte insists that cholera was the midwife to the birth of scientific medicine in France.

In fact the accepted texts on French history only mention cholera because it carried off Louis XVIII's prime minister at a critical time, despite the social effects of cholera and the importance given by French historians to French social thought. Chevalier mentions Villermé's critical publications on the statistics of cholera tens of years before Farr (4), and he is insistent that cholera increased the misery of Hugo's *miserables*. Villermé's figures disclosed an 'inequality of death' to range alongside the inequality of life. In Chevalier's words, the socially and economically disadvantaged now suffered a biological disadvantage. Paris was alive with rumours. It was said that the Tsar had sent the cholera to suppress the unrest. This had a certain aura of truth as the Tsar's efforts to suppress the Polish unrest had imported cholera to Poland and as the Polish 'agitators' fled to France they may have brought some cholera with them.

This satisfied the prejudices of all classes. To the bourgeoisie cholera was a disease of agitation; to the poor it was a disease sent by the oppressors. Though Paris had the foremost public health thinking in Europe and it had commissions which sat on the subject of cholera very little was done except to prepare hospitals which the victims eschewed as the chief places in which the privileged classes could further the plans to poison off the poor. Indeed almost all efforts to relieve cholera, misguided as these may have been in 1832, were viewed with great suspicion and efforts to isolate the victims for whatever purposes increased the persecution mania of the class most affected by the disease. A proclamation pinned up in the Faubourg Saint-Antoine stated: 'La cholera est une invention de la bourgeoisie et du gouvernment pour affamer le peuple.'

This proclamation goes on to claim that this put-up scourge was being used to isolate the poor in hospital for poisoning, or in gaol to be shot. Chevalier and

Delaporte claim that cholera was the cause of a great increase in class friction. Dineur & Engrand and Guiral read more or less the same lesson from events in Lille and Marseilles during the cholera months of 1832. Curiously Vidalenc finds that the rural Normans reacted differently and nursed the cholera victims with sympathy and generosity. Netchkina et al. present an unmarxist view of cholera in Russia in 1831 and 1832 and admit that a disease can exacerbate class struggle.

The Tsar Nicholas I was an autocrat who would have none of any popular unrest in his or anyone else's dominions. He believed himself to be the policeman of Europe and was ready to suppress insurrection with his own troops regardless of national frontiers. He represents the opposite pole in Europe to bubbling revolutionary Paris. He used his police ruthlessly to quarantine cholera, without an iota of success, and to suppress any consequent demands for greater equality. He was right to suspect cholera as an agent of unrest and a group of revolutionaries sprang up in Russia called the 'cholerics' who expressed the fears that the masses had of cholera and their desire for a better life. The people took to the streets of St Petersburg, destroying a hospital and ambulances and attacking and defying the police. They screamed that it was not cholera that was rife but a plot to kill off the poor. Nicholas had to call in the army to crush the uprising but even in the army secret societies had come into being and rumours of poisoning inflamed army opinion. This delayed but did not stop the army's extirpation of the rebellions in Tambov, Toula, Novgorod. Khakov and other centres. Nicholas ruled Russia with 130,000 policemen.

Events in Spain during the cholera epidemics have been examined by Santander & Grangal and Ortiz. Cholera struck Hamburg with great violence in 1892, and provided a fascinating insight into the reaction of a great commercial centre to the disease and also the medico-politics of the day. The observer of this crisis in Hamburg is Evans, who describes the events, not in epidemiological terms, but in terms of civic politics and it has to be said that cholera was the most political of diseases until the 1976 fiasco in the United States of America over influenza. Evans describes all the forces acting on the initiation and inception of civic public health. Hamburg had a sewerage system of which it was rightly proud though its building had involved the usual infighting between public welfare and 'market forces'. However the frugality of the city fathers of an intensely commercial city had prevented the addition of a filtering plant to the domestic water supply which hailed from the Elbe via some settling tanks and roof-top tanks.

Nearby Altona with the same water extraction had built a filtration system into their supply. In 1892 Hamburg was full of immigrants trying to reach the USA from eastern Europe. These immigrants represented good business to the Hamburg-Amerika shipping line. It is probable that it was the immigrants who brought cholera to the mouth of the Elbe and while Altona had only a few cases, Hamburg had 16,926 cases officially recorded. The ruling body of Hamburg, the Senate, dilly-dallyed over the declaration of cholera infestation, delayed the inception of a filtration plant which had to await another two years for its go-ahead and obstructed quarantine.

The Prussian government, with its much greater tendency towards intervention, sent Robert Koch to the Elbe. He had recently diagnosed the causative agent of cholera in Egypt as a vibrio and he rapidly diagnosed cholera in Altona. He now insisted on a number of anti-cholera measures in Hamburg with all the authority of Berlin behind him and with his own authoritative nature. He fired warning shots across the bows of the Hamburg doctors to cow them and anyone else who might stand in his way, not least the Senate and its politico-medical authorities. He insisted on a poster campaign designed to encourage the boiling of drinking water; he organised the introduction of paid sanitation teams who disinfected all houses of cholera cases.

The Senate choked on the payments and had to ask the help of the hated social-democrats in finding the necessary labour. Koch closed all public baths, schools, bars, public dance halls and disallowed any further committal to gaols and workhouses. He banned all raw fruit and all public gatherings. The market forces, of course, did not take it all lying down; they avoided the quarantine and sent out a liner with cholera on board. When cases of cholera started to appear on board it was called diarrhoea and vomiting. When they died it was called diabetis coma. Although all public gatherings were banned the exchange met as usual.

The other great debate apart from intervention versus laissez-faire was between the adherents of Snow/Koch and their water-borne vibrio theory and the adherents of Pettenkofer and his XYZ theory. This latter proposed that cholera could only be transmitted by the vibrio (X) if it was subjected to the influence of a fermentation provided by ground-water (Y) thus making a miasma (Z). This theory was a last ditch fight of the miasmatists against the contagionists. Koch's successful measures against cholera and directed at the drinking water did much to ensure the final victory of the direct contagion theory, though, even in 1912, a leading German medical textbook could still claim that the contagion theory of cholera spread was dead. Evans' excellent book contains much which need not concern us here though it should be read for the inevitable conclusion that the epidemiology of cholera contained a large social element, however it may look to us today.

It contains many fewer errors in medical fact than most of its like, though the organism found by Pasteur in bees was not a bacillus. Evans points out that cholera was unable to disturb the stability of Great Britain in 1832 and he expresses the belief that disease cannot bring about the breakdown of a social order without an extreme demographic loss. He even goes as far as to suggest that another extreme force is usually required concommittantly to bring about major change and he cites his belief that smallpox alone could not have brought about the downfall of the Aztec civilisation without the added force of Cortez. The argument is dubious, despite one's admiration for Evans' treatment of cholera in Hamburg. It is difficult to doubt that a population drop from 25,000,000 to 2,500,000 is insufficient to spell the end of a civilisation or, at the very least, most of the institutions of that civilisation and of course there will always be those around ready to pick up the pieces.

The other great organised government of relatively forward-looking nature which was called upon to face and organise against cholera was North America. Rosenberg is the chief source for the social and legislative effects of cholera on the east coast of the USA, while Chambers tells us of its spread and Bilson writes of cholera in Canada. In Canada the government was under attack for its handling of the cholera scare and doctors lost the respect of public at large. As in Europe cholera was said to have deepened the distrust between the classes in Canada and the disease became an election issue in 1832. Cholera brutally exposed the inadequacies of the hospitals and the organisation of public health. Cholera did not hold back the development of Canada in any meaningful way and it disappeared from the Dominion in 1871, discussion of this can be found in Godfrey's work.

In 1832 when cholera reached New York it was seen as the disease of the sinful, that is the poor, the Irish and the Negro. By 1866 it was the disease of poor drainage and inadequate sanitation. New York was a vigorous city of some one quarter of a million people. It viewed the advent of cholera with alarm and instituted vigorous and strict measures of quarantine directed at ships arriving from the Old World. Americans with their passionate view of the free, expanding, sturdy and healthy nature of their society believed instinctively that a disease of filth and poverty could not take a hold on a people dedicated to pushing back frontiers. This view took no cogniscance of the tenements of New York pullulating with newly arrived immigrants or of the successful visitations of yellow fever.

In 1831, with one eye on Russia, the city fathers of New York had formed a board of Health and it was this body which introduced quarantine. A people, passionately attached to the freedom of trade, who had fought the British on that very issue during the Napoleonic wars, did not take kindly to quarantine and felt it their duty to evade it. So cholera arrived in a city with no water for street cleaning, with only city pumps for the drinking water of the poor and with a reputation for delivering water of excellent purgative properties. Bathing and even washing was rare.

On the other hand New York had experience with epidemics in the form of frequent yellow fever oubreaks and there was an administrative machinery for handling epidemics in the form of the Board of Health and a health officer to promulgate and enforce its decrees. There was also a medical man available for diagnoses, who, should he be foolish enough to diagnose an epidemic disease, was immediately exposed to ridicule and vilification. When it was heard that cholera had reached the St Lawrence River, the Board actually started to build hospitals to cope with the expected epidemic. The Medical Society set up a special committee which recommended swilling down the streets with water, the disinfection of cesspools, temperance and chastity.

None of these measures took any real hold but it does show New York as better prepared and more sensible in anticipation of cholera than the Old World. As cholera advanced inexorably down from Canada to New York, medical boards were set up in the counties of New York State. Cholera arrived in New York to be greeted with scepticism and anger; those who diagnosed it were treated as if they had invented it and the officials were tardy in applying counter-measures. New Yorkers started to leave the city. New cholera hospitals were initiated, business stagnated and cholera reigned.

Cholera's reign did not last for long and it commenced to abate, partly perhaps because crowding was relieved by death and flight. Life started to return to normal and cholera went away to attack Chicago travelling on the USA's pride and joy – the system of canals and railroads. Cholera was driven by steam! As in Europe cholera had reinforced all the arguments between the classes though these were to some degree dissipated in the enormous spaces of the USA. The rich said that it was the poor who were to blame, the pious said it was the sinners who were to blame. The religionists, claiming as always to be in direct communication with the Almighty, called for a day of prayer and expiation. This proposal was to become a political issue and the side of self-proclaimed virtue claimed and owned several very unsavoury personalities. Opposition raised the issue of anti-clericism and the Guelphs and the Ghibbilines lived again in the Land of the Free. Immigration was called into question as the poor were the main carriers of the disease and immigrants were invariably poor and hailed from disease-ridden Europe.

To the eternal credit of the United States this anti-immigration sentiment was resisted. The New York City Board of Health was the only organisation to fight cholera and the state-wide boards were the basis for a country-wide health organisation but, alas, as cholera died down so did the boards. In 1848 cholera travelled from Le Havre to New York on, appropriately enough, the *New York*. The *New York* was quarantined as seven of its passengers had died during the voyage. But quarantine was in name only as there was nowhere to put the three hundred quarantined passengers. By the end of the year, sixty were sick and thirty dead. New York stiffened its backbone and waited for the outbreak with some confidence. After all they were a pious, clean, prosperous and intelligent citizenry. However what New York, like the rest of the world, did not know was that none of these virtues were as remotely as important as the provision of clean drinking water and this commodity was unknown in most areas of the city and the science of waste disposal was in its infancy.

Cholera tightened its grip. The Board of Health was given a new lease of life and ordered the streets cleaned. The severity of that winter gave cholera some stay, which was just as well for no cholera hospitals now existed. The disease spread into the red-light district to fuel the fire of Puritan conviction that cholera was one of the wages of sin. Eventually the Board of Health managed to get some hospitals opened for cholera patients but by now some panic had set in, the better-off fled the city and emigration into the city was non-existent. Business suffered. Despite the orders of the Board of Health for cleansing operations nothing was done and the city remained a wonder of filth with pigs roaming Wall Street.

No Board of Health was going to be allowed to interfere with the divine right of the free New Yorker for his hams and bacon. A day of prayer and fast was declared with a notable lack of enthusiasm for it on the part of the cholera victims who were the poor and the hungry. It was the immigrant, particularly the Catholic Irish, who suffered most from cholera and thus raised the spectres of chauvinism and religious intolerance. It says a great deal for American tolerance that these twin sentiments never affected official policy and they continued to receive your tired, your poor, your huddled masses as before.

In 1865 the Civil War had just ended and news that cholera was again sweeping over Europe reached New York, now a city of half a million people, many living in tenements riddled with typhus, typhoid, tuberculosis and dysentery and still without any form of city sanitation. There was no municipal waste disposal, no clean water supply. But by now the New Yorker had learnt that some personal liberty must be surrendered in the face of epidemics and a new Board of Health was given sweeping powers. This new Board had another inestimable ally – Snow – for now they knew that they must apply logical sanitation measures aimed specifically at the city's appalling arrangements for waste disposal and begin to organise the provision of clean drinking water supplies. This all relied on the acceptance of Snow's precepts and recognition was slow, though some help was at hand as many sanitation measures fitted either Snow's ideas or those of the miasmatists. Cholera, as always, slipped through the quarantine but was met with energy. Houses harbouring cholera were evacuated and cleansed. The public co-operated. Inspectors oversaw all the arrangements, the movement of patients to hospital and the provision for the victim's family. But true to the American ideal of freedom backed by litigation, street cleanliness was not achieved and quarantine was not enforced. New York, however, was cleaner than it had ever been and city cleanliness was the order of the day rather than more targeted measures, just the same New York had little cholera during the outbreak of 1869.

No other American city gave similar powers to health authorities and all suffered more than New York from cholera this time. Painful as it may have been to the American love of individual freedom the lesson was learnt and the other cities bit on the bullet and gave powers to their Boards of Health sufficient to deal with future epidemics The Protestants managed to reconcile their dislike of the poor and the new knowledge of the transmission of cholera by the belief that cholera remained God's punishment for sin but fell heaviest on the poor because they disobeyed God's sanitary laws (presumably Deuteronomy, XXIII, 12-14); a set of laws of which the heathen Irish were unaware. While the birth of the New York Board of Health was not the only great advance in the USA's public health record, it was a great advance and with vaccination must stand as one of the first successes in man's organised fight against infectious disease.

Indeed the one-man laboratory set up in Staten Island in 1887 to detect and

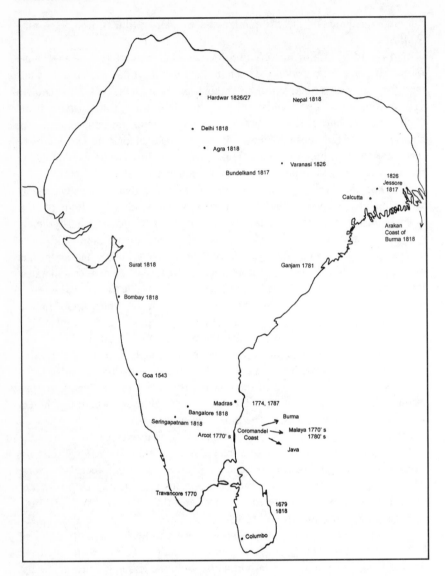

Hardwar 1826/27

Nepal 1818

Delhi 1818

Agra 1818

Varanasi 1826

Bundelkand 1817

1826
Jessore
1817

Calcutta

Arakan
Coast of
Burma 1818

Surat 1818

Ganjam 1781

Bombay 1818

Goa 1543

Madras

1774, 1787

Bangalore 1818

Burma

Seringapatnam 1818

Coromandel
Coast

Malaya 1770' s
1780' s

Arcot 1770' s

Java

Travancore 1770

1679
1818

Columbo

VI. Cholera

combat cholera and typhus was the forerunner of the Hygiene Laboratory of the 1930s which was to become the mighty National Institutes of Health, the greatest of man's institutions for the investigation of disease. Duffy (1971) makes two important points, first that general clean-up campaigns and cleanliness preceded the more logical schemes directed by Snow's discovery and secondly that cholera was also the time of burgeoning voluntary and charitable societies many of whom exist today. Cholera spread over the rest of the USA but it is the experience of New York which is grist to the particular mill grinding here.

CHAPTER 22
Cholera (part 4)

The sensational character of the novel visitation (cholera) scared society
into the tardy beginnings of sanitary self-defence.
G.M. Trevelyan. *English Social History*

In the Old World, the heartland of cholera, India continued to suffer epidemic
after epidemic. It would be impossible to trace the damage done without very
specialised studies done district by district, and these do not exist. India lost
millions of people to cholera just as it did to plague without there appearing to
be any demographic crisis. Jaggi records several outbreaks in India prior to
1817 when it broke out of Bengal to spread all over India in 1818. It faded in
1822 only to return in 1823, possibly exacerbated by the Pindari war. It receded
again in 1825 only to come back again in Bengal in 1826 and commenced to
move ominously up the Gangetic basin to Benares and the bathing and drinking
pilgrims. By November of that year two to three thousand were dying daily
from cholera and the disease moved on to Agra, the Jamuna River and Delhi.

Cholera kept up its advance reaching Hardwar, another centre of pilgrimage,
in April 1827 and the Himalayan foothills and the North-West Frontier by June.
Cholera's track now branched and went south to Bombay, Sind and the Punjab
also north to Afghanistan and on to the Middle East. Cholera was quiescent in
India for a time then broke forth again in 1833 spreading all over India. This
epidemic also reached China and from there went on to Russia killing at least a
million there. Another outbreak in India occurred in 1948 at Agra and Kanpur
going on to Bombay and eventually returning to Bengal and then moving south
it took in Madras. Jaggi blames the Ganges delta for all these cholera outbreaks.
He claims that Calcutta was totally insanitary and the villages of Bengal had
ponds which acted as both cesspits and as a source of drinking water. Between
1820 and 1860 twenty out of one hundred sick with cholera died, later the cholera
gained in virulence and the figure was seventy out of a hundred. Even among
the Europeans the odds against survival were three to one.

If an average death rate of 45 in 100 cases is accepted and the number of
cases in India as whole for the period of these epidemics was twenty million,

which is a reasonable though low figure, then nine million died. It appears that this death-rate was absorbed by a people growing in population without the incentive of the Industrial Revolution. There was no demographic decline. This problem of the growth of the Indian and Chinese populations without benefit of industrialisation will be discussed, if not resolved, in the last chapter. In 1921, towards the end of the 1898-1923 epidemic of cholera in India, the disease accounted for 6% of the deaths of the country or about half a million souls, and we know that India's population expanded enormously during this time.

As so often happens in the tropics, with its drop in temperature in the wet seasons which coincide with the summer of the temperate zones, cholera has peaks which differ in differing places, in the case of rivers it will depend on what happens upriver. According to Barua and Burrows, on the Brahmaputra delta cholera is at its worst towards the end of the monsoon, while in the Ganges delta it peaks in the dry season.

In China 1821 was a very bad year for cholera. The Imperial Prince Li in the *Hsiao-T'ing Hsu-Lu* mentions it but Ho gives it no especial mention in his study of the demography of China. This epidemic swept on to Japan. China suffered badly again from cholera in 1840, and again in 1854 and 1862 more discussion of this can be found in Maxwell's work. Inevitably the fifth pandemic struck China and 1881-3 saw wide-spread epidemics of cholera. Yamamoto says that Japan also suffered badly from cholera in 1881-1895. The sixth pandemic travelled east of India as far as Singapore. Whenever cholera visited China it enveloped Burma, South-east Asia, Indonesia and the Phillipines as well. Equally when cholera went on its peregrinations through Europe it attacked the Middle East as well, including, of course, Mecca.

There is even a case for saying that cholera is, par excellence, a disease of religious pilgrims with its great broadcasting foci at the areas of the Ganges sacred to the Hindus, Benares and Hardwar and at the town which has given the English language the word for an attracting and sacred gathering point, – Mecca – though none of these are the true home of cholera only the centres of further spread. The true home was and is the Ganges delta joined now by the Brahmaputra delta. In none of the Asian countries can it be claimed, without detailed studies of towns and districts, that cholera had or lacked any demographic effect locally in these countries, but given their burgeoning populations it must be assumed that cholera had no effect on demography in Asia as a whole, with the possible exception of Persia which Colnat claims was so weakened by cholera in the mid-eighteenth-century that it lost to Russia the Caucasus and the rivers running into the Caspian Sea.

In Africa cholera caused great fear and panic in such cities as Cairo and Alexandria. Hussein reports on its incidence and effects in Egypt where he identifies twelve epidemics and mentions in passing that it was at Alexandria that Robert Koch was to identify the causative agent of cholera in 1883. The first epidemic of 1831 claimed 36,000 victims in Cairo alone and 150,000 in all Egypt. In 1848 it claimed only 4,555 in Cairo and only 4,063 in 1855. The seventeenth epidemic (to Egypt), commencing in July of 1865 and coming from Mecca, killed over 60,000 in Egypt. July was the cholera month and Hussein gives a detailed account of the 1883 epidemic in Egypt in general and Cairo in particular. This epidemic killed nearly 60,000 people. Gallagher has made a detailed analysis of this epidemic and those of 1902 and 1947, the conclusion must be that while Egypt suffered dreadfully from cholera, none of the figures quoted begin to compare with those of plague.

Cholera reached the shores of East Africa directly from India or Sri Lanka only rarely. Usually cholera arrived from the Persian Gulf or the Red Sea. Christie and Stock have both made studies on the incidence of cholera in Africa and Christie is particularly harsh on the sanitary arrangements at Mecca. Christie is interesting on the incidence of cholera in Ethiopia in 1866 as its presence among the Emperor Theodore's troops coincided with his besiegement by Napier at Magdala, an area where 105 years later I was to encounter it myself. The dispersal of Theodore's defeated troops after the battle of Magdala carried cholera all over Ethiopia and on south to Kenya and central Africa. In these areas it seems to have been a dry season disease.

In North Africa cholera was rampant at the same times as it was ravaging Europe. Pollitzer records it as severe there in 1831-3, 1835-7, 1848-51, 1859-60, 1865-8, 1883-96, 1901-8 and the present pandemic. Gallagher believes that, although the great plague outbreaks of 1705 and 1784-5 did little damage to the fabric of the government of Tunis, the epidemic of cholera in 1849-1850, which caused 34,000 deaths, did cause a serious economic crisis, in the Regency. In the troubles of 1860-6 with its economic crisis cholera and typhus strode on stage to complicate events and by 1867 cholera was raging unchecked and uncontrollable. Typhus added to the misery of the winter of 1867/8 and in the crisis the weak government had to give way to French intervention which soon spread to take in the whole government of the country. Guyon, a French army surgeon, reports a rather charming story of cholera's visitation on Tunis which has been noted by Gallagher:

Cholera had travelled from France to Algeria and was now on his way to Tunis. While on the road he came upon, at Carthage, the marabout od Sidi Bu Said. The marabout sensing danger for the Muslims of Tunis who were under his protection awoke from his long sleep and asked: 'Where are you going, Oh bold one?' 'To Tunis', was the answer. 'What for?', the marabout wanted to know. Cholera said: 'To do what I do everywhere. I need victims'. The marabout ordered: 'Well take them from the Jews and the Christians too. I hold neither the one nor the other dear. As for the Muslims, they are mine. I cannot bear that you touch them.'

This was agreed and Cholera went on his way. Soon he found himself before the Chapel of St. Louis, the French saint. He proved no less jealous of his co-religionists. He, too, rose from his tomb and asked Cholera; 'Oh unhappy one, where are you going?'. 'You know where. To Tunis', was the slightly testy reply. The Saint then said: 'I am the protector of the Christians of Tunis. You must respect them. You must not touch them'. Again Cholera agreed and restarted on his road which led directly to Tunis with La Goulette, the Jewish quarter, on the left. Had there been a Jewish protector available to plead the cause of the Jews, he would never have entered the city at all. The fact is that the major outbreak of cholera in Tunis in 1849 began with an attack on the 'Hara' or Jewish quarter.

In conclusion what can be said of cholera and its effects on human society. It has to be said that despite its ravages it seems to have had very little lasting demographic effects and La Berge (1987) is rather fiercely dismissive of cholera's contribution to public health reform let alone social reform. It could be held that she is wrong to dismiss cholera so cavalierly, just as it must be said that McGrew (1960) attempts to load too much responsibility on to cholera for social reform. The best view seems to be that of Flinn published in the *Lancet* who believes that there is an indissoluble residue of fact to connect cholera with the growth of public health legislation and the growth of the whole public health movement, even if typhus, typhoid and tuberculosis were at least equal partners.

Of the degree of cholera's role in the class struggles of the 1830s and 1840s in Europe, particularly 1848, it is difficult to be certain and much deeper studies are necessary in this field before conclusions can be drawn. As important as anything was the growth of awareness that infectious disease could be controlled which the eventual arrest of cholera set in train. It was part and parcel of the Victorian belief in the eventual omnipotence of man in relation to his surroundings and the victory of the contagionists in medical thought.

Perhaps, above all cholera brought into being that remarkable feature of municipal life which runs unnoticed under our feet, the whole urban sewerage system and the pipes which supply our daily water filtered and oxidised. These are the result of our attempts to rid ourselves of cholera and dysentery by the safe disposal of waste and the provision of uncontaminated drinking water. Flinn notes that cholera was the midwife at the birth of the water engineer in our city society, even though the Metropolitan Commission of Sewers in London was born in a non-cholera year.

Dysentery has a much older and diffuse history than the well-defined pandemics of cholera, and doubt must be expressed if any of the epidemics of dysentery can lay claim to the name of pandemic. The history of dysentery is old in all the countries where it is possible to trace its existence. The *Lancet* says that Darius was checked by dysentery during the first Persian invasion of Greece and in the second invasion during the retreat of Xerxes after the defeats of Salamis and Plataea, thousands of the Persian troops died of dysentery, finishing Persian pretensions in Europe. The editorial writer of the *Lancet* also believes that dysentery affected Hannibal's campaign in Italy and may have been a factor in his turning away from Rome after Cannae. Cartwright (1972) lists a number of great men who died of dysentery in Europe, he believes that dysentery intervened in the Roman Empire in the critical period of 251-70. Felsen also lists a number of battles in which he believes dysentery was decisive.

Herodotus in Book 2 of his history says that the Great King (Cyrus) when marching on campaign carried boiled water from the River Choaspes (= Kerka).

Dysentery was described in the Ebers papyrus and in the Hippocratic writings. In Asia, Wong and Wu note that the Chinese Chang Chung-Ching wrote an essay on typhoid fever in 168. The Bible deals with dysentery (Acts, XXI, 8) and Josephus thought that the 'Plague of the Philistines' was dysentery. Preuss quotes the Lamentations Rabbi as saying that 'tears in the privy are not good tears', a phrase which seems to have lost something in the double translation, (Hebrew to German, German to English). Gregory of Tours records dysentery in France in the sixth-century. In India dysentery is mentioned in the Susrutas(1).

Briggs notes the report of the Chinese ambassador Chou Ta-Kuan to the Kmer Empire in 1296 as saying that eight to nine out of ten die of dysentery in the Empire. In the New World there is a Mayan hieroglyph (Codex Borgianus I Mixtec, section 51) which depicts a year's cycle of diarrhoea and vomiting. Moll reports dysentery in all parts of the twin continents of America. Dysentery is common in modern Africa and occurs in Oceana. In total dysentery is very widespread throughout the world and common in most areas still. It is an epidemic of crowding. Hill and Mitra examined 77 outbreaks of typhoid fever in the USA and the UK between 1870 and 1936. Huckstep believes that Molly Malone died, not of typhus but of typhoid, from eating her own shellfish no doubt.

Sandwith chronicles more incidents of dysentery in history. Dysentery still carries off millions of children in the Third World every year. War which brings large numbers of people together in insanitary conditions is a great friend to dysentery. Dysentery accompanied the Crusades and had a decisive effect on the Crusade led by Louis XI when it decimated the French crusaders camped near Carthage and killed Louis thus enabling his beatification. According to Runciman dysentery weakened the Normans in 1107 when Bohemund led them to the siege of Dyrrhachium. It was always present in the Jerusalem of the Crusading Kingdom and it killed the last effective King of Jerusalem, Almaric, in 1174 thus letting in Saladin. Albrecht of Germany was at the gates of Baghdad when dysentery sent him spinning back. The English army at Crecy in 1346 were derided by the French as 'barebottomed' because dysentery ordered the frequent dropping of the trousers. Dysentery was the inevitable companion of all medieval wars. It held up Frederick the Great after his victory over Maria Theresa's Austria. It halted the Prussian intervention into the French Revolution. It accompanied cholera on the Haj.

It dogged the footsteps of Napoleon and killed many in the American Civil War (81,360 dead of typhoid in the Army of the North) according to Marx, who even believes that dysentery may have lost Gettysburg for the South. Dysentery played its part in the Crimean War as so many pitiful letters from the soldiers at Balaclava and Inkerman were to show. It reared its head in the Boer War and at Gallipoli in the First World War. Berben reports typhoid at Dachau in the Second World War. Dysentery remains prevalent in the Mediterranean and everywhere in the tropics. But did typhoid fever and the *Shigella* dysenteries ever have a definable effect on history? The main answer has to be that this disease entity is too diffuse to make a judgement. There is no doubt that it frequently linked hands with cholera and could be said to have added its weight to the struggle for effective sanitary engineering, It weighed in on one side or the other in wars but it is doubtful if it can be said to have affected a whole campaign or altered a war aim let alone brought down a power. Despite the killing of millions its effect is rarely concentrated enough to have had a sudden demographic effect though it may have played its part in keeping up the pressure on populations affected by a greater and more concentrated disaster. The end of Persia' pretensions in Greece may have been the one exception.

CHAPTER 23
Influenza (part 1)

Coughs and sneezes spread diseases.

Influenza stands as a monument to the sin of *hubris*. It was an article of faith in the World Health Organisation of the 1960s that it was possible with the knowledge and tools then available that the scourge of malaria could be eradicated world-wide. Alas, it was learnt that the *Plasmodium* and the *Anopheles* had a few tricks up their sleeves, moreover a large portion of the blame for failure was laid quite correctly at the doorstep of the insufficient administrative infrastructure of many of the countries lying under the threat of malaria. When it was thought in the 1970s that influenza was to strike again as it had done regularly since the time of the disastrous 1919 influenza pandemic, the most advanced and powerful country in the world at the time, the United States of America, decided that it did have the administrative base, the knowledge and the skills, and the pharmaceutical industry to take on influenza within the confines of the USA. The result was an ignominious disaster. Influenza was called: 'The Last Great Plague' by Beveridge in 1977. AIDS also stands as a testament to the life and power of the danger of *hubris*.

Influenza is caused by a virus belonging to a family of viruses know as the Orthomyxoviridae, a fact and a word which need concern us no further. It is about 80-100 nanometres in diameter, (= about one ten millionth of a metre). The organism exists in slightly differing forms, a fact of enormous importance in the attempts to find a cure or a vaccine. The forms have the same general make-up but differ slightly in the configuration of the manner in which the pieces are put together. Even the major types have sub-types. For instance Type A flu virus has at least: human, swine, equine and avian sub-types and within these sub-types there are further identifiable divisions. The arrival of a new sub-type in a host will replace the former sub-type which then disappears.

It is Type A which has caused the great pandemics. Type B causes local epidemics of a lesser extent, usually among the old. Type C causes a mild disease among school children and does not appear to cause any damage either to the individual or to the world at large. The great complication in the search for a general vaccine is the variability of the virus and its ability to change that part of its make-up against which vaccines are directed. These are minor changes only but critical to the body's ability to detect and attack the virus; the dominant portion of the virus which may be the point of attack of the body of man will also be part of the new variant but now only a minor part and the difference is critical.

Both Type A and Type B show this antigenic drift. The virus tends to remain antigenically stable for the length of a particular epidemic. For a long time it was difficult to work with the influenza virus as no experimental animal was available, susceptible to the virus, until it was found that the ferret could be infected. The virus can be grown in fertilised eggs and sometimes in tissue cultures.

The influenza virus can also infect a number of wild and domestic animals and must be considered a zoonosis though not all influenza viruses of animals are infective to man. In an epidemic, of course, the transmission is from man to man. An influenza virus infective to man can be found in pigs, horses, poultry and a number of birds. In 1919, during the great pandemic of influenza, it was claimed in the USA that this virus had got into the pigs of Iowa. It may cause a high mortality among terns and seals (though this may have been called into question by the discovery of a fatal form of distemper virus among seals in 1989). Birds contain the influenza virus in their intestinal tract and it occurs there in various forms. According to Kaplan this reservoir of infection is for the present virtually ineradicable.

Influenza is an acute respiratory disease and the virus attacks the trachea and the bronchi. When fatal a secondary infection has usually supervened, such as a staphylococcal infection. The heart may be involved. The illness starts as a severe fever with copious sweating, lassitude and muscular pain which is followed, as the disease deepens, by prostration and possibly vomiting. The patient sneezes violently and there tends to be a dry cough and nasal irritation. The fever goes up and down and lasts about six days. It brings a flushed face and a slight cyanosis. The patient frequently subsides into pneumonia, particularly if old.

Transmission of the virus is by droplet following sneezing or coughing when the viruses are discharged into the air in minute droplets of bronchial fluid. These are taken up into the lungs of the next person to be infected. An epidemic of influenza occurs usually in winter but only if a large number of non-immunes have grown up since the last epidemic of the same virus and that it is a Type A virus which is circulating. Influenza is not an easy disease to diagnose without a laboratory diagnosis of the presence of the virus. Diagnosis becomes easier if an epidemic takes hold as it is the only prevalent respiratory disease which gives rise to a large number of cases simultaneously.

Even today there is a tendency to call any respiratory disease of any severity influenza and the common cold is often allowed the more distinguished sobriquet of influenza. Equally attacks of influenza can be called by more glamorous names such as 'an attack of my old trouble', i.e. malaria, if the subject has recently returned from the tropics to a flu area of the temperate zones. The best means of prevention, apart from vaccination, is by means of a barrier to the droplets such as a handkerchief held over the nose and mouth when coughing or sneezing. Hence the injunction at the head of this chapter.

It is possible to vaccinate against influenza provided one uses the contemporary strain of virus in the manufacture of the vaccine. Such a vaccine will give protection against that strain of virus for the normal length of an influenza epidemic, which tend to be short-lived. It will also give some cross-protection to closely related strains of the virus. This immunity seems to be largely cell-based and not antibody-based. Vaccines can occasionally give rise to an affliction called Guillain-Barre syndrome.

The early history of influenza is complicated by the arguments which rage about the identity of the 'sweating sickness' of the late fifteenth and early sixteenth centuries, particularly in Britain. This becomes even more complicated when the apparently related diseases on the continent of Europe are considered. Any final verdict on the identity of these diseases is not yet in and I am not qualified to join the argument. Suffice it to say that if influenza can be accepted as a known disease entity prior to 1500 then it is identified by Townsend as being the cause of the defeat of the Carthaginians before Syracuse in 412 and 393 BC (what a dreadful load of diseases the proponents of their speciality have heaped on those poor Phoenicians). Townsend sees influenza as the cause of an epidemic in Rome in 41 BC, and finds another epidemic in 591/2 in the same city. He also identifies more epidemics in 837, 876, 889 and 932; his paper should be read in the original for the reasons he puts forward for these assertions.

The earliest of the more generally accepted dates for an outbreak of influenza is 1170-13, which Hirsch places in Italy, Germany and Britain; acceptance of this date owes much to the reputation of Hirsch himself, though Burnett and White accept the attribution. Hirsch also identifies influenza in Italy in 1323, 1328, 1387, 1404 and 1411. All of these epidemics occurred elsewhere in Europe, France, Germany and the Low Countries, as well, except the one in 1328. Hirsch identifies about 300 epidemics of influenza up until 1875, practically all in Europe. For these he obtains the agreement of Townsend for most, though Townsend adds a few of his own. Marks and Beatty say that the first use of the word influenza or something like it was made in 1580 and referred to an epidemic in Florence in 1357 which would also have been a time of recovery from plague prior to the return of the plague in 1359.

From 1485 and during most of the sixteenth-century historians are likely to be talking about the sweating sickness when they speak of influenza epidemics as they are reluctant to rule it out as influenza. Creighton, the foremost expert on British epidemics, sees 1427 as the first date for an epidemic of influenza in Britain. It was this pandemic which was said to have killed off 5% of eastern Europe. Creighton does not commit himself on the identity of the sweating sickness but he notes that the 'English Sweats' or *Sudor Anglicus* became extinct after 1551. He has influenza on the continent in 1557, possibly, the 'Picardy Sweat'.

Creighton, too, accepts that the disease in Britain mentioned in the chronicle of Melrose in 1173 may have been influenza and that the 'rheum' in England under Henry VI in 1423-31 had many of the characteristics of influenza, but it must have been co-incident with the plague, which would complicate diagnosis. He notes that it was present in Paris too at this time. He records a great pandemic wave of influenza in Europe in 1510, though few died, and another wave in 1557. The pandemics of influenza in 1557/8 and 1580/2 were complicated by plague, typhus and diphtheria.

Stuart-Harris (1954), the great British influenza expert, is inclined to think that the 1510 epidemic was the first to be reliably recognisable as influenza and that the 1580 outbreak was the first pandemic. Castiglione notes that the Black Death years were complicated by influenza and that it had a name at that time, so was differentiated from plague. It was called *Influentia Coeli* or *Influentia del Diavolo*. It may have been a forerunner of the sweating sickness. Creighton set his face against the germ theory of infectious disease and this makes his views sometimes difficult to follow, particularly in his second volume, when speaking of the ague and influenza.

Thompson also records the great 1510 epidemic of influenza when it visited Ireland and calls it only a part of a far greater pandemic involving all Europe and North Africa, originating in the latter. He records many deaths in 1513. Thompson also notes the 1557 outbreak and puts it as particularly in Spain, France and Italy. This pandemic, he claims, came from Asia. The 1550s epidemic in England caused a serious mortality according to Clarkson and indeed some believe that it was the major cause of a demographic drop in England at that time, which led to an arrest of the inflation which had set in during the mid-sixteenth-century. Not, one feels, a recommended method of arresting inflation, despite the enthusiasm of some present-day politicians for such a stay.

Moll feels that the definition of influenza in Europe was too vague in the sixteenth-century for New World chroniclers to identify it in the Americas at that time but he does note the frequent respiratory diseases of the Amerindian of the day, particularly in the Andes. He believes that the 1510 outbreak was a pandemic and that it attacked the New World. This would require the virus to maintain itself for a long time at sea. Despite his doubts about diagnosis and symptomatology in the New World of the time Moll identifies outbreaks of what was probably influenza in San Domingo in 1518 and in Central America in 1523, 1526 and 1558 (pandemic). Dobyns also records an influenza pandemic in the Andes in 1558.

McBryde has more to say on the subject of American influenza. He sees evidence of it in Guatamala in 1523, 1559-62 (pandemic) and 1576 from a document of the Cakchiquel Indians. He maintains that these three epidemics were influenza and not, as has been claimed syphilis, smallpox or measles. The 1557 pandemic, which is thought to have commenced in Asia, got to Spain and hence to the New World. Crosby (1967) believes that the 1520/1 epidemic in Central America cleared the way for Alvarado's conquests south of Mexico. Recent evidence seems to show that some of these earlier epidemics and pandemics were as damaging as that of 1918/19. It would be wearisome and not to any great purpose to record all of the epidemics real or imagined during the seventeenth and eighteenth centuries (1). Many were, of course, recorded but influenza's modern history is both better documented and more interesting.

The first outbreak, of which we have good and reliable records, was that of 1889-91 in Great Britain, which was followed at the time by Parsons. He recommends, with cheer one imagines, champagne and quinine (the first for the physician and the second for the patient?) as a specific. The latter might control the temperature and the former the melancholy. Parsons notes that the previous great epidemic was in 1847-8, another affliction to add to the burdens of those eventually revolting in 1848. The 1889 pandemic was first noted in Paris on November 17 1889 and in Berlin and Vienna by the end of the month. It was thought to have arisen in Russia and Siberia where, according to Burnet and Clark, there was a pre-pandemic in 1886-7.

It spread to the USA in 6-8 weeks, to South Africa in two months, to India in four months, to Australia and New Zealand in five months and to the remotest parts of Africa in one year. This all assumes correct diagnoses. Parsons notes the freedom from infection at the time of those fishermen who had spent the critical time on the Dogger Banks and of lighthousemen. Greenwood (1918) has more to say on this pandemic. He describes four phases. A primary phase from December 1889 to February 1890; a secondary phase which was asymmetric and more fatal in the spring and summer of 1891; a third phase which seemed to be primary influenza in the autumn and winter of 1891-2 and a fourth phase from 1893 to January 1894. All this was an attempt to define the pandemic in order to predict the course of the 1918-19 pandemic.

This research seemed to predict relatively short outbreaks of about three months each time or for each community. This leads us to the greatest disease outbreak of our times: the pandemic of influenza which struck the world in 1918-19. With an attack rate of about 40-50% of the population and a death rate of between 0.5 and 1.2% of cases, this pandemic killed about 22,000,000 people world-wide. Both the attack rate and the death rate could be much greater among populations which had not been affected previously. Thus the USA suffered a mortality of about 0.5% of its population, that is about 500,000; the UK lost about 200,000 but Samoa, without previous experience of the disease, lost 25% of its population. Influenza wiped out whole Esquimo villages.

India, perhaps the worst affected of all, lost 12,000,000, but Das Gupta, cited by Vilmorovic, has shown that India's population rose by 85.9% in the period 1901 to 1961. There were great variations in both the attack rates and the death rates. In confined communities such as aboard ship passenger liners bound for Australia from the UK there was an attack rate of anything from 4% to 43%. Attack rates could also be higher for the younger age groups as they were unprotected by previous experience of the disease. The age-related attack rates of influenza can be very complicated, probably indicating previous exposures to the disease unsuspected at the time and also related to relative immunity conferred by varying strains of the virus.

Crosby (1977) in Osborn's book gives a conservative estimate of one-fifth of mankind as having suffered in the pandemic and a estimate of a 2-3% death-rate among cases. Many had sub-clinical infections, that is, that, while they were infected with the virus, they did not become ill with the disease. This particular pandemic was very dangerous to young adults, for unknown reasons as previous pandemics had attacked the very old and the very young. The crowding, due to the collection of young adult males in the armies being disbanded after the First World War, was a factor. Stuart-Harris (1954) believes that there were small epidemics of influenza in Europe in 1916 and 1917 and that it was from these small epidemics that the great pandemic sprang. The first cases were seen in Fort Riley in the USA among military personnel, though this time no-one blamed the Irish.

In fact, rather unfairly, Spain got the blame, hence the title of Collier's book on this pandemic: *The Plague of the Spanish Lady*, as it seems to have started in Europe in Madrid. In the USA 1,100 men at Fort Riley succumbed to the disease but such is man's perversity it became known as the 'Spanish Lady'. From Madrid it spread with frightening swiftness all over Spain and Portugal. All of a sudden it seemed, 8,000,000 Spaniards were down with influenza. It proceeded to blanket Europe and move quickly onto the New World, Asia, Africa and Australasia.

This pandemic was adequately reported by the medical authorities of the time and later. Greenwood, (1918) basing himself on the 1889-94 pandemic, predicted that the 1918 pandemic would last into 1919 at least. He noted the high attack rate and the very fast increase in the number of cases so that peak figures of cases came about early in the epidemic. From his studies of these outbreaks he laid down a number of criteria for influenza epidemics.

1. Primary influenza is a uniform disease.
2. The incidence of influenza is independent of climate and meteorology; epidemics may occur anywhere, at any time and during any climate .
3. Primary influenza is characterised by:
a) a tendency to become pandemic.
b) a fatality a little greater than the symptoms would lead one to expect.
c) a high rate of attack on people in the prime of life.

Greenwood also noted that there was little agreement between experts on
a) the periodicity of epidemics.
b) the influence of wind on transmission.
c) the contagiousness of the disease.

Greenwood answered these points himself and claimed no periodicity for influenza, allowed the wind no influence and affirmed the contagiousness of the disease.

The major point about the 1918-19 pandemic emphasised by all writers on it was that it killed more people than did the First World War. The other major point was that it was diffused as fast as man could carry it, thus slowly in 1767, fast in 1918 and very fast in 1957. The diffusion of the 1918-19 pandemic was both hindered and helped by the state of war which had engulfed most of the world, as one can imagine. As in 1889 the pandemic began slowly with mild attacks and a low mortality; then as it got into the enormous concentrations of men on the western front it picked up speed in April and May of 1918. During the summer it died down in virulence with fevers rarely over 102° F (= 38.9°C) and a duration of only three to four days.

In the autumn of 1918 a much more severe wave took over and bronchial pneumonia became a complicating feature; even septicaemia was seen. A dangerous central nervous system involvement caused alarm in the USA, and post-influenza encephalitis became a known entity, Jordan discusses this in greater detail. Despite this obvious severity and contagiousness influenza was not a notifiable disease in the UK at the time so death and attack rates cannot be given with any guaranteed accuracy for that country, according to Carnwarth.

Collier gives a rather more dramatic view. He notes that one quarter of the US Army were casualties to influenza and of these one in twenty-four contracted pneumonia as a sequel. He claims that 225,000 Germans died of the disease and it struck down Prince Max of Baden as he was to negotiate the peace treaty on behalf of Germany. Collier appears to claim that Damascus fell because the Turks were too ill with influenza to defend it, a claim which might be disputed by the adherents of Allenby and Lawrence. Collier even claims that the Germans were defeated as much by influenza as by the Allies, not a view acceptable to the military historians of the time or later and not really acceptable as influenza did not take sides and attacked the Allies fully as fiercely as it did the Central Powers. He notes the damage done among isolated populations, previously unaffected by the disease, such as in Fiji where 8,000 died and Madagascar where the disease was exceptionally severe.

Collier claims that the world was grinding to a halt, that crops were not harvested in the Ganges valley and potatoes not garnered in Poland. In Guatamala only half the normal amount of coffee was planted and in Malaya rubber was left untapped. Collier's tale of woe is unrelenting. He notes 500,000 dead in the Belgian Congo, the South African gold production down by £256,000, bankruptcies in New York, insurance companies reneging. The Prudential Insurance Company of Newark paid out a million dollars in three weeks at the end of 1918. He notes that Turin lost four hundred people a day and Paris five thousand a week; 228,000 died in Britain, 250,000 in the Punjab. Getting a seat in the train or underground was merely a matter of sneezing.

Collier calculates that influenza had attacked as many as a million people in Russia and killed 450,000 of its typhus-ridden inhabitants. Italy lost 375,000 and India 12,500,000. What he fails to mention is that the world scarcely hiccupped. Population losses were made up almost immediately and trade and industry recovered without difficulty except for a little delay in Germany for other reasons. While India may have lost 12,500,000 of its population, the total population was rising rapidly to 400,000,000 and so even here we are examining a population loss of about 5% compared with the 30-40% loss of the Black Death or up to 90% among Amerindians from smallpox. Overall death rates were in the order of 1% (or occasionally 2-4%), except in a few communities where it could be much higher; such a low death rate diffused all over the world was a pinprick to a rising population still, in a large part, under the demographic influence of the Industrial Revolution.

Hoehling has a rather more sober view but even he stresses that the civilised world stood amazed and shocked by a pandemic which could do such damage in such a short period of time (just a few autumn weeks in 1918) and he points out that only a few more weeks like October 1918 could have wiped out *Homo sapiens*. In the USA influenza let up on about November 11 1918, which must have puzzled the more logical of the epidemiologists. Hoehling gives a good account of the pandemic spread of the disease and its timing. He notes, with logic, that both sides in the Great War were equally affected by the disease. Smith confirms that the pandemic did not cause either panic or despair of the type seen during the great plague pandemics or even the cholera outbreaks even though Burnet and White estimate the total death toll at between 25,000.000 and 50,000,000, a staggering figure.

Crosby gives a good account of the start and the progress of the 1918-19 pandemic in the USA (particularly San Francisco), among the US armies and in the rest of the world and notes that it circled the world without benefit of air travel. Pettigrew has done the same for Canada. Greenwood makes the salutary point that even in the 1918-19 outbreak, diagnosis of influenza was still epidemiological. If there was enough of a respiratory disease in a sufficiently short space of time, then it was influenza, rather like bird-watching at a distance, if there are twenty black birds they are rooks, if there is one or two they are crows. If you have a cold you suffer alone, if two hundred have a cold it's influenza.

Greenwood (1935) was sure that, on the evidence of 1918-19 and the fact that 1922, 1927 and 1929 were all influenza years, the world would continue to suffer influenza outbreaks. He notes that an increase in deaths due to influenza is always accompanied by an increase in deaths due to pneumonia but not the other way around, so influenza predisposes to pneumonia but pneumonia does not predispose to influenza. However in death peaks during an epidemic of influenza pneumonia deaths always precede uncomplicated influenza deaths.

In the 1920s the epidemics did not become pandemics. The 1921 epidemic in the USA did not reach Britain and the 1929 British epidemic did not trouble the USA.

The next date of any significance was 1936 when an epidemic in Britain was the subject of an exhaustive report by a Medical Research Council team headed by Stuart-Harris (1976). This epidemic had broken out among Royal Air Force and Army personnel and was the first of its kind to be subjected to intense epidemiological, virological and immunological studies. All attempts to vaccinate either man or ferrets against influenza failed. Another outbreak in 1939 was also subjected to a similar study by Stuart-Harris' group, it was largely an infection of schools and service institutions. A new virus was isolated though the old 1937 virus may have been present simultaneously. We are now moving into epidemics and pandemics which have occurred in the lifetime of many alive today; indeed Britain and northern France are suffering an epidemic of influenza as I write.

In 1957 a pandemic of influenza struck the world and was called Asian flu. One of the major sufferers was the Soviet Union from whence Zhadanov has provided us with an excellent description of the Asian flu's spread and effects. It began in the first ten days of May in Tashkent, Stalinabad, Ashkabad and other towns of Central Asia and by the end of May it had reached the Trans-Siberian railway at the western Siberian towns of Omsk and Novosibirsk. From here influenza broke into the European Soviet Union in two waves, one in May/June and a second in September/October. By October the incidence of the disease was 870 per ten thousand and a considerable proportion of those had severe symptoms. Death was common, usually from intervening pneumonia. In October/November the mortality rate was twelve per hundred thousand in the big towns and probably about seven to eight per hundred thousand for the whole of the country. The highest death rate was among the 0-2 year old age group. Many strains of the virus were identified and most were A/Asia/57 type (= A2).

From Russia it spread to Turkey which suffered some million cases, and then, as we know, spread out all over the world. The 1957 pandemic has been characterised by Burnet and White as the most wide-spread and greatest of the pandemics whether of influenza or not. Its spread owes a great deal, of course, to man's spread over the world's surface. It started in China in 1956-7 and the virus, isolated in Beijing, was seen to be a new type. This was ominous but was ignored in the West; it should be remembered that China was not, at the time, a member of the World Health Organisation. In May of 1957 influenza had reached Singapore and Japan and the world began to awake to the fact that a new strain of influenza virus was on the rampage. June and July saw epidemics in the Southern Hemisphere and in the Northern Hemisphere influenza struck in two waves as we have heard from the Soviet Union. There were high death rates in October/November 1957 and again in February 1958.

After two years a new epidemic hit the USA and Australia in 1960. The next large visitation was the Hong Kong influenza pandemic of 1968, the virus being a variant of A2. Knowledge of the pattern of outbreaks and their causative viruses was building up; man was becoming confident of his ability to predict and master the influenza epidemics. A vaccine was now available so long as one had the right influenza virus for the epidemic in progress from which to manufacture the vaccine. This was merely millions of killed or inactivated viruses. Influenza was also now recognised as a threat to the god of Mammon as the 1968-9 pandemic had cost the USA an estimated $225,000,000 in Medicare alone and the total loss to the USA as a whole was estimated at 4,600,000,000 dollars. Vaccination would be a great deal cheaper if it worked. So the USA was led down the treacherous path of nationwide disease control and into an attempt to immunise the nation with influenza vaccine in 1976.

CHAPTER 24
Influenza (part 2)

There was no influenza in my young days. We called a cold a cold.
Arnold Bennett, *The Card*

The sad story of the failure of the attempt by the US health authorities to protect its population from an expected outbreak of influenza in 1976 has been exhaustively written up by the protagonists of either side. There are the apologists for the scheme and the more numerous critics, who, with the advantage of hindsight, have savaged the attempt (1). All combined they convey the facts; one may be permitted to draw one's own conclusions. The story starts during the cold and dreary winter of 1975-6 in the even colder north-east of the USA, specifically at Fort Dix in New Jersey near Philadelphia. Sputum from a few cases of upper respiratory infection were examined. Some of these showed influenza virus but most were type A/Victoria. However, two were difficult to identify and were sent to the Center for Disease Control (CDC) at Atlanta, Georgia. While this was going on recruits into Fort Dix were succumbing to what seemed like influenza and one died with an unidentified virus. CDC found this virus to be swine influenza-like. It looked as if a new swine influenza virus was circulating in the population, particularly at Fort Dix. Major pandemics of influenza were known to occur about every eleven years and the last had been in 1968.

Such a pandemic was usually predicted by the presence of a lesser epidemic during the previous year. Such a lesser epidemic seemed to be happening in Fort Dix. The USA had experience with vaccination against influenza as during the 1957 epidemic a large amount of vaccine had been prepared and inoculated into seven million people. This low level of coverage of only a section of the whole population was due to the lateness of the decisions to prepare vaccine and get inoculation under way. It was too little and too late and 70,000 died. In 1968 they were again late and the first vaccine appeared three weeks after the first cases appeared. Only ten million doses of the vaccine were available for a population of over two hundred million. The USA lost 33,000 dead. So at least they were improving.

Now they faced a situation where they had notice and perhaps six to ten months with which to play. By February 1976 the CDC had isolated the new strain of virus and it was available for growth as a vaccine. It was sufficiently different from other known strains that old vaccine stocks were useless, though it resembled the old 1918 strain and those over 50 years old carried antibodies against it. Swine influenza of this type was known to be able to be transmitted to man. So, to vaccinate or not to vaccinate? A large-scale production of this virus (A/New Jersey/6) by the private pharmaceutical industry would be necessary and time was short. Government would have to make up its mind with a speed to which it was wholly unaccustomed.

The choices for government were stark:

1. Stimulate the large scale production of A/New Jersey/6 virus and stock-pile it in readiness for the pandemic when and if it got underway.
2. Stimulate the production of A/New Jersey/6 virus and organise the vaccination programme itself.
3. Sit tight and hope the pandemic won't happen.

The last alternative had to take into account the normal annual loss to influenza of 17,000 dead and $500,000,000, let alone the losses in the event of a pandemic. The government's primary adviser was the CDC who favoured the direct intervention of the government on both the production side and the side of the delivery systems. CDC drew up a plan of action which involved the government accepting the responsibility for vaccinating the whole country, and a decision on the plan was required urgently, if the planners were to have time to get the programme off the ground before the projected start of the pandemic.

There was a bewildering array of influences on the decision. First CDC must decide whether an influenza pandemic was, indeed, on the way and whether they had the technical ability to stop it. CDC was faced with the failure, apparent by then, of the World Health Organisation's malaria eradication scheme. CDC decided that they had the ability, the skills, the tools and the organisation to do the job. The recommendation of the CDC involved the government in the ordering, purchase and distribution of enormous numbers of syringes and needles and vaccine 'guns', of large amounts of vaccine and in the organisation of vaccination at the local level – all of this after only 200 years existence as a state. There were principles involved, such as government intervention into health matters as opposed to the freedom of the public to combat the pandemic in their own way using the market economy.

As was to be seen later the whole question of indemnity in case of accidents and sequelae had not been addressed. Industry had not been fully consulted due to the speed needed in the decision-making. The CDC plan went up through channels from Dr Sencer, the head of CDC, via the Health, Education and Welfare Department to the President. It also reached him from the Management and Budget Office; the cost was modest, about $135,000,000. The President quickly approved the scheme. It has been said that Ford, the President could tolerate, politically, a health fiasco but not tens of thousands of deaths. The plan reached the relevant House and Senate sub-committees by mid-April 1976. It was obvious that the President would sign this bill in a hurry so the Democrats in the Senate slipped in a whole series of other health interventions into the bill which would never have passed the President otherwise. The President did sign the bill and the CDC got underway with the minimum of delay. The Bureau of Biologics went over entirely to A/swine virus production and everything was looking good. Then the errors started to creep in. Parke-Davis received the wrong vaccine. The production methods did not produce the projected amounts of vaccine. It became obvious that the target of one hundred and forty six million vaccine doses by October could not be reached. Internal fights broke out among the scientists; the timetable was thrown out of kilter and there was criticism from overseas.

The British, especially Stuart-Harris, and the World Health Organisation felt that there was insufficient information available for the decisions being made, though it should be remembered that they were not, for the present, under threat. Tests showed small errors in the estimate of the amounts of vaccine needed to achieve the necessary levels of protection and the spectre of two shots per person reared its head, with special interests demanding two shots for themselves.

All in all public approval and support was dropping away and some highly respected scientific voices could be heard advocating the stock-piling of the vaccine and a wait and see policy. The next blow was the question of indemnity, a real issue with the possibility of Guillain-Barre syndrome arising in a significant number of people as a direct result of vaccination. The US insurance industry was not willing to shoulder the possible burden and would not insure the drug firms for liability in the case of accidents.

Successful insurance claims in the case of the live polio vaccine had made both the insurance and the pharmaceutical industries wary. The pharmaceutical industry wanted the government to assume this responsibility but that would have been against the law and the insurance interests did not want the government in the insurance business. Congress thought that insurance companies should conduct insurance business, after all that was what they were there for, to insure and take risks. Congress would not accept governmental moves designed to take the responsibility for possible indemnity. It was all getting very messy and the projected date for the arrival of the pandemic was waiting for neither man nor organisation.

Then another distraction appeared. Legionnaires' disease turned up at a Philadelphia gathering and noone knew what it was. Congress got irritated with the CDC and stopped the pay of the CDC employees until they came up with a diagnosis. It was the last thing the CDC needed, distraction just as the vaccine programme was becoming critical, requiring tactical and logistical decisions to be made immediately, with unknown consequences. However it may have helped Congress to made up its mind to allow the government into the insurance business. CDC felt that it would not be able to deliver the two hundred million vaccine doses promised; the Department of Health, Education and Welfare insisted.

During all this time the programme was the target of continuous sniping from the *New York Times,* who claimed that decisions were being made too hastily and with insufficient time, thought and data. The outbreak of Legionnaires' disease was hailed by the press as the start of the influenza pandemic, which, though wrong, did clear some logjams. Though the promise of two hundred million vaccine doses was not forthcoming by the target date of October 1, the vaccination programme started on time and one million people were vaccinated in the first ten days. On October 11 in a Pittsburg clinic three old people dropped dead immediately after vaccination. Though any connection between the deaths was unproven the headlines made the connection for the public.

Other deaths turned up and one particular batch of vaccine came under public suspicion. Some vaccine programmes were suspended. CDC proved that there was no connection between the deaths and the vaccine, but had omitted to warn the public of the possibility of coincidental but unconnected deaths. The vaccine programme rolled on and two and a half million people were vaccinated by the end of the second week. By mid-November the acceptance rate was dropping off as the pandemic failed to make an appearance. This gave the breathing space necessary for a decision to give the 3-18 year-old age group two shots of the vaccine. By mid-December over forty five million vaccine doses had been delivered to civilians and a further half a million to the military. This represented about 24% of the population and so far very few side-effects had been reported. The number of vaccine related deaths with time was below the number of deaths expected by chance in any 48 hour period in the absence of vaccination. In the third week of November, however, an undoubted case of Guillain-Barre syndrome appeared in Minnesota not long after a dose of vaccine had been administered.

This was a blow of great importance to the programme. In the week following three more cases of the syndrome appeared in Minnesota with one death and three more in Alabama. Guillain-Barre syndrome, a paralytic disease rather like poliomyelitis, was not a reportable disease so the CDC had little epidemiological information on which to base a judgement. Such information as they did have showed only less than 1% of cases were influenza vaccine related. Then CDC began to be flooded with reports of Guillain-Barre syndrome cases but there was still no clear correlation with vaccine programme. By mid-December there had been five deaths due to Guillain-Barre syndrome and the cases showed a significantly greater number of them to be among vaccinees than among those unvaccinated. It was one in two hundred thousand as against one in a million and in the continuing absence of the expected pandemic this was the final blow to the programme.

It had become obvious that a vaccine based on A/swine virus gave a significant rise in the number of subsequent cases of Guillain-Barre syndrome. There was eventually a minor outbreak of swine influenza in man in the USA but the vaccine could not be used to bring it under control because of a total moratorium on the use of A/swine virus vaccine. The failure of the programme meant that heads would roll and both the Secretary of Health, Education and Welfare and the Chief of the CDC were sacked. Such is the fate of bold decision-makers if the decision turns out to be wrong, while those sitting on the sidelines or a convenient fence continue to sit in comfort. Neustadt and Fineberg cite one considered judgement delivered which seems to sum up the faults of the programme:
1. Too much confidence in the theory of the timing and causation of influenza pandemics with too little evidence upon which to base the conclusions.
2. Conviction about the value of the decision was influenced by the 'timing of personal agendas' (whatever that means).

3. The medical world overstepped its proper role in attempts to ensure governmental involvement.
4. Premature decisions were made to do more than was strictly necessary at any one time.
5. There was a failure to examine and list the uncertainties so that, if particular situations arose, they were expected and moves to counteract were planned.
6. There was too much confidence and insufficient questioning of scientific logic and prospects.
7. The medical authorities were too insensitive to the media and the public.

This is a particularly American view of the faults of the programme, but, as it was an American programme administered in the USA, that cannot be considered a criticism. Some of its lessons are not, however, exportable. The first criticism can be accepted in its entirety with the warning thought that it would be much less likely today with the computer-based mathematical models of vaccine programmes. The future of the fight against infectious disease seems at present to lie with vaccination so these lessons are vital. The second objection is an inevitable concomitant of any human activity and the hope is that if it is a significant element in failure the computer will iron it out. The third objection is peculiarly American and need not concern the world as a whole.

The fourth objection can be subsumed into the fifth and this is a vital point. It is paramount that planning should be such that the reaction to any event not predicted in the final scheme is simplified by plans for handling that event, which should be thrown up by a sophisticated computer programme even if very vague. Time is always of the essence and planning allows a measured response, particularly if the computer throws up the response in milliseconds. The sixth objection should also be taken up by such planning, which today would be on a computer programme with a built-in ability to examine all events occurring no matter how remotely relevant to the scheme.

The last objection is more American than universal. This is not to say that the favour of public opinion is not vital to success of any such scheme wherever it may operate, but the gathering of public opinion is a much more uncertain business in those countries afflicted with infectious disease. Even in the advanced countries sensitivity to the media must be accompanied by a little sensitivity by that notoriously insensitive estate. The question of indemnity is going to bedevil any vaccine programme and is obviously going to vary as a problem from state to state.

During the anti-malaria programme in Malaysia some people complained that the DDT was destroying the atap roofs of their huts. This, it was obvious to the scientists, was ridiculous as DDT had no effect upon leaves. Further complaints led to an investigation which showed that there was a moth which fed on atap palm leaves and that this moth had become resistant to DDT. It was normally kept in check by a parasitic wasp, which, however, remained susceptible to DDT and was greatly reduced in numbers. So DDT was indirectly responsible for the destruction of the atap roofs. No one is known to have sued the Malaysian government or the WHO for extensive damages, though one hopes some reparation was made.

Imagine the situation if some future vaccination programme started to lower the house values of certain areas of the Western World. The air would be impermeable with flying writs. It is advisable to remain sensitive to the opinions of the public, if for no other reason than that they may be right, but also if the co-operation of the public is required for the success of any scheme. Whether one should remain sensitive to the exaggerated legal claims being made in the USA against the medical profession, medical science and all their works remains in doubt.

During and immediately after this vaccination attempt there were 743 suits filed for damages for personal injury for over three hundred million dollars. There were 67 claims for wrongful death which gathered in a million or so. In total over six hundred million dollars were claimed and nine million one hundred thousand dollars were paid. One claimant filed for a thousand million dollars. New laws will have to accompany any new vaccination campaign in the USA limiting liability to real loss and only for a limited period.

So pride did indeed precede a fall in the 1976 vaccination campaign in the USA. It is hoped, however, that all concerned would do exactly the same or better if faced again with a similar situation. It should be asked only that it is done better and it is certain that it would. Their decisions were motivated by the highest ideals of public health. The same organs of government will be faced with the same sort of decisions if a new influenza pandemic threatens or if a vaccine for AIDS becomes available and they will face a much more helpful, much readier, much more understanding, but a much more factious and litigious public than the last time.

They themselves will be armed with the knowledge of some of what went wrong the last time. Did influenza have any effect upon human history? The answer must be an unequivocal – No. It may have had some effect upon human thinking about control of infectious disease, though nothing revolutionary. By the time the most disastrous pandemic of influenza occurred in 1918-19 and despite the timing just following a world war, civilisation had reached a point of development where it could absorb such a death toll with scarcely a blink. There was a blip in the birth rate in later years but due as much to the selective killing of young males in the war as due to unselective deaths from influenza. There was said to be a post-war psychosis involving immorality and much beloved by the self-appointed moralists of our society, but its advent, if it in fact occurred, was laid at the door of the war not the door of influenza.

The nature of this steady state, which could withstand the loss of 21,000,000 people, is a question for the sociologists if they can bring themselves to express the answer in a language comprehensible to the rest of mankind. The total population of the world and its continuing growth must be part of the answer. The confidence of the Industrial Revolution not yet dented by economic depressions might also have a role. It is not a question I am qualified to answer.

CONCLUSION

It has been the intention of this book to show that the course of history has been and can be affected by the major pandemics of infectious disease. The subsidiary aims have been:

1. To provide incidents, possibilities, disease descriptions and disease epidemiology over time as an assistance to future historians, and something of the vast bibliography of the incidence of infectious disease over recorded history.
2. To persuade historians that historical events cannot be studied satisfactorily and exhaustively without some attempt at the discovery of the state of health of the populace, the nature of any epidemic disease which might be present and the epidemiology and possible effects of that disease. It is recognised that the information may not be available for a diagnosis to be made, but effects can be noted and some investigation of the possible candidates among infectious diseases be pursued. To achieve such an aim some general conclusions must be drawn from the data presented to enable the reader to assess the importance of infectious disease in the fabric of history.

It seems axiomatic that all great powers, which have been the architects of social and economic systems, and all important systems themselves, have relied on and caused an increasing population and the expansion which naturally follows, to achieve and maintain power and erect those foundations upon which that power rests and feeds. The equivalent biological axiom would be that multiplication is a basic rule governing all organisms as natural selection favours the greater multiplication with its greater genetic plasticity.

It is tempting to call it a law but some mammals including man are known to use self-regulation of the rate of multiplication in times of stress and shortage and some advantage may be gained in terms of evolution in limiting populations in particular eco-systems, besides the short-term advantages. We simply do not know, but in the meantime the urge to multiply and even over-multiply does seem to be basic. It follows that the peak from which an organism will decline must be the maximum amount of population permitted by the environment or ecological niche occupied by that population. Once the source of power outruns the ability of the environment to maintain it, it and the population it supports become subject to a number of adverse pressures which bring about a decline or the acceleration of a decline already commenced. The problem is the definition and identification of the adverse pressures arising from population over-growth. Even when these are defined the problem of priority remains for any given situation.

It is obvious that the description of the lack of the ability of an environment to maintain a given population of mankind is complex, so complex indeed that rules cannot, as yet, be extracted. It is composed, to make an incomplete list of the elements involved, of:

1. Failure of the food supply.
2. Failure of other sources of power, such as fuel, water, metals or the means of purchasing these items.
3. Natural disasters, such as floods, droughts, volcanoes, earthquakes and presumably, in the decades to come, the warming of the earth.
4. Pandemics of infectious disease.
5. Aggression by other expanding populations requiring use of the particular environment.
6. Failure of the birth-rate.
7. On the other side of the coin. Emigration.

The last two are connected to rather nebulous concepts involving loss of confidence in the environment/population equation. Each of these categories contains a myriad of sub-categories. Any one of these categories may arise from an equal variety of causes and more often than not from one of the other categories and each may initiate, may contribute to the start of or may reinforce the decline. In that sense each is an element in the natural selection of the population. Detailed examination of each historical event is necessary to establish an order of importance for each or any of these categories.

It is held here that the state of susceptibility to adverse pressures must arise before these pressures, of the type listed above, can exert any significant effect. A state or a population of organisms seems able to absorb adverse pressures when expanding and it is only after the maximum expansion permitted by the environment has been reached that these pressures initiate or reinforce decline. There is nothing new in such a Darwinian view of historical events but the view is none the worse for that. It does express historical change in the terms of struggle and it is just from such a shackle that much modern political thinking is attempting to free mankind.

This view of major change in history omits the cause of the greatest alterations in man's state: the Agrarian Revolution and the Industrial Revolution, both the consequence of changes in technique. The view is, in fact, pre-Industrial Revolution. These revolutions also represent the temporal limits of the influence of infectious disease on history. The Agrarian Revolution brought about the crowding necessary for the leap forward in the incidence of infectious disease, while the Industrial Revolution began to bring the effects of infectious disease under man's control. However, these revolutions are not the league in which this book is intended to operate. Struggle, expansionism, compression and decline operate on states and their individual systems. Technical change is more universal and can be more all-embracing.

Of the categories listed above only that of natural disasters is free in its causation from the influence of others of the categories or the high populations susceptible to the influence of the categories. There is a sense, therefore, in which this is only a restatement of Malthusian doctrine which retains essential truths except among populations capable of controlling population growth or the environment or both. One of the watchwords of modern man must be, therefore, population contraction while struggling to maximise the use of the environment.

This leads to a question posed but not as yet answered. How did the large populations of Asia in India, China and the East Indies manage to continue to grow and absorb the shocks of plague, cholera and influenza in the eighteenth, nineteenth and twentieth centuries? They did not enjoy the benefits of the Industrial Revolution with its accompanying prosperity and confidence. It must be remembered, too, that the Industrial Revolution brought medical knowledge, a pharmaceutical industry and the ability to control many of the infectious diseases concerned whether by sewers, penicillin or DDT. The answer, in so far as it has been uncovered, seems to lie with a progressive increase in the efficiency in the use of land under cultivation and the opportunity to bring marginal land under the plough despite Ashton's gloomy view of the downtrodden, disadvantaged and diseased Asian peasant, unblessed by the Industrial Revolution.

The inter-relationships between the categories of pressure above are as important as the priorities, though rather more obvious. If crowding increases the chance of an infectious disease becoming epidemic, then a natural disaster, which almost always brings crowding in its wake, will also increase the likelihood of certain epidemics. War, which concentrates soldiers, camp followers and refugees, acts in the same way. Disease in its turn will bring about the failure of supply of labour and thus the supply of food and manufactures. Emigration will disseminate disease but also relieve over-crowding and other over-population stresses. Failures in supply will leave states subject to aggression. It is possible to go on and on with such inter-relations. Some suggested causes of decline, however, are illusory.

There is no proof that moral weakness or lack of confidence lays man more open to infection with the diseases studied here, unless *inter alia* they alter the life-style of man in such a way as to increase the quantum of infectious agent he may receive at any one time. Equally it can be claimed that there is no proof that lack of moral fibre ever brought about a major historical change though confidence does have some relationship to birth-rates. There is also no proof that famine or malnutrition are able directly to increase the susceptibility of man to the major infectious diseases treated here. Infectious diseases have their own logic which must be studied and applied to a particular situation just as one would with economics, geography or law.

It may seem entirely reasonable to assume that an adequate nutrition would enhance man's resistance to infection by most infectious diseases, but no scientist can allow himself the luxury of this type of thinking. After all it was entirely reasonable to assume that the world was flat, entirely reasonable to assume that the sun went around the earth, entirely reasonable to believe that infectious disease arose from a miasma. It remains entirely reasonable to a large body of living people that every rustle in the forest, every swirl in the river is informed by a spirit.

What is plain is that every fact about a particular event in history must be collected, whether thought relevant or not and these collated in a manner in which they can be brought to bear upon the event or system under study. These facts must include the state of health of the population and if an epidemic disease is present then that disease must be identified as far as possible and its incidence, nature, morbidity, mortality and epidemiology studied in order to assess its possible and probable effects on events. The computer with individual programs for individual diseases will be an invaluable tool in such enquiries.

This book does not attempt to fulfil the hope of Krause who wrote: 'Some day a man will write a new kind of history. Its keynote will be the shaping of human destiny by disease'. It does not fulfil this extravagant hope, partly because such a history would not be new but would only add to and employ existing knowledge and partly because disease is only one of the shapers of human destiny. None the less it can be hoped that this book will be a pale approximation of such a hope.

As a final comment I would like to insert a personal note in case anyone should be misled into believing that we have finished with the great infectious diseases described here. In my lifetime (and in that of all too many of my co-workers) I have seen the precautions, necessary in a sea-port of my youth, for the prevention of the arrival of plague; I have worked with and amidst malaria for much of my adult life; I missed by a bare year a major outbreak of yellow fever in the area in which I had been working; I saw a large outbreak of smallpox with its many victims; I have brushed with typhus when it broke out 45 kilometres away at a time when I was, myself, lousy; I have been in the midst of two cholera outbreaks and finally I have survived, as has anyone of my age, a number of influenza epidemics.

We are still in the midst of the recent plague pandemic and it still exists in the USA, in south-east Asia and in Africa. The El Tor pandemic of cholera is still with us. We have our very own pandemic of the 1980s and 1990s in AIDS. We have conquered smallpox but failed to do so with malaria and influenza. Yellow fever and typhus are still with us. We are on the brink of a revolution in biology and medicine which will bring at least some of these diseases under the control of man armed with the modern techniques of biological engineering, but it will not be tomorrow or even next year.

That rather feverish dreamer of Patmos, St John the Divine has given unexpected support to this book. Seven plagues have been examined just the number his seven angels had. It is also my personal belief that he was right to put the rider of the white horse first.

CHAPTER NOTES

PREFACE

(1) Even with rabies and AIDS the immune system works, but inadequately or inefficiently.

CHAPTER 1
(Early Civilizations)

(1) These included a plague in Thebes due to the murder of Laius by Oedipus, another following the first Heraclid (children of Heracles) invasion of the Peloponnese (if one equates that with the first Dorian invasion of the Mycaenian civilisation then that conquest was accompanied by infectious disease), another following the killing of Linus and Psamanthe in Argos, stopped by Crotopus' confession at Delphi, another plague at Orchomanus attended the escape from sacrifice by Phrixus who fled to Cholcis on Zeus' golden ram whose fleece was later sought by the Argonauts. A plague in Greece after the Trojan War was cured, at least locally, by the reburial of Hector's bones in Boetia. A plague in Elis was cured by the shoulder-blade of Pelops. In East Locris Athene sent a pestilence which lasted 1,000 years, despite the sending of Locrian girls as hostages to Athene in Troy (as this plague subsided in 246 BC this dates the end of the Trojan War to about 1264 BC). While all these plagues are mythological, probably all reflect real events and some may represent the same plague in differing localities.

(2) Shrewsbury really should have known better. He was a Professor of Bacteriology but of a pugnacious nature, which, allied to an extraordinary ability to take a firm grasp of the wrong end of the stick, made him a very unreliable source. The idea that a whole male population should be given over to a single and unusual sexual activity hardly bears a moment's examination. That such an activity leads to haemorrhoids is unproven.

(3) Not for the first time as field mice were said to have eaten the bow-strings of Scamander and his people as they founded Troy

(4) I must confess to some bias as I have a distinct partiality for the late Lieutenant-General Sir William MacArthur. An ex-president of the Royal Society of Tropical Medicine and Hygiene, an ex-Director-General of the Army Medical Services, an ex-Commandant of the Royal Army Medical College, an ex-Colonel-Commandant of the Royal Army Medical Corps, an ex-Editor of the Transactions of the Royal Society for Tropical Medicine and Hygiene, an ex-pupil of Robert Koch, Sir William was a formidable scholar and a physician of considerable experience and scope. He retained from his schooldays an ability to read Latin and ancient Greek and, more unusually, he possessed the facility to read ancient Irish. His experience with the great epidemic diseases was transcendent, an advantage not always shared by his fellow commentators and critics. My personal partiality

arises from an occasion when a paper of mine was submitted to the learned journal of which he was the editor. The paper included numerous references to an eminent pathologist and nineteenth-century German nobleman. I had referred to this gentleman as Kuppfer. The General's hand-written note accepting the paper for publication also mentioned- 'When I knew the Graf von Kupffer he was spelling his name with one P and two Fs.' Rarely has my appalling spelling received a more gentle admonition.

(5) for instance Bullock and Goodall.

(6) Crawfurd – erysipelas; Zinnser – smallpox. Ergotism and plague were also put forward as candidates. Hare, Conrad, Henschen, Wells and Patrick all favoured typhus.

(7) Though many commentators refer to Alexander's army turning back on the banks of the Indus, a more accurate description would be the Beas, a tributary of the Sutlej, itself a tributary of the Indus

CHAPTER 2
(Rome)

(1) Parker, the Littmans, Gilliam, Grant, Finley, Will, Salmon and Marks & Beatty all have views relevant to Boak's thesis. Others who have medical comments on the Roman Empire include Castiglione, Henschen and Maenchen-Haelfen.

CHAPTER 3
(Plague, Justinian's Plague, part 1)

(1) In a footnote to p. 14.

CHAPTER 4
(Plague, Justinian's Plague, part 2)

(1) The Asian nomads did give themselves some memorable names: Celestial Turks, the Golden Horde, the Turcomen of the White Sheep, the Seljuks of Rum, the Volga Bulgars.

(2) These included Conrad, Dols, Biraben & Le Goff and Allen.

(3) Or Byzantine Empire. There is a terminological disagreement between historians as to when the Eastern Roman Empire became the Byzantine Empire. To its inhabitants of the time it would have been the Roman Empire.

CHAPTER 5
(Plague, Justinian's Plague, part 3)

(1) The book in question: *The Plague in the Early Medieval Near East*, is in fact Conrad's thesis for a degree of Doctor of Philosophy at Princeton University. His University must have been proud of such a scholarly, perceptive and penetrating student.

(2) It is rather more complicated than this but it is not desirable to embark upon a dissertation on the genetics of plasmid control of bacteria in a book such as this, even if the facility to do so were available.

(3) See Burroughs & Bacon, Burroughs and Rosqvist et al.

(4) I am not sure about black rats which have not been reported to my knowledge to demonstrate periodic rises and crashes in population; other field rodents, in my experience, show such population movements every four to five years which would not seem to fit with plague periodicities which are in the ten to twenty year range.

CHAPTER 6
(Plague, The Black Death, part 1)

(1) Twigg's suggestion that the Black Death was not bubonic plague is based primarily on a belief that there were insufficient black rats in the Europe of the fourteenth-century to support a massive zoonosis like the Black Death. Twigg suggests that it may have been anthrax. It has been stressed here as well that it is difficult to believe that a zoonosis could reach the dimensions of the Black Death but, rather than putting forward an alternative disease it is suggested here that there were large elements of pneumonic and septicaemic plague in the Black Death. It has been pointed out that there were, in fact, a number of reports of *Rattus rattus* in Europe in the period before the Black Death and indeed before the Crusades, the time when black rats were thought by many to have been introduced into Europe. These reports, however, do not support the notion that the black rat was either ubiquitous or present in great numbers. There are many objections to Twigg's thesis and it would be wearisome to list them all. Suffice it to say that the substitution of another zoonosis, anthrax, not known to produce pandemics in man for plague, raises more questions than it answers. Anthrax is a sparse disease in man rarely epidemic for long and not transmitted directly between men except in very special circumstances. It must be said, however, that zoonotic plague did cause a pandemic in man in the late nineteenth and early twentieth-century.

(2) This is the recently published account of the Black Death in Scandinavia by Benedictow, O.J. (1992) *Plague in the Late Medieval Nordic Countries*. Middelalderforget, Oslo. This book advances the theory that the rat flea is better able to withstand cold than the human flea because it is a 'fur flea' (*X. cheopis*) as opposed to a 'nest flea' (*P. irritans*) and so benefits to a greater degree from the hosts' warmth.

(3) As has been shown by Bolin et al, Burroughs & Bacon and Rosqvist et al.

(4) Such as Gottfried, Dols .

(5) Ibn Batuta was in China at the time and says nothing about an epidemic. It would be strange indeed if a major epidemic of plague was raging and that ubiquitous, inquisitive and voluble globe-trotter failed to note it, particularly as he was to experience it himself in Damascus prior to his writing of his travels and to say so.

CHAPTER 7
(Plague, The Black Death, part 2)

(1) The recent general accounts include Pollitzer, Ziegler, Biraben, Dols, Gottfried and Twigg.

(2) The more particular and localised accounts are those of Herlihy in Pistoia, Carpentier in Orvieto, Verlinden in Spain. Prat in Albi and numerous others in Switzerland, Germany and the Low Countries.

(3) Josiah Russell has written a number of articles and books on the medieval population of Britain. These can be found in the bibliography.

CHAPTER 8
(Plague, The Black Death, part 3)

(1) Shakespeare noted this tendency when, in *Romeo and Juliet*, (Act III, Scene I) he has Mercutio say of Benvolio :– 'Thou! why, thou wilt quarrel with a man that hath more hair, or a hair less, in his beard than thou hast: thou wilt quarrel with a man for cracking nuts, having no reason but because thou hast hazel eyes, thy head is as full of quarrels as an egg is full of meat.'

(2) This view of medicine can be culled from reading Gerlitt, Cipollo and Carmichael.

(3) Petrach's Laura died of pneumonic plague and Petrach was gripped with a life-long hatred of doctors as a consequence. The story that the doctor in question was Gui de Chauliac has been discounted.

(4) See Singer and Allyn.

(5) There must be some doubt cast upon this belief as Gibbon states that in Rome one might say 'Jupiter bless you' if you sneezed which would cast considerable doubt on the term 'bless you' having anything to do with a disease not known in the Western Roman Empire or the Roman republic

(6) Carmichael has put in a disclaimer to this view. She has thrown her cap into the ring with these words:– 'It has become very popular to assume that changes in the natural world, especially the influence of disease-causing organisms, have repeatedly altered the course of history'. She goes on to say:– 'It is the purpose of this (her) book to offer weight to the argument that conscious decisions influence patterns of mortality.' As she chooses northern Italy in the fourteenth and fifteenth centuries as her battle-ground her arguments should be addressed here. One of her main contentions is that of the epidemic diseases of the fifteenth-century by no means all were caused by *Yersinia pestis*. She believes that typhus and smallpox, in particular, played a part. It has already been pointed out that the nature of the disease would not affect the thesis that it was disease *in toto* that caused certain effects, particularly a population decline. Carmichael goes on to argue that some of this disease was brought under control by deliberate human agency (as opposed to immunity in, say, smallpox). Some of her guesses as to the nature of the diseases which might have been concerned are a little too widely put.

To interpret 'colds and fever' as influenza would alarm those physicians of today who are trying to persuade the general public not to assume that they have influenza whenever they sneeze and have a little fever. A more likely translation is 'chills and fever' which would open the diagnosis much more widely and include malaria which was common in the Po valley and the lands of the Gonzaga of Mantua at the time. It would help if we knew what sweating sickness was and whether it was sweating sickness which was involved. Her introduction of flea-borne typhus onto the scene seems irrelevant as flea-borne typhus would be zoonotic and sporadic and if one has to call upon the rat and its fleas why not choose bubonic plague with its known track record? The objections to anthrax as a candidate have already been expressed. The introduction of African meningococcal meningitis as a possible contributor to the diseases of fifteenth-century Florence is rather eccentric; it is a disease of the hot dry savannah of sub-saharan Africa.

She feels strongly that smallpox was mixed up in the organisms causing the post-Black Death epidemics in Italy and she may well be right though it is surprising that no descriptions of this highly distinctive disease have come down to us from the period, (see Cook for a discussion of the differences between smallpox and plague). In the later fifteenth-century when the population ceased to fall or remain stagnant in Europe Carmichael separates major from minor pestilences. The minor pestilences she categorises as clustered in space and tending to be confined to classes and occupations and she argues strongly that such clustering is atypical of plague. This is largely true of the Bombay plague, a zoonosis. However, she also discounts any involvement of pneumonic or septicaemic plague at the time on not wholly convincing grounds. She finds that the outbreaks which she categorises as smallpox occurred at intervals of twenty-five to thirty years, starting among the children and spreading to the adults and the elderly. This seems a little dubious, the elderly should have been largely immune in any concentrated community. Carmichael rejects the claim that the same progression would have occurred for plague and that the loss among the pre-breeding children would have had the effect of lowering the fertility of the population leading to the inability of the population to recover in the first part of the fifteenth-century. Carmichael is most interesting about fifteenth-century Florence and its sanitation laws. She claims that these attempts to control disease were partially successful and were the basic cause of the slowing down of the epidemics of the later fifteenth-century, though earlier she had implied that a loss of virulence of plague had played a part, and though she will have nothing to do with the two truly contagious forms of plague as contributory factors in the fifteenth-century.

She notes all the new precautions taken which include the opening of hospitals, quarantine of active cases, quarantine of people from plague areas, general cleansing operations and isolation of the poor, generally believed to be the source and major reservoir of contagion. The major difficulty with the acceptance of this hypothesis of man's partial control of the disease of the time lies with cities other than Florence, notably Venice and Milan. Both instituted all, some or more of the measures adopted by Florence with no apparent benefit at all. Venice, which had the greatest number of hospitals, health officers and quarantine restrictions still suffered major plague outbreaks in 1575 and 1630. Milan, likewise, instituted many anti-plague measures and suffered badly in the late fifteenth and early sixteenth centuries. It would appear that even if Carmichael had proved her point that man had slowed down the incidence of post-1348 epidemics of disease and that these diseases were by no means wholly plague, she is still far from proving or starting to prove that infectious disease has not altered the course of history, if that was her intention.

CHAPTER 9

(The Bombay Plague)

(1) It has been claimed that the bacillus found by Kitasato was not the plague bacillus.

(2) See Wu, Hirst, Crumpston & MacCullum and van Zwanenberg.

(3) See Rosqvist et al., Brubaker and Lenski.

(4) The scientific method of apportioning priority and praise on the basis of first past the publication post can lead to injustice. Yersin published his short account of *Y. pestis* first though Kitisato had been the first to find an organism which he claimed was *Y. pestis*. Not for the first or the last time the French were able to claim priority because of their habit of publishing letters quickly in their medico-scientific press, even, sometimes, letters to colleagues rather than to editors of journals.

(5) For India see Hirst; for South Africa see Pirie; for Australia see Crumpston & MacCullum; for the USA see Smith and Gregg; for England see van Zwanenberg and for South America see Moll.

CHAPTER 10

(Malaria, part 1)

(1) Jones put forward his thesis in two books and a paper and these included notes from Ronald Ross. Both were convinced from their observations of malaria in Greece in the early part of this century and from the poverty to be seen at the time in the areas to the north of Athens that malaria could bring the Greece of earlier times to its knees.

(2) The malariology gets a little complicated here as it all depends on the species of *Anopheles* involved and its preferences for breeding places. In parts of West Africa sea water can be used to flush out drains containing compounded fresh water as the dangerous local vector *A. gambiae* will not breed in sea or brackish water; in other parts it could be dangerous as another efficient vector *A. melas* will breed in brackish water. To complicate matters the level of brackishness necessary for *A. melas* may be achieved in one part of West Africa in the dry season when the sea creeps back up the less strongly flowing

rivers, but in others it may in the wet season when the greater amounts of fresh water commence to dilute the tidal sea water. In Agrigentum if the *Anopheles* bred in brackish water, then the prevention of the entrance of sea water would have resulted in fresh water inimical to the mosquito. If the mosquito bred in fresh water the blockage of sea water would do harm. de Zulueta's argument about which species of *Anopheles* was present is critical to this tale of Agrigentum.

(3) Is such a term permissible in the tideless Mediterranean?

CHAPTER 11
(Malaria, part 2)

(1) Celli's *The History of Malaria in the Roman Campagna* and his *Malaria* should be read in association with Russell, de Zulueta, Bruce-Chwatt & de Zulueta, Bruce-Chwatt and Hackett to obtain a balanced and up-to-date view of malaria in Rome.

CHAPTER 12
(Malaria, part 3)

(1) Brigadier John Sinton of the Indian Medical Service who not only made notable contributions to research in tropical medicine, for which he was made a Fellow of the Royal Society, but also was awarded the Victoria Cross for bravery in the First World War when attending the wounded in no-man's-land between the trenches of the Western Front. He was the only Fellow of the Royal Society to be the recipient of the Victoria Cross. He was described by a colleague as 'a strange fellow' because he infected himself with a parasite from his dog to prove that the parasite also infected man. The same colleague, of course, tested plague and rabies vaccines on himself. The RAMC were known as 'rather a mad crowd'; the IMS earned the soubriquet of 'infinitely more so'.

(2) *Anopheles minimus*, an efficient local vector today, would have done well in the conditions of the Great Lake.

CHAPTER 13
(Yellow Fever)

(1) See Germain et al, Meunier et al and Baudon & Robert.

(2) See Marks & Beatty, Creighton, Moll and Cloudesley-Thompson.

CHAPTER 14
(Smallpox, part 1)

(1) This version of the story of the Elephant War can be found in Hopkins, Guillaume and Muhammed Ali.

(2) by Moore, Wu and Wong.

(3) This group includes Smith, Wong again, MacGowan and Wong & Wu.

(4) see also Rosen.

(5) such as Cartwright and Nicholas.

CHAPTER 15
(Smallpox, part 2)

(1) for the early history of the Spanish Carribean possessions relative to Cortez see Prescott, Collis and Diaz.

CHAPTER 16
(Smallpox, part 3)

(1) Including Hare, Marks & Beatty, Hobson, Crosby, Parry, Thursfield, Williams, Hauptman, Woodward, Bardell, Cook and Hirsch.

(2) The figures tell their own story:– N-E. USA & S-E. Canada, from 55,000 reduced to 22,000. N-W. USA, several nations destroyed, from 90,000 reduced to 15,000. The plains of the USA, from 142,000 reduced to 53,000. S. USA, from 52,000 reduced to 2,170. W. Canada, from 86,000 reduced to 25,000. A reduction of over 70%. What chance did the North American Indian stand?

(3) One of the important books devoted to this subject and others concerning the effect of disease on world history is *Plagues and People* by William, H. McNeill. It is time to consider this book and examine McNeill's theories in some detail. There are two main difficulties with McNeill's book. The first is with his introduction where he states the answer to the ease with which Cortez and Pizarro had defeated whole nations with a few men, primitive arms and some horses came to him from a chance remark by a forgotten interlocutor; it was only after mulling over the thought for some time that the blinding truth struck him, – smallpox had intervened. Surely his reading must have been a little on the sparse side. The idea is embedded in the contemporary account of Bernal Diaz, another of those matter-of-fact chroniclers in the mould of Thucydides.

Prescott says there was not any requirement for warfare in order to capture the Aztec capital as the inhabitants were no longer capable of resisting due to starvation and disease. Moore in 1815 gave a vivid account of the victory of smallpox before Tenochtitlan. In our day Rolleston, Moll, Stearn & Stearn, Ashburn, Duffy, Henschen, Hare, Hobson, Dobyns, Cooray, Parry, Crosby and the *Cambridge Modern History of Latin America* all set forth the idea that the conquest of the Aztecs and the Incas was enabled by smallpox. It does seem that the idea was in circulation well before McNeill's sudden realisation.

The second sticking point arises from his historical theories based on the behaviour of parasites. Here the problems spring from what McNeill believes are the principles of parasitology. His theory of mutual adaption and a consequent state of balance between host and parasite which is reached after a long interval of change and adaption is unproven. It is challenged by those who see parasitism as a state of open warfare where mutual agreements are not possible. As this view of adaption is central to McNeill's ideas perhaps the opposite view should be set out here:– it states that parasites always attempt to multiply to the greatest degree possible and this is an invariable rule; that multiplication and the resultant numbers are the basis of the parasite's virulence in the host; that the host, on the other hand, always strives to rid itself of the parasite and that this too is an invariable rule. So all mutations of the parasite that are useful and selected for survival are those which bring about greater numbers and therefore greater virulence, including those which evade the host's defence mechanism. Mutations in the host which limit the multiplication of the parasites also have survival value and are therefore selected. The opposite to this open warfare cannot exist as selection would then be required to select for a loss of multiplication of parasites or protection of the host. The two opponents have no means of communication to indicate that they are going to weaken so the other side could weaken simultaneously. No negotiation is possible so a sympathetic weakening of response has no mechanism whereby it can be agreed. Selection is of advantage not disadvantage. If the parasite were to change to a more conciliatory form it would be eliminated. If the host let down its defences it would be killed if not by the parasite then by other parasites ready to take advantage of any weakening of the host. We see today the results of treatments resulting in immuno-deficiencies or infection with human immuno-deficiency virus where previously harmless organisms are allowed to multiply to life-threatening proportions. So mutual tolerance systems between host and parasite cannot exist.

The proponents of this view of host-parasite relationships have some proof on their side, arising out of work done on mutant flax rusts and mutant host flaxes, but they have to lay down rules for behaviour, always a dangerous exercise in biology. They have to say for instance that multiplication is an invariable rule, but animals are known voluntarily to limit the size of their litters in times of stress and so to alter their multiplication rate within one generation.

The supporters of the view that mutual adjustments are possible between host and parasite, argue that they are not only possible but operating in a number of situations today and point to the relationships between the older species on our planet such as lizards and some of their parasites which appear to be relatively non-pathogenic and apparently undamaging relationships do exist. The problem is that they do not do any experiments to find out the degree to which the lizard is suffering and whether it has given up any of its defences. In summary the whole question is *sub-judice* and no conclusions from it can be recruited for macro-parasitic theories of history.

McNeill's examples of this state of mutual peace between host and parasite also bear little examination. His first example is *P. falciparum*, the parasite causing malignant tertian malaria, which he says entered man recently and is therefore the most virulent of the human malaria parasites. The late arrival of *P. falciparum* is a common view, but it is only a guess and is assumed largely because it is pathogenic, so making a wholly circular argument. It also completely ignores the fact that a virtually indistinguishable parasite exists today in chimpanzees. In fact *P. falciparum* is something of an enigma as recent work has tended to relate it to the bird malaria parasites rather than the other primate malaria parasites. If it entered into the primate stock from birds then any adaptions it made in the birds are irrelevant to its existence in primates. On the other hand chimpanzees have a malaria parasite almost identical with *P. falciparum* so the entry from birds would have to have occurred before man split from the ancestral primate stock some five or so million years ago. Again the argument is *sub-judice* and far more complicated than McNeill gives it credit for.

McNeill says of malaria that it is not surprising that this very ancient form of infection should be harmless to mosquitoes and still preserve its malignancy to the recent man. This statement contains so many errors that it is difficult to know where to start. It assumes that the parasite in man is new to man but old to the mosquito. Why? It must have changed in some way to have infected man (the *P. falciparum* – like parasite of chimpanzees does not infect man) and so it will also be new to the mosquito, at least in some way (the mosquito transmitting chimpanzee malaria is not the same as the one transmitting human malaria). After this the progression gets very complicated indeed.

There are those who believe that it is axiomatic that the malaria parasite does affect the mosquito, and, of course, *vice versa*. In other words that a host-parasite relationship must include some effects on both host and parasite. It should be said that an effect of malaria parasites on mosquitoes has not yet been shown.

What happens if one starts to apply these principles inherent in McNeill's theories to plague? Here too we have an insect host where the relationship is presumed to be ancient, a rodent host where the relationship is also of some age and a human host where the relationship is new. *Y. pestis* does not care, it kills them all indiscriminately. There is no proof for McNeill's assumption that rodents acquire an immunity to plague so the disease becomes sylvatic and quiescent. In the tarabagan colonies of Manchuria it is known that the bacillus continues to kill rodents and those experiments which have shown that some species of rodent are more resistant to plague than others have not shown that this resistance was due to some past exposure to plague. Indeed, in general, it would seem that such innate resistance to a particular disease as does occur among rodents is the result of some mutation selected for a wholly different reason which then turned out to confer resistance to the disease.

All too many of McNeill's assumptions are expressed as facts for a scientist to be anything else than uncomfortable. He says that the probability of picking up a disease lying in wait for man in the rain forests is the 'principal obstacle to human domination over the rain forests'. An agriculturalist or a member of the Green Party would be unlikely to agree. He designates these lying-in-wait organisms as free-living potential parasites. It is certain that a parasitologist would not agree.

Later he touches a raw nerve with his statement that:– 'Low grade infections and infestations probably flared up into fatal complications whenever serious injury or some severe stress (famine for instance) upset the host's internal physiological balances'. This statement wholly lacks any experimental proof.

Elsewhere McNeill states:– 'Many of the parasitic worms and protozoa that abound in Africa do not provoke immune reactions, ie the formation of anti-bodies in the bloodstream'. McNeill can be forgiven for not realising that blood-stream antibodies are not the only specific immune reaction when he was writing in 1975/6 but not for building a theory of balance on such a bold and wholly incorrect statement. The fact is that all foreign bodies of reasonable molecular size cause an immunological reaction in man. Zoology is not yet in the state of mathematical physics where permanent rules can be extracted within the limits of the uncertainty principle, which have stood the test of time. That time may come when the fundamentals of zoology are reduced to physical chemistry, but for the present few general principles of animal behaviour can be adduced which do not have exceptions and are thus unacceptable as laws. In zoology and biology we must content ourselves with natural selection and the necessity to multiply as seeming general principles. It follows that it is not possible to extract rules of the behaviour for parasites, which can hold up against any challenge, and apply them to events in human history. This is not to say that the attempt to do so may not be illuminating and even enlighten aspects of history but it will establish no rules.

CHAPTER 17

Typhus (part 1)

(1) Baker sets out this progression of typhus from simple rat-flea-rat transmission through the zoonotic stage where both man and rat are involved and occasionally the tick and mite as well, eventually to the anthroponotic epidemic man-louse-man situation. The final step of direct man-man transmission has not occurred in typhus as it has in pneumonic plague.

(2) **AD1083** The monastery at La Cava near Salerno. Hirsch, Zinnser, Castiglione, Henschen, Ackerknecht. **AD1157** Frederick Barbarossa's army before Rome. Zinnser, Cloudesley-Thompson. **AD1196** In Britain. Bonser. MacArthur thinks it may have been in Britain earlier. **AD1347** In Florence. Crawfurd. **AD1419** Possibly in Newgate Gaol, London. Creighton. **AD1480** In Carinthia and Carniola following a famine. Marks & Beatty. **AD1489** Granada where the troops of Ferdinand and Isabella fought the Moors; the decisive battle of the Reconquista. The Spaniards were supposed to have brought the disease back from Cyprus where they had been fighting with the Venetians against the

Ottoman Turk. Hirsch, Crawfurd, Prinzing, Hobson, Hare, Cartwright. **AD1505**. Fracastorius, the father of the theory of infectiousness, gave the first valid description of epidemic typhus in 1546 and mentioned outbreaks in 1505 and 1528. Zinnser, Ackerknecht, Marks and Beatty. **AD1528** The German and Spanish Habsburg Emperor Charles V was disputing the hegemony of Europe with the French Francis I. The French troops were besieging the Imperial troops in Naples when they were struck by typhus and had to withdraw. Charles V was confirmed in his role of Holy Roman Emperor and arbiter of Europe by grace of typhus. Later the Imperial army was besieging the French at Metz when typhus reversed its allegiance and attacked the troops of Charles V, thus releasing the French. Greenwood, Major, Colnat.

(3) Wallenstein enjoyed the certainties of a horoscope cast by no lesser cosmologist than Kepler himself.

CHAPTER 18
Typhus (part 2)

(1) Larrey had had typhus himself a year or so before in Konigsberg.

(2) For accounts of typhus and Napoleon's retreat from Moscow see Fuller, Crawfurd, Burnet & White, Greenwood, Zinnser, Major, Hare, Henschen , Marks & Beatty, Chandler.

(3) This can be found in the descriptions of typhus in Hort, Davey & Brown, Prinzing, and Strong et al.

(4) This belief has been noted by Crawfurd, Moore, Hare, Gale, MacArthur, Woodham-Smith, Ackerknecht, Creighton, Clarkson and Post.

(5) I can remember being on the so-called 'Long March' from Pomerania to Hannover as a prisoner-of-war in 1944/5 and being told, when in a barn in Demmin, that typhus had broken out among Russian prisoners-of-war at Neubrandenburg, some 35 miles to the south. Not news to fill any of us with joy as we were all inevitably lousy. We ended up in a camp at Fallingbostal on the Lunerberger-Heide, fortunately escaping typhus, when one day our water supply was cut off. Our protests evinced the news that typhoid and typhus had broken out in a camp nearby and it was for our own protection that the mains water supply had been cut. Later it was realised that the nearby camp was Belsen, where some 3,500 victims of typhus lay.

CHAPTER 19
Cholera (part 1)

(1) The very few gaps which might have been left by MacNamara are plugged by Pollitzer and Proust.

(2) There is something about Archangel, just below the Arctic Circle, which acts as a magnet for so-called tropical diseases; it saw malaria immediately after the First World War and was the home of a moujik in whom was made the first discoveries of the agent of amoebic dysentery.

(3) See Bourdelais & Raulot, Delaporte and Chevalier.

(4) See Delaporte, Chevalier and Tudesq.

CHAPTER 20
Cholera (part 2)

(1) Such as Greenwood, Hare, Smith and Hobson.

CHAPTER 21
Cholera (part 3)

(1) for commentaries on the social and legislative effects of cholera in the United Kingdom see McGrew, Briggs, Singer & Underwood, Morris, Durey and Cartwright.

(2) See Chevalier and Ocana.

(3) Napoleon's campaigns had spawned a group of doctors and surgeons well aware of infectious diseases among crowds. See Ackerknecht, La Berge and Coleman.

(4) For the pre-eminence of French medical statistics and municipal public health at the time see Coleman and Flinn.

CHAPTER 22
Cholera (part 4)

(1) Kinnear-Wilson believes that the demoness who strikes the belly seven times with her long fingernails in the Babylonian Lamastu text may have been typhoid which tends to cause seven rose spots as a rash.

CHAPTER 23
Influenza (part 1)

(1) these are well documented by Hirsch, Creighton, Gale, Crookshank, Burnet & White and Clarkson.

CHAPTER 24
Influenza (part 2)

(1) There is the sober chronicle of Millar & Osborn and that of Viseltear in the 1977 book on influenza edited by Osborn. The more critical writing have been by Silverstein and Neustadt & Fineberg.

Bibliography

B.H.M. = *Bulletin of the History of Medicine*
B.J.M. = *British Medical Journal*
C.U.P. = *Cambridge University Press*
E.H.R.2 = *Economic History Review, 2nd Series*
H.M.S.O = *Her Majesty's Stationary Office*
O.U.P. = *Oxford University Press*
T.R.S.T.M & H. = *Transactions of the Royal Society of Tropical Medicine and Hygine*
W.H.O. = *World Health Organisation*

Ackerknecht, E.H. (1948) Hygiene in France, 1815–1848. *B.H.M.*, 22, 117–55.
Ackerknecht, E.H. (1965) *History and Geography of the most Important Diseases*. Hafner, New York.
Adamson, P.B. (1970) The Babu'tu' lesion in antiquity. *Hist. Med.*, 14, 313–18.
Allen, P. (1979) The 'Justiniac' plague. *Byzantion*, 49, 5–20.
Allyn, H.B. (1925) The Black Death and its social and economic results. *Ann. Hist. Med.*, 7, 226–36.
Appleby, A.B. (1980) The disappearance of plague: a continuing puzzle. *E.H.R.2*, 33, 161–73.
Ashburn, P.M. (1947) *The Ranks of Death*. Coward McCann, New York.
Ashton, T.S. (1968) *The Industrial Revolution, 1760–1830*. Claredon, Oxford.
Aubrey, P. (1979) L'expédition Française de Madagascar de 1895. Un disastre sanitaire. *Méd. Armées*, 7, 745–52.
Bailey, N.T.J. (1975) *The Mathematical Theory of Infectious Disease and its Applications*. Griffon, London.
Baker, A.C. (1943) The typical epidemic series. *Am. J. trop. Med.* 23, 559–66.
Bardell, D. (1976) Smallpox during the American war of independence. *Am. Soc. Med. News*, 42, 526–30.
Barkhuus, A. (1947) Diseases and medical problems of Ethiopia. *CIBA Symposium*, 9, 710–23.
Bartsocas, C.S. (1966) Two fourteenth century Greek descriptions of the Black Death. *J. Hist. Med.* 21, 395–401.
Barua, D. & Burrows, W. eds (1974) *Cholera*. Saunders, Philadelphia.
Baudon, D & Robert, V. (1984) Epidemic yellow fever in the Upper Volta. *Lancet*, ii, 42.
Bean, J.M.W. (1963) Plague, population and economic decline in England in the later middle ages. *E.H.R.2*, 15, 423–37.
Bean, J.M.W. (1982) The Black Death and its social and economic consequences in *The Black Death, the Impact of the Fourteenth Century Plague*. ed. D. Williman. Medieval and Renaissance Texts. Studies, Binghampton.

Berben, P. (1975) *Dachau*. Norfolk, London.

Bercovier, H., Mollaret, H.H., Alonso, J.M., Brault, J,Fanning,G.R. Steigervalt A.G. & Brenner D.J. (1980) Intra-and interspecies relatedness of *Yersinia pestis* by DNA hybridization and its relationship to *Yersina pseudotuberculosis*. *Current Immunology*. 4, 225–9.

Bethell, L. ed. (1984)*The Cambridge History of Latin America*. Vol. 1. C.U.P., Cambridge.

Beveridge, W.I.B. (1977) *Influenza: The Last Great Plague*. Heinemann, London.

Bilson, G. (1980) *A Darkened House: Cholera in Nineteenth century Canada*. Univ. Toronto Press, Toronto.

Binnie, G.M. (1981) *Early Victorian Water Engineers*. Telford, London.

Biraben, J-N. & Le Goff, J. (1969) La peste dans le haut moyen âge. *Ann. Econ. Soc. civil.*, 24, 1484–1510.

Biraben, J-N. (1975) *Les Hommes et la Peste en France et dans les Pays Européens et Mediterranéens*. Mouton, Paris.

Blanc, G. & Baltazard, M. (1941) Récherches expérimentales sur la peste. Infection de la puce de l'homme. *C.R. Acad. Sci.*, 213, 813–16.

Blanton, W.B. (1942) Medical references in Bernal Diaz' account of the discovery and conquest of Mexico, (1517–1521). *Ann. Med. Hist.*, (3rd ser.), 4, 399–05.

Boak, A.E.R. (1955) *Manpower Shortage and the Fall of the Roman Empire*. Univ. Mich. Press, Ann Arbor.

Boccaccio, G. (1966) *The Decameron*. Folio Soc., London.

Bodenheimer, F.S. (1972) *Animal and Man in Bible Lands*. Brill, London.

Bolin, I., Forsberg, A., Norlander, L., Skurnik, M. & Wolf-Watz, H. (1988) Identification and mapping of the temperature inducible plasmid encoded proteins of *Yersinia* spp. *Infect. Immun.* 56, 343–8.

Bonser, W. (1944) Epidemics during the Anglo-Saxon period. *J.Brit. arch. Soc.* (3rd ser.), 9, 48–71.

Borges, J.L. (1973) *A Universal History of Infamy*. Allen Lane, London.

Bourdelais, P. & Raulot, J-Y. (1987) *Une Peur Bleue: Histoire de Cholera en France. 1832–1854*. Payot, Paris.

Bowsky, W.M. (1964) The impact of the Black Death on Sienese government and society. *Speculum*, 39, 1–35.

Bowsky, W.M. (1971) Siena: stability and dislocation. in *The Black Death. A Turning Point in History?* ed. W.M. Bowsky, pp. 114–21. Holt, Rhinehart & Winston, New York.

Boyle J. (1831) *A Practical Medico-Historical Account of the West Coast of Africa*. Highly, London.

Bray, J. (1988) *The Emperor's Doorkeeper*. pp. 104–20, Univ. Adelaide Foundation, Adelaide.

Bridbury, A.R. (1973) The black death. *E.H.R.2*, 26, 557–92.

Briercliffe, R. (1935) *The Ceylon Malaria Epidemic, 1934-35*. Ceylon Govt. Press, Colombo.

Briggs, A. (1961) Cholera and society in the nineteenth century. *Past & Present*, 19, 76–96.

Briggs, L.P. (1951) The Ancient Khmer Empire. *Trans. Am. phil. Soc.* n.s. 41, part 1, Am. Phil. Soc., Philadelphia.

Brubaker, R.R. (1979) Expression of virulence in *Yersinia* in *Microbiology* – 1979. ed. D. Schlessinger. pp. 168–71. *Am. Soc. Microbiol.*, Washington D.C.

Bruce-Chwatt, L.J. & de Zulueta, J. (1980) *The Rise and Fall of Malaria in Europe*. O.U.P., London.

Bruce-Chwatt, L.J. (1989) History of malaria from pre-history to eradication in *Malaria. Principles and Practice of Malariology*. eds. W.H. Wernsdorfer & I.A. McGregor, pp

1–59. Vol. 1. Churchill-Livingston, London.

Brunt, P.A. (1971) *Italian Manpower, 225 BC – AD 14*. Clarendon, Oxford.

Bullock, W. (1930) History of bacteriology, in *A System of Bacteriology in Relation to Medicine*. ed. F.W. Andrews et al., H.M.S.O., London.

Burnet, M. & Clark, E. (1942) *Influenza*. MacMillan, London.

Burnet, M. & White, D.O. (1972) *Natural History of Infectious Diseases*. C.U.P. Cambridge.

Burroughs, T.W. & Bacon, G.A. (1958) The effects of loss of various virulence determinants on the virulence and the immunogenicity of strains of *Pasteurella pestis*. *Brit. J. exp. Path.*, 39, 278–91.

Burroughs, T.W. (1963) Virulence of *Pasteurella pestis* and immunity to plague. *Ergb. Mikrobiol. Immunatsf. exp. Therap.*, 37, 59–113.

Bury, J.B. (1958) *History of the Later Roman Empire*. Dover, New York.

Butler, T. (1983) *Plague and Other Yersinia Infections*. Plenum, New York.

Campbell, A.M. (1966) *The Black Death and Men of Learning*. A.M.S. Press, New York.

Carlson, D.G. (1984) *African Fever*. Sci. Hist. Publ, Canton.

Carmichael, A.G. (1983) Plague legislation in the Italian Renaissance. *B.H.M.*, 57, 508–25.

Carmichael, A.G. (1986) *Plague and the Poor in Renaissance Florence*. C.U.P., Cambridge.

Carnwarth, T. (1919) Lessons of the influenza epidemic. *J. State Med.*, 27, 142–57.

Carpentier, E. (1962A) *Une Ville Devant la Peste. Orvieto et la Peste Noire de 1348*. S.E.V.P.E.N., No 7 of the collection Demographie et Sociétés, Paris.

Carpentier, E. (1962B) *La Peste Noire: Famines et épidémies au XIV siecle*. Ann. Econ. Soc. Civil., 17, 1062-1092.

Carpentier, E. (1971) Orvieto: institutional stability and moral change. in *The Black Death. A Turning Point in History?* ed. W.M. Bowsky, pp. 108-113. Holt, Rhinehart & Winston, New York.

Carter, H.R. (1931) *Yellow Fever*. Williams & Wilkins, Baltimore.

Cartwright, F.F. (1972) *Disease and History*. Hart-Davis, McGibbon, London.

Cartwright, F.F. (1983) Pandemics past and present. in *Disease in Ancient Man*. ed. G.D. Hart, pp. 267–80. Clarke-Irwin, Toronto.

Castiglione, A. (1947) *History of Medicine*. Routledge & Kegan Paul, London.

Cavanaugh, D.C., Elisberg, B.L., Llewellyn, C.H., Marshall, J.D., Rust, J.H., Williams, J.E. & Meyer, K.F. (1974) Plague Immunization. Indirect evidence for the efficacy of plague vaccine. *J. inf. Dis.*, 129 suppl. 537–40.

Celli, A. (1900) *Malaria*. Longmans Green, London.

Celli, A. (1933) *The History of Malaria in the Roman Campagna*. Bale, London.

Chambers, J.D. (1972) *Population, Economy and Society in Pre-Industrial England*. O.U.P., Oxford.

Chambers, J.S. (1938) *The Conquest of Cholera*. MacMillan, New York.

Chandler, D.G. (1978) *The Campaigns of Napoleon*. Weidenfeld & Nicholson, London.

Chevalier, A.G. (1941) Hygienic problems in the Napoleonic armies. *CIBA Symposium*, 3, 974–80.

Chevalier, L. (1958) Paris. in *Le Choléra. La Première Epidémie du XIX Siècle*. ed. L. Chevalier, pp. 3–45. *Imprimerie Centrale de L'Ouest*, La Roche-sur-Yon.

Christie, J. (1876) *Cholera Epidemics in East Africa*. MacMillan, London.

Christophers, S.R. (1911) Malaria in the Punjab. *Mem. Off. med. san. Dept. Govt. India*, No. 46, Govt. Printer, Calcutta.

Christophers, S.R. (1924) What disease costs India: being a statement of the problem before malaria research in India. *Ind med. Gaz.*, 59, 196–400.

Cipolla, C.M. (1974) *The Economic History of World Population*. Penguin, Harmondsworth.

Cipollo, C.M. (1973) *Christofano and the Plague*. Collins, London.

Clarke, G. (1947) *The Seventeenth Century*. Clarendon, Oxford.

Clarkson, L. (1975) *Death, Disease and Famine*. Gill & MacMillan, Dublin.

Cloudesley-Thompson, J.L. (1976) *Insects and History*. Weidenfeld & Nicholson, London.

Cockburn, A. (1963) *The Evolution and Eradication of Infectious Diseases*. John Hopkins Press, Baltimore.

Coleman, W. (1982) *Death is a Social Disease*. Univ. Wisconsin Press, Madison.

Coleman, W. (1984) Epidemiological methods in the 1860s. Yellow fever at St. Nazaire. *B.H.M.*, 58, 145–63.

Collier, R. (1974) *The Plague of the Spanish Lady*. MacMillan, London.

Collis, W. (1954) *Cortes and Montezuma*. Faber & Faber, London.

Colnat, A. (1937) *Les Epidémies et L'Histoire*. Editions Hippocrate, Paris.

Concannon, R.J.G. (1967) The third enemy: the role of epidemics in the Thirty Years War. *J. wld. Hist.*, 10, 500–11.

Conrad, L.I. (1981) *The Plague in the Early Medieval Middle East*. Univ. Microfilms Internat., Ann Arbor.

Cook, S.F. (1946) The incidence and significance of disease among the Aztecs and related tribes. *Hisp. Am. hist. Rev.*, 26, 320–35.

Cook, S.F. (1973) The significance of disease in the extinction of the North American Indians. *Human Biol.*, 45, 485–508.

Cooray, M.P.M. (1965) Epidemics in the course of history. *Ceylon med. J.*, 10, 88–91.

Corlett, W.T. (1935) *The Medicine Man of the American Indian and his Cultural background*. Thomas, Springfield.

Cornebise, A.E. (1982) *Typhus and Doughboys*. Univ. Delaware Press, Newark.

Coulton, G.G. (1925) *The Medieval Village*. C.U.P., Cambridge.

Councell, C.E. (1941) War and infectious disease. *Publ. Hlth. Rep.*, 56, 547–73.

Cowie, L.W. (1972) *The Black Death and Peasants' Revolt*. Wayland, London.

Crawford, E.M. (1981) Indian meal and pellagra in nineteenth century Ireland. in *Irish Population, Economy and Society*. eds J.M. Goldstream & L.A. Clarkson, pp. 113 Clarendon, Oxford.

Crawfurd, R. (1914) *Plague and Pestilence in Literature and Art*. Clarendon, Oxford.

Creighton, C. (1956) *A History of Epidemics in Britain*. Cass, London.

Crew, F.A.E. (1962) *The Army Medical Services*. H.M.S.O., London.

Crookshank, F.G. ed. (1922) *Influenza*. Heinemann, London.

Crosby, A.W. (1967) Conquistador y Pestilencia. The first New World pandemic and the fall of the great Indian empires. *Hist. Am. Hist. Rec.*, 47, 321–77.

Crosby, A.W. (1976) *Epidemic and Peace*. Greenwood, Westport.

Crosby, A.W. (1977) The influenza pandemic of 1918. in *Influenza in America, 1918–1976*. ed. J.E. Osborn, pp. 5–13. Prodist, New York.

Crumpston, T.H.L. (1914) *The History of Smallpox in Australia, 1788–1908*. Commonw. Austral. Quarant. Serv. Publ. No. 3.

Crumspton, T.H.L. & MacCullum, F. (1926) *The History of the Plague in Australia*. Govt. Printer, Melbourne.

D'Irsay, S. (1925) The Black Death and the medieval universities. *Ann. Hist. Med.*, 7, 220–5.

Davey, P.C.T. & Brown, A.J. (1915) Clinical aspects of typhus fever. *B.M.J.*, ii, 737–40.

Davis, D.E. (1986) The scarcity of rats and the Black Death: an ecological history. *J. interdiscip. Hist.*, 16, 455–70.

de Zulueta, J. (1973) Malaria and Mediterranean history. *Parassit.*, 15, 1–15.

de Zulueta, J. (1987) Changes in the geographical distribution of malaria through history.

Parassit., 29, 193–205.

De, S.N. (1961) *Cholera.* Oliver & Boyd, London.

Defoe, D. (1966) *A Journal of the Plague Year.* Penguin, Harmondsworth.

Delaporte, F. (1986) *The Cholera in Paris, 1832.* M.I.T. Press, Cambridge.

Delatouche, R. (1971) European crisis: the plague or moral decline. in *The Black Death. A Turning Point in History?* ed. W.M. Bowsky, pp. 47–55. Holt, Rhinehart & Winston, New York.

Devignat, R. (1953) La peste antique de Congo Belge dans le cadre d'histoire et de la géography. *Mem. Inst. Roy. Coll. Belge, Sect. Sci. nat. et Med.*, 23, 3–47.

Diaz, B. (1963) *The Conquest of New Spain.* Penguin, Harmondsworth

Dineur, M. & Engrand, C. (1958) Lille. in *Le Choléra. La Première Epidémie du XIX Siècle.* ed. L. Chevalier, pp. 49-95. Imprimerie Centrale de L'Ouest, Roche-sur-Yon.

Dobyns, H.F. (1963) An outline of Andean epidemic history to 1720. *B.H.M.*, 37, 493–515.

Dodwell, H.H. ed. (1969) *The Cambridge History of India.* vol. 6, S. Chand, Delhi.

Dols, M.W. (1974) Plague in early Islamic history. *J. Am. orient. Soc.*, 94, 371–83.

Dols, M.W. (1977) *The Black Death in the Middle East.* Princeton Univ. Press, Princeton.

Dols, M.W. (1978) Geographical origin of the Black Death. Comment. *B.H.M.*, 52, 112–13.

Dols, M.W. (1979) The second plague epidemic and its recurrences in the Middle East. 1347-1894. *J. econ. soc. Hist. Orient*, 22, 162–89.

Droz, J. (1967) *De la Restauration à la Revolution, 1815–1848.* Colin, Paris.

Dryden, J. (1697) *Virgil's Aeneid.* (1981 edition) Routeledge, London.

Duby, G. (1962) *L'Economie Rurale et la Vie des Campagnes dans L'Occident Medièval.* Vol. 2, Montaigne, Paris.

Duffy, J. (1951) Smallpox and the Indians in the American colonies. *B.H.M.*, 25, 324–41.

Duffy, J. (1953) *Epidemics in Colonial America.* Louisiana State Univ. Press, Baton Rouge.

Duffy, J. (1966) *Sword of Pestilence.* Louisiana State Univ. Press, Baton Rouge.

Duffy, J. (1971) The history of asiatic cholera in the United States. *Bull. N. Y. Acad. Med.*, 47, 1152–68.

Dumbell, K.R. & Huq, F. (1975) Epidemiological implications of the typing of variola isolates. *T.R.S.T.M.& H.*, 69, 303–6.

Durey, M. (1979) *The Return of the Plague.* Gill & MacMillan, Dublin.

Dutt, A.K., Akhata, R. & Dutta, H.M. (1980) Malaria in India with particular reference to two west-central states. *Soc. sci. Med.*, 14D, 317–30.

Elgood, C. (1951) *A Medical History of Persia.* C.U.P., Cambridge.

Ell, S.R. (1979) Some evidence for interhuman transmission of medieval plague. *Rev. inf. Dis.*, 1, 563–6.

Ell, S.R. (1984) Immunity as a factor in the epidemiology of medieval plague. *Rev. inf. Dis.*, 6, 866–79.

Ell, S.R. (1985) Iron in two seventeenth century plague epidemics. *J. interdisciplin. Hist.*, 15, 445–57.

Emery, R.W. (1967) The black death of 1348 in Perpignan. *Speculu*, 42, 611–23.

Evans, R.J. (1987) *Death in Hamburg.* Clarendon, Oxford.

Eversley, D. (1958) L'Angleterre. in *Le Choléra. La Première Epidèmie du XIX Siècle.* ed. L. Chevalier, pp. 157–88. Imprimerie Centrale de L'Ouest, La Roche-sur-Yon.

Farr, W. (1852) *Report on the Mortality of Cholera in England in 1848–1849.* H.M.S.O., London.

Farris, W.W. (1985) *Population, Disease and Land in Early Japan.* Harvard Univ. Press, Cambridge.

Felsen, J. (1945) *Bacillary Dysentery, Colitis and Enteritis.* Heinemann, London.

Felsenfield, O. (1967) *The Cholera Problem*. Green, St Louis.

Fenner, F. (1982) The global eradication of smallpox. *Rev. inf. Dis.*, 4, 916–30.

Fiennes, R. (1964) *Man, Nature and Disease*. Weidenfeld & Nicholson, London.

Finley, M.I. (1958) Review of Boak. (28). *J. Roman Studies*, 48,156–64. 3

Fisher, F.J. (1965) Influenza and inflation in Tudor England. *E.H.R.2*, 18, 120–9.

Flinn, M.W. (1965) Introduction. in E. Chadwick, *The Sanitary Condition of the Labouring Population of Great Britain*. ed. M.W. Flinn, Univ. Press, Edinburgh.

Frederich, C.J. (1952) *The Age of the Baroque*. Harper, New York.

Fuller, J.F.C. (1970) *The Decisive Battles of the Western World*. Granada, London.

Gale, A.H. (1959) *Epidemic Diseases*. Penguin, Harmondsworth.

Gallagher, N.E. (1977) *Epidemics in the Regency of Tunis*. Univ. Microfilms Internat., Ann Arbor.

Gasquet, F.A. (1893) *The Great Pestilence*. Simkin, Marshall, Hamilton & Kent, London.

Gelfand, M. (1964) *Rivers of Death in Africa*. O.U.P., London.

Gerlitt, J. (1940) The development of quarantine. *CIBA Foundation Symposium*, 2, 566–72.

Germain, M., Francey, D.B., Monath, T.P., Ferrara, L., Bryan, J., Saloun, J.J., Heme, G., Renaudet, J., Adam, C. & Digouette, J.P. (1980) Yellow fever in the Gambia, 1978–1979: Entomological aspects and epidemiological correlations. *Am. J. trop. Med. Hyg.*, 29, 929–40.

Gibbon, E. (1983) *The History of the Decline and Fall of the Roman Empire*. Folio Soc., London.

Gilliam, J.F. (1961) The plague under Marcus Aurelius. *Am. J. Philol.*, 82, 225–51.

Glasscock, R.E. (1973) England circa 1334. in *A New Historical Geography of England*. ed. H.C. Darby, pp. 136–85. C.U.P., Cambridge.

Godfrey, C.M. (1968) *The Cholera Epidemics in Upper Canada, 1832–1886*. Secombe House, Toronto.

Goodall, E.W. (1934) *A Short History of Epidemic Infectious Diseases*. Bale, Sons & Danielsson, London.

Gordon, C.A. (1884) *An Epitome of the Reports of the Medical Officers to the Chinese Imperial Customs Service*. Balliere, Tyndal & Cox, London.

Gordon, R. (1983) *Great Medical Disasters*. Stein & Day, New York.

Gore, A.A. (1876) *A Contribution to the Medical History of our West African Campaigns*. Balliere, Tyndall & Cox, London.

Gottfried, R.S. (1978) *Epidemic Disease in Fifteenth century England*. Leicester Univ. Press, Leicester.

Gottfried, R.S. (1983) *The Black Death*. Hale, London.

Grant, M. (1968) *The Climax of Rome*. Weidenfeld & Nicholson, London.

Grant, M. (1980) *The Etruscans*. Lane, London.

Greenwood, M. (1918) The epidemiology of influenza. *B.M.J.*, ii, 563–6.

Greenwood, M. (1935) *Epidemics and Crowd Diseases*. Williams & Northgate, London.

Gregg, C.T. (1978) *Plague*. Scribner, New York.

Gregory of Tours (1974) *The History of the Franks*. Penguin, Harmondsworth.

Groslier, B. & Arthaud, J. (1957) *Angkor, Art and Civilization*. Thames & Hudson, London.

Guillaume, A. (1955) *The Life of Muhammad*. O.U.P., London. Being a translation of Ibn Ishaq's book of AH140 Sirat Rasul Allah.

Guiral, P. (1958) Marseilles. in *Le Choléra. La Première Epidémie du XIX Siècle*. ed. L. Chevalier, pp. 121–40. Imprimerie Centrale de L'Ouest, Roche-sur-Yon.

Hackett, L.W. (1937) *Malaria in Europe*. O.U.P., London.

Halawani, A. & Shawarby, A.A. (1957) Malaria in Egypt.*J. Egypt med. Assoc.*, 40, 753–92.

Hankin, E.H. (1905) On the epidemiology of plague. *J. Hyg.*, 5, 48–83.

Hankin, E.H. (1930/31) The pied piper of Hamlyn and the coming of the Black Death. *Torquay nat. hist Soc. Trans. & Proc.*, pp. 23–31.

Hare, R. (1954) *Pomp and Pestilence*. Gollanz, London.

Hare, R. (1967) The antiquity of diseases caused by bacteria and viruses, a review of the problem from a bacteriologist's point of view. in *Diseases in Antiquity*. ed. D. Brothwell & A.T. Sanderson, pp. 115–31. Thomas, Springfield.

Hart, G.D. ed. (1983) *Disease in Ancient Man: an Illustrated Symposium*. Clarke Irwin, Toronto.

Hartwig, G.W. (1981) Smallpox in the Sudan. *Int. J. Afr. hist. Studies*, 14, 5–33.

Hatcher, J. (1977) *Plague, Population and the English Economy, 1348–1530*. MacMillan, London.

Hauptman, L.M. (1979) Smallpox and the American Indian. *N. Y. State J. Med.*, 79, 1945–9.

Hecker, J.F.C. (1846) *The Epidemics of the Middle Ages*. Sydemham Society, London.

Henneman, J.B. (1971) France: a fiscal and constitutional crisis. in *The Black Death. A Turning Point in History?* ed. W.M. Bowsky, pp. 86–9. Holt, Rhinehart & Winston, New York.

Henschen, F. (1962) *Sjukdomarnus Historia och Geografi*. Bonniers, Stockholm.

Herlihy, D. & Klapisch-Zuber, C. (1979) *Les Toscans et leur Familles*. S.E.V.P.E.N., Paris.

Herlihy, D. (1967) *Medieval and Renaissance Pistoia*. Yale Univ. Press, New Haven.

Herlihy, D. (1971) Malthus denied. in *The Black Death. A Turning Point in History?* ed. W.M. Bowsky, pp. 60–4. Holt, Rhinehart & Winston, New York.

Hill, A.B. & Mitra, K. (1936) *Enteric fever in milk-borne and water-borne epidemics*. Lancet, ii, 589–94.

Hirsch, A. (1883) *Handbook of Geographical and Historical Pathology*. Sydenham Soc., London.

Hirst, L.F. (1953) *The Conquest of Plague*. Clarendon, Oxford.

Ho, P-T. (1959) *Studies on the population of China*. Harvard Univ. Press, Cambridge, Mass.

Hobson, W. (1963) *World Health and History*. Wright, Bristol.

Hoehling, A.A. (1961) *The Great Epidemic*. Little Brown, Boston.

Hollingsworth, T.H. (1969) *Historical Demography*. Cornell Univ. Press, Ithaca.

Holmes, G. (1975) *Europe: Hierarchy and Revolt*. Fontana, London.

Hopkins, D.R. (1983) *Princes and Peasants*, Smallpox in History. Univ. Chicago Press, Chicago.

Hort, E.C., (1915) Typhus fever. *B.M.J.*, i, 673–5.

Howard-Jones, N. (1975) Kitasato, Yersin and the plague bacillus. *Clio Med.*, 10, 23–7.

Huckstep, R.L. (1962) *Typhoid Fever*. Livingston, London.

Hughes, J.M., Boyce, J.M., Levine, R.J., Khan, M., Aziz, K.M.A., Huq, M.I. & Curlin, G.T. (1982) Epidemiology of eltor cholera in rural Bangladesh: importance of surface water in transmission. *Bull. W.H.O.*, 60, 395–404.

Hurtrel, B., Alonso, M., Lagrange, P.H. & Hurtrel, Maryse. (1981) Delayed-type hypersensitivity and acquired resistance to plague in mice immunised with killed *Yersinia pestis* and immunoregulators. *Immunology*, 44, 297–304.

Hussein, A.G. (1949) Epidemiology of Cholera in Egypt. *Med. Press Egypt*, 60, 627–76.

Hutcheson, C. (1895) Mahamari, or the plague, in British Garhwal and Kuamon. *Trans. 1st Ind. med. Congr.*, 1, 304–312.

Ilvento, A. (1934) The reclamation of the Pontine marshes. *League Nations quart. Bull. W. H. O.*, 3, 157–201.

Ingram, A. (1927) Plague investigations in South Africa from an entomological aspect.

Publ. *S. Afr. Inst. med. Res.*, 3, 222–56.

Jaggi, O.P. (1979) Epidemics and Tropical Diseases. Vol. 12 of *History of Science, Technology and Medicine in India*. Atma Ram, Delhi. 69.

Jones W.H.S. (1907) *Malaria, a Neglected Factor in the History of Greece and Rome*. MacMillan & Bowes, Cambridge.

Jones, W.H.S. (1908) Malaria and history. *Ann trop. Med.* Parasit., 1, 529–46.

Jones, W.H.S. (1909) *Malaria and Greek History*. Manchester Univ. Press, Manchester.

Jordan, E.O. (1927) The influenza epidemic of 1918. 1. Encephalitis and influenza. *J.A.M.A.*, 89, 1603–06.

Jorge, R. (1932) Summa epidemiologia de la peste, épidémies anciennes et modernes. *Comm. Off. internat. Hyg. publ.*, Oct, 1932, 425–50.

Judson, S. & Kahane, A. (1963) Underground drainage ways in southern Etruria and northern Latium. *Papers Brit. School, Rome.*, 31, 74–99.

Kaplan, C. (1975) Smallpox eradication – a narrative account. *T.R.S.T.M.& H.*, 69, 293–8.

Kaplan, M.M. (1981) Influenza in nature. *Abstracts from a symposium on animal diseases in relation to animal conservation*. Zool. Soc., London.

Keil, H. (1951) The louse in Greek antiquity. *B.H.M.*, 25, 305–23.

Kennear Wilson, J.V. (1967) Organic diseases of ancient Mesopotamia. in *Diseases of Antiquity*. eds, D. Brothwell & A.T. Sandison, pp. 191–208. Thomas, Springfield.

Kennedy, P. (1988) *The Rise and Fall of the Great Powers*. Unwin Hyman, London.

Kister, M.J. (1965) The Campaign of Huluban, a new light on the expedition of Abraha. *Le Muséon*, 78, 425–36.

Kitasato, S. (1894) The bacillus of bubonic plague. *Lancet*, ii, 428–30.

Korobova, E.I., Pavlova, L-P. & Bakhrakh, E.E. (1961) The intradermal allergic test as an index of immunity against plague. *J. Microbiol. Epidemiol. Immunol.*, 32, 1608–14.

Kosminskii, E.A. (1971) The plague de-emphasised. in *The Black Death. a Turning Point in History?* ed. W.M. Bowsky, pp. 38–46. Holt, Rhinehart & Winston, New York.

Krause, A.K. (1928) Tuberculosis and public health. *Am. Rev. Tuberc.*, 18, 271–83.

La Berge, A.F. (1984) The early nineteenth century French public health movement: the disciplinary development and institutionalization of Hygiene Publique. *B.H.M.*, 58, 363–79.

La Berge, A.F. (1987) Review of Delaporte *J. Hist Med.*, 42, 378–80.

La Berge, A.F. (1988) Edwin Chadwick and the French connection. *B.H.M.*, 62, 23–41.

Laiou-Thomadikis, A.E. (1977) *Peasant Society in the Late Byzantine Empire*. Princeton Univ. Press, Princeton.

Lancet (1949) Editorial. i, 68–9.

Langer, W.L. (1958) The next assignment. *Ann. Hist. Med.*, 63, 283–304.

Langmuir, A.D., Worthen, T.D., Soloman, J., Ray, C.G. & Petersen, E. (1985) The Thucydides syndrome. *New Engl. J. Med.*, 313, 1027–30.

Lebrun, F. (1967) *Le XVII Siècle*. Colin, Paris.

Lehman, J. (1977) *The Hittites*. Collins, London.

Lenski, R.E. (1988) Evolution of plague virulence. *Nature*, 334, 473–4.

Levine, M.M. (1985) Immunization against infectious diarrhoeas. in *Diarrhoeal Disease and Malnutrition*. ed. M. Gracey. pp. 183-200. Churchill-Livingstone, Edinburgh.

Liston, W.G. (1905) Plague, rats and fleas. *J. Bombay nat. Hist. Soc.*, 16, 253–71.

Littman, R.J. & Littman, M.L. (1969) The Athenian plague: smallpox. *Trans. Proc. Am. Philo. Assoc.* 100, 261–75.

Littman, R.J. & Littman, M.L. (1973) Galen and the Antonine plague. *Am. J. Philol.* 94, 243–55.

Lividas, G.A. (1959) *Malaria in ancient Greece*. Riv. Parassit., 20, 299–304.

Longmate, N. (1966) *King Cholera*. Hamish Hamilton, London.

Longrigg, J. (1980) The great plague of Athens. *Hist. Sci.*, 18, 209–25.

Loosjes F,E. (1956) Is the brown rat (*Rattus norvegicus, Berkenhout*) responsible for the disappearance of plague in Western Europe?. *Doc. Med. Geograph. Trop.* 8, 175–8.

Lowson, J. (1898) as stated in *Manson's Tropical Diseases* (16th edn.) p. 223.

Lucas, H.S. (1930) The great European famine of 1315, 1316 and 1327. *Speculum*, 5, 343–77.

Lutge, F. (1971) Germany: the black death and a structural revolution in socio-economic history. in *The Black Death. A Turning Point in History?* ed. W.M. Bowsky, pp. 80–5. Holt, Rhinehart & Winston, New York.

Lynch, J. (1969) *Spain under the Hapsburgs*. 2 vols, O.U.P., Oxford.

M'William, J.O. (1843) *Medical History of the Expedition to the Niger during the Years 1841–1842*. Churchill, London.

MacArthur, W. (1959) The medical identification of some pestilences of the past. *T.R.S.T.M.& H.*, 53, 423–439.

MacArthur, W.P. (1926) Old-time plague in Britain. *T.R.S.T.M.& H.*, 19, 355–72.

MacArthur, W.P. (1951) A brief history of English malaria. *Oxford med. School Gaz.*, 3, 21–6.

MacArthur, W.P. (1952) The occurrence of the rat in early Europe. *T.R.S.T.M.& H.*, 46, 209–12.

MacArthur, W.P. (1957) The occurrence of the rat in early Europe. *T.R.S.T.M.& H.*, 51, 91–2.

MacGowan, D.J. (1881) Report on the health of Wenchow for the half-year ended 30th September 1881. in *An Epitome of the Reports of the medical Officers to the Chinese Imperial Customs Service*. ed. C.A. Gordon. Balliere, Tyndal & Cox, London.

MacNamara, C. (1876) *A History of Asiatic Cholera*. MacMillan, London.

MacNiocaill, G. (1972) *Ireland before the Vikings*. Gill & MacMillan, Dublin.

MacPherson, J. (1872) *Annals of Cholera*. Ranken, London.

Maenchen-Helfen, J.O. (1973) *The World of the Huns*. Univ. Calif. Press, Berkeley.

Major, R.H. (1936) *Disease and History*. Appleton-Century, New York.

Marks, G. & Beatty, W.K. (1976) *Epidemics*. Scribner, New York.

Martin, C.J. (1913) Discussion on the spread of plague. *B.M.J.*, ii, 1249–61.

Marx, R. (1958) The fifth column at the battle of Gettysburg. *Surg. Gynecol. Obstet.*, 100, 375–8.

Maxwell. J.L. (1927) The history of cholera in China. *Chin. med. J.*, 41, 595–7.

McBryde, F.W. (1940) Influenza in America during the sixteenth century, (Guatamala: 1523, 1559–62, 1576). *B.H.M.*, 8, 296–302.

McGowan, J. (1897) *The Imperial History of China*. Curzon, London.

McGraw-Hill Encyclopedia of Science & Technology. McGraw-Hill, New York.

McGrew, R.E. (1960) The first cholera epidemic and social history. *B.H.M.*, 34, 61–72.

McGrew, R.E. (1965) *Russia and the Cholera: 1823–1832*. Univ. Milwaukee Press, Madison.

McNeill, W.H. (1976) *Plagues and People*. Blackwell, Oxford.

Meiss, M. (1951) *Painting in Florence and Siena after the Black Death*. Princeton Univ. Press, Princeton.

Meunier, D.M.Y., Avon, N. & Mazzariol, M.J. (1988) The 1947 yellow fever epidemic in Mali: viral and epidemiological diagnosis. *T.R.S.T.M.& H.*, 82, 767.

Millar, G.D. & Osborn, J.E. (1977) Precursers of the scientific decision-making process leading to the 1976 national immunization programme. in *Influenza in America, 1918–1978*. ed J.E. Osborn, pp. 15–17. Prodist, New York.

Miller, E. & Hatcher, J. (1978) *Medieval England – Rural Society and Economic Change, 1086-1348*. Longman, London.

Mitchell, J.A. (1927) Plague in South Africa: historical study. *Publ. S. Afr. Inst. med. Res.*, 3, 89–104.

Mitra, A. & Sachdev, R.P. (1980) *Population and Area of Cities, Towns and Urban Agglomerations, 1872–1971.* Allied, Bombay.

Moll, A.A. (1944) *Aesculapius in Latin America.* Saunders, Philadelphia.

Moore, J. (1815) *The History of Smallpox.* Longman. London.

Moore, J.W. (1928) Epidemiology in Ireland. Past and present. *Irish J. med. Sci.*, 6, 626–39.

Moore, R.L. & Brubaker, R.R. (1975) Hybridization of oxyribonucleotide sequences of *Yersinia enterocolitica* and other selected members of the Enterobacteriaciae. *Int. J. system. Bact.*, 25, 336–9.

Morley, S.G. (1946) *The Ancient Maya.* Stanford Univ. Press, Stanford.

Morris, R.J. (1976) *Cholera 1832. The Social Response to an Epidemic.* Croom Helm, London.

Muhammed Ali, (1972) *Muhammad the Prophet.* Ahmadiyyah Anjuman Isha'at, Lahore.

Mullet, C.F. (1956) *The Bubonic Plague and England.* Univ. Kentucky Press, Lexington.

Nakasone, M., Iwanaga, M. & Eeckels, R. (1987) Characterisation of *Vibrio cholerae* 01 recently isolated in Bangladesh. *T.R.S.T.M.& H.*, 81, 876–8.

Needham, J. & Lu, G-D. (1962) Hygiene and preventive medicine in ancient *China. J. Hist. Med.*, 17, 429–78.

Netchina, M-V., Skirov, K-V. & Siderov, A-L. (1958) *La Russie. in Le Choléra. La Premiere Epidémie du XIX* Siècle. ed. L.Chevalier, pp. 143–55. Primerie Centrale de L'Ouest, Roche-sur-Yon.

Neustadt, D. (1946) The plague and its effects upon the Mamluk army. *J. R. asiatic Soc.*, 67–73.

Neustadt, R.E. & Fineburg, H. (1982) *The Epidemic that Never Was.* Random House, New York.

Nicholas, R.W. (1981) The Godess Sitata and epidemic smallpox in Bengal. *J. Asian Studies*, 41, 21–44.

Nicholls, L. (1921) Malaria and the lost cities of Ceylon. *Ind. med. Gaz.*, 56.121–30.

Norris, C. (1971) Review of Shrewsbury (71). *Hist J.*, 14, 205–24.

Norris, J. (1977) East or west? The geographic origin of the Black Death. *B.H.M.*, 51, 1–24.

North, W. (1896) *Roman Fever.* Sampson, Low & Marston, London.

Norwich, J.J. (1988) *A History of Venice.* Penguin, Harmondsworth.

Ocana, E.R. (1983) *El Colera de 1834 en Granada: Enfermedad Catastrofia y Crisis Social.* Univ. del Granada, Granada.

Ortiz, M.Y. (1978) *Epidemias de Colera en Viscaya en el siglio XIX.* La Gran Enciclopedia Vasca, Bilbao.

Pallottino, M. (1955) *The Etruscans.* Lane, London.

Pankhurst, R. (1965) The history and traditional treatment of smallpox in Ethiopia. *Med. Hist.*, 9, 343–55.

Parker, E.H. (1907) Smallpox and inoculation in China. *B.M.J.*, i 88–9.

Parker, H.M.D. (1935) *A History of the Roman World from AD 138 to AD 337.* Methuen, London.

Parry, J.H. (1966) *The Spanish Seaborne Empire.* Hutchinson, London.

Parsons, H.F. (1891) The influenza epidemics of 1889-90 and 1891 and their distribution in England and Wales. *B.M.J.*, ii, 303-308.

Patrick, A. (1967) Disease in antiquity. Ancient Greece and Rome, in *Diseases in Antiquity*. ed. D. Brothwell & A.T. Sandison. Thomas, Springfield.

Pettigrew, E. (1983) *The Silent Enemy.* Western Producer Prairie Books, Saskatoon.

Piontkovskaya, S.P. & Korshanova, O.S. (undated) Asian tick typhus. in *Human Diseases with Natural Foci.* ed. Y.N. Pavlovsky, pp. 98–137. Foreign Languages Publ. House,

Moscow.

Pirenne, H. (1936) *Economic and Social History of Medieval Europe*. Routledge & Kegan Paul, London.

Pirie, J.H.H. (1927) Miscellaneous bacteriological observations. *Publ. S. Afr. Inst med. Res.*, 3, 207–21.

Pollitzer, R. & Li, C.C. (1943) Some observations on the decline of pneumonic plague epidemics. *J. infect. Dis.*, 72, 160–2.

Pollitzer, R. (1951) Plague Studies. 1. A summary of the history and a survey of the present distribution of the disease. *Bull.* W.H.O., 4, 475–533.

Pollitzer, R. (1954) Cholera Studies: i. History of the disease. *Bull.* W.H.O., 10, 421–61.

Pollitzer, R. (1954) *Plague*. W.H.O. Monograph series No. 22. W.H.O., Geneva.

Poole, J.C.F. & Halliday, A.J. (1979) Thucydides and the plague of Athens. *Classic Q*, 29, 282–300.

Post, J.D. (1976) *Man, Nature and Disease*. Weidenfeld & Nicholson, London.

Postan, M. (1950) Some economic evidence of declining population in the later middle ages. *E.H.R.2*, 2, 221–6.

Postan, M. (1971) Malthusian pressure and population decline. in *The Black Death. A Turning Point in History?* ed. W.M. Bowsky, pp. 56–9. Holt, Rhinehart & Winston, New York.

Powell, J.H. (1949) *Bring out your Dead*. Univ. Penn. Press, Philadelphia.

Prat, G. (1952) *Albi et la peste noire*. Ann. Midi, 64, 15–25.

Prescott, W.H. (1843) *History of the Conquest of Mexico*. The Modern Library, New York.

Preuss, J. (1978) *Biblical and Talmudic Medicine*. Sanhydrin Press, New York.

Prinzing, F. (1916) *Epidemics Resulting from Wars*. Clarendon, Oxford.

Procopius. (1914) *The Persian War*. Loeb Classical Library, Heinemann, London.

Prothero, R.M. (1961) Population movements and problems of malaria eradication in Africa. *Bull.* W.H.O., 24, 405–25.

Prothero, R.M. (1964) *Continuity and change in African population mobility in Geographers in the Tropics: Liverpool Essays*. eds. R.W. Steel & R.M. Prothero. Longman, London.

Proust, A. (1892) *La Défence de L'Europe contre le Cholera*. Masson, Paris.

Pym, W. (1848) *Observations on Bulam, Vomito-Negro or Yellow Fever*. Churchill, London.

Rackam, D.J. (1979) *Rattus rattus*: the introduction of the black rat into Britain. *Antiquity*, 53, 112–20.

Renouard, Y. (1948) Consequences et interet demographique de la peste noire de 1348. *Population*, 3, 459–66.

Robert, R.S. (1966) The place of plague in English history. *Proc. R. Soc. Med.* (Hist. Med.), 59, 101–5.

Roberts, J.I. (1935) The endemicity of plague in East Africa. *E. Afr. med. J.*, 12, 200–19.

Rolleston, J.D. (1937) *The History of the Acute Exanthemata*. Heinemann, London.

Rosen, G. (1954) Acute communicable diseases. in *The History and Conquest of Common Diseases*. ed. W.R. Bett, Ch. 1. Univ. Oklahoma Press, Norman.

Rosenberg, C.E. (1962) *The Cholera Years*. Univ. Chicago Press, Chicago.

Rosenthal, R. (1959) The history and nature of smallpox. *Lancet*, 79, 298–505.

Rosqvist, R., Skuerik, M. & Wolf-Watz, H. (1988) Increased virulence of *Yersinia psuedotuberculosis* by two independent mutations. *Nature*, 334, 522–5.

Ross, R. (1906) Malaria in Greece. *J. trop. Med.*, 9, 341–7.

Runciman, S. (1962) *A History of the Crusades*. C.U.P., Cambridge.

Russell, J.C. (1948) *British Medieval Population*. Univ. New Mexico Press, Albuquerque.

Russell, J.C. (1966) Effects of pestilence and plague 1315–85. *Comp. Studies Soc. Hist.*, 8, 464–73.

Russell, J.C. (1968) That earlier plague. *Demography*, 5, 174–84.

Russell, J.C. (1971) England: pre-plague population and prosperity. in *The Black Death. A Turning Point in History?* ed. W.M. Bowsky, pp 100-107, Holt, Rhinehart & Winston, New York.

Russell, J.C. (1985) Late Ancient and Medieval Population Control. *Am. Phil. Soc.*, Philadelphia.

Russell, P.F. (1955) *Man's Mastery of Malaria*. O.U.P., London.

Russell, W.H. (1966) *Dispatches from the Crimea*. ed. N. Bentley. Deutsch, London.

Russell, W.M.S. (1983) The paleodemographic view. in *Disease in Ancient Man*. ed. G.D. Hart, pp. 217–53. Clarke-Irwin, Toronto.

Salaman, R.N. (1949) *The History and Social Influence of the Potato*. C.U.P., Cambridge.

Salmon, P. (1974) *Population et Depopulation dans L'Empire Romain*. Latomus, Bruxelles.

Saltmarsh, J. (1941) II. Plague and economic decline in England in the later middle ages. *Camb. Hist. J.*, 7, 23–41.

Sandwith, F.M. (1914) Dysentery. *Lancet*, ii, 637–44.

Santander, L.S-G. & Granjel, L.S. (1980) *El Colera y la Espana och Ocentista*. Univ. Salamanca, Salamanca.

Seal, S.C. (1969) Epidemiological studies on plague in India. *Bull*. W.H.O., 23, 283–92.

Shipley, A.E. (1915) *The Minor Horrors of War*. Smith Elder, London.

Shortt, H.E. (1951) History of recent researches on tissue phases of the malaria parasite at the London School of Hygiene and Tropical Medicine. *T.R.S.T.M.& H.*, 45, 175–88.

Shrewsbury, J.F.D. (1949) The yellow plague. *J. Hist. Med.*, 4, 5–47.

Shrewsbury, J.F.D. (1950) The plague of Athens. *B.H.M.*, 24, 1–25.

Shrewsbury, J.F.D. (1964) *The Plague of the Philistines and Other Medico-Historical Essays*. Gollanz, London.

Shrewsbury, J.F.D. (1970) *A History of the Bubonic Plague in the British Isles*. C.U.P., Cambridge.

Silverstein, A.M. (1981) *Pure Politics and Impure Science*. Johns Hopkins Press, Baltimore.

Simond, P.L., (1898) La propagation de la peste. *Ann. Inst. Pasteur*, 12, 625.

Singer, C. & Underwood, E.A. (1962) *A Short History of Medicine*. Clarendon, Oxford.

Singer, C.S. (1915) 13th centuries minatures illustrating medical practice. *Proc. R. Soc. Med.* (Hist. Med.), 9, 29–42.

Singer, C.S. (1962A) Some plague tractates. *Proc. R. Soc. Med. (Hist. Med.)*, 9, 159–214.

Singer, C.S. (1916B) The figures of the Bristol Guy de Chauliac MS. *Proc. R. Soc. Med. (Hist. Med.)*, 10, 71–90.

Sinton, J.A. (1935/36) What malaria costs India, nationally, socially and economically. *Rec. Mal. Survey India*, 5, 223–64; 413–89; 6, 91–169.

Smith, C.E.G. & Gibson, M.E. (1986) Yellow fever in South Wales. *Med. Hist.*, 30, 322–40.

Smith, F.P. (1871) Smallpox in China. *Med. Times Gaz.*, ii, 277.

Smith, G. (1943) *Plague on us*. O.U.P., London.

Smith, G.E. & Dawson, W.R. (1924) *Egyptian Mummies*. Allen & Unwin, London.

Soubiran, A. (1966) *Le Baron Larrey*, Chirugien de Napoleon. Fayard, Paris.

Spooner, F.C. (1970) The European economy, 1609–1650. in *The New Cambridge Modern History*. Vol. 4, ed. J. Cooper. C.U.P., Cambridge.

Stearn, E.W. & Stearn, A.E. (1945) *The Effect of Smallpox on the Destiny of the Amerindian*. Bruce Humphreys, Boston.

Stirn, D. (1985) *Histoire de la Revolution de 1848*. Bolland, Paris.

Stirns, I. (1983) Care of sick brothers by the Crusade orders in the Holy Land. *B.H.M.*, 57, 43–69.

Stock, R.F. (1976) Cholera in Africa. *Int. Afr. Inst.*, London.

Stowman, K. (1945A) The epidemic outlook in Europe. *U.N.R.R.A. epid. Inf. Bull.*, 1, 101–11.

Stowman, K. (1945B) Typhus during the war. *U.N.R.R.A. epid. Inf. Bull.*, 1, 289–310

Strode, G.K. ed. (1951) *Yellow Fever.* McGraw Hill, New York.

Strong, R.P., Shattuck, A.M., Sellards, A.W., Zinnser, H. & Hopkins, J.G. (1920) *Typhus Fever with Particular Reference to the Serbian Epidemic.* Harvard Univ. Press, Cambridge.

Stuart-Harris, C.H. & Schild, G.C. (1976) *Influenza. The Viruses and the Disease.* Arnold, London.

Stuart-Harris, C.H. (1954) *Influenza.* in *The History and Conquest of Common Diseases.* ed. W.R. Bett, pp.71–3. Univ. Oklahoma Press, Norman.

Stuart-Harris, C.H., Andrews, C.H., Smith, W., Chalmers, D.K.M., Cowan, E.G.H.& Hughes, D.L. (1938) *A Study of Epidemic Influenza with Special Reference to the 1936/37 Epidemic. Med. Res. Counc., H.M.S.O.,* London.

Teall, J.L. (1965) The barbarians in Justinian's army. *Speculum,* 40, 294–322.

Thompson, E.S. (1890) *Influenza.* Percival, London.

Thorndyke, L. (1927) The blight of pestilence on early modern civilization. *Ann. Hist. Rev.,* 32, 455–74.

Thucydides (1954) *History of the Peloponnesian War.* Penguin, Harmondsworth.

Thursfield, H. (1940) Smallpox in the American war of independence. *Ann. Hist. Med.,* (3rd ser.), 2, 312–18.

Titow, J. (1960) Evidence of weather in the account rolls of the Bishopric of Winchester. *E.H.R.2,* 12, 360–407.

Torres, C.M. (1935) Further studies on the pathology of Alastrim and their significance in the Variola-Alastrim problem. *Proc. R. Soc. Med.,* 29, 1525–40.

Townsend, J.K. (1933) History of influenza epidemics. *Ann. Hist. Med.* (new ser.), 5, 533–47.

Tudesq, A.J. (1970) La France romantique et bourgeoise, 1815–48. in *Histoire de la France.* ed. G. Dubey, pp. 374–93. Larousse, Paris.

Twigg, G. (1984) *The Black Death.* Batsford, London.

Udovitch, A.L. (1971) Egypt: crisis in a Muslim land. in *The Black Death. A Turning point in History?* ed. W.M. Bowsky, pp. 122–5. Holt, Rhinehart & Winston, New York.

Vallin, J. (1989) *La Population Francaise.* Découverte, Paris.

van Zwanenberg, D. (1970) The last epidemic of plague in England? Suffolk, 1906–1918. *Med. Hist.,* 14, 63–74.

Verlinden, C. (1938) La grand peste de 1348 en Espagne. *Rev. Belge Philol. Hist.,* 17, 103–46.

Verlinden, C. (1971) Spain: a temporary set-back. in *The Black Death. A Turning Point in History?* ed W.M. Bowsky, pp. 89–90. Holt, Rhinehart & Winston, New York.

Vidalenc, J. (1958) *Les departments Normands.* in *Le Choléra. La Première Epidémie du XIX Siecle.* ed. L. Chevalier, pp. 99–108. Imprimerie Centrale de L'Ouest, Roche-sur-Yon.

Vilmorovic, B. (1972) Plague in south-east Asia. *T.R.S.T.M.& H.,* 66, 479–504.

Viseltear, A.J. (1977) *A short political history of 1976 swine influenza legislation.* in *Influenza in America, 1918–1976.* ed. J.E. Osborn, pp. 29–58. Prodist, New York.

Viswanathan, D.K. (1949) A study of the effects of malaria and of malaria control measures on population and vital statistics in Kanara and Dharwar districts as compared to the rest of the province of Bombay. *Ind J. Malariol.,* 3, 69–99.

von Grimmelshausen, H.J.C. (1964) *Simplicimus Simplicissimus.* Calder, London.

W.H.O. (1982) Rickettsioses: a continuing disease problem. *Bull. W.H.O.,* 60, 157–64.

Wake, A., Morita, H. & Morita, Michico. (1978) Mechanisms of long and short term immunity to plague. *Immunology*, 34, 1045–52.

Warshaw, L.J. (1949) *Malaria, the Biography of a Killer*. Reinhart, New York.

Wedgewood, C.V. (1938) *The Thirty Years War*. Cape, London.

Wells, C. (1964) *Bones, Bodies and Diseases*. Thames & Hudson, London.

Wernsdorfer, W.H. & McGregor, I.A. (1989) *Malaria. Principles and Practice of Malariology*. 2 vols. Churchill-Livingstone, London.

Will, E. (1956) Review of Boak (28). *L'Antiquite Classique*, 25, 219–20.

Williams, H.U. (1909) *The epidemic of the Indians of New England, 1616-1620*. Johns Hopkins Hosp. Bull., 20, 340–9.

Winslow, C-E.A. (1943) *The Conquest of Epidemic Disease*. Princeton. Univ. Press, Princeton.

Wise, T. (1976) *Medieval Warfare*. Osprey, London.

Wong, F.C. & Wu, L-T. (1932) *History of Chinese Medicine*. Tientsin Press, Tientsin.

Wong, K.C. (1918) Smallpox in China. *Nat. med. J.*, 4, 94–7.

Woodham-Smith, C. (1962) *The Great Hunger, Ireland 1845/49*. Hamish Hamilton, London.

Woodward, S.B. (1932) The story of smallpox in Massachussetts. *New England J. Med.*, 206, 1181–91.

Wu, L-T. (1930) Rodents of Manchuria and Mongolia and their significance in disease. *Bull. Dept. Biol.*, Yenching Univ, Peking, 1, 95-101. 9–23.

Wu, L-T., Chun, J.W.H., Pollitzer, R. & Wu, C.Y. (1936) Plague. *Nat. Quarant. Serv.*, Shanghai.

Wu. L-T, (1926) *A Treatise on Pneumonic Plague*. League of Nations Publ., Geneva.

Wu, L-T. (1930) The history of certain infectious diseases in China. Rep. North Manchurian Plague Prevention Service for 1929-1930. 7, 127–42

Yamamoto, S-i. (1985) Cholera in Japan. in *Advances in Research on Cholera and Related diseases*. eds S. Kuwahara & N.F. Pierce, pp. 55–9. R.T.K. Sci. Publ., Tokyo.

Yersin, A. (1894) Sur la peste de Hong-Kong. *C.R. Acad. Sci.*, 119, 356.

Yersin, A. (1894) La peste bubonique à Hong Kong. *Ann. Inst. Pasteur*, 8, 662–7.

Zeigler, P. (1970) *The Black Death*. Penguin, Harmondsworth.

Zhdanov, V.M. (1959) The 1957 influenza pandemic in the U.S.S.R. *Bull.* W.H.O., 20, 489–94.

Zinnser, H. (1935) *Rats, Lice and History*. Routledge & Sons, London.

Index

Don, River 55
Dorian 213
Dneiper River 5, 146
Drake 109, 151
Dresden 143, 146
Droplets 21, 32, 53, 66, 114-5, 194
Dryden, J 96
Duby, G 60
Dudgeon, J 158
Duffy, J 110, 126, 186
Dundalk 144
Durer 139
Durey, M 178, 223
Dushan 72
Dutt, A K *et al* 102
Dyrrachium 98, 191
Dysentery 3, 4, 8, 10, 109-10, 118-9, 130, 140, 142-45, 185; amoebic 139, 222; bacillary 139, 154, 157, 173, 180; viral 139
East Anglia 100
East Indies 121, 158-59, 165, 170, 211
Eastern Europe 31
Ebers Papyrus 92, 191
Eco Systems 209
Edward I 58
Edward III 69
Egypt, Egyptians 2, 5, 7, 11-12, 14-6, 31, 35-6, 45, 47, 62, 73-4, 117, 151, 161, 167-71, 182, 188-9
Ekron 9
Elbe, River 170, 181-2
Elephant War 32, 39, 116-4, 122, 218
Elgood, C 117
Elis 213
Elisha 4, 92
Ell, S R 30, 38, 53
Elteken 10
El Tor 154-5, 171-2, 212
Emengol 86
Emerods 2-3
Emery R W 69
Empedocles 93
Encephalitis 199
Endemic 89, 94, 102, 105, 159
Engehein 142
England, English 25, 27, 29, 47, 58-9, 64-6, 69, 71, 74, 77, 80, 82, 84, 100, 119-10, 123, 131, 148, 159, 162, 167, 176, 191, 196, 217
"English Sweats" 195
Enteric Disease 59
Entomologist 105
Enzyme 41
Epidemic 1, 4, 9-11, 16-4, 20, 28, 30, 66,

69, 72, 83-93, 89, 91-9, 94, 102, 107-9, 119-20, 126, 130-34, 138, 147, 149-50, 152, 156, 158, 160, 162, 167-8, 170, 174, 183, 185, 187-8, 191, 194-8, 200, 202, 211-13, 215, 217
Epidemic Fever 135
Epidemiology, Epidemiologists 22, 35, 82-3, 103, 107-8, 110, 114-5, 135, 139, 181-2, 200, 209, 212
Epizootic 20, 108
Eradication 115-6, 203
Erevan 160
Ergotism 15
Erin 45
Eruption 115
Erysipelas 214
Esquimos 119, 133, 197
Essex 82
Ethiopia, Ethiopians 5, 7, 26-7, 112, 122, 136, 151, 165, 169, 189
Etruria, Etruscans 17, 45, 96-7, 99
Eubel 61
Europe, Europeans 4, 25, 30-1, 47-8, 53, 57, 59-60, 62-63, 66, 68-9, 72, 76, 78-9, 81-84, 87, 97-8, 101, 103-4, 108-9, 111-3, 118-10, 126, 129, 136, 138-9, 141-4, 149, 153-4, 156-7, 159, 162-65, 167-8, 170-2, 174-6, 178, 180-1, 183-5, 187-90, 195-6, 198, 201, 215-6, 222
Eusebius 118
Evagrius Scholasticus 22, 26-7, 33, 44
Evans, R J 181-2
Evolution 209
Exanthematic Typhus 135
Eye 115, 136

Face 115, 136
Factory Acts 178-9
Faeces 136
Faeland of the Lagan 46
Fallingbostal 222
Famine 17, 40, 59, 63, 65-6, 102, 120, 135, 146-7, 151, 211, 221
Famine Fever 135, 147
Far East 24, 47, 54, 84, 113, 159
Farr, W 167, 175, 180
Farris, W W 120
Fatimids 62, 74
Faubourg St Antoine 180
Febris Militarius 135
Feichen of Fore 46
Felsen, J 190
Felsenfelt, O 159, 161
Fenner, F 115

Hill, A B & Mitra, K 191
Himalaya Mountains 82-84, 187
Himera 94
Himilco 94
Himmler 133
Hinayama Buddhism 105
Hindu 121-2, 171, 188
Hinton 45
Hippocrates, Hippocratic (Greek) 4, 8, 32, 75, 89, 93, 137, 191,
Hippocrates (Carthaginian) 94
Hiroshima 57
Hirsch, A 135, 145, 151, 170, 195, 219, 221-3
Hirst, L F 82, 217
Hisham ibn al-Malik 40
Historians 39
Hittler 133
Hittite Empire 1, 116
Ho, P-T 54, 88, 188
Hobson, W 149-51, 219, 222
Hoehling, A A 200
Hogarth 177
Hohenstauffens 58-9
Holbein 76
Hollingsworth, T H 42, 44
Holmes, G 74
Holstein 140
Holy Roman Empire, Emperor 59, 137-43, 222
Homer 1, 93
Hong-Kong 81-2, 84, 87, 201
Honolulu 84
Hopkins, D R 116, 118-22, 129, 218
Horace 99
Horses 194
Hort, E C 136, 222
Horus 9
Hospitals 75, 98, 147, 164, 178, 180-1, 183, 185, 217
Host 37, 219
Host-Parasite Relationships 220
House of Representatives 204
Hsiung-Nu 47, 117
Hualan 160
Huayna Capac 126, 151
Hubris 193
Huckstep, R L 191
Hudson Bay 129, 1 31
Hughes, J M et al 173
Hugo, Victor 180
Humans (Homo sapiens) 37, 81, 135
Humming Bird 125
Hundred Years War 60, 66, 69

Hungary, Hungarians 28, 72, 100, 138, 143, 162, 164, 169, 171, 178
Hunger Typhus 135
Huns 16-8, 47, 116-8
Hunyadi 138
Hurons 130
Hurtrel, B et al 38
Hussein, A G 188, 99
Hutchenson, C 82
Huts 207
Hydra 93, 106

Iberia 36-7, 107
Ice Age, Little 57, 59
Ice Cream 161
Iceland 61, 119
Iliad 1
Illinois, River 130; People 130
Illyria 31
Ilvento, A 99
Immunity 17, 34-9, 63, 91, 104, 107-8, 111, 115, 118, 122, 124, 126, 133, 136, 151, 156-7, 169, 194-5, 197, 200-1, 216, 221
Immuno-Deficiency 220
Immunoglobulin G 37-8
Immuno-suppression, Immuno-depression 31, 36
Inca 126, 219
Indemnity 206, 207
India, Indians 10, 27, 45, 54, 82, 84, 87-8, 91-9, 94, 101, 106, 116-8, 120-2, 151, 154, 157-61, 165, 167-73, 177, 187-9, 210, 217
Indo China 84, 165
Indonesia 105, 188
Indus, River 27, 29, 116, 174, 214
Industrial Revolution 162, 172, 188, 200, 208, 210
Infant Deaths 102
Inflammation 2, 30
Influenza 9, 38, 42, 53, 92, 107, 114, 116, 181, **193-208**, 211-2, 216, 223; Influenza Virus, Type A 193-4, 202-5; Type B 193-4; Type C 193
Ingolstadt 144
Inkerman 191
Insecticides 100
Insurance Industry 204
Intestine 91, 107
Iowa, 194, 197; People 132-3
Iran 27, 47, 151, 165, 168, 171, 183, 198, 213
Iraq 40, 47, 55, 165, 168, 171, 183, 198, 213
Ireland, Irish 27, 29, 111, 120, 144, 147-8,

151, 163-4, 185, 196
Iron 18, 108
Iroquois 130-1
Irrigation 43
Isaurian Dynasty 36
Isfahan 161
Islam 29-33, 35, 39, 42, 43, 47, 55, 62, 116, 171
Isle de Bourbon 158-9
Isles d'Hyeres 148
Israel, Israelites 9
Istamboul 162, 164, 167, 169
Istria 25, 34
Italy, Italians 18-20, 24, 29, 46, 48, 55-61, 66, 69, 71-2, 80, 84, 97-100, 111, 137-8, 142, 145, 164, 167, 169, 178, 190, 195-6, 199; Northern 31, 140, 145, 171, 216; Southern 34
Itch 115

Jacquerie 74
Jaffa 76
Jaggi, O P 45, 54, 117-8, 151, 158, 161, 187
Jago, St, Island of 109
Jahangir 76
Jamaica 110
Jamuna, River 191
Japan, Japanese 84, 120-1, 149, 151-2, 160, 165, 170, 172, 188, 201
Jaundice 107
Java 84, 158, 160, 165
Jayvarman 105
Jefferson 110, 132
Jehovah 9
Jenner 115, 118, 120, 162, 172
Jerusalem 3, 27, 100, 191
Jessore 160
Jews, Jewish 43, 61, 78-9, 150, 190
Joachim of Brandenburg 138
John of Ephesus 22, 27, 44
John, St, the Divine 212
Joints 115
Jones, W H S 93-4, 97-8, 217
Jordan, E O 199
Jorge, R 53
Joseph I 120
Josephus 3, 191
Judah, Judaism 3, 43
Julian Alps 23
Julich-Cleves-Berg 139
Julius Caesar 97-8
Jupiter 216
Jusserand 79

Justin II 46
Justinian 12-3, 18, 24, 28, 31, 44, 46-7

Ka'aba 166
Kachin 83
Kalispe 132
Kaplan, C 117, 194
Kanpur 187
Kansas 133
Karachi 85
Kara Khiti 55
Karkov 111
Kashmir 77
Kazakistan 55
Keil, H 137
Kenya 91, 122, 168-9, 189
Kennedy, P 143
Kennistos 132
Kent 100
Kepler 222
Khamsin Wind 62
ibn Khatimah 52, 61
Khiti 55
Khmer 98, 105-6, 191
Kickapos 133
Kidneys 91
Kilwa 168
Kennear-Wilson, J V 223
Kiowa 132-3
Kipchak Khanate 55
Kissi People 109
Kister, M J 117
Kitasato, S 81, 84, 217
Kites 166
Klikitat, River 133
Koch, R 81, 84, 162, 182, 188, 213
Ko Hung 117
Kolosh 133
Konigsberg 146, 222
Konsa 133
Koran 117
Korobova, E I et al 38
Krause, A K 212
Krishna 106
Kuamon 82-3
Kublai Khan 54
Kunming 83
Kupffer 214
Kurdistan, Kurds 54-5
Kush 33
Kyakta 160

Laing 103
Laiou-Thomadikis, A E 47